Probing Parapsychology

Probing Parapsychology
Essays on a Controversial Science

Edited by GRANT R. SHAFER
Foreword and Conclusion by Jay Harold Ellens

McFarland & Company, Inc., Publishers
Jefferson, North Carolina

LIBRARY OF CONGRESS CATALOGUING-IN-PUBLICATION DATA

Names: Shafer, Grant R., 1951– editor. | Ellens, Jay Harold, 1932–2018, writer of foreword.
Title: Probing parapsychology : essays on a controversial science / edited by Grant R. Shafer ; foreword by Jay Harold Ellens.
Description: Jefferson, North Carolina : McFarland & Company, Inc., Publishers, 2023 | Includes bibliographical references and index.
Identifiers: LCCN 2023004082 | ISBN 9781476680385 (paperback : acid free paper) ∞
 ISBN 9781476648910 (ebook)
Subjects: LCSH: Parapsychology.
Classification: LCC BF1031 .P774 2023 | DDC 133.8—dc23/eng/20230310
LC record available at https://lccn.loc.gov/2023004082

BRITISH LIBRARY CATALOGUING DATA ARE AVAILABLE

ISBN (print) 978-1-4766-8038-5
ISBN (ebook) 978-1-4766-4891-0

© 2023 Grant R. Shafer. All rights reserved

No part of this book may be reproduced or transmitted in any form or by any means, electronic or mechanical, including photocopying or recording, or by any information storage and retrieval system, without permission in writing from the publisher.

Front cover images © WhataWin/Shutterstock

Printed in the United States of America

McFarland & Company, Inc., Publishers
 Box 611, Jefferson, North Carolina 28640
  www.mcfarlandpub.com

This volume is dedicated to the memory of my mother, Grace Kortman Ellens on whose birthday, February 1, it was finished. She lived ninety years and died on the eve of her seventieth anniversary of marriage. Her character reflected her excellent name, a woman full of grace and truth.
—Jay Harold Ellens

* * *

To Jay Harold Ellens, soldier, pastor, psychologist, prolific author, generous friend.
"Blessed are the dead who die in the Lord from now on. Yes, says the Spirit, so that they rest from their toils, for their works follow after them."

To Oskar Fischer, pioneer in the study of dementia and parapsychology, murdered by the Nazis.
"And those who are wise shall shine like the brightness of the firmament; …"

To Heather Leah Shafer.
"When people see her, they will say, 'She's better than her father.'"
—Grant R. Shafer

Acknowledgments

I thank my co-authors for their patience and industry in making the changes needed to prepare *Probing Parapsychology* for publication. Jens Schlieter was generous in giving me a copy of his *What Is It Like to Be Dead? Near-Death Experiences, Christianity, and the Occult*, likewise Madelaine Lawrence in giving *The Death View Revolution: A Guide to Transpersonal Experiences Surrounding Death*. Stanley Krippner provided wise advice and kind encouragement about reviving this book after Jay Harold Ellens' death in 2018. V.G. Miller took the initiative in contacting us co-authors, which started the process of reviving the book. Layla Milholen, our editor at McFarland, has been patient, professional in her guidance, and encouraging throughout the arduous process of editing. Dan Ellens, Harold's son, generously permitted us to continue publishing what was his father's book. Penultimately, I thank my former wife Cathy and our daughter Heather for dealing with a stressed-out ex-husband and father. Et Deo gratias.

Table of Contents

Acknowledgments   vi

Foreword
    Jay Harold Ellens   1

Preface
    Grant R. Shafer   3

Introduction
    Stanley Krippner *and* Everton Maraldi   7

The History of Parapsychology
    V.G. Miller   17

Extrasensory Perception: Telepathy, Clairvoyance, Precognition, and Retrocognition
    Grant R. Shafer   38

Psychokinesis: Famous Cases Around the World
    V.G. Miller   63

Reincarnation and Past-Life Memory
    James G. Matlock   78

An Overview of Research on Mediums: History and Cautions
    Stephen J. Pullum, Carole M. Van Camp,
    and Wendy Donlin Washington   96

Talking to Your Dead Uncle Teddy: Probing the Validity and Persuasiveness of TV Mediums
    Stephen J. Pullum   118

Serpent-Handling as Near-Death Experience
    Ralph W. Hood, Jr.   140

viii Table of Contents

Near-Death Experiences 1: History, Explanations, Anecdotes
    Grant R. Shafer   159

Near-Death Experiences 2: More Rigorous Studies
    Grant R. Shafer   185

Revising Our Concepts About Reality: The Challenge of Consciousness
    Dean Radin   206

Theoretical Criticism of Psychical Research
    Grant R. Shafer   215

Conclusion
    Jay Harold Ellens   231

Epilogue
    Grant R. Shafer   234

About the Contributors   237

Index   239

Foreword

Jay Harold Ellens

Parapsychology is an intriguing field of study. It has been a subject of research for a century or so. It has come under intense scientific investigation since the beginning of the twenty-first century. Research on the numinous or paranormal experiences that many human beings have reported is now being taken seriously. This opens a frontier of scientific inquiry with the potential of unveiling an entirely new world of knowledge.

I am certain that if we had kept a careful account of the wide range of parapsychological events humans have experienced on a daily basis throughout history, we would now have a well-developed science of the psychospiritual world of reality. A large percentage of humans have reported such experiences. It is estimated that all or nearly all persons have the kind of parapsychological experiences that result in changes in the directions of their lives. If these experiences had all been taken seriously and documented, we would have an enormous amount of data, and would be able to look for patterns indicating similarities and differences of experiences. From those patterns we could likely have discerned various categories of data. In terms of such categories we would almost certainly have been able to develop scientific hypotheses.

Hypotheses tested against a larger field of data reveal the laws of nature. Laws describe what kinds of things are true, for example, of the science of parapsychology. That would expand our paradigm of reality. We would have a phenomenological and heuristic science of the parapsychological. We would likely see that what we now call "paranormal" is really a very normal part of the real world in which we live every day.

This volume intends to provide an introduction to that intriguing world of experience and that area of study. It is intended for persons who are willing to examine evidence without presupposing conclusions. It is for those who are serious-minded about reaching beyond the boundaries of the familiar and the routine and grasping that which lies beyond the borders of our present knowledge.

2   Foreword

The scholars who have composed the essays of this book include some of the most notable investigators of parapsychological events today. Their publications have received notable prizes, wide-ranging acclaim, and worthy esteem. They are authorities in this field. We were fortunate that we could assemble such an estimable stable of authors who provide varied insights and scientific work.

This is a special kind of reference work. It is designed on the one hand, to be an engaging narrative, so it is possible for the student or new investigator in the field of the paranormal to find easily various sub-topics of parapsychology. Many concepts, experiences, notable personages, and components of the field are set forth in systematic fashion. Throughout our book major items are appropriately titled as subtopics. Categories are named. Major issues are defined. If the reader is seeking information about many components of parapsychology, he or she will be able to find it by means of the table of contents or by consulting the index.

Preface

Grant R. Shafer

> Jesus said, If the flesh came into being because of spirit, it is a wonder. But if spirit came into being because of the body, it is a wonder of wonders. Indeed, I am amazed at how this great wealth has made its home in this poverty.
> —Gospel of Thomas 29, Robinson 13

This book was planned and first put together by Jay Harold Ellens. His death, on 13 April 2018, coincidentally my sixty-seventh birthday, the end of his earthly life of achievement as a soldier, pastor, scholar, psychotherapist, and author of nearly two hundred books, derailed the composition. V.G. Miller, author of our essays on the history of parapsychology and famous cases of psychokinesis, asked whether the other authors wanted to finish the book. I answered "yes" and began recovering what the authors had written for Dr. Ellens and finding a new publisher, with the help of Stanley Krippner.

Dr. Ellens had envisioned something like a dictionary or encyclopedia. Our new publisher, McFarland, and I decided that what we had would work better as a collection of essays. The essays that survived the process of editing are on the history and future of parapsychology, extrasensory perception, psychokinesis, various aspects of the question of survival of the human personality after death, i.e., reincarnation, mediums, and near-death experiences, and philosophical aspects of parapsychology.

It is difficult to fit the phenomena of parapsychology within a materialist framework. That worldview has given us incalculable material advantages. Even in very poor societies lifespan has increased, which is a good measure of the progress of science in improving human life, not to mention the reduction of suffering and the growth of entertainment and education.

On the other hand, two world wars, oppressive governments and businesses, and environmental destruction, all enabled by science, have put the very survival of our species in doubt. Likewise, the reduction of life and mind to the interactions of unconscious matter and energy yield a world view which is empty for many people.

The materialist world view began with Leucippus of Miletus (fl. 450–420 BCE) and Democritus of Abdera (460–370 BCE). They proposed that everything comes from the interactions of very small particles, which they called "atomos," meaning "indivisible." Their theory was picked up by Epicurus (341–270 BCE), but was mostly overshadowed by Christianity and Islam in the Middle Ages.

Isaac Newton's (1642–1727) work was so successful in explaining motion on earth and in space that Democritus' theory was revived by John Dalton (1766–1844). By 1900, with the help of Charles Darwin's explanation of life on earth, religion, which had provided structure to society and comfort to the individual, seemed illusory.

Largely in response to this challenge, intellectuals such as the founders of the Society for Psychical Research (1882) hoped to find in reports of clairvoyance, telepathy, ghosts, etc., proof that materialism was incomplete. Help would also come from physics. Relativity, and more so quantum mechanics, undermined materialism by redefining matter, time, space, and causality. Although some physicists maintain that quantum mechanics did nothing to weaken materialism, others disagreed, and some, such as Schroedinger and Weizaecker, even turned to Eastern religion (Schroedinger, "The Vedantic Vision," *My View*; Chari 813).

Given that there is no compelling theoretical reason to exclude extrasensory perception (ESP), psychokinesis (PK), and afterlife, the efforts of parapsychologists to study these questions are justified. Unfortunately for believers, research has not been unambiguous in its results, but further research is justified.

Some of the contributors to this book are parapsychologists who can draw from their own experimental data. Others, such as myself, are trained in other fields and have investigated others' research.

The book begins with the history of parapsychology. It proceeds with extrasensory perception (ESP), the purported ability of humans to acquire knowledge without use of the five senses, and psychokinesis (PK), the ability to make changes in matter and energy without physical contact. It continues with several aspects of the question of survival after death, reincarnation, mediums, and near-death experiences. It concludes with philosophical consequences of parapsychology.

The ontogeny of my interest in parapsychology repeats the historical phylogeny of the field. I had a very thorough religious training as a child and pursued New Testament studies at the doctoral level. I find a positivistic explanation of the origin of Christianity intellectually persuasive but emotionally wanting. I met Dr. Ellens when he pursued a doctorate in New Testament studies, already possessing one in communications. I had contributed to several of his books, was happy to write about parapsychology, and succeeded him as editor following his death.

Several books on parapsychology have been most helpful to me. Jesse Hong Xiong's *The Outline of Parapsychology* has much useful information but lacks documentation and a critical approach. Benjamin Wolman's *Handbook of Parapsychology* is much more reliable, but was published in 1977, likewise *Foundations of Parapsychology* by Hoyt Edge et al. (1986). Harvey Irwin and Carolyn Watt's *Introduction to Parapsychology* is a more up-to-date (5th ed., 2007), equally reliable source of basic information.

Probing Parapsychology: Essays on a Controversial Science is a snapshot of some aspects of the field from a diverse group of observers. I hope that it is more readable than the more comprehensive works above. We present it as our understanding of a fascinating and vital field at an interesting historical moment and hope that our readers will find it helpful.

WORKS CITED

Chari, C.T.K. "Some Generalized Theories and Models of Psi: A Critical Evaluation." Wolman et al., pp. 803–22.
Robinson, James M., editor. *The Nag Hammadi Library*. 3rd ed. HarperSanFrancisco, 1988.
Schroedinger, Erwin. *My View of the World*. Cambridge U, 1964.
Wolman, Benjamin B., Laura A. Dale, Gertrude Raffel Schmeidler, Montague Ullman, editors. *Handbook of Parapsychology*. Van Nostrand Reinhold, 1977.

Introduction

Stanley Krippner
and Everton Maraldi

During World War II, a young American woman living in England had a strange and distressing dream about her fiancé, who was based several miles away from her. In her dream she saw him in an office, working on a typewriter. He seemed to be disturbed; sweat was dripping from his face. She woke up crying, with the strong impression that there was something wrong with him, wherever he was. On the following day she received a letter from him in which he described a situation that matched her dream. He had to work overtime in the office, and one day he was ordered to type out secret orders for a troop movement. Although he was feverish, he worked for hours with no rest, almost developing pneumonia as a result. Nevertheless, he managed to complete his assignment.

The two persons described in this vignette are not fictitious characters. This experience—extracted from the extensive collection of cases presented by Louisa Rhine in her book *Hidden Channels of the Mind* (88–89)—is just one example of many reported by people all over the world in which visions, dreams, or feelings concerning distant events (in time or in space) are later found to coincide with real-life situations.

Such experiences can be explained in many ways. Probably the most parsimonious explanation would be chance occurrence. Ordinary people, who are generally not aware of probability, can be easily misled by finding patterns where none exist (Kahneman 115). They often tend to remember only those occasions in which internal and external events coincided, usually forgetting or dismissing other situations in which nothing surprising had happened. Such biases may create the impression that something extraordinary or anomalous is taking place, when, in fact, what is recalled is merely a coincidence.

A series of other psychological explanations could be proposed for these experiences. These would include attributing meaning to something that is actually devoid of significance, fitting an experience into a particular religious belief system, or inadvertently creating distortions in the remembering, reporting, and presentation of the case. There is also the possibility of deliberate distortion or outright fabrication from someone who wants to gain attention. Moreover, in some cases, these reports might be symptoms of an underlying mental disorder.

But there is another possibility. What if such experiences reveal processes that are unknown to or not well understood by contemporary science? What if, instead of a chance occurrence, the experience between the two young people during World War II represented an actual phenomenon in which the girl provided an accurate description of her fiancé's activities by relying on an ability overlooked by contemporary science?

Anecdotal reports, which suffer from a series of observational and methodological problems, may not represent the best evidence in favor of these alleged phenomena. But what if we could reproduce these experiences (or their important aspects) in a controlled setting in order to understand the specific variables and processes underlying them? What would we discover by systematically observing, describing, and classifying these and similar phenomena, instead of just relying on personal accounts? These are precisely the questions that parapsychologists have been exploring for more than a century, in their pursuit of rational and verifiable answers.

What Is Parapsychology?

Parapsychology can be defined as "the scientific study of experiences which, if they are as they seem to be, are in principle outside the realm of human capabilities as presently conceived by conventional scientists" (Irwin and Watt 10). This definition does not imply that such experiences cannot be subjected to scientific methods, nor does it mean that they will always remain outside the "realm of human capabilities." It is simply a description of potentially controversial and currently unexplained phenomena (in terms of Western science's available physical, biological, and psychological knowledge) that are meaningful and impactful enough in people's lives to deserve a rigorous investigation and understanding.

In this sense, parapsychology is not exclusively concerned with *unconventional* explanations, but also addresses the study of conventional physical, biological, and psychological processes involved in these reports. The fact that someone describes his or her experience as "telepathic" is not sufficient, in principle, for a parapsychologist to consider it anomalous. This possibility is open, but it will have to be verified empirically, against other hypotheses. It may turn out, for example, that certain reports of telepathy are better explained by delusions and cognitive biases than by any unconventional form of communication at a distance. That is why parapsychology is not directly concerned with *psi*—a neutral (and non-explanatory) term used by parapsychologists to name the presumed anomalous processes underlying parapsychological phenomena (Irwin and Watt 15; May and Marwaha 1: 1)—but with *experiences* apparently involving "psychic" processes.

An important point to note here is that, although the term parapsychology may sometimes be employed by people outside the scientific community (or even by members of it) with the purpose of legitimizing religious, spiritual, or esoteric belief systems, these opinions and speculations should be understood as such, rather than as a fundamental part of the definition of parapsychology as a scientific field. Indeed, to avoid particular connotations and stereotypes frequently related to the words *psychic* or *paranormal*, some authors have suggested describing these experiences in terms of their status as scientific anomalies, thereby preferring the broader (and more neutral) term *anomalous experiences* (Cardeña et al., *Varieties* 4).

Although usually referred to as the starting point of the modern scientific interest in parapsychological research, the founding of the Society for Psychical Research in 1882 is just one of the many crucial events in the long history of investigations of these experiences. The origins of these investigations are actually much older, being traceable to the ancient world, as when Croesus investigated the Delphic oracle (Herodotus 1.46–56, 71–95). But the interest in parapsychological phenomena is not restricted to science; it is, indeed, widespread in Western culture, and constitutes an important aspect of science fiction, art, and spiritual movements. The study of the psychosocial and cultural implications of these phenomena has served an important function in different areas, such as anthropology and depth psychology; some of these aspects are explored by V.G. Miller.

The Varieties of Parapsychological Experience

Given that the phenomenology of parapsychological experiences is varied, a series of its examples and classifications will be found by the reader throughout the several essays in this book. Certain areas of inquiry that have attracted particular attention from parapsychologists include phenomena such as alleged *telepathy*—in which specific information is apparently and somehow directly transferred from one mind to another, as when someone senses when loved ones are in danger even when physically far away and in the absence of ordinary communication; alleged *clairvoyance*—in which specific information is somehow directly obtained by the individual concerning distant (and sometimes obscure) events, such as information about lost objects or hidden locations with no previous knowledge about them; alleged *precognition*—the purported ability to gain information regarding future events, such as dreaming about a disaster that is later confirmed to have occurred; or alleged *psychokinesis*—the purported direct influence of mind on matter, such as reports of table levitation without a mechanical or other established scientific explanation (Cardeña et al., "Reintroducing Parapsychology" 10–11). For more information on psychokinesis, see essays by V.G. Miller. Telepathy, clairvoyance, and precognition are often subsumed under the term *extrasensory perception* (May and Marwaha 1: 2), discussed in Grant R. Shafer's essay.

Another topic of relevance to parapsychology is *mediumship*—the supposed ability of an individual to be in regular contact with the deceased, or to serve as an instrument of communication and action for alleged spirits or other non-corporeal beings. Mediumistic experiences, which have been investigated since the days of psychical research (the original term for parapsychology), have since then fueled discussions on the mind-brain relationship as well as the possibility of life after death, or what some parapsychologists define as the *survival hypothesis* (Rock 11). Claimant mediums and channelers are frequently said to possess privileged or private information about the living or the deceased that could not be obtained by ordinary sensory means, sometimes concerning future as well as past events. Some mediums are said to "materialize" or move objects without physical contact. Purported mediumistic messages from spiritual beings or deceased people have sometimes inspired entire spiritual movements and doctrines, as well as apparently helping some people cope with bereavement. Mainly because of these characteristics, mediums have attracted considerable attention from the media and the public, but there are controversies regarding their authenticity and the phenomena under consideration. Some parapsychologists distance themselves from mediumship studies, given both the history of fraud by mediums and the presence of alternative, psychological explanations (Irwin 25). A more detailed description and analysis of mediumship, channeling, and their underlying social context can be found in essays by Stephen J. Pullum, Carole M. Van Camp, and Wendy Donlin Washington.

Other topics of interest to parapsychological research that are closely related to speculations on survival after death and/or the mind-body problem include *out-of-body experiences*—the perception that the mind or one's self-identity is somehow located outside of the physical body (see essays by Ralph W. Hood, Jr., and Grant R. Shafer). Also related to these issues are putative past-life memories and cases of children who claim to remember previous lives (see the essay by James G. Matlock), as well as apparitions, hauntings, and poltergeists, and near-death experiences (see essays by Ralph W. Hood, Jr., and Grant R. Shafer).

Parapsychologists do not all hold the same perspectives regarding these phenomena, nor use the same terminology to describe them. For example, *psychokinesis* has also been called "non-local perturbation" or "psi kappa." *Extrasensory perception* is also referred to as "non-local perception" or "psi beta." *Clairvoyance* is sometimes termed "remote viewing," especially if it occurs at a distance. *Survival research* has been called "psi theta," and *past-life reports* have been conceptualized as examples of "post-cognition," "retrocognition," or anomalous information about past events. Some of these alternative terms, including "psi kappa," "psi beta," and "psi theta," are no longer employed (or are uncommon) in contemporary parapsychological literature. Thus, the reader cannot expect to see them used throughout the essays of this book. Such terminological variations partly reflect the lack of a consistent theory concerning anomalous phenomena, their nature and causes, thereby indicating the need for more and better studies (Irwin and Watt 11).

Some researchers, who are not convinced that any psi phenomena have been indisputably demonstrated, nonetheless believe that the field is worthy of study. Some parapsychologists describe themselves as "dualists" (who see the mind as fundamentally independent from the body and the brain) some as "relative monists" (who believe that mind and matter are facets of the same reality or substance), and some as "physicalists" or "materialists" (who regard anomalous experiences as reducible to physical processes or explanations), while others position consciousness as fundamental to all reality (e.g., Baruss and Mossbridge 3 ; Kelly et al. 607).

Criticisms and Controversies

Parapsychology has faced several criticisms throughout its history, mainly concerning its validity as a scientific field and the methodological adequacy of its experiments. One common allegation by critics is that parapsychology is not a science, and its subject matter is not scientific. However, what defines a discipline as scientific is not necessarily its object of study, but rather its commitment to the scientific method. In this regard, the scientific research on parapsychological phenomena is no less rigorous than the work done in mainstream areas of science; moreover, parapsychologists have actually collaborated with the creation and development of important scientific methods such as meta-analysis and masked designs (Cardeña et al., "Reintroducing Parapsychology" 15).

It is true, however, that some of the topics of interest to parapsychologists may be hard (or even impossible) to test experimentally. Let us consider here, for example, the survival hypothesis. Some of the assumptions of survivalists include processes that allegedly occur in a hypothesized spiritual world or dimension, for which there is no direct verification. These propositions are sometimes immune to refutation, since they are based on metaphysical and ad hoc speculations (Maraldi and Krippner, "Biopsychosocial Approach" 561–562). A similar problem may occur with alternative hypotheses to survival, such as the so-called super-psi hypothesis (Rock 7). It is thus plausible to consider that certain claims regarding psychic phenomena are, in principle, outside the scientific scope, despite their philosophical importance. On the other hand, the fact that some mediums apparently provide veridical information about deceased people that they could not obtain by ordinary sensory means is a phenomenon that requires investigation, to which the scientific method can certainly contribute, regardless of a supposed other-worldly origin. It is also important to be open-minded, taking into consideration the possibility that some metaphysical speculations may one day prove to be testable enough to be confirmed or refuted.

It must also be stressed that there is some difference between the experimental evidence obtained in the context of parapsychology and popular conceptions of the field. The evidence usually obtained in the laboratory is far less impressive and extraordinary than are the presentations of these phenomena in science fiction, or in the reports of religious "miracles" and unconventional "cures." Experimental designs often control for a series of confounding variables, including trickery, sensory leakage, and selective reporting, and thus many ordinary explanations for these experiences are routinely discarded. With the exception of observational studies, for which the evidence may be regarded as *suggestive* (see the essay by James G. Matlock on claims of reincarnation), the results of parapsychological experiments are interpreted in terms of statistical deviations from chance expectation, as in many mainstream areas of science.

Another common assumption is that psychic experiences could be explained away as instances of psychopathological symptoms. Although these experiences have indeed been shown to be associated with variables such as dissociation, schizotypy (mild symptoms of schizophrenia), and psychotic symptoms, the evidence is mixed, indicating differences between subgroups of participants as well as positive correlations between anomalous experiences and well-being or other health indicators (e.g., Kennedy et al. 353). It is thus not possible to generalize a psychopathological explanation for all reports of parapsychological experiences. A possible motivation underlying this or similar hypotheses (see also the *cognitive deficits hypothesis* described by Irwin and Watt 255) consists in denigrating so-called "believers" and experiencers by associating them with negative stereotypes, such as mental illness, thereby neglecting the heterogeneity of the available evidence (Maraldi and Krippner, "Cross-Cultural Research" 311).

In all fairness, after examining the data, some scholars have found sound reasons why parapsychology has been rebuffed by mainstream science. James Alcock has cited several reasons, including some negative definitions that "tell us not what the phenomena are but only what they are not" (37). He adds lack of replicability, unpredictability, unfalsifiability, lack of significant progress, and the absence of psi-related anomalies in physics and other fields where one would expect their presence, if the experimenter's mind were affecting the outcome (37–41).

Despite all the barriers and criticisms faced by parapsychologists, proponents maintain that the field has, in fact, advanced. It has produced rigorous experimental evidence in favor of anomalous processes, while uncovering some of the mechanisms apparently involved in their elicitation. In an influential review and critical examination of the evidence, Cardeña argues that psi phenomena "cannot be readily explained away by the quality of the studies, fraud, selective reporting, experimental or analytical incompetence, or other frequent criticisms" ("Experimental Evidence" 663). Reber and Alcock subsequently responded to Cardeña's article by stating that "claims made by parapsychologists cannot be true" (391). They point to a series of theoretical and methodological shortcomings—basically reiterating the criticisms raised by Alcock in his previous article ("The Parapsychologist's Lament")—and affirm "the existential impossibility of psi phenomena" (391) since "paranormal effects violate basic scientific principles" (392). Ellens, Shafer, and Dean Radin assert that psi is compatible with scientific principles. In his rejoinder, Cardeña ("Data") contested the argument for the ontological impossibility of psi phenomena and urged researchers to look at the data and analyses instead of permanently refusing to consider the evidence solely on philosophical or conceptual grounds. Cardeña also discussed the findings of a series of surveys showing that scientists are generally open to the possibility of psi—in contrast to Reber and Alcock's views (391–99).

Still, parapsychology faces many problems, such as lack of funding, inability to institute and maintain longitudinal studies, and difficulty in finding acceptance as a valid topic of investigation by mainstream science (Cardeña et al., "Reintroducing Parapsychology" 17). Additional inquiry is necessary to clarify the different variables involved in these phenomena, especially if such complex matters as quantum mechanics and geomagnetic fields are found to be relevant. Cardeña also provided a series of methodological and theoretical recommendations, including project and data repositories, inter-disciplinary studies with sufficient power, nonconscious measures of psi, falsifiable hypotheses, analyzing elements of useful sessions and subjects, better "ecological validity" of research (the extent to which the findings of an experiment can be generalized to real-life settings), experimenting about how to increase effect sizes, finding more researchers at least willing to consider the reality of psi, and placing psi in larger areas, e.g., consciousness studies ("Experimental Evidence" 663).

These are important issues, not only because of potential implications for the understanding of the limits and reach of human capabilities, but also because of their consequences in everyday life. Such experiences are reported worldwide, with prevalence percentages ranging from around 50 percent to 80 percent depending on the country (Maraldi and Krippner, "Cross-Cultural Research" 308). Influencing the way people make decisions in their lives, they have sometimes saved individuals from danger and death (Rhine 88–89). Scientific investigation is crucial to understand these ancient but still relevant human experiences; thus, the essays in this book are excellent examples of parapsychology's current directions and perspectives.

Works Cited

Alcock, James. "The Parapsychologist's Lament." *Mysterious Minds: The Neurobiology of Psychics, Mediums, and Other Extraordinary People.* Edited by Stanley Krippner and Harris Friedman, Praeger/ABC-CLIO, 2010, pp. 35–43.

Baruss, Imants, and Julia Mossbridge. *Transcendent Mind: Rethinking the Science of Consciousness.* 1st ed., American Psychological Association, 2017.

Cardeña, Etzel. "'The Data Are Irrelevant': Response to Reber and Alcock (2019 [sic])." *Journal of Scientific Exploration,* vol. 33, no. 4, 2019, pp. 593–98.

_____. "The Experimental Evidence for Parapsychological Phenomena: A Review." *American Psychologist,* vol. 73, 2018, pp. 663–77.

_____ et al. "Reintroducing Parapsychology." Etzel Cardeña, John Palmer, and David Marcusson-Clavertz, editors. *Parapsychology: A Handbook for the 21st* [sic] *Century,* McFarland, 2015, pp. 9–27, [e-book version] www.amazon.com.br/Parapsychology-Handbook-21st-Century-English-ebook/dp/B014RWX8TQ/ref=tmm_kin_swatch_0?_encoding=UTF8&qid=&sr=.

_____ et al. *The Varieties of Anomalous Experience: Examining the Scientific Evidence.* 2nd ed., American Psychological Association, 2014.

Herodotus. *The Histories.* Trans. A.D. Godley. Loeb Classical Library. Harvard UP, 1920–1925. 4 vols., penelope.uchicago.edu/Thayer/E/Roman/Texts/Herodotus/1B*.html. Accessed 15 July 2021.

Irwin, Harvey. "Is Scientific Investigation of Postmortem Survival an Anachronism? The Demise of the Survival Hypothesis." *Australian Journal of Parapsychology,* vol. 2, 2002, pp. 19–27.

_____, and Caroline Watt. *An Introduction to Parapsychology.* 5th ed., McFarland, 2007.

Kahneman, Daniel. *Thinking, Fast and Slow.* 1st ed., Farrar, Straus and Giroux, 2011.
Kelly, Edward, et al. *Irreducible Mind: Toward a Psychology for the 21st* [sic] *Century.* Rowman and Littlefield, 2007.
Kennedy, Jim, et al. "Psychic and Spiritual Experiences, Health, Well-Being and Meaning in Life." *The Journal of Parapsychology*, vol. 58, 1994, pp. 353–83.
Maraldi, Everton, and Stanley Krippner. "A Biopsychosocial Approach to Creative Dissociation: Remarks on a Case of Mediumistic Painting." *NeuroQuantology*, vol. 11, no. 4, 2013, pp. 544–72.
_____. "Cross-Cultural Research on Anomalous Experiences: Theoretical Issues and Methodological Challenges." *Psychology of Consciousness: Theory, Research, and Practice*, vol. 6, no. 3, 2019, pp. 306–19.
May, Edwin, and Sonali Marwaha. *Extrasensory Perception: Support, Skepticism, and Science.* 1st ed., Praeger/ABC-CLIO, 2015. 2 vols.
Reber, Arthur, and James Alcock. "Searching for the Impossible: Parapsychology's Elusive Quest." *American Psychologist*, vol. 75, no. 3, 2020, pp. 391–99.
Rhine, Louisa. *Hidden Channels of the Mind.* William Morrow, 1965.
Rock, Adam. *The Survival Hypothesis: Essays on Mediumship.* 1st ed., McFarland, 2014.

The History of Parapsychology
V.G. MILLER

Introduction

Parapsychology is broadly concerned with the study of extrasensory perception (ESP), psychokinesis (PK), out of body experiences (OBEs), and near-death experiences (NDEs). ESP is defined as knowledge that is acquired without the use of the sense organs. Specifically, the study of ESP can be broken down into three main sub-species: telepathy; clairvoyance; and precognition; and to a lesser extent, retrocognition (Kahn 3). The ability hypothesized by parapsychology is called "psi."

Telepathy concerns the communication of information directly from one mind to another. An example of this phenomenon is known as the "distress call." In this phenomenon a person's distress is communicated ordinarily to a loved one who "knows" that his or her loved one is hurt without reaching this conclusion by way of reason or empirical data (Kahn 10). *Clairvoyance* concerns the knowledge of objects, places or people that has not been mediated by the sense organs, nor by another person by means of telepathy. Clairvoyants often use objects to assist them. For instance, the clairvoyant who helps the police with investigations of missing persons may receive information about the victim by means of holding onto something that belonged to a specific missing person. Both telepathy and clairvoyance concern the acquisition of knowledge in real time (Kahn 62). *Precognition* concerns the acquisition of knowledge of the future, such as is believed in prophetic dreams (Kahn 95). Also of note is the lesser-known area of *retrocognition* in which knowledge that is obtained, without the aid of the sense organs, pertains to past events. An example of this kind of phenomena is past-life regressions (Gauld 6). Past-life regressions use hypnosis to recall supposed experiences of past lives.

PK in contrast to ESP concerns the ability of a person to affect objects, events, or people around them without using their muscles to do so. This is different from knowing information about objects, events, or people, as is the case with ESP. A famous exponent of PK was Uri Geller, who claimed to be able to bend metal objects with only the slightest stroking (Douglas 289). This is an example of PK that can be seen by the naked eye and is classified as *macro*-PK as opposed to *micro*-PK which is only noticeable by means of a statistical evaluation, as occurs in laboratory testing (Beloff 42).

Other notable areas of paranormal activity which are of interest to parapsychology are OBE and NDE. OBE (out of body experience), as the name suggests, concerns cases in which the mind appears to be detached from the body. OBE may be otherwise known as astral projection or travel. NDE (near-death experience) is the phenomenon in which a subject is clinically dead and appears to move into another realm of existence. These cases often involve the "dead" person levitating above his or her body, claims of ESP, being met by deceased persons or religious figures, and/or entering into a tunnel which ends in a bright and peace-inducing light (Long and Perry 1–10).

All of the accounts so far noted, including ESP, PK, OBE, and NDE, can be grouped into two distinct categories: *anecdotal accounts* and *experimental accounts*. Anecdotal accounts of paranormal activity ordinarily cover spontaneous paranormal events, which include any of the phenomena just discussed that have not been solicited. Examples include hunches, prophetic dreams, premonitions, the manifestations or hallucinations of persons or voices, visions, strong impulses to act in a certain way, and strong emotional upsurges which point to a distant, or future/past event, otherwise unknown to the percipient. A widely known collection of anecdotal accounts of paranormal experience was published by Edmund Gurney on behalf of the British Society for Psychical Research four years after the society was formed. The book was published in 1886 and is called *Phantasms of the Living*.

Experimental accounts include those occasions in which paranormal activity is tested in a laboratory. Influential laboratory experiments include Professor J.B. Rhine's pioneering experiments with card-guessing and dice-throwing. These experiments were conducted at Duke University in the early 1930s. In the 1960s the experiments changed to electronic machinery and were characterized by the presentation of randomized target sequences and comprehensive recording of the percipient's guesses (Gauld 18).

Parapsychological Events in the Bible

In the ancient world events that we now call parapsychological experiences were recorded as though they were significant yet normal events.

For instance, in primitive religions the belief in magic was commonplace. Moreover, it has been argued that cave-paintings show evidence of shamanism—the practice of a shaman making contact with the spirit world (Wallis 54). A detailed account of the way the ancient world perceived parapsychological events is most evident in the Bible. In the Bible we find the antecedents for nearly all of the main branches of parapsychological studies. Saul's encounter with the witch of Endor (1 Sam. 28:3–25), who summoned the deceased Samuel, was not dissimilar from the séances popularized in the Spiritualism movement in the 1800s. (Cf. Pullum, "Talking.") In both cases the spirits of dead people allegedly manifested in order to communicate information to the one who summoned them. Usually, this information pertained to future events.

Stories of ancients divining the future also abound in the Bible, most notably through the accounts of prophetic dreams (Gen. 37:3–11, 40:1–41:56). Moreover, the practice of haruspicy (Ezek. 21:21), concerned the inspection of the entrails of a dead animal in order to divine future events. Telepathy or clairvoyance is suggested in the Bible when Elisha is reported as being in the Israelite town of Dothan and knowing what the King of Syria was speaking, in his bedchamber, probably in Damascus, one hundred miles away (2 Kings 6:8–23). Indeed, listing all of the parapsychological events in the Bible would take some time. Yet this sampling is enough to demonstrate that what we now call parapsychological activity is nothing new, and that parapsychological activity was once respected as a significant part of everyday life.

Mesmerism

This easy acceptance of parapsychological activity had changed dramatically in the eighteenth century when the Viennese physician Franz Anton Mesmer (1734–1815) first made a name for himself for his particular type of hypnotism that was called mesmerism. Instead of perceiving parapsychological events as everyday events, the world of the eighteenth century was both exceedingly fascinated by such events and highly skeptical of their authenticity. However, regardless of how mesmerism was perceived, mesmerism is generally considered to be the earliest area of parapsychological activity that was observed and tested under scientific conditions. As such mesmerism can be considered one of the first fruits of the type of psychical research that would later be called parapsychology.

In the early 1700s the popular understanding of astrology and alchemy was that there was a pervasive energy in the universe, including in human beings, which was influenced by the sun, moon, and the stars. In

1760 Mesmer developed this theory further. Mesmer believed that he could use magnets to manipulate the pervasive energy he believed was in human beings, which Mesmer called magnetic fluid, and in doing so improve the health and wellbeing of his subjects (Beloff 18).

Mesmer eventually dropped the use of magnets but not the idea of magnetism. Instead of magnets Mesmer focused on the transfer of what he called the animal magnetism of one person to another. Or to be more specific, he claimed that the animal magnetism of a healthy person could be transferred to a person who was ill with the result that the animal magnetism of the healthy practitioner would heal the sick patient. Mesmer allegedly achieved this transfer of energy by stroking his patients and putting them in sleep-like trances called somnambulism. In this state Mesmer's patients were said to feel no pain even if they were undergoing surgery. As can be imagined, this was incredibly important at a time when there were no chemical anesthetics (Beloff 21–25).

Moreover, mesmerism, as Mesmer's hypnotism was called, could allegedly bring forth the hitherto unknown remarkable powers of some of its patients. One case in point is the story of Victor Race. Victor was a seemingly inarticulate peasant boy who was treated in hospital for an inflammation of the lungs. In hospital Victor was visited by Armand Marie Jacques de Chastenet, marquis de Puységur (1751–1825), one of Mesmer's famous followers, who put Victor into a trance-like state. As the story goes, whilst in this state Victor changed into a highly articulate and educated person who not only diagnosed his own condition but suggested treatment which was superior to the treatment that the doctors had given him. So impressed were the doctors with Victor's abilities, they took him around the ward where Victor apparently suggested effective treatments for his fellow patients (Beloff 21).

However, despite these seeming successes, mesmerism all but died out in the 1850s. This may have been in part as a result of the findings of a French royal commission, chaired by Benjamin Franklin, investigating mesmerism, which concluded in 1784 that Mesmer's successful results were the product of suggestion. However, the focus on the psychological benefits of mesmerism as opposed to belief in the power of magnetized fluid proved to be advantageous to the rising study of psychiatry. Indeed, it has even been argued that mesmerism was the precursor to hypnotism, that later gave rise to the concept and theory of the unconscious. This ultimately culminated in Jung's and Freud's ground-breaking work on the unconscious mind (Beloff 17).

According to John Beloff (26) the Chinese art of *qi gong* could be spoken of as the present-day equivalent of mesmerism. Certainly, the Chinese concept of qi as a pervasive energy in the universe is compatible with

Mesmer's concept of magnetic fluid. In both instances the health and well-being of a person are dependent on the correct balance of this energy. Moreover, mesmerism and qi gong are both accepting of paranormal phenomena.

Spiritualism

Spiritualism emerged in the 1850s as mesmerism waned. However, it could be argued that mesmerism served to popularize Spiritualism, as spiritualists believed that the mesmeric trance-like state was the perfect state for communicating with the dead. Yet, Spiritualism was particularly distinct from mesmerism as Spiritualism was a quasi-religious phenomenon, whereas mesmerism was not. Indeed, if the claims of the Spiritualists are to be believed, then Spiritualism was the first "religion" to provide consistent and substantial evidence for life after death. However, this claim is contentious as the Spiritualist movement was tainted by fraudsters and charlatans who were attracted to its popularity and the assurance of fame and financial benefits (Kurtz 177).

The Spiritualist movement is credited with beginning with the teachings of Emmanuel Swendenborg (1688–1772), who believed that he could communicate with the dead, and with the events of the Fox family in upstate New York which began in 1848, which are discussed in detail in Pullum et al., "Overview."

After the Fox sisters, Spiritualism developed in two distinct ways: (1) physical phenomena, as was consistent with the rapping of the Fox sisters, and (2) coded messages.

The most famous exponent of the physical category of Spiritualism was Daniel Dunglas Home (1833–1886). Home was born in Edinburgh but grew up and found fame in the United States. In America, Home conducted a number of spectacular séances which were observed by many skeptical investigators including scientists and academics who had uncovered fraudulent practices by other mediums. Yet Home was never shown to be deceptive in his practices (Beloff 56). Indeed, Home was amenable to working in environments which were not conducive to trickery. For instance, he worked in bright gaslight, as opposed to the darkness spiritualists preferred; and he worked in private homes at little notice, not giving him a chance to stage his "spirit manifestations." (Beloff 56).

The alleged paranormal phenomena that were observed in Home's séances were typical of the very physical category of the spiritualist movement. These phenomena included unseen hands playing musical instruments, levitations of things and people, and manifestations of objects and people. Indeed, the extravagance of the physical phenomena that was experienced at Home's séances was unparalleled. For instance, a typical séance for Home began with what became known as the earthquake effect, a phenomenon whereby the room and everything in it would appear to shake, including the very chairs that the participants were sitting on. This would ordinarily be followed by the table tilting and the objects on the table falling off. While this was happening, musical instruments would play of their own accord. The big event of the evening would occur as Home's very heavy mahogany table would levitate (Beloff 41-57).

Robert Barrett Browning, son of the poet, claimed that his father caught Home in fraud (Houdini 41-42). However, letters of the poet and his wife only express suspicion (Phelps 125-35; Huxley 218-21). Stein says, "While the statement that Home was never caught in fraud has been made many times, it simply is not true.... It is simply that Home was never *publicly exposed in fraud*. Privately he was caught in fraud several times," and that Home was a "fraud, just as were all of his fellow spiritualists. He was just a more clever and politically sophisticated fraud" (328-29). Beloff says that it is generally believed today that Home was a gifted illusionist (41-57). Much later the study into past-life regressions and NDEs became popular (Beloff 58).

A Scientific Approach to the Parapsychological

After the Spiritualist movement, psychical research was focused on a scientific approach to paranormal phenomena. The first society to take on this task was the British Society for Psychical Research (SPR). It was founded in 1882 in London by Henry Sidgwick (1838-1900), its first president and distinguished professor of moral philosophy at Cambridge University. Three professors of physics, Sir William Barrett (1844-1925), Sir William Crookes (1832-1919), who had pronounced Daniel Home to be genuine, and Sir Oliver Lodge (1851-1940), one of classics, Fredrick W.H. Myers (1843-1901), and Edmund Gurney (1847-1888), outstanding student of music, law, physics, and chemistry, were also founders. Frank Podmore (1856-1910), a writer, well-known skeptic, and founder of the socialist Fabian Society, and Sidgwick's wife Eleanor Balfour Sidgwick (1846-1936), mathematician and physicist, and her two brothers also assisted. Philosopher Arthur Balfour (1848-1930), prime minister of England from 1902 to 1905, is better known as the author of the Balfour Declaration, which declared that establishment of a "national home" for Jews in Palestine was British policy. Gerald Balfour (1853-1945) was a classicist. Although not on the original board, the Australian-born attorney and skeptic Richard Hodgson (1855-1905) joined the SPR within a few years of its inception.

American psychologist and philosopher William James (1842–1910) likely was the most famous member of SPR (Shepard 2: 1543).

At its founding SPR included the Rev. W. Stainton Moses (1839–1892), a medium, Dawson Richards, and Dr. George Wyld, all important Spiritualists. Later, British physician Arthur Conan Doyle (1859–1930), creator of Sherlock Holmes, likewise a Spiritualist, joined SPR and investigated mediums. Spiritualists and non–Spiritualists in SPR originally got on well, but time passed and SPR did not formally promote Spiritualism, bringing conflict, even though many of SPR's founders, skeptical in the beginning, became convinced Spiritualists (Shepard 2: 1543–44).

Founders of SPR, who believed in afterlife, as did almost all in the late nineteenth century, refused to accept that science disproved life after death. They hoped that science could substantiate "survival." "[A] desire to challenge what they regarded as the depressing mechanistic worldview proposed by nineteenth-century science, combined with an intense curiosity about the evidence for life after death, formed an explicit and openly acknowledged part of the motivation of many of those who founded the Society for Psychical Research in 1882" (Carter 41).

The society's objectives were outlined succinctly in the same sentence that appeared in every issue of the society's journal (*Journal of Parapsychology*). It read that the society's purpose was "...to examine without prejudice or presupposition and in a scientific spirit those faculties of man, real or supposed, which appear to be inexplicable on any generally recognized hypothesis" (Beloff 61). Its current web page says that SPR was "the first society to conduct organized scholarly research into human experiences that challenged contemporary scientific models." SPR proposed to investigate "the various physical phenomena commonly called spiritualistic; with an attempt to discover their causes and general laws" as well as to gather and/or organize "existing materials bearing on the history of these [paranormal] subjects" (Shepard 2: 1238). In addition, the SPR was particularly interested in studying the concept of "survival" of death and the related, albeit separate, question of whether the dead actually communicated with the living.

The scope of the parapsychological activity that the SPR studied can be divided into two different types: (1) spontaneous occurrences of parapsychological phenomena which are unsolicited such as premonitions or precognitive dreams or hunches. Also, in this category can be found spirit manifestations and poltergeist-like events, and (2) parapsychological phenomena that can be performed more or less on demand. This kind of phenomenon is traditionally that of mediums or clairvoyants. The six committees that were established by the SPR in 1883 to investigate psi covered the following phenomena: (1) thought-transference (telepathy); (2)

mesmerism; (3) Reichenbach's phenomenon and suchlike (auras); (4) physical phenomena; (5) haunted houses; and, (6) literary material reporting psychic phenomena (Beloff 72).

Of note, thought-transference was explained as "...any influence which may be exerted by one mind upon another, apart from any generally recognized mode of perception" (*Proc. S.P.R.* 1882, qtd. in Beloff 72). The experiments which were considered to prove thought-transference were guessing experiments using cards, symbols, and words. These experiments will be explained later in more depth when we discuss Rhine's contribution to parapsychological research. The study into Reichenbach's phenomena researched Baron Carl von Reichenbach's claim that he was able to see auras. Or to be more precise, Reichenbach argued that some sensitives in mesmeric trances were able to see luminous emanations coming from the magnets used in mesmeric treatment, or that they saw auras surrounding crystals and people. Reichenbach called these auras "odyles," after Odin, king and magician of the Norse gods. Yet thought-transference was the most prevalent area of research for the British SPR in the early days (Beloff 74).

Apparitions

SPR founders Edmund Gurney, Frederic Myers, and member Frank Podmore published their research on ghosts as *Phantasms of the Living* in 1886. However, the theories concerning ghosts have changed dramatically over time. There has always been a long-held belief that ghosts are material objects, albeit transparently material, and that they occupy the space they are seen in. However, in the domain of psychical research a psychological explanation of ghosts is preferred. It is believed that ghosts emanate from the minds of the people who see them, in much the same way as hallucinations do. However, in the case of ghosts it would appear that the hallucination is not a product of the participant's imagination, as ghosts often appear in a historical authenticity and setting that is unknown to the participant. Moreover, the same ghost is often seen by more than one person, and thereby the manifestation is thought to be created by the mind intuiting a real phenomenon. This connection has been explained as a kind of telepathic connection between the two persons who see the ghost or from the person who is the ghost and the person receiving the message (Gurney et. al. 1: xxxv).

Myers proposed that there is a person who sends a telepathic message which the recipient converts into a manifestation of the sender's distress. However, not all cases of apparitions are connected with distress. In response to this difficulty in Myer's claim, Tyrrell argued that what he called the mid-level of a person's mind is permeable and potentially connected to the mind of another person. Thereby, it is possible that we are all connected at the mid-level of our minds according to Walker (55).

More Communication with the Dead

In Paris nearly four decades later, in 1919, the Institut Métapsychique Internationale was created. The institute was founded by an important wine merchant and Spiritualist named Jean Meyer (Marmin 29). Its first president was the eminent psychologist Charles Richet. The most influential case of clairvoyance that the Institut Métapsychique researched was that of the medium, Pearl Curran (1883–1937), and her supposed contact, Patience Worth. Pearl, a simple housewife, claimed that she made contact with Patience by means of a Ouija board. Patience, it appears, was a woman who lived in the seventeenth century and who was a gifted writer. Indeed, when (1913–1937) Pearl was in contact with Patience, she wrote seven novels with a historical authenticity that was said to have been beyond Pearl's ability. Yet it has also been argued, by a leading professor on the Elizabethan period, that the alleged historical information in Curran's novels was not historically accurate. That said, there was and is still some doubt concerning the veracity of Pearl's claims. For instance, James Hyslop, the head of the American Society for Psychical Research, considered Pearl to be a fraud. On the other hand, his successor, Walter Franklin Prince, held that "some cause operating but not originating in.... Mrs. Curran must be acknowledged" (qtd. in Carroll 1). Prince, who had a daughter with multiple personality disorder, found that Pearl's case was not consistent with a personality disorder (Carroll 1).

Around the same time the SPR expanded its operations in America, and psychical research was being shared at congresses for experimental psychology. Experimental psychology was distinct from the depth psychology popularized by Freud because experimental psychology focused on universal properties of the mind as opposed to a focus on an individual person—the arena of depth psychology. Parapsychology could be said to be akin to experimental psychology, in as much as it is focused on a universal property of the mind (Beloff 125).

The Rhine Revolution in Research

Psychical research into card-guessing was popularized by Joseph Banks Rhine. In the 1920s, Rhine, a professor at Duke University, developed the first long-term program into psychical research which was to be carried out in a university. The objectives of the Rhine "revolution" were summed up by Beloff. Rhine had three main goals. First was the effort to start a progressive program of experiments about the paranormal, founded on a valid methodology. This was planned to establish "an ever-expanding sphere of knowledge." The second, founded on the first, tried to obtain academic status and scientific recognition for the discipline. Rhine's third goal was to ascertain and demonstrate that psi ability is not restricted to unusual creatures but was potentially ubiquitous in everybody (Beloff 127).

This development in the study of psi phenomena divested the study of much of the fraud and deception which had tainted research into paranormal phenomena. No longer were mediums dictating how paranormal phenomena were to be observed, making conditions favorable for cheats. Rhine insisted on strict conditions which lessened the possibility of deception. In short, the experimenter was now responsible for creating and maintaining the conditions of the experiment. Notably, Rhine favored card-guessing exercises which relied on statistical evidence to prove whether a percipient's guesses were above average or not and to indicate how far these guesses deviated from the average (Beloff 133).

The cards which Rhine used to carry out these experiments are called Zener cards, named after their creator, Karl Zener, Duke psychology professor. Rhine commissioned Zener to create cards on which it was easy to focus. There are five Zener cards including a square, a circle, a star, a cross, and wavy lines. Rhine's most famous achievement was his monograph entitled *Extra-Sensory Perception* (1934). This book, which became a runaway success, detailed Rhine's alleged successful experiments in his laboratory at Duke and generated the popular acronym, ESP. However, Oskar Fischer, pioneer in parapsychology and Alzheimer's disease, had already coined the synonym "aussersinnlichen Wahrnehmung" in 1924 (Fischer 186, 196–197, 199). Rhine also started the *Journal of Parapsychology*, which is still published today. It explained that the word parapsychology was used to describe the experimental area within psychical research (Beloff 139).

Within this period the study of parapsychology was to enlarge and to include precognition and psychokinesis (PK). In experiments for precognition the subject had to guess the card before the pack was shuffled as opposed to afterwards for other types of ESP. Another development at this time was that ESP and PK became known generically as psi-phenomena. R.H. Thouless in Britain coined this term as he believed that ESP and PK were so closely connected, being as they were mind-matter interactions, that they represented a single fundamental two-way process (Douglas 336).

Another important development at this time concerned "bidirectionality." Gertrude Schmeidler wrote about bidirectionality in her paper,

"Separating the Sheep from the Goats" (Schmeidler). Schmeidler found that believers in ESP, "sheep," tended to score above chance while disbelievers, "goats," tended to score below chance. Consequently, both groups deviated significantly from chance. Schmeidler named this phenomenon as the bidirectionality of psi because it appeared that ESP may function in either a positive or negative mode depending on the personality of the subject.

Further Developments in Psychical Research

The study of parapsychology soon became internationally recognized. Of note, the Parapsychology Foundation of New York, founded by medium Eileen Garrett, came into being in 1951. However, the growth in parapsychological research was not reserved for the UK and the USA. Advances could soon be found in many countries.

Of note was the way in which parapsychology expanded in China. During the Cultural Revolution (1966–76) study into the parapsychological was considered to be a decadent Western study. However, this changed in 1978 when a 12-year-old boy, Tang Yu, convinced a group of scientists that he had psychic ability, called "exceptional functions of the human body" (EFHB). In 1981 a documentary of the boy's ability was made and shown in cinemas and on televisions across China. As a result of this documentary, *Do You Believe*, hundreds of children claimed to have abilities similar to the boy in the documentary (Beloff 159–161; Central Intelligence Agency 403).

In October 1981 Stanley Krippner led American and Canadian scientists in visiting China and attending five formal technical meetings. Harold Puthoff reported in 1985 that he tried to duplicate Chinese experiments with partial success. The claims that the children made were investigated in over a hundred different Chinese research centers, and the findings of these investigations were published in peer-reviewed journals, including *Ziran Zashi* ("*Nature Journal*"), which spun off the monthly *EFHB Bulletin* (Beloff 160; Central Intelligence Agency 403–406).

Some of the conclusions of this research are as follows: the best candidates for ESP research are girls between the ages of six and twelve; natural psychic ability diminishes or disappears as children mature, and psychic ability diminishes or disappears in the presence of a "hostile person" (Smith). A strong difference between the Western and Eastern view of psi phenomena developed at this time. The Chinese diverged with the Western tradition that viewed psi phenomena as abnormal. The Chinese term, "Exceptional Human Body Function" expresses this idea. Between 1984 and 1987, the Chinese military sponsored psi research, and in 1987 the Communist Party informally reversed its early opposition (Beloff 160; Central Intelligence Agency 403–406).

In the 1960's research into psi phenomena became more creative, across the globe. This was the time when free-choice or free-response testing begun to emerge. The free-choice test was not limited to one pre-determined test answer as was the case with the early testing methods, such as Zener cards and dice throws. A free-choice test could incorporate an object, person, location, or piece of writing, and allowed for a wider range of responses in its test subjects. Areas of free-response testing can be noted in dream testing, the ganzfeld technique, and remote viewing (Beloff 182).

Dream studies were particular to the Maimonides Dream Laboratory, which was founded in 1962 by Montague Ullman, who hired Stanley Krippner in 1964 (Krippner). Krippner observed that dreams figured highly in ESP phenomena, and he sought to modify dreams as they were happening. His method for doing this was as follows. The dreamer would be hooked up to an EEG (electroencephalograph), and another agent would be focusing on a target picture. The dreamer would be awakened during the night and asked to record his or her dreams. In the morning the dreamers would be asked to record their belief that a certain postcard, which was shown them, was used in the previous night's activities. It must be said that Krippner's studies did not produce remarkable evidence of psi phenomena. However, Krippner did introduce parapsychology to the psychophysiology of sleep. He also popularized the free-response technique (Wehrstein).

Charles Honorton, on the other hand, became the leading exponent of free-response ESP testing. Honorton induced altered states of consciousness by means of putting participants into a ganzfeld state, a state which restricted external stimuli. Honorton achieved this by restricting the participant's vision perception by covering his/her eyes with glasses that were constructed from ping-pong balls that were cut in half, and by restricting the participant's audio perception by means of headphones playing white noise. The ganzfeld replicated the state just before sleep, which is known to be particularly hypnotic, meaning that it is easier for people to move into an altered state of consciousness. It is also the time when a person is particularly vulnerable to suggestion. The ganzfeld technique is still used today in parapsychological investigations (Douglas 355–56; Radin, "Revising").

Another area of free-response psychical investigation was that of remote viewing. Unlike the ganzfeld technique, remote viewing did not require the participant to be in an altered state of consciousness in order to achieve psi activity. The precursors to remote viewing were the travelling clairvoyants who held objects in their hands and who supposedly gave information about remote people and locations. In remote viewing experiments, a target was in a remote location, and the subject's task was to discern and indicate in what location the target was.

The most famous case of remote viewing concerned the Stargate Project. The Stargate Project concerned research into paranormal phenomena commissioned by the U.S. Army and conducted at a research center in 1979 at Fort Meade, Maryland. Regarding remote viewing the research concluded that although remote viewers could be used to gather intelligence, their information should not stand on its own. The merit of this research was questioned in 1995 when it was decided to close the center. Moreover, an independent review of the center argued that even though there were statistically significant findings in the center's reports, they did not prove the existence of remote viewing. Also, it was decided that so-called cases of remote viewing were too vague to be actionable intelligence. That said, the center *was* funded for two decades which suggests that the army had an interest in their work (American Institutes of Research).

Other modes of research into psi phenomenon that occurred from the 60s to the 90s included the Schmidt machine and Bio-PK among other things. Helmut Schmidt, a physicist, was the namesake of the Schmidt machine—an automated electronic device that was used to test precognition. The innovation in Schmidt's machine consisted in the fact that it produced completely blind tests. It did this by using radioactive decay to light random lights that the participants had to pick. Bio-PK was the study of PK exerted on living things mainly for the purposes of healing diseases and disorders (Beloff 171).

Other Areas of Psychical Research

Divining

Another enduring area of paranormal activity is that of divining. Water divining or dowsing has been practiced for hundreds of years. Water is found or divined underground by means of a divining rod. The two-pronged end of the stick is held by the diviner, one prong in each hand, and the other end is held out in front. When water is found the free end moves forcefully up or down, and occasionally the stick is known to break in two. This same method of divining is used by diviners who assist police in their inquiries. However, in modern times diviners are more likely to use pendulums or nothing at all. Diviners are said to feel a tingling in their hands when a divining rod or a pendulum is moving, and some practitioners maintain that they do not need the instruments of a divining rod or a pendulum as the slightest trembling of their hands is enough to suggest the anomaly they are seeking—the other instruments merely exaggerate this effect (Broughton 163).

Radionics

The art of divining provided the backbone for the modern-day field of radionics. Radionics is a branch of radiesthesia, which plainly means a sensitivity to radiations. Radionics uses, in some instances a pendulum, and in other instances, more elaborate instruments to diagnose and to treat illnesses. Radionics also has a great deal in common with mesmerism as radionics works on the premise that there is a unified energy in the patient that can be balanced by guiding that energy, usually by a healthy practitioner (Broughton 165).

Radionics was introduced by Albert Abrams (1864–1924). He claimed that he could detect the electromagnetic frequencies of disease and heal it (Ades 196). However, Abrams was denounced by *Scientific American* and the American Medical Association (Lescarboura; "The Scientific American"). Yet, although radionics as proposed and practiced by Albert Abrams appears to be fraudulent, electromagnetic fields are often effective medical tools, which is demonstrated by the use of X-rays, magnetic resonance imaging (MRI), radiofrequency and microwave ablation, et al.

Indeed, Vavken et al. conclude specifically: "Pulsed electromagnetic fields improve clinical scores and function in patients with osteoarthritis of the knee and should be considered as adjuvant therapies in their management. There is still equipoise of evidence for an effect on pain in the current literature," and generally: "Even though mainstream medicine has adopted techniques such as electric cardioversion and has accepted, more grudgingly, transcutaneous electric stimulation and electroconvulsive therapy, its interests have never strongly focused on electromagnetic therapeutics."

Modern Survival Research

Reincarnation

The study into past-life regressions is reliant on hypnosis—an element which has been common with paranormal experiences for as long as psi research has been around. However, it must be noted that this reliance on hypnosis is fraught with problems, as people are known to make up information under hypnosis if there are gaps in their knowledge. Moreover, memories can be distorted, as is evident in cases of cryptomnesia, where people mistake the source memories. This sometimes causes "unintentional plagiarism," in which an author mistakes an idea from another as the author's own. It has been argued that this was the case in the most famous example of so-called past-life regression, that of Virginia Tighe (Gravitz 3–10).

Tighe was a young woman who lived in Chicago in the 1950s but who claimed that she had also lived the life of Bridey Murphy in Cork, Ireland, in the early nineteenth century. This so-called previous life emerged under hypnotic sessions with Morey Bernstein from 1952 to 1953. The public interest in this case developed in response to Bernstein's bestselling book, *The Search for Bridey Murphy*, that outlined the results of the sessions Virginia had with Bernstein. However, skeptics claim that Virginia had constructed a "past-life" as Bridey Murphy, based on knowledge of Ireland that she had received in childhood from her Irish neighbors in Chicago, including an immigrant named Bridey Murphy Corkell (Root 1).

Yet stories remain regarding past-life regressions. Notably, past-life regressions of children have been the subject of some interest. Children were typically studied for past-life regressions because it was believed that the supposed previous life had been lived in the not-too-distant past. For instance, it was claimed that the birth-marks on a particular child subject were similar to the wounds of the violent death of a supposed past life. It was also argued that behavioral problems could be related to past lives (Stevenson 403).

Near-Death Experiences

In modern times parapsychology has become interested in near-death experiences (NDE). There are today more documented cases of NDE because more people are resuscitated after being declared clinically dead due to advances in medical techniques. There is persuasive evidence for NDE in these cases. However, the question of whether these experiences are testimonies of the afterlife or whether they are the product of other causes is still debated. For example, a lack of oxygen to the brain can cause hallucinations (Atwater 3).

Ordinarily NDEs are similar, so much so that psychiatrist Raymond Moody, psychology professor Kenneth Ring of the University of Connecticut, and others outlined the psychospiritual stages of death. The first stage Ring argues for is the stage in which the dying person experiences a sense of peace and wellbeing. This stage was reported by 60 percent of the participants in his exhaustive study. The second stage that Ring posits is an out-of-body or autoscopic experience. In this stage the self appears to be separated from the physical body and appears to look down on itself from a point near the ceiling. This experience was reported by 37 percent of the subjects. Of note, in this stage sight and hearing become exceptionally acute while the dying person's attitude toward the body and world with which they are familiar becomes detached (Ring ch. 3).

The third stage is characterized as "entering the darkness," and involves the widely known effect of traversing a tunnel. Twenty-three percent of participants reached this stage. This stage is described as being pleasant, and the participants of the study felt as though they were moving away from their earth-bound miseries, and that they were moving towards Heaven. The final stage, which is characterized by "entering the light" was achieved by 10 percent of the participants. In this stage the dying are met by religious figures or deceased people that they knew when they were living, or the dying are met by beautiful gardens or other peaceful scenes. Two other common features of NDE are (a) a panoramic life-review and (b) the decision which has to be confronted whether to go back into the ailing body and continue the struggle (Ring ch. 3).

Philosophical Perspectives

Not only have academics and scientists observed psi phenomena, they have also tried to make sense of them. Theories which conceptualize psi phenomena fit into two categories (a) the physical or quasi-physical and (b) the transcendental. Beloff summarizes both of these categories in the following way.

> By a "physical theory" [sic] I imply one that is compatible with contemporary physics and by "quasi-physical" I mean one which would be compatible with physics, granted some extension of, or modification to, the existing paradigm. By a "transcendental theory" I mean one which invokes another plane of reality, be it mental, spiritual, occult, or whatever, over and above that of mundane material existence (Beloff 215).

It appears that physics is the scientific discipline which can best cope with psi activity. Of particular interest is Observational Theory, that is, a quasi-physical solution associated with quantum physics. It grew from the fact that Schroedinger's wave equation specifies the probability of many outcomes, but only one is observed, for no known reason. In terms of transcendental theories, one might consider Jung's theory of synchronicity and radical dualism. Synchronicity might loosely be called a cluster of meaningful co-incidences (Beloff 221).

Not unlike Jung, scholars such as Kenneth Walker have argued that parapsychological occurrences are normal but misunderstood processes of the unconscious mind. He argues that these processes are often ignored as they do not happen in accordance with sense perception followed by reason. Walker instead describes these experiences as direct experiences, as the mind is the most direct mode of information for a human being. These direct experiences are known to most people as inspirations which rise up from within us but at the same time seem to come from somewhere beyond our conscious apprehension (Walker 55).

For instance, Blake had always believed that his poetry came from somewhere beyond him. Similarly, Mozart and Chopin were known to "receive" entire pieces of music through inspiration. In the case of Chopin, it would often take him weeks on end to try and write down the individual parts of a piece of music that he would hear in his head. It has even been argued that the subliminal self, in some instances, is more impressive than the primary consciousness in some individuals. This was thought to be the case with Pearl Curran, the seemingly ordinary peasant woman who wrote numerous historical novels by means of automatic writing. Here it is interesting to note the suggestion from neuroscience that the brain spends 80 percent of its energy and metabolism in the resting state (Northoff 71). Walker, in line with Tyrrell, suggests that our minds are less private than we imagine them to be. For instance, he writes, "I prefer the idea that our minds are less well insulated from other systems of thought than we believe them to be; and that mind-substance and mind-energy is to be found everywhere in the universe, just as matter and other forms of energy are to be found everywhere in the universe" (Walker 55).

Methodological Limits

As has been explained, parapsychological phenomena have been reported for thousands of years and have been treated in large part as ordinary aspects of life. Yet, in the scientific age parapsychological phenomena have been looked on with suspicion. This is not surprising as parapsychological experience often cannot be tested empirically very easily, as other phenomena can be. Parapsychological activity largely involves the mind or psyche—something which is not examined readily. Walker explains this difficulty. When researching happenings neither in the physical world nor in our conscious minds, ordinary methods are not useful. One deals here with phenomena which one cannot control or observe directly. The unconscious mind is invisible, and its products are only visible when they become conscious (Walker 231). Moreover, as we have little control over the unconscious mind, producing verifiable results is difficult.

Another difficulty with parapsychological research is the phenomenon of precognition and retrocognition. These phenomena would seem to challenge the linear concept of time that is generally accepted. However, other concepts of time have been put forth which would include paranormal experiences. For instance, there is the idea that time is understood to encompass past, present, and future simultaneously, but that our minds ordinarily process one phase of time at any given moment. This is in keeping with L.C. Robinson's view of time. Certainly, it would seem reductive to believe that the entirety of the universe is understood by way of our senses (Walker 231). To begin with, the limitations of our senses are well-documented. For instance, it is common knowledge that we cannot hear sounds on all wavelengths. Similarly, we cannot see everything on the electromagnetic spectrum that surrounds us (Saleem).

Conclusion

Parapsychological phenomena are not new. Indeed, some of the earliest recorded events in human history are parapsychological events. In this study we have looked at the Bible as an example of the way ancient people viewed what we now call the paranormal. As mentioned, the paranormal events in the Bible are reported as though they were significant everyday events. However, it is also worth noting that not all paranormal events were seen to be morally acceptable in the ancient Near East. For instance, God and the dead Samuel looked upon Saul poorly for using a witch to call Samuel up in order to divine the future. It was argued that this act showed Saul to be faithless (1 Sam. 28:16; 1 Chron. 10:13). Yet other events such as prophetic dreams were looked upon favorably—presumably as these events came to the participant without his or her solicitation. This line of criticism appears to have weakened in the time of Spiritualism when spirits were seemingly raised from the dead on a nightly basis. Conservative Christians still look on psi with suspicion (Pullum, "Talking"). Instead, most criticism of this time concerned the large number of frauds who used the Spiritualist movement in order to achieve fame and fortune. Yet despite the dubious practices in Spiritualism, the enduring line of inquiry from this practice raises the question as to the plausibility of life after death. As far as parapsychology is concerned the phenomena of NDEs are the most compelling possible cases suggesting life after death.

Other paranormal events that we have spoken of concern the here and now, such as mesmerism, which used hypnotism in order to heal people and was said to enhance the hitherto unknown potential of certain individuals. This essay discussed Victor Race, who was thought to have diagnosed illnesses beyond his conscious comprehension. Victor's story is not entirely dissimilar from other participants, spoken of in this essay, who were more intellectually gifted in a hypnotic or altered state. This was also the case with Pearl Curran who wrote seven historical novels by way of an undetermined form of inspiration. Of note, in the cases of Race and Curran, we find observable instances in which an otherwise untapped ability of healing and otherwise unknown talent have manifested. (See Radin, "Revising.") Therefore, to dismiss parapsychology means disregarding the possibility of improvement in individual and community lives thereby. Similarly disregarding the sizeable evidence for life after death means dismissing a datum that could potentially ameliorate the deep anxiety of dying persons. This is particularly true given the fact that NDEs are known to be generally positive experiences.

We have also discussed laboratory experiments into the paranormal, which were largely institutional responses to paranormal experiences. These experiments were not always successful in proving psi phenomena and were frequently difficult to replicate. Indeed, it may be argued that laboratory experiments test the more difficult modes of parapsychological phenomena such as Rhine's card-guessing tests. It may also be argued that the more common form of telepathy or clairvoyance is known to most people by way of hunches, for instance, having an urge to call somebody the moment before they call. This kind of paranormal event would appear to be common, yet it is almost impossible to test in a laboratory environment. However, the SPR, Rhine, and the other pioneers of parapsychology did manage to make psi research more attractive and accessible to scientists and academics, thus giving some credibility to the studies.

Lastly, we have touched on a few of the prevailing theories that claim to explain parapsychological events. These theories regard new understandings of the workings of time, space, and the unconscious mind. The theory with the greatest amount of traction appears to be that our minds are more permeable than we otherwise imagine them to be, and also that our minds have a greater capacity than we think they have. Moreover, the theory of a unifying consciousness is profoundly significant if it can be proven that we are psychically connected to one another.

Works Cited

Ades, Terri, et al., editors. *American Cancer Society Complete Guide to Complementary and Alternative Cancer Therapies*, 2nd ed. American Cancer Society, 2009, archive.org/details/americancancerso0000unse/page/196/mode/2up. Accessed 30 July 2021.

American Institutes of Research. "Executive Summary." *An Evaluation of Remote Viewing: Research and Applications*, 1995, fas.org/irp/program/collect/air1995.pdf. Accessed 5 Aug. 2020.

Atwater, P.M.H. *Beyond the Light. What Isn't Being Said About Near Death Experience.* Transpersonal Publishing, 2009.

Beloff, John. *Parapsychology: A Concise History.* The Athlone Press. 1993.

Broughton, Richard. *Parapsychology. The Controversial Science.* Ballantine Books. 1991.

Carroll, Robert Todd. "Patience Worth." *The Skeptic's Dictionary*, www.skepdic.com/patienceworth.html. Accessed 1 July 2020.

Carter, Chris. *Science and Psychic Phenomena: The Fall of the House of Skeptics*. Simon & Schuster, 2012.

Central Intelligence Agency. "XI. Chronology of Recent Interest in Exceptional Functions of the Human Body in the People's Republic of China." 403–407. www.cia.gov/library/readingroom/docs/CIA-RDP96-00792R000400300011-9.pdf. Accessed 20 Nov. 2020.

Davenport, Reuben Briggs. *The Death Blow to Spiritualism: Being the True Story of the Fox Sisters, as Revealed by Authority of Margaret Fox Kane and Catherine Fox Jencken*. D.W. Dillingham Co. Publishers. 1987.

Douglas, Alfred. *Extra-Sensory Powers. A Century of Psychical Research*. Victor Gollancz Ltd., 1976.

Fischer, Oskar. *Experimente mit Raphael Schermann: Ein Beitrag zu den Problemen der Graphologie, Telepathie, und des Hellsehens*. Urban and Schwarzenberg, 1924.

Gauld, Alan. "ESP and Attempts to Explain it." Shivesh C. Thakur, editor. *Philosophy and Psychical Research*. Allen and Unwin Press, 1976, pp. 17–46.

Gravitz, Melvin A. "The Search for Bridey Murphy: Implications for Modern Hypnosis." *American Journal of Clinical Hypnosis*, vol. 45, no.1, 2002, pp. 3–10.

Gurney, Edmund, Frederic W.H. Myers, and Frank Podmore. *Phantasms of the Living*. Trubner and Co, 1886. 2 vols.

Hannemann, P.F.W., et al. "The Effects of Low-Intensity Pulsed Ultrasound and Pulsed Electromagnetic Fields Bone Growth Stimulation in Acute Fractures: A Systematic Review and Meta-Analysis of Randomized Controlled Trials." *Archives of Orthopaedic and Trauma Surgery*, vol. 134, 2014, pp. 1093–1106, pubmed.ncbi.nlm.nih.gov/ 24895156/. Accessed 29 June 2021.

Houdini, Harry. *A Magician Among [sic] the Spirits*, Harper and Bros., 1924.

Huxley, Leonard. *Elizabeth Barrett Browning: Letters to Her Sister: 1846 to 1859*. 1st ed., John Murray, 1929.

Kahn, Samuel. *An Introduction to Parapsychology*. Vantage Press, 1965.

Karolyi, George. *An Excursion into the Paranormal*. Paranormal Phenomenon Research Foundation Inc., 2003.

Krippner, Stanley. "The Maimonides ESP-Dream Studies." *The Journal of Parapsychology*, vol. 57, no. 1, 1993, www.questia.com/read/1G1-14527221/the-maimonides-esp-dream-studies.

Kurtz, Paul, editor. "Spiritualists, Mediums and Psychics: Some Evidence of Fraud." *A Skeptic's Handbook of Parapsychology*. Prometheus Books, 1985, pp. 177–224.

Lescarboura, A.C. "Our Abrams Verdict: The Electronic Reactions of Abrams and Electronic Medicine in General Found Utterly Worthless." *Scientific American*, vol.131, 1924, pp. 158–159.

Long, Jeffrey, and Paul Perry. *Evidence of the Afterlife*. HarperCollins Publishers, 2010.

Marmin, Nicolas. "Métapsychique et psychologie en France (1880–1940)." *Revue d'Histoire des Sciences Humaines*, vol. 1, no. 4, pp. 145–171, DOI:10.3917/rhsh.004.0145. Accessed 20 Nov. 2020.

Northoff, Georg. "Psychoanalysis and the Brain--Why did Freud Abandon Neuroscience?" *Frontiers in Psychology*, vol. 3, 2012, p. 71.

Phelps, William Lyon. "Robert Browning on Spiritualism." *Yale Review*, vol. 23, Autumn 1933, pp. 129–135.

Pullum, Stephen J. "Talking to Your Dead Uncle Teddy: Probing the Validity and Persuasiveness of TV Mediums." Shafer, *Probing Parapsychology*.

Radin, Dean. "Revising Our Concepts about Reality: The Challenge of Consciousness." Shafer, *Probing Parapsychology*.

Ring, Kenneth. *Life at Death: A Scientific Investigation of the Near-Death Experience*. William Morrow and Company, 1980.

Root, Chris. "The Bridey Murphy Saga: Yesterday's News." Denver Public Library, *News and Events*, 22 Oct. 2019, history.denverlibrary.org/news/bridey-murphy-saga-yesterdaysnews-vol-v. Accessed 11 July 2021.

Saleem, Ammar. "Limitations of Our Senses." 20 Oct. 2012. prezi.com/h3msftelbmly/limitations-of-our-senses/. Accessed 5 Aug. 2020.

Schmeidler, Gertrude. "Separating the Sheep from the Goats." *Journal of the American Society for Psychical Research*, vol. 39, 1945, pp. 46–49.

"The Scientific American on Abram's 'Electronic Reactions.'" *Journal of the American Medical Association*, vol. 83, no. 12, pp. 939–40, babel.hathitrust.org/cgi/pt?id=mdp.39015082605836&view=1up&seq=969. Accessed 1 July 2021.

Shafer, Grant R., editor. *Probing Parapsychology: Essays on a Controversial Science*. McFarland, 2023.

Shepard, Leslie, editor. *Encyclopedia of Occultism & [sic] Parapsychology*, 3rd ed. Gale Research, 1991. 3 vols.

Smith, Daz. "The Real Story behind Indigo Children," www.topsecretwriters.com/2010/11/thereal-story-behind-indigo-children/. Accessed 7 July 2020.

Stein, Gordon, editor. "Daniel Dunglas Home." *The Encyclopedia of the Paranormal*. Prometheus Books, 1996, pp. 325–329.

Stevenson, Ian. "Birthmarks and Birth Defects Corresponding to Wounds on Deceased Persons." *Journal of Scientific Exploration*, vol. 7, no. 4, 1993, pp. 403–10.

Vavken, Patrick, Ferdi Arrich, Othmar Schuhfried, and Ronald Dorotka. "Effectiveness of pulsed electromagnetic field therapy in the management of osteoarthritis of the knee: A metaanalysis of randomized controlled trials." *Journal of Rehabilitation Medicine*, vol. 41, no. 6, 2009, www.archives-pmr.org/article/S0003-9993(01)22503-9/fulltext. Accessed 29 June 2021.

Walker, Kenneth. *The Unconscious Mind*, Arrow Books, 1961.

Wallis, Robert J. "Art and Shamanism: From Cave Painting to the White Cube." *Religions*, vol. 10, no.1, 2019, p. 54.

Wehrstein, Karen. "Stanley Krippner." *Psi Encyclopedia*, 2008. psi-encyclopedia.spr.ac.uk/articles/stanley-krippner. Accessed 7 July 2020.

Extrasensory Perception

Telepathy, Clairvoyance, Precognition, and Retrocognition

GRANT R. SHAFER

Introduction

Extrasensory perception, or ESP, is the ability to learn of persons, places, and events without physical access to them. While Joseph Banks Rhine is credited for coining the term in 1934, Oskar Fischer, also a pioneer in the study of dementia, wrote of "aussersinnlicher Perzeptions-qualitaeten" and "aussersinnlichen Wahrnehmung" in 1924 (Goedert; Fischer 186, 196–7, 199). Humans have believed in this ability since prehistory, shamanism rather than prostitution probably being the world's oldest profession.

ESP can be roughly divided between telepathy, or communication from one mind to another by extrasensory means, and clairvoyance, or the power or faculty of discerning objects not present to the senses. This essay will cover the history of research into ESP, experimental methods, major divisions of ESP, i.e., telepathy, clairvoyance and its divisions into precognition, which is clairvoyance of future events, retrocognition, clairvoyance of past events, and remote viewing, a technique of clairvoyance researched by U.S. intelligence services from 1973 until 1995 (Popkin), ESP in popular culture, and finally criticism of ESP research.

Although there are other variants of ESP, such as dowsing (detection of things underground), skin vision, crystal vision, clairaudience (paranormal hearing), clairolfaction (smelling), clairgustance (tasting), clairsentience (touching), and channeling (contact with disembodied spirits) (Xiong, 93–97, 111–114), they are mostly omitted from this essay as unusual or covered in another essay in this book. Intuition, i.e., "the power or faculty of attaining to direct knowledge or cognition without evident rational thought and inference" (*Merriam* 615), is on the borderline of ESP because it is often psychologically explicable and will also not be further discussed.

John A. Palmer says, "...In practice, it is impossible to isolate fully these subspecies of ESP..." ("Experimental Methods" 116). If a subject shows ESP, did they read the sender's mind (telepathy), sense the targets themselves (clairvoyance), see the future results of the trial (precognition), or make the results happen? The last alternative would be psychokinesis (PK), i.e., "the movement of physical objects by the mind without use of physical means" (*Merriam* 942). Some possibilities can be eliminated by experimental procedures, e.g., telepathy by machine generation and scoring, but others cannot, so that researchers "define types of ESP operationally rather than metaphysically," referring to "general ESP" (GESP) (Palmer, "Experimental Methods" 116). A related problem is called "experimenter psi," e.g., when the researcher unconsciously sets up a sequence which favors the subject's responses, the "psychic shuffle," where the researcher affects the card sequence by PK, or when the researcher unintentionally stops shuffling when the card sequence matches the subject's responses (Palmer, "Experimental Methods" 124). In other cases, the researcher would need to foresee the subject's responses (precognition). Although these phenomena certainly would confuse the type and agent of ESP or PK, it would imply the existence of some variety of "psi" (Palmer, "ESP Research" 214–15, 218–20). "Psi" is "parapsychological psychic phenomena or powers" (*Merriam* 942).

Ironically Palmer says, "Target selection by REGs [random event generators] is the method most susceptible to this potential bias, because the selection mechanism is very sensitive to minute physical forces, and thus to PK as well..." ("Experimental Methods" 124).

History of ESP Research

Psychical research grew out of interest in fortunetelling and ghosts. Francis Bacon (1561–1624), "prophet and protector of the dawning scientific revolution" (Blackburn 34), thought that he had a premonitory dream of his father Nicholas' death and that Francis himself cured warts by magic (Bacon par. 986, 997, pp. 214, 216). Bacon told of a "jugler" [sic] who did a card-guessing trick (par. 946, p. 207) and said of it, "The experiment of binding of thoughts would be diversified and tryed [sic] to the full: and you are to note whether it hit for the most part though not alwaies [sic]" (par. 956, p. 210). In 1848 Hydesville, New York, Maggie and Katie Fox claimed to communicate with spirits, initiating modern Spiritualism. The loss of life in the American Civil War and the First World War encouraged the growth of Spiritualism, a common practice of which was the séance, in which people sat around a table trying to communicate with the dead, usually with the aid of a medium, who claimed a special connection with spirits of the dead.

Early experimental research began in 1876, when William Barrett asked hypnotized subjects telepathically to identify what sensations the hypnotist experienced in another room (J. Rhine, "History" 26). In 1881, Edmund Gurney and Frederick William Henry Myers had the five Creery sisters guess a playing card or 2-digit number thought by a sender, but it was later revealed that the sisters cheated (Irwin and Watt 49). A more quantitative approach followed in 1884, when Charles Richet tested a number of people with long sequences of playing cards (J. Rhine, "History" 26). Richet reported 789 correct responses to a series of 2927 cards, where 732 would occur by chance (Irwin and Watt 49). The probability of Richet's result was 15 out of 1000 (Carpenter 205).

In 1882 the British philosopher Henry Sidgwick founded the Society for Psychical Research (SPR). SPR attempted to develop precise criteria for reports of psychic phenomena. For example, if a mother dreamed of her child's death, evidence was needed that the dream had occurred before knowledge of the event became available through normal means, such as a diary entry or a witness to whom the dream had been told before the news arrived. Meticulous documentation of such reports, including witness reports, character references, and death certificates, was required for publication. SPR collected hundreds of such reports primarily for purposes of authentication (Irwin and Watt 29–30). H. Sidgwick published "Census of Hallucinations" in 1894. It "attempted to show statistically that in the hallucinatory form of telepathic experience a relationship exists between the dying person and the percipient's experience...." (L. Rhine 63). The researchers gathered 17,000 responses about such claims over 3 years, of which 2272 were affirmative. Comparing this number with the number of deaths in the same period, H. Sidgwick and his collaborators concluded that there were too many accurate reports to be explained by chance (L. Rhine 64).

John Coover tested telepathy in 1917 by asking 100 pairs of subjects to identify 5135 playing cards seen by a sender, the experimental series. However, he also asked other subjects to identify 4865 cards not seen by the sender, the control series. Whether the sender looked at the card was decided by a die roll. Coover concluded that the difference between the success rates for seen and unseen cards was statistically insignificant, and that telepathy was not demonstrated. F.C.S. Schiller countered that although the difference between the experimental and control rates did not demonstrate conscious telepathy, the fact that both rates were higher than chance, with which Robert Henry Thouless agreed, suggested clairvoyance. Samuel George Soal also said that Coover's experimental method was flawed (Hansel 25–29).

In 1927, J. Rhine began a systematic experimental program at Duke University. The fact that each playing card has 2 identifying marks, i.e., suit and number or face, complicates scoring, as does the preference of subjects for some characters (Irwin and Watt 51–52). Karl E. Zener, Duke colleague, invented a series of cards for J. Rhine, each of which has one of 5 symbols, a cross, circle, square, star, or 3 wavy lines. Decks of 25 cards, containing 5 of each symbol, are used to test telepathy or GESP, when a sender looks at a card, and a receiver tries to guess the card (Beloff 18; Palmer, "Experimental Methods"116). Clairvoyance is tested when the receiver tries to guess the card before the sender looks at it (Rush, "Parapsychology" 31–32). Precognition is tested when the receiver tries to guess the card before the sender shuffles the deck (J. Rhine, "History" 32).

J. Rhine constructed a statistical protocol for measuring ESP. Chance would allow a subject to guess ("call") the correct card (a "hit") 1/5 of the time. On average the subject would call 5 of a "run" of 25 correctly, which Rhine called "mean chance expectation" (MCE). The statistic comparing a particular subject's success rate with MCE is the "critical ratio" (CR) (Irwin and Watt 52–53). CR is now called "z-test," a test in which the distribution of results is statistically normal (Palmer, "Statistical Methods" 147–48). It is expressed as a standard or Z score, which is the number of standard deviations from the average (Irwin and Watt 53; Hoel 116). Standard deviation is a mathematical expression of the degree to which a measurement differs from the average (Hoel 19–21; Uvarov and Chapman 285).

After establishing his method, J. Rhine looked for people who could score high on his tests. From 1931 to 1932, J. Rhine tested 24 subjects who achieved 207 hits in 800 trials (MCE 160, probability less than 1 in 1 million). Rhine worked to exclude error, e.g., by ensuring that the backs of cards were identical, and separating subject from experimenter (Irwin and Watt 53).

J. Rhine published *Extra-Sensory Perception* in 1934. Critics pointed to errors in his early research, but the book convinced others that ESP could be studied scientifically. Reasonable criticisms were statistical error, uncontrolled sensory cues, recording errors, insufficient randomizing, omission of negative results, deception, and optional stopping (Irwin and Watt 53–54). Optional stopping is "[i]n sequential data collection, halting the process in the light of the data collected up to that point, as when a researcher continues collecting scores just until the data support the hypothesis under investigation. This procedure is unacceptable, and it undermines the validity of any statistical tests that are later performed on the data" ("Optional Stopping"). Shuffled decks of cards vary in randomness depending on the number of shuffles. the skill of the shuffler, and how ordered the deck was originally. Five riffles, also known as dovetail shuffles, or "leafing the cards," in which the shuffler holds half the deck in each hand and releases them with the thumbs so that they are interleaved, are considered adequate. J. Rhine and other researchers have also used random number tables, such as that published by RAND Corp. in 1955 (Palmer, "Experimental Methods" 123).

In 1942 George Nugent Merle Tyrrell analyzed 61 hallucinations. The "perfect" apparition, which he constructed from them, differed from the "popular 'ghost' of fiction," suggesting something objective (L. Rhine 66).

Louisa Ella Rhine theorized that unauthenticated cases were useful for purposes other than authentication, such as studying conditions associated with ESP (Irwin and Watt 30). She divided ESP into four categories, (1) intuitive impression, a vague unexplained sense that something is the case, (2) hallucination, such as a vision or audition which relates to an event at that time otherwise unknown, (3) realistic dream, which is clear realistic mental images, awake or asleep, and (4) unrealistic dream, which is fanciful unrealistic imagery like Pharaoh's dream in Genesis 41:2–7 (L. Rhine 71; Irwin and Watt 32–34). In 1962 America L. Rhine reported a distribution of 26 percent intuitions, 9 percent hallucinations, 44 percent realistic dreams, and 21 percent unrealistic dreams. In 1963 Western Europe G. Sannwald observed 27, 10, 48, and 15 respectively. Although Sybo Schouten arrived at somewhat different results in 1982, the correlation between L. Rhine and Sannwald's results suggests real psychological, if not parapsychological, forces at work (Irwin and Watt 34). As L. Rhine's work progressed, she became more confident of the "evidential value" of unauthenticated cases, which allowed critics to say that parapsychologists accepted delusions as fact. Such critics did not pay attention to L. Rhine's rationale and methodology (Irwin and Watt 30–32, 34; Rush, "Spontaneous Psi" 52).

One source of error in J. Rhine's methods was the "closed deck," "sometimes called selection without replacement* [sic] because once a picture is selected for a trial it is not put back in the pool and thus is not available for subsequent trials. On the other hand, an *open deck* [italics GRS] is generated by selection with replacement*; once a picture is selected it is put back in the pool and has as much chance as any other picture of being selected for a subsequent trial...." A subject can do "card counting" (which can get one thrown out of casinos) of a closed deck, e.g., in a standard trial of 25 Zener cards, and the subject with a good enough memory will know the last card with certainty (Palmer, "Experimental Methods" 125).

Despite weaknesses, J. Rhine's techniques dominated the field until 1969 when Helmut Schmidt invented the "random event generator" (REG), controlled by particles from a radioactive or electronic source (Irwin and Watt 54). Pseudo-random sequences of numbers which are usually unpredictable enough for ESP research are also available from microcomputers and pocket calculators (Palmer, "Experimental Methods" 123–24).

J. Rhine relied on "forced-choice" trials (Burdick and Kelly 109). A subject must choose from a fixed set of possible targets, such as Zener cards (Irwin and Watt 55). Toward the end of the twentieth century, "free-response" techniques regained popularity among researchers. These techniques require a subject usually to choose from a fixed set of targets, called the "target pool," but a subject may draw, write, speak, or choose their response (Irwin and Watt 54–55). Forced choice is like a multiple-choice exam, and free-response like an essay test. Montague Ullman, Stanley Krippner, and Charles Honorton used free-response in dream experiments, and Russell Targ and Harold E. Puthoff in remote viewing (Burdick and Kelly 109; Irwin and Watt 55).

Experimental Methods

ESP research is divided between authentication, i.e., "Does ESP exist?" and process, i.e., "How does ESP work?" Many scientists object that process research is premature because ESP has not been proven to exist. Palmer counters that we need only to accept ESP as a "working hypothesis." Process research actually is relevant to authentication. It could show that psi is the product of a "normal physical" process. On the other hand, "The demonstration of a significant and reliable relation between psi and some other variable is itself evidence for the reality of psi..." (Palmer, "ESP Research" 185). Also, if research uncovers such correlates of psi, psi can more easily be produced for research. Process research is finally necessary for a theory of psi (Palmer, "ESP Research" 185).

Irwin and Watt divide ESP evidence between spontaneous cases (29–47), which are reports from members of the public, and experimental research, conducted by professionals in a laboratory (48–82). They think that spontaneous cases cannot demonstrate the authenticity of ESP because (1) memory is interpretive and creative rather than exact and passive, (2) people misinterpret ambiguous situations, (3) subconscious perceptions are mistaken for ESP, (4) fraud is well-documented, especially among professional "psychics," and (5) chance is difficult to rule out because the odds of a given occurrence are as often as not virtually impossible to calculate (40–45). L. Rhine (61) reports that Gurney et al. already in 1886 devoted 58 pages to errors of memory, inference, narration, and observation. Donald J. West and J. Rhine decided that spontaneous cases did not authenticate ESP, but J. Rhine thought that they should suggest directions for experiment (L. Rhine 67).

Gertrude Raffel Schmeidler (131–50) describes necessary methods to facilitate valid ESP tests. Targets must be concealed and randomized. Closed decks allow subjects to infer targets through "card counting." Open decks preclude this. In forced-choice, displacement from the target, i.e., consistent choice of targets before or after the correct one, is often scored. Optimal forced-choice responses also vary with subject populations. Free-response requires that (1) the person who records the subject's attempt to describe the target and the subject's physiological responses and (2) the judge of the attempt both be unaware of the correct target, and (3) the experimenter for whom the reading is held be absent. Targets can be nearly anything appropriate to the variable tested, especially when the variable is probability levels for the subjects chosen (Schmeidler 131–40).

Subjects may be motivated by various rewards, intrinsic, such as giving them a feeling of inclusion, or extrinsic, such as theater tickets. Animals and diverse populations of humans, i.e., general, or preselected for psi ability, are used. When an experiment uses two procedures or sets of targets with a subject, the one which the subject prefers usually yields significantly higher scores. Experimenters should test subjects for the "sheep-goat effect" (SGE), because believers in ESP score higher than chance and unbelievers lower than chance. To avoid "decline effects," in which a subject is decreasingly accurate as a trial progresses, experimenters often use no more than 5 responses to complex targets, 100 calls for ESP symbols, and 1000 button pushes on Schmidt machines. Experimenters sometimes rate different hypotheses for targets about which a subject shows different biases (Schmeidler 140–44).

In order to prove either telepathy or clairvoyance, an experimenter must exclude the other. Likewise, care must be taken to distinguish precognition from PK, here a sort of self-fulfilling prophecy. A very interesting proof of retrocognition would be if a subject could successfully interpret ancient records which have baffled experts. G. Spencer-Brown attempted to show that random number tables are not completely random. Schmeidler suggests that his thesis be checked by computer, which she said would be expensive. It would be less expensive today, forty years after she wrote. Schmeidler says that distance experiments might be distorted by the subject's attitude about the distance, which might be nullified by keeping the subject unaware of the distance. Once again, the difficulty of isolating types of psi appears because the subject could clairvoyantly know the correct target, telepathically read the experimenter's mind, or precognitively know the experiment's results. Schmeidler's thoughts about dowsing and auras are outside the scope of this essay. Investigations initiated by subjects, such as mediums and professional psychics, are especially vulnerable to fraud and error (Schmeidler 144–50).

Irwin and Watt (64–66), Palmer ("ESP Research" 214–19), and Rhea A. White discuss the effect of the experimenter on results, i.e., (1) the experimenter may allow or perpetrate error or cheating, (2) psychologically supportive experimenters seem to conduce psi, while less supportive experimenters inhibit it, and (3) the experimenter's own psi may affect results. For example, Palmer ("Experimental Methods" 123–24) tells how the experimenter may use ESP or PK to choose an entry point in a random number table or a "seed number ... which activates a complex mathematical formula which generates each number in sequence" for a pseudo-random sequence from a computer, either of which would produce a target sequence matching the subject's response sequence.

Selection of subjects is an important procedure in ESP research. Palmer ("Experimental Methods" 118–20) distinguishes four subject populations, (1) psychics or "gifted subjects," (2) special subject populations, who are selected by mass screening or who have traits associated with ESP, e.g., practice of biofeedback, meditation, or hypnotic suggestibility, (3) unselected subjects, relying on the idea that ESP is distributed throughout our whole species like other psychological characteristics, and (4) animals, mostly rodents and cats. J. Rhine also thought that psi extends to animals (Morris 693–95). There are advantages and disadvantages in all of these groups.

Irwin and Watt (71) say that (1) hypnosis, (2) sensory deprivation or ganzfeld, (3) meditation, (4) progressive relaxation, (5) hypnagogic states (of drowsiness preceding sleep), and (6) dreaming, but less probably (7) drug intoxication, conduce ESP. William G. Braud (1975) proposed a "psi-conducive syndrome" including (1) physical relaxation, (2) reduced physiological arousal, (3) reduced sensory input and processing, (4) increased awareness of internal processes, (5) receptive-mode or "right-hemisphere" functioning, (6) altered view of the natural world, and (7) the sense that psi is momentarily important (Palmer, "ESP Research" 193).

Honorton and Braud separately introduced "ganzfeld," a sensory deprivation technique, to parapsychology (Palmer, "Experimental Methods" 127). Ganzfeld usually includes half ping pong balls over the eyes, "a moderately bright white or colored light (red is generally preferred) ... white, or preferably pink noise (something like soft radio static) ... lying down or seat[ing] in a reclining chair ... between 20 and 45 minutes ... observ[ing] and/or report[ing] their imagery during the reception period ... [or] afterward" (Palmer, "Experimental Methods" 127). Irwin and Watt conclude that the "effect size" of ganzfeld is "impressive" (72–73). Edge and Morris say that ganzfeld studies have replication rates better than chance (Edge and Morris 319). Dean Radin's essay in this volume references more recent meta-analyses of ganzfeld.

Palmer suggests that feedback, informing subjects of their performance, counteracts decline and enhances ESP. He tells how Honorton (1970), Charles T. Tart (1976), and Braud (1977) think that feedback could sharpen ESP through learning (Palmer, "ESP Research" 210–14).

Irwin and Watt (66–67) and Carpenter (205) describe a number of aspects of ESP performance. "Psi missing" (ψM) is scoring lower than chance, as opposed to "psi hitting" (ψH), scoring higher than chance. Irwin and Watt say that ψM is not simply the negative end of the normal curve of scoring because the frequency is much lower than for ψH and suggests that it is due to mood, attitude, and personality, which cause inaccurate focus of ESP. Jephson (1928) noticed that subjects' accuracy was often high at beginning and end and low in the middle, which J. Rhine (1941) called "terminal salience" (Carpenter 206). "Position effects" are "groupings which reflect changes in scoring direction from one part of the test to another" and "decline effects" are that scores at the start of the test tend to be above chance but decline to chance or below toward the end of a process (Palmer, "Statistical Methods" 154). Tart explains decline as "extinction," as defined in behaviorism (Palmer, "ESP Research" 210). "Displacement" is the tendency to choose "targets other than the one for which [the response] was intended, generally targets in the immediate vicinity of the intended one" (Carpenter 217).

Famous and Notable Cases

Ancient literature, such as the Bible, is full of claims of ESP, most of which are not credible. Exceptions are that Apollonius of Tyana described the assassination of Domitian, and Swedenborg the burning of Stockholm. Predictions of the Lincoln assassination and the *Titanic* sinking also come to mind, but all such cases are better discussed within the individual sections on telepathy and on forms of clairvoyance.

Telepathy

In 2 Kings 6:8–23, apparently in Dothan, Elisha hears the plan which the king of Syria spoke in his bedroom, presumably a hundred miles away in Damascus, and Elisha strikes a "great" Syrian army with blindness. The fact that neither the king of Syria nor of Israel is named does not lend credibility to the story. Xiong asserts that sponges and plants possess telepathy because of the ways in which their cells organize themselves and react to their environment (Xiong 84). It is more likely that physical communication is happening which has not yet been observed, as when a dog appeared to do arithmetic but was really responding to its trainer's subtle cues.

Francis Bacon proposed testing telepathy by guessing cards or names and "to note whether it hit for the most part though not alwaies [sic]" (par. 956, p. 210). Early experiments in telepathy concerned "remote hypnosis," in which subjects were placed under and out of hypnosis over long distances, beginning with D. Velinski in 1818 Russia (Xiong 89). Leonid Leonidovich Vasiliev resumed this research between 1928 and 1966. Vasiliev worked under a Soviet mandate to uncover the physical basis of telepathy. In 1959 Vasiliev received a hoaxed report that telepathy had been achieved between the submerged USS *Nautilus* and a lab on the American mainland. This confirmed his conclusion of the 1930s that telepathy was not electromagnetic because such radiation could not traverse deep water (Pratt 887, 890–91). Later studies of extremely low frequency (ELF) radiation as the medium of ESP have been inconclusive. Puthoff and Targ say that ELF cannot efficiently carry information (Xiong 305). The Soviet government was interested in the military aspect of the story, and Vasiliev was able to publish his research on the occasion of the founding of a telepathic laboratory (Pratt 887–88). Vasiliev claimed to replicate the 1897 work of P. Joire in eliciting responses to silent commands to hypnotized subjects. Vasiliev also reported "unmistakable" accuracy of 14 percent and partial or symbolic accuracy of 34 percent in having someone send a target image to someone who would draw or describe it. Vasiliev claimed that a third series of studies mimicked Pierre Janet's 1886 efforts at remote hypnosis with 90–100 percent success in 1933–1934 and statistically highly significant success in more rigorous trials in 1935–1936 (Pratt 887–90). Pratt (890) says that Soviet parapsychology has "its own value" but not "a place of major importance" in the field.

J. Rhine called the traditional definition of telepathy "untestable" ("Extrasensory Perception" 165–66). However, Tart stimulated a sender with electric shocks, measured the receiver's physiological response, and later compared brain waves of separated pairs, one of whom was stimulated with a light, for example (Xiong 90). Ullman and Krippner tested telepathy by having a receiver sleep wired for brain waves in a soundproof room. When the receiver began to dream, evidenced by rapid eye movements, the sender concentrated on a picture. When brain waves showed that the dream had ended, the receiver was awakened. The receiver described their dream on audio tape and chose one of eight to twelve pictures with the help of their recording. This research was successful enough for Hansel to call it an exception to inconclusive, poorly designed experiments (Xiong 91–92).

Clairvoyance

An early report of clairvoyance is that Apollonius of Tyana described in Ephesus the assassination of the Roman emperor Domitian at the same time (18 September 96 CE) as it happened in Rome, 500 miles away (Philostratus 8.26).

Bacon (par. 987–88, pp. 214–15) tells how the archbishop of Vienna [sic; probably Vienne, France] told king Louis XI that Charles, Duke of Burgundy, had been killed by the Swiss, at the time when it happened, 5 January 1477, likewise how Pope St. Pius V suddenly adjourned his law court to tell that the Turks had been defeated at Lepanto, again at the time when it happened, 5 October 1571, by the Holy Alliance, which he had engineered.

A report documented by Immanuel Kant is that Emanuel Swedenborg (1688–1772) described the burning of Stockholm (19 July 1759) as it happened 300 miles away. However, Lars Bergquist (*Swedenborgs Hemlighet* 312–13) says that Swedenborg's description was on 29 July 1759, which was ten days after the fire, only commenting that Kant's date, "in the end of September 1756," was incorrect. Bergquist seems to have been misled by R.L. Tafel, who gives 2 dates for the Stockholm fire, 19 July 1759 (2: 616), which is correct, and 29 July 1759 (2: 629 note), which is incorrect. Perhaps "29" for "19" is just a misprint. The point is that Swedenborg is reported by primary sources to have described the fire as it happened. The English translation of *Hemlighet*, *Swedenborg's Secret* (269–71), does not include Tafel/Bergquist's error. *Hemlighet* was published by Natur och Kultur, an academic press, while *Swedenborg's Secret* was edited by the Rev. Norman Ryder, a Swedenborgian clergyman, and published by the Swedenborg Society, dedicated to the propagation of Swedenborg's teachings.

Another story is that Swedenborg correctly reported to Swedish queen Louisa Ulrika the content of a letter from her late brother Prince August Wilhelm of Prussia on the basis of Swedenborg's conversation with the deceased. A third is that Swedenborg told Countess Marie Louise Ammon de Marteville, the widow of the Dutch ambassador in Stockholm, where to find a lost receipt for a very large payment of a debt after Swedenborg talked to her dead husband.

There are "several different versions" of these stories as well (Bergquist, *Swedenborg's Secret*, 271–273, *Swedenborgs Hemlighet*, 312–316).

Remote viewing

Apollonius and Swedenborg could be classified as remote viewers. Upton Sinclair's *Mental Radio* (1930) described his experiments with what would be called remote viewing, a form of clairvoyance at great distance. When parapsychological research sponsored by the Soviet Union was revealed in 1970, the U.S. government became interested. Various U.S. intelligence agencies experimented with remote viewing from 1972 until 1995, starting with SCANATE and ending with the Stargate Project. The CIA contracted with the Stanford Research Institute (SRI), where Russell Targ, Harold Puthoff, and Edwin C. May worked with remote viewers (Federation of American Scientists). Charles Tart, Puthoff, and Targ's remote viewing research was published in *Science* and *Nature* (Tart; Tart et al.).

The chief researcher picked 100 locations nearby, another researcher stayed 30 minutes at each one, and a 3rd researcher stayed with a subject who was asked to describe or draw the location. An "independent judge" visited the locations and judged the likeness of the drawings and descriptions to the locations. Although the researchers reported a high degree of success, critics suggested that the judges were clued, intentionally or not (Palmer, "ESP Controversy" 177–79). Tart enlisted a different judge, who corroborated the researchers' success. Robert G. Jahn wrote a computer program to obtain more precise results. In 1995 the CIA said that although Stargate had achieved higher-than-chance results, ESP had never been used to guide an intelligence operation. May said that the CIA had selected data and used a discredited evaluation of parapsychology to achieve a predetermined result (Xiong 109–10).

Targ and Puthoff reported 51 trials with 9 different subjects. Their net results had probability of less than 1 in 100 million. David Marks and Richard Kamman (1980) saw unedited transcripts of trials with their dates and other indications of when they had occurred. They thought that this information could bias the judge if the order of targets was not randomized, as with subject Pat Price. However, Marks and Kamman misinterpreted the judge's letter to say the same for subject Hella Hammid, whose targets were randomized (Palmer "ESP Controversy" 177–78). Hansel (162) quotes Marks and Kamman that cues available to Price enabled one of them to achieve success with probability less than 1 in 50,000, but Hansel never mentions Hammid.

Ingo Douglas Swann (1933–2013) was one of Targ and Puthoff's more prominent subjects (Rush, "Spontaneous Psi" 55–56; Xiong 108). Harold Sherman and Swann, at the same time but in Arkansas and "on the West Coast" respectively, remote viewed the planet Jupiter on 27 April 1973 with remarkably similar results (Central Intelligence Agency, "Experimental Psychic Probe" 2, 5).

Joseph McMoneagle is another renowned remote viewer. The U.S. Army Security Agency recruited him in 1964. After a near-death experience in 1970, he began to have out-of-body and mind-reading experiences. In 1977 he became Remote Viewer 001. He claims over 1000 viewings with accuracy between 65 and 75 percent. He resigned the Army in 1984 and received the Legion of Merit, the citation of which mentions the CIA, DIA, FBI, Secret Service, Department of Defense, Customs Service, and Coast Guard. The citation honors McMoneagle for supplying "critical information unavailable from any other source" (Popkin). McMoneagle also claimed to have viewed ancient inhabitants of Mars (Central Intelligence Agency, "Mars").

L. Storm claimed higher-than-chance results for remote viewing in 2003 (Irwin and Watt 57).

Precognition

Belief in precognition is older than history. Astronomy began with the correlation of the seasons with the movement of the sun among the stars. From this recognition came the belief that events could be predicted from the movements of the planets, which created astrology, which was expelled from astronomy only in the eighteenth century.

Besides predicting the future from the planets or the entrails of animals, some individuals were believed to be able to see the future intuitively. South Asians, Chinese, Greeks, and Hebrews trusted experts to tell the future. This belief persists in the fascination with Biblical prophecy of conservative Christians. However, the accuracy of predictions in the Old Testament can be explained by hypothesizing that the predictions were written after the events predicted, or, in the case of Jesus' fulfillment of prophecy, the gospel stories were created to accord with prophecy. The book of Daniel is the best example, accurately predicting events through 167 BCE, but failing afterward, so that the book seems to have been written after that date (May and Metzger 1080, 1086 notes; Hartmann 408).

In the sixteenth century, as the scientific revolution was beginning, Michel de Nostredame (1503–1566), better known as Nostradamus, convinced French nobles, most prominently Catherine de Medicis, wife of King Henry II, whose death Nostradamus was believed to have predicted (*Compleat Works,* Century 1, Quatrain 35), that Nostradamus could predict the future. His following persists today, although it is the vagueness of his predictions which allows them to fit real events.

Bacon thought that he had a premonitory dream of his father's death (par. 986, p. 214).

Elizabeth Reynolds, maid and second wife of Richard Shearsmith, Swedenborg's landlord, said that Swedenborg predicted his death a few days before (Tafel vol. 2 [part 1]: p. 546). When John Wesley proposed that he and Swedenborg meet in 6 months after a missionary trip, Swedenborg replied that he would die on 29 March 1772, in 1 month, and so it happened.

The attestation for this reminds one of a hadith. S. Noble, a Swedenborgian minister, said that J. I. Hawkins, a Swedenborgian layman, and M. Sibly, a Swedenborgian minister, said that Samuel Smith, a Methodist minister, said that Swedenborg proposed the meeting in a letter in late February 1772, Wesley replied and proposed a meeting in 6 months, and Swedenborg said that he would die on 29 March 1772 (Tafel 2 [part 1]: pp. 564–69). Tafel and all but 1 of the 4 witnesses were Swedenborgians, so that a skeptic would not be convinced.

There are many other anecdotes about precognition. On 4 April 1865 Abraham Lincoln dreamed of his death, confiding in his wife Mary and his friend Ward Hill Lamon. Many people claimed to have foreseen the 1912 sinking of the *Titanic*. Morgan Robertson published the novel *Futility* in 1898, in which an iceberg sank the *Titan*, a huge passenger ship, with great loss of life (Xiong 119–20, 123–25). John William Dunne, an aeronautical engineer, dreamed of the eruption of Mt. Pelee on Martinique in 1902 before the news arrived (Xiong 119–20, 123–25). In 1927, he published *An Experiment with Time*, in which he developed his belief in precognitive dreams into the theory of serial time (Knight).

Erik Jan Hanussen (1889–1933) coached Adolf Hitler on public speaking and predicted his appointment as chancellor. Hanussen was acquitted of fraudulent claims to psychic power in what is now the Czech Republic in 1928. Oskar Fischer was an expert witness against Hanussen. It was an open secret that Hanussen was Jewish. Although he claimed to be a Danish nobleman, he was actually born Hermann (Hershmann Chaim) Steinschneider in Vienna. Hanussen's ancestors included miracle working, perhaps heretical, rabbis. After the Reichstag fire, Hanussen was killed by the Nazis, probably because he knew too much about the fire (Goedert, Portnoy, Spence).

Jeane L. Pinkert Dixon (1904–1997) convinced many that she had predicted the assassination of John F. Kennedy. In 1956 she told *Parade* magazine that a Democratic president elected in 1960, a tall young man with blue eyes and thick brown hair, would die in office. ("Jeane L. Dixon") Despite her many failed predictions, she had a very large following.

On 19 October 1966, in Aberfan, Wales, Eryl Mae Jones dreamed that a huge black mass engulfed the town. On 21 October, she and 143 others were killed when a mound of mine tailings collapsed onto her school (Lynch). J.C. Barker reported 24 predictions of the disaster ("Aberfan Disaster").

Formal research began in 1889 when Eleanor Mildred Sidgwick, wife of Henry, published a study of precognitive cases, which had been excluded by Gurney et al. She concluded that some could not be attributed to chance (L. Rhine 64). In 1934 H.F. Saltmarsh found 349 cases of precognition, 100 of death. L. Rhine (65–66) calls them "statistically significant." J. Rhine speculated that precognition might be explained in terms of PK (J. Rhine, "Extrasensory Perception" 166). E. Sidgwick (1888–1889), Saltmarsh (1934), L. Rhine (1954), C. Green (1960), G. Sannwald (1963), J.E. Orme (1974), F. Steinkamp (2000), and A.A. Drewes (2002) report "high incidence of dreams" in precognitive cases (Irwin and Watt 86).

J. Rhine (1938) reported statistically significant precognition for a group of subjects and very high scores with theological student Hubert E. Pearce (Irwin and Watt 88). Whether a precognized event can be averted is confusing, because if the event is averted, the precognition arguably is invalidated. L. Rhine (1955), Steinkamp (2000), and Drewes (2002) nevertheless claim cases in which the precognized event was averted. In such cases it might be clear that, without intervention, the precognized event would have occurred. William E. Cox (1956) showed that ridership was lower on days of train crashes and suggested that precognition might be a cause, although bad weather might account for both (Irwin and Watt 87). That the future is not immutable is suggested by 1933 Nobel laureate in physics Erwin Schroedinger's equation, which gives probabilities of multiple subatomic outcomes rather than only one. A more serious objection to precognition is that the statistical support for it is weaker than for other ESP (Irwin and Watt 92). Dean Radin (1997, 2004) claims to have demonstrated unconscious responses to future events. Electrodes measured skin conductance, heart rate, and blood volume in the left third fingertip. A computer randomly displayed "calm" or "emotional" pictures. All 3 physiological measures changed consistently before "emotional" but not "calm" pictures were seen. Dick Bierman (1996), A. Bechara, H. Damasio, D. Tranel, A.R. Damasio (1997), J. Spottiswoode, May (2003), Z. Vassy (2004), and L. Sartori, S. Macassessi, M. Martinelli, P. E. Tressoldi (2004) reported similar results, but J. Dalkvist, J. Westerlund, Bierman (2004) and J. Wackermann (2004) suggest that subjects actually have increasing electrodermal activity (EDA) because they anticipate distress after a period of little stimulation (Xiong, 126–27; Irwin and Watt 90). Libet provided a more philosophical interpretation of seeming precognition.

Retrocognition

Xiong (129) cites Jesus' interview with the Samaritan woman (John 4:16–19) as telepathy and retrocognition, but the story is not historical in its present form (Shafer, "Saint" 25–32). In 1911 Annie Moberly and Eleanor Jourdain published *An Adventure* (under the pseudonyms Miss Morison and Miss Lamont). They claimed to have traveled to Versailles at the time of Louis XVI. There were similar reports by Sir Kelvin Spencer and Sir William Rees-Mogg. J. Rhine abandoned research on retrocognition because he could not separate it from clairvoyance, coming to no conclusion on its existence. Edgar Cayce (1877–1945) is supposed to have seen the past (Xiong 129–31). Stanislaw Poniatowski tested retrocognition of Stefan Ossowieski connected with archeology from 1936 to 1942, with disputed results (Feder, Weaver). Retrocognition often is tied to places and battles, such as the Dieppe raid of 1942, reportedly heard by two women in neighboring Puys in 1951 (Irwin and Watt 84). A problem in authenticating retrocognition is that it may be merely fantasy based on natural knowledge of the past, i.e., cryptomnesia, as with "Bridey Murphy," the purported past life of Virginia Tighe, published in 1956 (Edge, "Survival" 342).

Criticism of ESP Research

Here we will deal with empirically-based criticisms of ESP. Most theoretical objections to ESP are discussed in Shafer, "Theoretical Criticism of Psychical Research" because they are objections to psi in general. I will only say here that such objections are based on obsolete physics, and a more general problem with such objections is that data should dictate theory rather than theory exclude evidence from consideration.

Nevertheless, ESP has not convinced most scientists. Irwin and Watt (57–61) lay out 3 approaches to establishing the authenticity of ESP: (1) Does a definitive experiment exist? (2) What is the weight of cumulative evidence? (3) What is the logical status of ESP experiments? Irwin and Watt conclude that no definitive experiment can be devised because fraud can never absolutely be excluded, recalling Hume's claim that extraordinary claims require extraordinarily convincing proof. Irwin and Watt set an unreasonable standard because while fraud can never be categorically excluded, researchers can make it so improbable as to be negligible.

Irwin and Watt say that even if a definitive experiment or cumulative data would demonstrate a statistically significant effect, other explanations than ESP are logically possible, such as something like a natural tendency to coincidence independent of minds (Jung's "synchronicity"?)

or unaccounted variations of known, ordinary processes such as an operation of chance different than what we understand (Irwin and Watt 40–45, 61). Once again Irwin and Watt are unrealistic because there is no way categorically to exclude alternative explanations, practically speaking this objection can be falsified statistically, i.e., if results deviate sufficiently from chance, coincidence can be ruled out, and procedurally, if experimental methods exclude known explanations, as Radin ("Revising") has attempted to demonstrate.

Another objection is that much research has not been replicated. However, both social and natural scientific journals discourage replication in favor of original research. Further, replication is more difficult than imagined because (1) Human subjects cannot be replicated, and (2) replication is difficult also in the "hard" sciences (Edge and Morris 317–18). H.M. Collins (1978) found that universities could not replicate "the TEA laser on the basis of written reports or discussions with third parties, ..." More direct contact and work with the original builders were necessary (Edge and Morris 317–18).

Palmer ("ESP Research" 186–87) gives 4 possible reasons for the "lack of repeatability" (1) Psi does not exist, and apparent psi is due to faulty method and statistical quirks. (2) Sampling error rises from the fact that most "hits" result from chance, which by definition varies from study to study. This suggests that even if it exists, psi is less significant than chance. (3) Factors which facilitate or inhibit psi are unknown, so that they are impossible to control. (4) Psi is real but inherently "unlawful," which would make it inaccessible to science.

(See Shafer, "Theoretical Criticism" for speculation on the "Trickster.")

Becker (12) thinks that the "sheep-goat effect" (SGE) may explain the fact that researchers who have a strong disbelief in psi do not replicate results of believers. This is a hazardous explanation. Whenever those who claim paranormal powers fail to demonstrate them, they can blame their failures on the bad influence of nonbelievers, as in the Bible (Mark 6:5; Matt. 13:58). Some degree of replicability is necessary for verification. Even the Bible calls for 2 witnesses to capital crimes, (Num. 35:30, Deut.17:6, 19:15), as does the U.S. Constitution to treason (Art. 3 Sec. 3).

Irwin and Watt conclude that authentication of ESP depends on understanding how it works, which requires process-oriented research (61). Such process-oriented research has had impressive results. REG PK, and the correlation of ESP with certain psychological traits have produced higher-than-chance results (Edge and Morris 319).

Other such research confirms that psi is affected by the attitude of the subject. Further, starting with Bacon, researchers have noticed that ESP is associated with objects of personal significance. Bacon recommended that it be "thorowly inquired, whether there be any Secret Passages of Sympathy between Persons of near Bloud; As Parents, Children, Brothers, Sisters, Nurse-Children, Husbands, wives, &c. [sic]" (par. 986 p. 214). J. Rhine ("Extrasensory Perception" 171), Schmeidler (1952), Schmeidler and McConnell (1958), Palmer (1977), T.R. Lawrence (1993), B.E. Lovitts (1981), R. Wiseman, and M.D. Smith (2002) reported that believers scored higher than chance (psi hitting, ψH) and skeptics lower than chance (psi missing, ψM). These belief-correlated deviations from chance are SGE. (Irwin and Watt 74–75) Also "…As far as its implications for process-oriented research is [sic] concerned, arguably the most interesting ideas thrown up by Louisa Rhine's analysis of spontaneous case reports is [sic] that ESP seems purposive in its orientation and that it may well be instigated by the experient rather than being passively received by him or her" (Irwin and Watt 35–37). However, higher-than-chance results for believers and lower-than-chance for unbelievers might be explained by confirmation bias combined with experimental error which allows the subjects unconsciously through their 5 senses (subliminally) to choose correct or incorrect responses consistent with their expectation.

Another method of verification was suggested by J. Rhine ("Extrasensory Perception" 167), who reported "characteristic indications of psi" in many studies by different researchers, such as the fact that the scoring rate of subjects declines as testing proceeds. That the "indications" were very frequent but unrecognized by the researchers conducting the tests and uncovered later by others who analyzed earlier research is a "source of psi evidence of unquestionable quality."

One such "indication" is that neurotic subjects score at or below chance, while well-adjusted subjects score above chance (Irwin and Watt 75). Extraverts also score higher than introverts (Palmer, "Attitudes" 185–86). L. Sartori, S. Massacessi, M. Martinelli, and P.E. Tressoldi (2004) reported elevated heart rate of subjects viewing targets over non-targets, although subjects' guesses were at chance level (Irwin and Watt 77), suggesting unconscious psi. Dissociative tendencies, i.e., "mental processes are divided or lacking integration in a situation where their integration would be expected," e.g., traumatic amnesia, also correlate with high ESP performance (Irwin and Watt 74–79). Johnson and Haraldsson reported a negative correlation between ESP and scores on Ulf Kragh and G.W. Smith's Defense Mechanism Test. In other words, defensiveness inhibits ESP. (Palmer, "ESP Research" 205–06; he says that there is a "positive" correlation, which seems to be a clerical error.)

Objections to J. Rhine's higher-than-chance results were that other researchers could not duplicate his results, researchers and subjects were in the same room, cards could be read from their backs, subjects could do card-counting, and there may have been statistical errors, uncontrolled sensory cues, recording errors, inadequate shuffling, optional stopping, suppression of null results (no divergence from chance), and fraud (Hansel 50–51; Irwin and Watt 53–54).

Gregor Mendel, or an assistant, seems to have committed scientific fraud (Judson; Fisher 132). Fraud was a serious enough problem in science that the American Association of Universities issued "Guidelines for Integrity of Research" in 1983 (Edge and Morris 317–18). J. Rhine's bona fides is suggested by the fact that when W.J. Levy confessed fraud to Rhine, he fired him and published a report on the incident, warning not to use Levy's publications (J. Rhine, "New Case"; "Science").

Hansel (63–73) argued that J. Rhine and Pratt did not correctly report the details of the experiments with Pearce, Rhine's most successful subject, and that Pearce had been left alone and snuck from his assigned place to look at research assistant Pratt's papers and to copy information to be sent by ESP. However, Pearce's initial reluctance to participate in psychical research (Xiong 102) might be inconsistent with fraud. J. Rhine and his supporters pointed out that the cards used in the experiments were better than commercial ones, and the windows which Hansel assumed in his explanation did not exist. Hansel responded that Pearce likely drilled a hole in the ceiling (Xiong 103, Hansel 66). Hansel (78–80, 87–88, 92) also suggested fraud by Pratt and his assistant Joseph Leroy Woodruff in their 1938–1939 card-guessing experiment, facilitated by the fact that Woodruff served as both experimenter and subject (Xiong 103–04). J. Rhine's later results were not as successful as those obtained before he applied stricter protocols (Xiong 103). Nevertheless, after almost a half-century, Palmer ("ESP Controversy" 165) concluded "that the ball is now in the critic's court."

Palmer agrees with Hansel that Soal faked results with his subject Basil Shackleton (1941–1943; Palmer, "ESP Controversy" 165–67). Eighteen scientists wrote 27 papers on Pavel Stepanek. Pratt (1973) reported that Stepanek's hit rate for guessing the color of cards in envelopes was 53.9 percent (probability less than 1 in 1 million). However, Stepanek first seemed to prefer certain envelopes, then when the envelopes were covered, certain covers, and when the covers were jacketed, certain jackets. Stepanek's accuracy declined as more layers were added (Palmer, "ESP Controversy" 167–69). Hansel (257) might be correct: "The Stepanek investigations can hardly be called experimental...."

Schmidt (1969) used REG to test precognition in 3 subjects who were relatively successful in screening. One experiment yielded 26.1 percent hits (probability less than 1 in 100 million), another 27 percent hits (probability less than 1 in 10 billion). He also tested clairvoyance in 6 subjects from the same screening. Their hit rate was 26.7 percent (probability less than 1 in 100,000) (Palmer, "ESP Controversy" 169–70). Hansel objects that electronic defects, such as irregular power supply, could cause nonrandomness in Schmidt's apparatus. He adds that the paper-tape recorder and mechanical counters could be turned on and off (134–35). Subject Bill Delmore achieved an "exact hit" rate of 6 percent (probability less than 1 in 1 nonillion, 1 followed by 30 zeroes), was successful at the "psychic shuffle," and got 28.7 percent hits (probability less than 1 in 1 billion) on a Schmidt REG at J. Rhine's laboratory. Persi Diaconis (1978, 1979), magician and statistician, accused Delmore of magician's tricks (Palmer, "ESP Controversy" 171–72).

Charles T. Tart used his 10-choice trainer (TCT) to test telepathy. The hit rate was 3.61 (probability less than 1 in 1 septillion, 1 followed by 24 zeroes). Lila L. Gatlin (1979) and J.E. Kennedy (1980) claimed nonrandomness in the target sequence. Kennedy also suggested cheating (Palmer, "ESP Controversy" 172–73).

Ullman, Krippner, and Honorton tested ESP in dreams in the late 1960s. An agent used a random number table to select a famous painting on which to concentrate during the night. The subject slept with electrodes measuring brain waves and eye movements. Several minutes after these physiological measures indicated dreaming, the experimenter wakened the subject and tape-recorded the subject's description of the dream. Again the next morning the subject's description was recorded. Later the subject and 1 to 3 outside judges ranked the similarity of the descriptions to the target. Descriptions in the top 50 percent of ranks were deemed hits. For example, dreams of a ceremony with Winston Churchill and an indigenous sacrifice were ranked as a hit on Max Beckmann's *The Descent from the Cross*. Ullman et al. reported success with Robert Van de Castle, but David Foulkes and Edward Belvedere (1971, 1972) claimed that their replication produced "nonsignificant" results (Palmer, "ESP Controversy" 174–76). Hansel (152) speculates that Van de Castle succeeded with Ullman et al. because of experimental error, and that Van de Castle failed with Foulkes and Belvedere because of proper experimental rigor.

Unlike other ESP studies, which tend to be diverse and isolated in particular institutions, Honorton claimed 28 successful ganzfeld experiments out of 42 conducted at 9 laboratories and a success rate of 55 percent for them. The distribution of the studies in different labs and their unselected subjects made fraud less an issue. Hyman (1983, 1985) countered that (1) only statistically significant studies were submitted for publication, (2) scoring was statistically flawed, and (3) studies where multiple conditions were used were deemed successful if just one condition gave a significant outcome, (4) one-tailed tests (statistical tests in which whether deviation is above or below chance is specified in advance) counted ψM as success, and (5) methods were flawed. Honorton (1985) countered by recalculating his analysis and obtained a composite CR with probability less than 1 in 1 billion (Palmer, "ESP Controversy" 179–81). Hansel (153–159) deconstructs several ganzfeld experiments and maintains that most experiments "fail to confirm ESP." Dean Radin ("Revising") disagrees based on meta-analyses cited in his essay.

J. Utts' survey of meta-analyses, i.e., analyses of many studies, suggested that apparent ESP cannot be attributed to suppression of null, i.e., chance, results. Irwin and Watt countered that meta-analysis of the cumulative record of studies up to then (2007) could not authenticate ESP because of subjectivity and bias in the selection of studies for meta-analysis. However, they add, if the criteria for inclusion and coding were set in advance by competent and trustworthy professionals, as suggested by J.E. Kennedy in 2004, meta-analysis of subsequent experiments could validate ESP to the same degree as other psychological phenomena (Irwin and Watt 59–60). Radin's essay ("Revising") presents meta-analyses of ganzfeld experiments which yield success rates of around 32 percent, where chance would yield 25 percent. Radin ("Revising") also argues that these meta-analyses have excluded the problems which Irwin and Watt criticized. This would satisfy Irwin and Watt's criterion (2), "cumulative data."

In Popular Culture

It has been said that no one ever went broke by underestimating the intelligence of Americans. This is supported by the popularity of psi in popular culture, especially the prevalence of TV programs on ghosts and psychics. Ipsos polling found that 1 in 7 people around the world believed that it would end in 2012 because of the Mayan calendar. Belief in psi expresses discomfort with materialism, which offers little hope in the face of death. John Edwards, Uri Geller, and Jeane Dixon have made careers out of popular parapsychology. Their claims have not been substantiated scientifically. On the contrary, like faith healers, psychics have sometimes been exposed as frauds by debunkers such as Harry Houdini and James Randi.

Conclusion

Does ESP exist? The prevalence of fraud in popular parapsychology might suggest not. However, contemporary physics has so undermined materialism, the philosophy in which everything is a process of matter and energy, that consciousness, as Schroedinger thought, may need to be considered as a third, irreducible, part of nature (Shafer, "Theoretical Criticism").

There is no compelling theoretical objection to psi, so that the next logical question is whether empirical research supports the existence of psi. If we follow Hume, the evidence is not sufficient. Nevertheless, Hume was privileging materialism because relativity and quantum mechanics were as yet unknown. Therefore, Hume's objection is invalid.

What does the empirical evidence suggest? There are anecdotes and "spontaneous cases" of psi back to the dawn of history, but in themselves they cannot authenticate psi. What does experimental research suggest? Many studies show much higher-than-chance accuracy for ESP. Critics such as Hansel maintain that all of these can be explained by experimental error, including fraud. However, the length to which Hansel has gone to discredit the Pratt-Pearson trials, for example, is so far-fetched as to discredit Hansel's reasoning. Meta-analysis of ganzfeld in particular argues that ESP is real (Radin, "Revising").

I conclude that psi exists. Even if further research does not uncover more dramatic evidence of psi, it seems that psi exists, but is very weak compared to physical forces. Physics has demonstrated four basic forces: gravity, electromagnetism, the strong nuclear force, and the weak nuclear force. The two nuclear forces operate only over the tiny distances within the nucleus, and gravity is very weak compared to electromagnetism, as is shown by the fact that a small magnet can overcome the gravitation of the earth. So it may be with psi.

Works Cited

"Aberfan Disaster." *Ghost Theory.* www.ghosttheory.com/2013/03/01/the-aberfan-disaster. Accessed 5 Aug.2020.
Bacon, Francis. *Sylva Sylvarum: A Natural History in Ten Centuries*, William Lee, 1658, archive.org/stream/sylvasylvarumo00baco?ref=ol#page/210/mode/2up. Accessed 19 July 2021.
Bechara, Antoine, Hanna Damasio, Daniel Tranel, and Antonio R. Damasio, "Deciding Advantageously Before [sic] Knowing the Advantageous Strategy," *Science*, vol. 275, no. 5304, 28 Feb. 1997, pp. 1293–95.
Becker, Carl B. "Extrasensory Perception, Near-Death Experiences, and the Limits of Scientific Knowledge," *The Journal of Near-Death Studies*, vol. 9 ,1990, pp. 45–54, https://digital.library.unt.edu/ark:/67531/metadc799152/m2/1/high_res_d/vol9-no111.pdf. Accessed 30 Jan. 2021.
Beloff, John. "Historical Overview." Wolman et al. pp. 3–24.
Bergquist, Lars. *Swedenborgs hemlighet: Om ordets betydelse, anglarnas liv och tjansten hos Gud: en biografi*, Natur och Kultur, 1999.
_____. *Swedenborg's Secret: The Meaning and Significance of the Word of God, the Life of the Angels, and Service to God*, The Swedenborg Society, 2005.
Bierman, Dick J. "FMRI-Meditation Study of Presentiment: The Role of 'Coherence' in Retrocausal Processes." Paper presented at the symposium of the Bial Foundation, Porto, Portugal, Mar. 2008, www.uniamsterdam.nl/D.J.Bierman/PUBS/2010/ JoP_74_ pp273_299_CIRTS_proof.pdf. Accessed 2 Mar. 2021.
Blackburn, Simon. "Bacon, Francis." *The Oxford Dictionary of Philosophy*. Oxford University Press, 1996, pp. 34–35.

60   Probing Parapsychology

Brown, Raymond E., Joseph A. Fitzmyer, and Roland E. Murphy, editors. *The New Jerome Biblical Commentary*. Prentice-Hall, 1968.
Burdick, Donald S., and Edward F. Kelly. "Statistical Methods in Parapsychological Research." Wolman et al., pp. 81–130.
Carpenter, James C. "Intrasubject and Subject-Agent Effects in ESP Experiments." Wolman et al., pp. 202–72.
Central Intelligence Agency. "An Experimental Psychic Probe of the Planet Jupiter. Harold Sherman, Ingo Swann, April 27, 1973," www.cia.gov/readingroom/docs/NSA-RDP96X00790R000100040010-3.pdf. Accessed 29 Jan. 2021.
———. "Mars Exploration May 22, 1984," www.cia.gov/readingroom/docs/CIA-RDP96-00788R001900760001-9.pdf. Accessed 29 Jan. 2021.
Edge, Hoyt L. "Survival and Other Philosophical Questions." Edge et al., pp. 325–360.
———, Robert L. Morris. "Psi and Science." Edge et al., pp. 295–324.
———, Robert L. Morris, Joseph L. Rush, and John A. Palmer. *Foundations of Parapsychology: Exploring the Boundaries of Human Capability*. Foreword by Theodore Xenophon Barber, Routledge and Kegan Paul, 1986.
Feder, Kenneth L. "Ossowiecki, Stefan." *Encyclopedia of Dubious Archaeology: From Atlantis to the Walam Olum*. Greenwood, 2010, p. 203, archive.org/details/ encyclopediaofdu0000fede/page/202/mode/2up. Accessed 15 January 2022.
Federation of American Scientists. "Stargate [Controlled Remote Viewing]." Intelligence Resource Program, fas.org/irp/program/collect/stargate.htm. Accessed 21 Dec. 2020.
Fischer, Oskar. *Experimente mit Raphael Schermann: Ein Beitrag zu den Problemen der Graphologie, Telepathie, und des Hellsehens*, Urban and Schwarzenberg, 1924.
Fisher, R.A. "Has Mendel's Work Been Rediscovered?" *Annals of Science*, vol. 1, 1936, pp. 115–137, drmc.library.adelaide.edu.au/dspace/bitstream/2440/15123/1/144.pdf. Accessed 16 Jan. 2022.
Goedert, Michel. "Oskar Fischer and the Study of Dementia." *Brain: A Journal of Neurology*, vol. 132, no. 4, Apr. 2009, pp. 1102–11, www.researchgate.net/publication/23415937_Oskar_Fischer_and_the_study_of_dementia. Accessed 29 Jan. 2021.
Hansel, Charles Edward Mark. *The Search for Psychic Power: ESP and Parapsychology Revisited*, Prometheus, 1989.
Hartman, Louis F., and Alexander A. Di Lella. "Daniel." Brown et al., pp. 406–20.
Hoel, Paul G. *Elementary Statistics*. 4th ed., John Wiley and Sons, Inc., 1976.
Ipsos. "One in Seven (14%) Global Citizens Believe End of the World is [sic] Coming in Their Lifetime," www.ipsos.com/sites/default/files/news_and_polls/2012-05/5610rev.pdf. Accessed 29 Jan. 2021.
Irwin, Harvey J., and Caroline A. Watt, *An Introduction to Parapsychology*, 5th ed., McFarland, 2007.
"Jeane L. Dixon; Psychic Predicted JFK's Death." *Los Angeles Times*, 26 Jan. 1997, www.latimes.com/archives/la-xpm-1997-01-26-mn-22407-story.html. Accessed 29 Oct. 2020.
Judson, Horace Freeland. *The Great Betrayal: Fraud in Science*. Harcourt, 2004.
Knight, Sam. "The Psychiatrist Who Believed People Could Tell the Future." *New Yorker*, 25 Feb. 2019, www.newyorker.com/magazine/2019/03/04/the-psychiatrist-who-believed-people-could-tell-the-future. Accessed 29 Jan. 2021.
Libet, Benjamin. "Subjective Antedating of a Sensory Experience and Mind-Brain Theories: Reply to Honderich." *Journal of Theoretical Biology*, vol. 114, no. 4, 21 June 1985, pp. 563–70. doi: 10.1016/s0022–5193(85)80043–6. PMID: 4021506, The Determinism and Freedom Philosophy Website, www.ucl.ac.uk/~uctytho/ Libethimself.html. Accessed 2 Mar. 2021.
Lynch, Patrick. "10 [sic] Premonitions of Doom from History That Actually Came True." *History Collection*, historycollection.com/10-premonitions-of-doom-and-from-history-that-actually-came-true/2/. Accessed 29 Jan. 2021.
May, Herbert G., and Bruce M. Metzger, editors. *The New Oxford Annotated Bible with the Apocrypha*. Oxford University Press, 1977.
Merriam-Webster's Collegiate Dictionary, 10th ed., Merriam-Webster, 1996.
Morris, Robert L. "Parapsychology, Biology, and ANPSI." Wolman et al., pp. 687–715.

Nostradamus. *The Compleat* [sic] *Works of Nostradamus*, zelalemkibret.files.wordpress. com/2012/02/the-complete-works-of- nostradamus.pdf. Accessed 29 Jan. 2021.
"Optional Stopping." *Oxford Reference*. www.oxfordreference.com/view/10.1093/oi/ authority.20110803100252397. Accessed 22 Aug. 2021.
Palmer, John A. "Attitudes and Personality Traits in Experimental ESP." Wolman et al., pp. 175–201.
_____. "The ESP Controversy," Edge et al., pp. 161–83.
_____. "ESP Research Findings: The Process Approach," Edge et al., pp. 184–222.
_____. "Experimental Methods in ESP Research," Edge et al., pp. 111–37.
_____. "Statistical Methods in ESP Research," Edge et al., pp. 138–69.
Philostratus. *The Life of Apollonius of Tyana*. .. Trans. by F.C. Conybeare, William Heinemann/Macmillan, 1912, archive.org/details/in.ernet.dli.2015.183421/page/n399/mode/2up. Accessed 29 Jan. 2021.
Popkin, Jim. "Meet the Former Pentagon Scientist Who Says Psychics Can Help American Spies," *Newsweek*, 12 Nov. 2015, www.newsweek.com/2015/11/20/meet-former-pentagon-scientist-who-says- psychics-can-help-american-spies-393004.html. Accessed 29 Jan. 2021.
Portnoy, Eddy. "Strange Tale of Hitler's Jewish Psychic." *Forward*, 8 Nov. 2011, forward. com/culture/145806/strange-tale-of-hitlers-jewish-psychic/. Accessed 29 Oct. 2020.
Pratt, Joseph Gaither. "Soviet Research in Parapsychology." Wolman et al., pp. 883–903.
Radin, Dean. "Electrodermal presentiments of future emotions." *Journal of Scientific Exploration*, vol. 18, no. 2, June 2004, pp. 253–273, www.researchgate.net/publication/279770368_Electrodermal_presentiments_of_future_emotions. Accessed 2 Mar. 2021.
_____. "Revising Our Concepts about Reality: The Challenge of Consciousness." Shafer, *Probing Parapsychology*.
Rhine, Joseph Banks. "Extrasensory Perception." Wolman et al., pp. 163–74.
_____. "History of Experimental Studies." Wolman et al., pp. 25–47.
_____. "A New Case of Experimenter Unreliability." *Journal of Parapsychology* 33, 1974, 136–75.
Rhine, Louisa Ella. "Research Methods with Spontaneous Cases," Wolman et al., pp. 49–80.
Roback, A.A. "Review of Oskar Fischer, *Experimente mit Raphael Schermann. Ein Beitrag zu den Problemen der Graphologie, Telepathie und des Hellsehen*." *American Journal of Psychology*, vol. 38, no.1, January 1927, pp. 146–47.
Rush, Joseph H. "Parapsychology: A Historical Perspective." Edge et al., pp. 9–44.
_____. "Spontaneous Psi Phenomena: Case Studies and Field Investigations." Edge et al. pp. 47–69.
Schmeidler, Gertrude Raffel. "Methods for Controlled Research on ESP and PK," Wolman et al. pp. 131–59.
"Science: The Psychic Scandal." *Time*. 26 Aug. 1974. content.time.com/time/subscriber/article/0,33009,944971-2,00.html. Accessed 18 July 2021.
Shafer, Grant R. *St. Stephen and the Samaritans: An Evaluation of, and a Contribution to, the Samaritanology of the New Testament*, unpublished dissertation, University of Michigan, 1995.
_____. "Theoretical Criticism of Psychic Research." Shafer, *Probing Parapsychology*.
_____, editor. *Probing Parapsychology: Essays on a Controversial Science*. McFarland.
Spence, Richard. "Erik Jan Hanussen: Hitler's Jewish Psychic." *New Dawn*. Vol. 8 no. 3, June 2014, www.newdawnmagazine.com/articles/erik-jan-hanussen-hitlers-jewish-psychic. Accessed 30 Jan. 2021.
Tafel, Rudolf Leonhard. *Documents Concerning the Life and Character of Emanuel Swedenborg*, 2 vols., Swedenborg Society, 1877, archive.org/details/documentsconcern21tafe/page/542/mode/2up. Accessed 29 Jan. 2021.
Tart, Charles T. "States of Consciousness and State Specific-Sciences," *Science*, vol. 176, no. 4040, 16 June 1972, pp. 1203–10, www.academia.edu/25585623/States_of_Consciousness_and_State-Specific_Sciences Accessed 25 Aug. 2021.

———, Harold E. Puthoff, Russell Targ. "Information Transmission in Remote Viewing Experiments," *Nature*, vol. 284, no. 5752, 13 Mar. 1980, p. 191, www.researchgate.net/publication/15839349_Information_transmission_in_remote_viewing experiments. Accessed 30 Jan. 2021.

Thouless, Robert Henry. *From Anecdote to Experiment in Psychical Research*. Routledge and Kegan Paul, 1972.

Troffer, Suzanne A., Charles T. Tart. "Experimenter Bias in Hypnotist Performance," *Science*, vol. 145, no. 3638, 18 Sep. 1964, pp. 1330–31, science.sciencemag.org/content/145/3638/1330. Accessed 30 Jan. 2021.

Uvarov, E. B., and D.R. Chapman. "Standard Deviation." *A Dictionary of Science*, 3rd ed., rev. by Alan Isaacs, Penguin Books, 1964, p. 285.

Weaver, Zofia. "Stefan Ossowiecki." *Psi Encyclopedia*. Society for Psychical Research, psi-encyclopedia.spr.ac.uk/articles/stefan-ossowiecki#footnote25_gmhnaz6. Accessed 15 January 2022.

White, Rhea A. "The Influence of Experimenter Motivation, Attitudes, and Methods of Handling Subjects on Psi Test Results." Wolman et al., pp. 273–301.

Wolman, Benjamin B., Laura A. Dale, Gertrude Raffel Schmeidler, Montague Ullman, editors. *Handbook of Parapsychology*. Van Nostrand Reinhold, 1977.

Xiong, Jesse Hong. *The Outline of Parapsychology*, rev. ed., University Press of America, 2010.

Psychokinesis
Famous Cases Around the World

V.G. MILLER

Introduction

The words psychokinesis (PK) and telekinesis (TK) are interchangeable. The word psychokinesis is a combination of the Greek words *psyche*, which means "mind" or "soul," and *kinesis*, which means "movement" or "motion." The word telekinesis uses the Greek word *tele*, which means "far away." This illustrates that the kind of movement that is being discussed in this phenomenon involves objects that are said to be moved at a distance from the person who is making them move. The study of PK covers a wide range of phenomena including moving objects without physical intervention, distorting objects from a distance, the production of light or sound without physical intervention, spontaneous ignition, interfering with the functioning of mechanical, electrical or electronic devices without touching them, imprinting photographic film psychically, and the materialization and dematerialization of objects and living things.

The antecedent of PK in the ancient world is the practice of magic. In magical ceremonies it was thought that the shaman or the priest could affect the material world through his directed thoughts and rituals (Karolyi 3). The word "telekinesis" was first used in 1890 by the Russian psychical researcher Alexander N. Aksakof. Aksakof coined the term to describe the phenomena that surrounded the Italian spiritualist and medium Eusapia Palladino. Among other things Aksakof believed that Palladino could make tables levitate. However, like most spiritualists of the time Palladino was observed in fraudulent practices ("Aksakof"; "Alexander").

Notwithstanding this, the word telekinesis endured. The word psychokinesis was invented in 1914 by the horror writer Henry Holt who wrote of paranormal events in his fictional work, *On Cosmic Relations*.

The word then made its way into the field of parapsychology by way of J.B. Rhine, who conducted experiments to see if a person with psychic ability could influence the outcomes of falling dice, among other things. In 1934 Rhine stated that PK is the phenomenon whereby objects and events are influenced by mental powers alone and not by the use of physical energy.

Spiritualism

The most famous instances of PK phenomena are associated with the Spiritualist movement. So-called examples of PK in séances include the following: musical instruments being played by themselves; the movement of objects and items of furniture similarly without human intervention; the levitation of pieces of furniture and people; apportation (the manifestation of objects in the séance); teleportation (when objects are moved into another location without human intervention), and manifestations (Beloff 38).

The most famous exponent of PK in the Spiritualist movement was Daniel Dunglas Home (1833–86). Notably, Home allowed himself to be tested by skeptics in a laboratory environment. In 1871 he was tested by William Crookes, a Fellow of the Royal Society and a physical scientist of note. One such test involved a wooden beam that was placed on a table at one end while the other end was suspended from a spring balance. The object of the experiment was for Home to place his fingers on the end of the wood that was placed on the table and to try and exert pressure psychically that would register on the other end. Crookes reports that there was clear evidence of downward pressure that had been exerted on the end that was suspended by the spring-balance. Notwithstanding this, most modern-day skeptics regard the phenomena that occurred in the Spiritualist movement to be clever conjuring, not unlike famous illusionists in the twenty-first century including David Copperfield and Dynamo (Beloff 41–51).

Famous Cases of PK from Around the World

Uri Geller

Undoubtedly the most famous and controversial exponent of PK today is the Israeli Uri Geller. Geller is most often remembered for his talent of bending spoons with the slightest stroking. He is also thought to have caused objects to bend and to move without touching them and by using only the power of his mind. Of his more impressive feats, Geller is thought to have made objects dematerialize and to reappear in different places. Geller controversially claimed that his powers came to him from extra-terrestrial intelligence with which he was in communication (Beloff 192–200).

Geller first came to the public's attention in Israel, where he performed tricks similar to stage magic. However, there was a point of difference between Geller and other stage magicians, notably in that he claimed that he was using psychic ability and not merely faking his effects (Targ and Puthoff 136). Yet, the authenticity of Geller's claims have been challenged, importantly by members of his staff, including his manager at the time, Yasha Katz. Indeed in 1977 James Randi interviewed Katz who confessed to the numerous tricks that were used in Geller's stage shows. For instance, Katz would signal to Geller the words that were written on a blackboard on stage behind Geller. Katz also told Randi that Geller would take notes on unusual cars and number plates that he later revealed as "psychic intuitions" on stage. Furthermore, Katz would stand near the box-office and note down information about the audience that he would relay to Geller to use on stage. Katz also said that he witnessed Geller throw things over his shoulder ostensibly to make them "materialize," among other fraudulent practices. Geller admitted to cheating on certain occasions, to follow the advice of Katz, who wanted his shows to be more impressive, but stated that he did not cheat on other occasions, when he manifested true psychic phenomena. Geller also maintains that some of the claims against him were made by people who were motivated by jealousy (Randi 122–28). Randi himself has confirmed his own occasional dishonesty (Storr).

Notwithstanding the debate concerning the veracity of his stage performances Geller has been tested rigorously in laboratories across the world by researchers who are convinced of his paranormal abilities. Geller was first studied by John Taylor at King's College for his ability to bend metal without exerting physical pressure. For instance, Taylor measured the downward pressure that Geller's strokes applied to a copper sheet. It is claimed that the brass bent upwards by ten degrees despite the fact that Geller applied no more than one-half ounce of downward pressure—this is an anomalous result. Moreover, Taylor reports that the needle in the gauge also bent despite this not being the focus of the experiment. Furthermore, Geller was tested for his spoon bending techniques at the Birkbeck College of London. This spoon bending practice was later dubbed the "plasticization" of spoons due to the apparent rubber-like quality of spoons after they were stroked by Geller. Of interest in the Geller case is the number of children, in particular, who watched Geller perform and subsequently claimed that they had the same ability. It has been estimated that these children number into the thousands (Broughton 164).

Nina Kulagina

Other cases of alleged PK emerged from the Soviet Union. One of the most documented cases of PK was that of Nina Kulagina (1926–1990), who was continuously observed in laboratory conditions for twenty years. Kulagina was first tested for PK by the Soviet parapsychologist Leonid L. Vasiliev in 1963. When Vasiliev died in 1966, Nina then went on to be investigated by Zdenek Rejdak, who was a parapsychologist and scientist at the Prague Military Institute. Kulagina was also studied by other scientists including Genady Sergeyev, who was a physiologist and a mathematician at the A.A. Uktomskii Physiological Institute in Russia. Sergeyev had studied Kulagina's PK ability for many years and was convinced of the veracity of her phenomena and that Kulagina could summon her ability at will (Ostrander and Schroeder 58–62).

An ordinary demonstration of Kulagina's alleged PK activity involved her concentrating on a small object, such as a matchbox case, holding her hands above the object and seemingly moving it a matter of inches. Kulagina was also thought to move matchsticks and other small objects, including objects that were kept in sealed containers in order that Kulagina could not be using trickery to move the objects (such as by attaching very fine threads to the objects so as to move them fraudulently). Sergeyev argued that Kulagina was closely monitored for the presence of fraudulent behavior. For instance, he claimed that Kulagina was routinely searched for magnets, strings, and the presence of any other objects that might go towards fraudulently simulating PK phenomena. Moreover, he argued that Kulagina was even x-rayed at one point to test for the presence of hidden magnets, to discount the theory that she was magnetizing the objects that she appeared to move (Ostrander and Schroeder 68).

Kulagina was said to expend an enormous amount of physical energy in order to produce PK. Her pulse was often recorded as increasing up to 240 beats a minute when she performed. Similarly, it was claimed that her blood sugar levels were elevated and her weight could drop by as much as 3 pounds in a single session. Some of the other feats that Kulagina is claimed to have performed included moving a compass head and decreasing the intensity of a laser beam. One of the more interesting examples of PK that Kulagina was said to have performed was splitting the egg white from the egg yolk and then restoring the egg. This is not a feat that could be performed with hidden threads or magnets. Kulagina could even be said to cause her own skin to burn (Ostrander and Schroeder 72). Work with Kulagina stopped in the 1980s when her health declined, and she claimed she could no longer cope with the physical demands of performing PK (Beloff 187).

Inspired by what she had learned researching Kulagina's case, Felicia Praise of the Maimonides Dream Laboratory in New York claimed to have taught herself PK. Praise reported that she would come home every night and concentrate her energy on a small container that was used to contain her false eyelashes in the hope that the container would move by PK. After many weeks of concerted practice Praise believed that she was able to move the container by her mind's power alone. Praise claimed that she was profoundly emotionally stressed on the first day that she was able to move the container with her mind. She claimed that the experiment would always be a success if she could work herself up into a physically and emotionally charged state, rather than purely focusing on the task ahead (Douglas 342). Indeed, as stated above, it is often claimed that changes in physical energy are associated with PK (Ostrander and Schroeder 58). Likewise Ellwood and McGraw observe that Tibetan shamans exhibit abnormally great strength, are exhausted after performances, and do not generally live long (39).

However, notwithstanding endorsements of her PK ability Kulagina was the object of much criticism. Some critics took an indirect approach and claimed that the testing conditions were favorable for fraudulent activity (e.g., Massimo Polidoro). Polidoro also argued that Kulagina's feats were easy to reproduce. For instance, static electricity could be used to move objects at a distance. He also claimed that there was a strong motivation for the researchers to falsify their findings as, he claimed, there was a "Psi Race" which was analogous to the Space Race (Polidoro). Others, such as Martin Gardner, made direct accusations that Kulagina had been caught cheating by Soviet Establishment scientists (Gardner 244).

Zhang Baosheng

A notable case of PK from China is Zhang Baosheng, who was a live-in psychic at Beijing's Institute of Space-Medico Engineering in the 1980s. Some of Zhang's alleged feats included moving small objects and live insects in and out of sealed containers. In one particular experiment paper that was marked and treated chemically was put into the bottom of a modified test-tube (the test-tube was melted in the middle in order to constrict the test-tube). At the top of the test-tube were placed cotton wool pieces that had been treated with a chemical that would react with the chemical that the piece of paper contained. The top of the test-tube was then sealed closed. Zhang was asked to move the piece of paper out of the test-tube. Within five minutes of the request being made the piece of paper was claimed to be on the outside of the test-tube and the cotton wool indicated that a chemical reaction had occurred suggesting that the piece of paper had passed through or come in contact with the cotton wool (Beloff 159–161). Zhang was arrested for fraud in 1995 (Damiani 1).

Poltergeist Activity

Another related area of PK testing is poltergeist phenomena. The word poltergeist is a German word that means "noisy spirit" and describes the mischievous activities of spirits in folklore. However, the term was later adopted in psychical research to describe a range of unexplained cases of moving objects, rapping noises and other phenomena traditionally associated with hauntings. What was once called poltergeist activity is now referred to by parapsychologists as "recurrent spontaneous psychokinesis" (RSPK). This shift in the study of "poltergeist" phenomena developed as it appeared in most cases that there was a live person, often a child, around whom the phenomena happened. Thereby researchers shifted their attention from trying to calm mischievous spirits to finding a person who was using PK (Irwin and Watt 145–56). Famous cases are those of Julio Vasquez and Annemarie Schaberl.

Miami

In one such story, in January 1967, the police were called to a warehouse in Miami that sold novelty items as it appeared there had been a break-in because a number of items were broken and boxes were strewn across the floor of the warehouse. Yet it appeared that this was not a break-in after all as over two hundred isolated instances of objects falling onto the floor were reported over the next three weeks. Of note, these boxes did not appear to have simply fallen off their respective shelves; instead it was argued that some force had been exerted on the boxes. For instance, in one case a box was found 22 feet away from where it should have been. These boxes were largely full of fragile items including glasses that smashed when they hit the floor (Roll ch. 10).

The police officers tested the shelves and found that they were in good working order. The boxes were seen to fall to the ground, and it appeared as though they were being tilted and tipped off the shelves despite the fact that there was nobody behind them to push them. These events were eventually subject to scrutiny by two leading parapsychologists, William Roll and J.G.

Pratt, who decided that the poltergeist activity was surrounding a 19-year-old Cuban refugee who was called Julio Vasquez. All of the activities happened when he was at the warehouse, and the activities ceased when he was not there.

The activities stopped entirely at the end of January 1967 when Julio stopped working at the warehouse. At this time Roll and Pratt invited Julio to undergo a psychological investigation. From this investigation they found out that Julio was not happy in his environment and that he was angry and rebellious due to a perceived lack of success in his life. His fantasies at this time were all of a violent nature. The unusual events at the warehouse began at a time of trauma in Julio's life. He confessed that he felt tense and nervous in the warehouse when everything was moving along as it should, and that these feelings of nervous tension were abated when there was a breakage, leading him to feel happy (Roll ch. 10).

Of further interest Roll and Pratt have suggested that the pattern of objects moving in the warehouse conformed to the same pattern as a vortex field that followed a decay function. This pattern, which is found in a number of physical phenomena, such as how light dims as water deepens, led Roll and Pratt to conclude that RSPK phenomena conforms to some physical laws as it converts "psychic" energy into kinetic energy (Roll ch. 10; Roll and Joines).

As with the other examples that are given in this essay, Julio was accused of fraud, and his supporters challenged the accusations. For instance, the warehouse was broken into, stock was stolen, and Julio was the number-one suspect. The police sergeant who interviewed Julio later told reporters that Julio had confessed to the crime and to staging the supposed paranormal activity. Julio purportedly attached threads and placed objects near the edges of shelves. Shaking from passing jets made them fall. Roll said that Susy Smith, writer on parapsychology, who helped in the investigation, told him that the sergeant never "examined" the warehouse. When Al Laubheim, the owner, met with Julio and the sergeant, Julio said that the sergeant lied, and that Julio had not confessed to faking the activity. Laubheim added that the sergeant did not contradict Julio but became "red in the face." (Roll 170).

Rosenheim

A similar case occurred in November 1967 in lawyer Sigmund Adam's office in Bavaria. Sigmund and his staff observed a number of odd happenings including lights inexplicably turning on and off, light bulbs exploding, and unexplained phone calls both to the office and from the office. To investigate the phenomena Sigmund called in the maintenance department who checked the electricity supply to their satisfaction and even connected an emergency generator to see whether or not it was the electrical supply that was faulty. They found that the happenings occurred while the office was connected to the emergency generator which seemed to discount the theory that it was the electricity supply that was the cause of the unexplained phenomena. The telephone company was also called in to investigate the unexplained telephone calls. It was found that the phone number which gave the time of day was being called excessively, sometimes fifty times in a row without the phone being dialed (Broughton 216).

This case was investigated by the eminent West German parapsychologist, Hans Bender. Not unlike the case with Julio, Bender observed that the phenomena only occurred when the young employee Annemarie Schaberl was working. Also, not unlike Julio's case, the phenomena happened in close proximity to Annemarie. When Bender told Sigmund that he suspected that the phenomena were linked to Annemarie, the happenings were said to intensify and it was claimed that pictures on the wall spun on their hooks, among other things. Annemarie then moved on to a different job and the paranormal happenings followed her in her new position (Broughton 218; "Dreh").

Subsequently Annemarie was invited to be tested by Bender in his laboratory in Freiburg. There she was tested for PK abilities, and it was found that her PK abilities were above chance but only when she was emotionally disturbed. Upon talking to Annemarie it was discovered that she was desperately unhappy in her job and thought excessively about her home-time later in the evenings when the unexplained telephone calls were being made. The commonalities in these cases when compared with other famous cases of RSPK suggest that, if true, these kinds of phenomena are more common in young people who are unhappy and going through disturbances in their lives. RSPK phenomena are also said to be common in children at the age of puberty (Broughton 219).

Interestingly, the reported early days of Kulagina's alleged PK phenomena were not unlike "poltergeist" phenomena. Kulagina was said to be aware of objects moving around her, but she did not attribute this phenomenon to her own alleged PK abilities. She did, however, observe that these events happened spontaneously when she was very angry or upset. For instance, on the first occasion when it is alleged that Kulagina noticed the phenomenon, she came home angry and upset from work and watched a water pitcher move to the edge of the cupboard before it fell off and broke in front of her. Consequently, unlike other cases of poltergeist phenomena Kulagina concluded that she was the cause of the objects moving in her presence and that she could control the energy that was making them move (Ostrander and Schroeder 78–79).

Interestingly, the famous psychotherapist Carl Jung is said to have experienced the same phenomenon in his family home. Jung recounted that he came from a family where paranormal experiences were a part of everyday life. Jung's grandmother was a spirit medium, his father was said to converse with his dead first wife, and Jung's mother kept a diary of her precognitive dreams. There are a few notable events in the Jung family home that are consistent with "poltergeist" phenomena. For example, a heavy walnut table is said to have split in two without having any physical force exerted on it. Similarly, a knife and a glass vase apparently shattered without explanation. Jung reasoned that the emotional energy in the house at those times had caused the otherwise unexplained phenomena (Jaffe).

Psychic Photography

Although the study of PK is best known as the study of objects that are moved or distorted without having physical force exerted on them, the study of PK also involves the ability of a subject to directly influence any kind of physical process. The study of psychically imprinting images on a photograph (thoughtography) is the kind of PK phenomena that falls into the latter category. In this case the subject is believed to have the ability to alter the chemical constituents of film emulsion. However, this area of paranormal investigation is the area of PK investigation that has been most associated with fraudulent practices. Indeed, the founders of the Society for Psychical Research (SPR) refused to consider thoughtography as a worthy area of continuing investigation as they could not find any evidence of genuine psychic activity in this case (Eisenbud, *Psychic Photography* 5). This decision was made despite the large numbers of people who claimed to be psychic photographers. The position of the SPR was not unreasonable considering some of the characters who were involved in the early days of what was called spirit photography. For instance, in the Spiritualist movement a number of unscrupulous mediums were known to produce photographs that were supposedly of dead spirits who were trying to communicate with them. However, in a number of cases these "dead" people were discovered to be living, thus throwing the practice of psychic photography into disrepute (Broughton 194).

The first notable case of psychic photography was recorded in Japan in 1910 under the supervision of Tomokichi Fukurai (1869–1952), who was at the time a professor at Tokyo University. Fukurai is known for his tests that required subjects to imprint a Japanese character onto a photographic plate psychically. Fukurai alleged that he had a number of successful subjects whom he later wrote about in his book, *Clairvoyance and Thoughtography*. However, the book was wildly controversial at the time, and Fukurai resigned from his position at Tokyo University ostensibly to continue his research; however, it is evident that there was pressure on Fukurai to resign (Takasuna 164).

The most famous case of supposed psychic photography was that of Ted Serios. Ted, a lift operator and bellboy from Chicago, was tested by Julie Eisenbud who was a psychiatrist and an associate professor of the University of Colorado. She supervised tests on Serios from 1964 to 1967. Ted's big claim was that he could imprint an image onto a polaroid film while the film was still in the camera. It was Eisenbud who came up with the term "thoughtography" as Eisenbud believed that Serios was imprinting his own thoughts onto the polaroid film (Beloff 187–88).

Serios famously had to be drunk before he found himself in a state where he could perform. He would then stare into the camera lens while an assistant would depress the shutter button. Occasionally, when the film was removed from the camera it would not be the usual picture of Ted's face but would instead be a picture of a place, person, or item that was not in the room. However, Ted's case did not manage to lift the reputation of psychic photography. In the late experiments Ted aroused suspicion by the use of a device he called his "gizmo." The gizmo was a cardboard tube which was either open or sealed with cellophane at the top and had a piece of unexposed film negative covered with cellophane at the bottom. Ted would point his "gizmo" at the camera and stare down the tube whilst he produced his imprints. Photographers have discredited Ted's gizmo by arguing that it is possible to conceal a small lens and a photographic slide in the device and to imprint a photographic slide remotely. However, it must be noted that Ted's gizmo was scrutinized closely by his investigators, who never accused him of fraudulent practices (Beloff 190).

It must also be noted that many of Ted's imprints of the photographic slides appeared to be his impression of certain people and places and not exact representations of those people and places (Beloff 189). For instance, Ted, not having a good education, was a poor speller. In one example the imprint on the film had a significant misspelling. This particular imprint was that of a warehouse belonging to the Royal Canadian Mounted Police. However, the word Canadian was misspelled as "Cainadain." The original site did not have this misspelling (Eisenbud, *World* 96).

Generally, today it is believed that Ted Serios was a talented fraudster (Beloff 191).

Pyrokinesis

Pyrokinesis is a lesser-known species of PK. Indeed, the word pyrokinesis was not the creation of a parapsychologist. Instead the term was coined by the horror writer Stephen King in his novel *Firestarter* (1980). In this novel, that utilizes a range of psi activity for narrative effect, King created a character who could start and control fires with her mind. As mentioned, he spoke of this power as being pyrokinesis. *Pyr* is the Greek word which means "fire," and *kinesis* is the Greek work that means "movement" or "motion." Yet, the phenomenon that is associated with pyrokinesis is not a fiction that was created by King. Pyrokinesis in terms of paranormal study is described as the ability to "excite the atoms within an object until they create enough energy to burst into flames" (Gresh and Weinberg 38–39).

Micro-Kinesis

So far the kind of PK that we have been talking about is macro-PK. This is PK that deals with large cases, or rather PK that is directly observable with the eyes. The other kind of PK that is tested in a laboratory is called micro-PK. This PK can be "proven" by statistical analysis, or by experiments where the PK cannot be examined with the naked eye (Beloff 171).

The clinical study of PK began in Duke University in 1934 under the skillful guidance of J.B. Rhine. Rhine's interest in the study of PK was aroused when a student who was a gambler informed Rhine that he believed that he could influence the fall of a die with the power of his mind. The student was immediately tested by Rhine with impressive results. Consequently, Rhine devised further tests using dice that could test a wide range of people and rely on statistical analysis as evidence of PK. For instance, in early experiments Rhine decided that the subjects should intend the dice to make the high score of 7. These tests were conducted in runs that comprised of 12 throws of the die. Statistical analysis showed that the chances of throwing a combination of 7 in a run, without psychic influence, were 2 in 12. Twenty-five people participated in the initial experiment, which consisted of 562 runs and 24 die casts each run, which totaled 13,488 casts, and the number of "hits" was 3,110. Statistically the number of hits that could be attributed to chance would have been 2,810. Therefore, according to Rhine, these results were 300 higher than the chance score. The odds of getting this score by chance, according to Rhine's calculations, is 1 billion to 1 (Broughton 69).

An interesting finding to emerge from Rhine's experiments was that the test results were U-shaped. Or, in other words, it was observed that the subjects had high scores in the first and last quadrants of testing, whereas the second and third quadrants of results were usually lower than the others (Rhine 140). This U-shaped result is similarly seen in psychological testing of learning and recall processes which has led to the suggestion that PK is more of a psychological process than a physical one. This U-shaped result also confronts the "unconscious" nature of PK phenomena and goes towards advancing the idea that the subjects' motivation in an experiment directly affects the results of the experiments. It is a well-known premise that interest is usually high at the start of a task, only to wane as the task continues, and to increase when the end is in sight (Broughton 68).

Another popular example of micro-PK is the coin-tossing experiment. In this experiment a subject with PK is tested, and he or she may be asked to try and influence the fall of the coin as it is spinning in the air so as to make the coin fall with the head facing upwards. In tests where a coin is tossed by a catapult device a coin will fall with the head side facing up an average of 56 percent of the time in a run of two hundred tosses, assuming that there is no bias in the toss. Any result with a probability of 5 percent or less is argued to be "significant" and may be considered for causative factors. However, if the result has a probability of 1 percent or less, then chance is rejected, another causative factor is considered, and this kind of test result is called "highly significant." For example, if the results show that heads come up 120 times out of 200 then the findings are called "highly significant" because by chance the probability of this result is 0.29 percent (Broughton 172).

If a subject tests in the range that is called highly significant, then it is preferred that the subject be examined further. For instance, the subject may be tested for 10 runs of 200 tosses at a week's interval. It would be expected that the results over this time would vary, but if the results were consistently highly significant, then it would be prudent to assume that the subject has PK ability (Broughton 172).

Another development in micro-PK research emerged from Helmut Schmidt's experiments in the 1960s and 1970s, which, he claims, suggest that it is possible for a person with PK ability to move an atomic particle. To prove this claim Schmidt created a box with lamps in a circle attached to a Geiger counter. The Geiger counter would register when the atoms had hit it, which would in turn cause the lamps to light up. Without PK intervention the atoms would decay in a random fashion, so that some of the atoms that hit the Geiger counter would cause the lamps to light clockwise, but others would cause them to light counter-clockwise, alternating randomly. Schmidt asked his subject "Bob" to decide in which direction he was going to light the lamps and to maintain the lamps' lighting in that direction. Schmidt claimed that Bob was able to achieve this. Schmidt claimed that this was a significant laboratory experiment for PK, as it appeared to show that it was PK, and not precognition, that had achieved the results in the test. This experiment was the beginning of Schmidt's work with random number generators (Schmidt 175–81). There have been numerous criticisms of Schmidt's work. For instance, Leonard Zusne and Warren Jones claimed that his findings were not statistically significant, given that the deviation from normal in many cases was small, sometimes only 2 percent (Zusne and Jones 183). Victor Stegner was critical of Schmidt's claims given that his test results have not been duplicated in over thirty-five years (Stegner 1).

Possible Explanations

Genady Sergeyev argued for a possible solution to the cause of PK, building on the work of Harold Burr (1889–1973) and Leonard Ravitz (1923–2005) of Yale. Burr argued that all living matter is surrounded by and controlled by electrodynamic fields. It is claimed that this energy ensures that tissue takes the correct form when the body renews itself. Ravitz argued that the mind could influence this force field which surrounds the body. Sergeyev claimed that this force field was utilized in and invented a machine that was said to detect biological fields up to 4 yards away from a person. Sergeyev claimed to have tested Kulagina with this machine, and he argued that the electromagnetic field around her body was 10 times that of a normal person. He also claimed that the electrical voltage that Kulagina generated from the back of her head was 10 times more than average—a characteristic that is said to be more common among psychics. Sergeyev also claimed that the magnetic field surrounding Kulagina's body would pulse when she was about to perform PK. Her brain and her heart were also said to pulse in unison with the pulsing of the magnetic field. Sergeyev posited that this pulsing action caused magnetic waves that either attracted or repelled whatever was the focus of Kulagina's attention (Ostrander and Schroeder 71).

Notwithstanding Sergeyev's claims, it is difficult to explain how PK may be possible given the ordinary understanding of the laws of physics, which does not think through the implications of quantum mechanics. Skeptics have widely argued that PK phenomena are a product of delusions, hallucinations, or fraud. Certainly, all three of these explanations are possible for many cases of supposed PK activity. Notably, there are numerous examples of fraud, particularly where subjects have themselves confessed to manipulating events physically (Brownlee). However, it would be dismissive to reject all of the different claims of PK based on an overarching prejudice that these events are impossible.

That said, PK has proven to be one of the most difficult areas of paranormal activity to reproduce with any success under controlled conditions. Indeed, it is worth noting that most experiments require certain positive conditions in order to be able to occur. Most importantly, it is reported that the belief of the researchers or the observers is crucial to the positive outcome of the results. Many psychics, including Geller have refused to be tested in laboratories by skeptical scientists.

Moreover, a number of claims by researchers appear to show signs of other types of phenomena, particularly hypnotic or hallucinatory experiences rather than true PK events. Take for instance the account of Russell Targ and Harold Puthoff, who examined Geller. Notably, Targ and Puthoff were unsuccessful in recording PK events in their laboratory; however, they were stunned by the number of PK events that surrounded Geller. In particular, Targ and Puthoff found bent metal objects around their apartment, but even more astounding they found that a traffic sign at the front of their apartment was not only bent in half but twisted in a spiral fashion. They concluded that this event must have had something to do with Geller (Targ and Puthoff 164). Interestingly, we are not told if the traffic sign remained bent, or if Targ and Puthoff investigated the bent traffic sign any further. Was this a hallucination brought about by suggestion?

In the case of Praise there are reported instances where Praise was certain that an object had moved, although another observer was not. In the case that the observer did notice an object move, it often settled back into its original position (Douglas 342). Yet, not all of the tests mentioned are so easy to explain; tests that record if any pressure has been applied to a remote object are difficult to dismiss as hallucinations or trickery. These results have been explained away as resulting from the fraudulent practices of researchers. Indeed, there have been many cases of researchers cheating, even Mendel (Rhine, "New Case;" Judson). However, surely all claims of potential fraudulent behavior on the part of academics should be carefully investigated.

Works Cited

"Aksakof, Alexander N. (1832–1903)." Encyclopedia.com, www.encyclopedia.com/science/encyclopedias-almanacs-transcripts-and-maps/aksakof-alexander-n-1832-1903. Accessed 19 July 2021.

"Alexander N. Aksakof." *Kook Science Research Hatch*, hatch.kookscience.com/wiki/Alexander_N._Aksakof. Accessed 19 July 2021.

Beloff, John. *Parapsychology. A Concise History*. The Athlone Press, 1993.

Blackmore, S.J. "Review of *The Supernatural A-Z: The Truth and the Lies* by James Randi." *Journal of the Society for Psychical Research*, vol. 61, 1996, pp. 270–72.

Broughton, Richard S. *Parapsychology. The Controversial Science*. Ballantine Books, 1991.

Brownlee, John. "The Confession of James Hydrick." *Wired*, 28 Mar. 2007, www.wired.com/2007/03/the-confession-/. Accessed 21 Nov. 2020.

Damiani, Matteo. "Supernatural Powers in China." *China Underground*, 2012, chinaunderground.com/2012/03/23/11-rare-videos-of-chinese-with-supernatural-powers/. Accessed 6 Aug. 2020.
Douglas, Alfred. *Extra-Sensory Powers. A Century of Psychical Research*. Victor Gollancz Ltd., 1976.
"Dreh mit Lilien." *Der Spiegel*. Mar. 1968, www.spiegel.de/politik/dreh-mit-liliena-9b9cf 97f-0002-0001-0000-000045465380. Accessed 16 Jan. 2022.
Eisenbud, Julie. *Psychic Photography and Thoughtography*. Cosimo Classics, 2015.
_____. *The World of Ted Serios*. Pocket, 1968.
Ellwood, Robert S., Barbara A. McGraw. *Many Peoples, Many Faiths*, 8th ed. Pearson Prentice Hall, 2005.
Gardner, Martin. *Science: Good, Bad and Bogus*. Oxford University Press, 1983.
Gresh, Lois H., and Robert Weinberg. *The Science of Stephen King: From Carrie to Cell, The Terrifying Truth Behind* [sic] *the Horror Master's Fiction*. Wiley and Sons, 2007.
Irwin, Harvey J., and Caroline A. Watt. *An Introduction to Parapsychology*. 5th ed., McFarland, 2007.
Jaffe, A. "C. G. Jung and Parapsychology." *Science and ESP*. Edited by J.R. Smithies, Routledge and Kegan Paul, 1967, pp. 263–80.
Judson, Horace Freeland. *The Great Betrayal: Fraud in Science*. Harcourt, 2004.
Karolyi, George. *An Excursion into the Paranormal*. The Paranormal Phenomena Research Foundation Inc., 2003.
Ostrander, Sheila and Lynn Schroeder. *Psychic Discoveries Behind* [sic] *the Iron Curtain*. Prentice-Hall, Inc., 1970.
Polidoro, Massimo. "Secrets of a Russian Psychic." *CICAP*, 2000, www.cicap.org/n/articolo.php?id=101003. Accessed 2 July 2020.
Randi, James. "New Evidence in the Uri Geller Matter." *Paranormal Borderlands of Science*, edited by Kendrick Frazier, Prometheus Books, 1981, pp. 122–28.
Rhine, Joseph Banks. *Extra-Sensory Perception*. Faber & Faber, 1935.
_____. "A New Case of Experimenter Unreliability." *Journal of Parapsychology*, vol. 33, 1974, 136–75.
Roll, William G. *The Poltergeist*. Signet, 1972.
_____, and William T. Joines. "RSPK and Consciousness." *Journal of Parapsychology*, vol. 77, no. 2, 2013, pp. 192–211.
Schmidt, Helmut. "A PK Test with Electronic Equipment." *Journal of Parapsychology*, vol. 34, 1970, pp. 175–81.
Stegner, Victor J. "Can Prayer Change the Past?" *Skeptical Briefs*, vol. 14, no. 1, 2004.
Storr, W. "James Randi: Debunking the King of the Debunkers." *Metaphysics and Psychology*, www.soulask.com/james-randi-debunking-the-king-of-the-debunkers/. Accessed 6 Aug. 2020.
Takasuna, Miki. "The Fukurai Affair." *The History of the Human Sciences*, vol. 25, no. 2, 2012, pp. 149–64.
Targ, Russell, and Harold E. Puthoff. *Mind-Reach: Scientists Look at Psychic Ability*. Delacorte Press/Eleanor Friede, 1977.
Zusne, Leonard, and Warren H. Jones. *Anomalistic Psychology: A Study of Magical Thinking*. Psychology Press, 2014.

Reincarnation and Past-Life Memory

JAMES G. MATLOCK

Reincarnation is the idea that some part of what comprises a human being survives the death of one body and returns to animate another body later. The belief in reincarnation is very old and widespread, probably going back to prehistoric indigenous culture (Haraldsson and Matlock 169–73; Matlock, *Signs* 63–75), but the possibility that reincarnation actually might occur was not taken seriously by Western science until the twentieth century. The sustained and systematic study of evidence for reincarnation began only in 1960, when psychiatrist Ian Stevenson at the University of Virginia (UVA) published a review article of claims of past-life memory (Stevenson, "Evidence"). In that article, Stevenson pointed to forty-four published reports of people, mostly children, whose memories of previous lives had been confirmed. Since then, he and his colleagues have investigated over 2500 cases from all over the word, identifying the previous person in about 1700 of them (Mills and Tucker 318). Stevenson died in 2007, but the research program he initiated continues at UVA, and other workers are making independent contributions. The most recent survey of this domain is James Matlock's *Signs of Reincarnation*, published in 2019.

A central problem in reincarnation research is determining what it is that reincarnates. Many people assume this to be the "soul," but what is the soul? Matlock suggests that what reincarnates is best thought of as the mind or consciousness. Consciousness may be considered equivalent to soul, or the soul may be imagined as the self, that which supplies the first-person "I" perspective to experiences. In any event, Matlock proposes, what reincarnates is a stream of consciousness continuous with embodied life. Moreover, he thinks, consciousness has a duplex nature, consisting of a subconscious stratum along with conscious awareness.

Memories, dispositions to act in certain ways, and psychological traits are carried in the subconscious part of the mind, conveyed to the new body when it is possessed by the reincarnating consciousness stream. From time to time, memories of previous lives may penetrate into conscious awareness, but they persist in the subconscious and may influence our lives even in the absence of conscious awareness (Matlock, *Signs* 199). This chapter adopts Matlock's understanding of what reincarnates and how it does so.

Stevenson summarized decades of research findings in *Children Who Remember Previous Lives*, whose second edition appeared in 2001. In addition to conscious memories of previous lives, the cases he studied included behavioral and physical features such as birthmarks and other congenital anomalies. The most developed cases were those of young children, generally aged two to five years when they began to relate their memories. Adults also sometimes recall events from previous lives, but adults' memories tend to be vaguer and are less often verified than children's memories (Matlock, *Signs* 209–10). It is also easier for investigators to rule out the possibility that children have learned what they say they remember by hearing others talk about the previous person or by reading or seeing something about him or her. For these reasons, Stevenson and his colleagues worked mostly with young children.

Stevensonian reincarnation research has been concerned almost entirely with memories that occur spontaneously, most often in the waking state, but sometimes in dreams. Little attention has been paid to apparent memories appearing during regressions under hypnosis or to the past-life readings of psychics. These types of case are much less often verified. Whereas previous lives recalled spontaneously mostly transpired in the recent past, and usually within about twenty-five kilometers (15.5 miles) of the case subject's home (Stevenson, *Children* 242), regressions and past-life readings tend to refer to lives from long ago, often in different parts of the world. These factors make the cases harder to investigate, but when they are investigated, they turn out to include more mistakes, distortions, and fantasy elements than spontaneous cases do (Matlock, *Signs* 219–20).

Unsurprisingly, Stevenson's work has received a good deal of pushback from critics (e.g., Angel, Edwards, Wilson) and any introduction to reincarnation research must take account of their objections. It is noteworthy that many of the potential problem areas were addressed by Stevenson himself (in *Twenty Cases Suggestive of Reincarnation*, his first book of case reports, as well as in *Children* and elsewhere) and that the best examples of processes such as fraud, mistaken inference, and parental guidance have been supplied by field researchers rather than armchair critics (Matlock, *Signs* 111–12). As we shall see, many of the charges critics have made are overblown or demonstrably false. Critics have failed to come to grips with the case data in all its complexity. The evidence for reincarnation is much harder to explain away than is commonly supposed, and this moves the problem to issues of theory. How can the case data be harmonized with what is known from psychology and biology? Must the acceptance of reincarnation entail the rejection of large areas of established science, or have we just not been looking at things in the right way? The less adjustment the reincarnation case data demand from mainstream science, the easier it will be for mainstream scientists to accept them and their implications.

Early Accounts of Past-Life Memory

Where did the belief in reincarnation originate? Scholars have advanced various suggestions, including India, Egypt, the Eurasian steppe, Mongolia, and Tibet (Matlock, *Signs* 39–40). Victorian anthropologist Edward Burnett Tylor offered a different suggestion in his classic *Primitive Culture*. Tylor made an extensive comparison of beliefs and customs of tribal societies worldwide. He wrote before modern ethnographic fieldwork and based his account on the reports of travelers, missionaries, and colonial administrators. He found beliefs in reincarnation connected again and again to signs such as birthmarks on newborns, the telltale behaviors of toddlers, and dreams in which figures of deceased persons indicated their intention to be reborn to the dreamers or to someone close to them. Tylor (2: 4–6) thought that these observations and experiences had inspired the belief in reincarnation among primitive peoples. He considered reincarnation "a highly philosophical theory, accounting as it does so well for the general resemblance between parents and children and even for the more special phenomena of atavism" (2: 3–4).

The signs Tylor identified as linked to a belief in reincarnation are among the signs that Stevenson later studied as evidence for reincarnation. Although Tylor did not cite any past-life memory claims, they have been reported from numerous tribal societies since he wrote (Matlock, *Signs* 53–63; Mills and Slobodin). It is an axiom of anthropology that the more widespread a trait is, the older it is likely to be. The same signs appear so regularly in association with reincarnation beliefs in tribal societies that we may justifiably wonder whether they are present along with the beliefs even when they are not recorded by ethnographers, and if that is so, then it may well be that Tylor was right that signs of reincarnation gave rise to the belief in reincarnation in the far distant past.

Before 1960, memories of previous lives were so little known that having them was widely assumed to be impossible and other signs, especially child prodigies and déjà vu experiences, were adduced as evidence for reincarnation by its advocates (Matlock, *Signs* 96). There were, however, a fair number of past-life memory accounts in the published record by that time. The earliest concerns Pythagoras (580?–500? BCE), who is reputed to have remembered being Euphorbus, a Greek hero from the Trojan War immortalized by Homer in the *Iliad* (17.9–50), and to have recognized Euphorbus's shield when he saw it displayed it in a temple (Diogenes Laertius, *Lives of Eminent Philosophers* 8.1.4–5). Another of the ancient Greeks, Apollonius of Tyana, said he recalled being on a ship boarded by pirates on the Mediterranean Sea (Philostratus, *Vita Apollonii* 3.23–24).

More detailed accounts begin to appear in first-millennium CE China (Matlock, "Reincarnation Accounts"). In one of them, a dying child told his mother that he would be reborn to another family, with whom he had past-life connections. His mother made a black mark on his right elbow. His new mother dreamed that he appeared to her, saying, "I must become your descendent," and she became pregnant. After her baby's birth, a black mark was noticed on his right elbow, in the place his previous mother had marked her son's body. When he was three years old, the boy led the way back to his former house, without anyone showing him the way (De Groot 144).

These old accounts are similar to better documented modern cases. Recognitions of people, places, and articles, such as Pythagoras's identification of Euphorbus' shield, are mentioned again and again. Cadaver marking related to birthmarks, as described in the Chinese case, has been reported up to the present throughout East Asia (Matlock, "Experimental Birthmarks"; Tucker and Keil). The Chinese case includes two other common features: the new mother's dream, called an "announcing dream" (Matlock, "Announcing Dreams"), and the boy's finding his way unaided to his former home. Another child who did this was the Japanese Katsugoro, in the 1820s. Katsugoro was eight when he first talked about his memories of having been a boy named Tozo, who had died of smallpox the year after his father's death and his mother's remarriage. He gave the name of his previous father, mother, and stepfather, and told his family where he had lived with them. When he was taken to that village, he led the way to Tozo's house, where all he had been saying about Tozo was confirmed (Hearn 267–90).

John Wortabet (308–09 note) described a Syrian Druze case in his 1860 book, *Researches into the Religions of Syria*. A 5-year-old boy from a mountain village said he remembered being a rich man from Damascus. He was so eager to return to that city that his relatives finally took him there. He astonished them by calling out the names of the places they passed on their journey, and when they reached the city, led the way through the streets to his former home. He knocked on the door, called the woman who answered it by name, and told her he was her husband reborn. He asked about their children, other relatives, and friends, and recalled other things from his past life. Everything he said was corroborated, except for a small amount of money he said he was owed by a certain weaver. When this man was summoned, he acknowledged the debt, pleading his poverty as the reason he had not repaid it to the man's heirs.

The boy then asked his past-life widow whether she had found the money he had buried in the cellar. She had not, so he showed her where it was. The widow and her children, by this point convinced that the boy was their deceased husband and father, returned, gave him some of the recovered money and went home with him to meet the rest of his family.

The first well-attested European case is the case of Alexandrina Samona (as her name is usually spelled in English). Her father was a physician, and he first reported it in Italian medical journals in 1911. Stevenson summarized the case in *European Cases of the Reincarnation Type* (23–27). Five-year-old Alexandrina died of meningitis, leaving her mother distraught. Three days after the death her mother dreamed that she came to her and told her not to grieve, because she would be returning as a baby. Three days later, her mother dreamed the same thing again. The family heard knocks on the door, answered it, but no one was there. They tried to contact the girl through a medium, and she responded at once. She said that she had made the knocks and that she would be returning before the end of the year with a twin sister. Her mother became aware she was pregnant, and in time, gave birth to twin girls. One of the twins looked so much like her deceased sister that she was given the same name, Alexandrina. The new Alexandrina was lefthanded, her left eye was engorged, her right ear was inflamed, and her face was slightly asymmetric—all like her namesake, but unlike her twin. As she grew older, she behaved in many ways like the first Alexandrina. Then one day when the family was planning a trip to Monreale, she said she had already been there and correctly described a scene that the first Alexandrina had witnessed shortly before her death.

Reincarnation Research: Method and Criticism

Because claims of past-life memory were a new area of investigation in 1960, Stevenson had to devise a research methodology appropriate to them. In doing this, he drew on techniques that had been developed in the early years of parapsychology to study spontaneous cases of apparitions and other experiences considered paranormal by mainstream science. These techniques had been applied to reincarnation case investigations by the Indians R.B.S. Sunderlal and K.K.N. Sahay in the 1920s but had gone unnoticed by Anglo-American parapsychologists. Stevenson followed Sunderlal and Sahay in gathering information about both the case subject and the person whose life he recalled, if this person had been or could be identified, in order to confirm or disconfirm the memories. He interviewed multiple witnesses with firsthand knowledge, returning to them repeatedly over a period of years to check on the reliability of memories and to fill in gaps in the record. He collected all supporting written documentation he could. Stevenson was impressed that his case subjects not only recalled many names and events accurately, they displayed personalities and behaviors similar to the people whose lives they recalled. Moreover, there might be physical features, such as birthmarks, that linked the lives as well. Stevenson's methods, together with their strengths and limitations, have been described by him (CORT I 8–35; *Twenty Cases* 1–14; "Reincarnation" 648–50) and by his colleagues (Cook 90–95; Pasricha 53–61; Tucker *Life* 17–29) on several occasions.

Critics, especially self-identified skeptics, have gone after Stevenson's methods in an effort to undermine the evidence he presented. Matlock has addressed criticisms of Stevenson's work prior to 1990 ("Past Life Memory" 238–55) and more recent appraisals by Leonard Angel and Michael Shermer (Matlock, *Signs* 103–8, 110–12), but the critique of Paul Edwards has not been treated in detail. Although Edwards' *Reincarnation: A Critical Examination* was published in 1996, it is deemed by commentators like Shermer to be "still the best work on the topic" (102) and so deserves consideration.

Edwards (255) opens his chapter on Stevenson with an outline of "the initial presumption against reincarnation." He explains that reincarnation includes "a host of collateral assumptions," such as that the reincarnating "pure mind" might come to Earth from other planets. After intervals varying "from a few months to hundreds of years," minds enter the wombs of their new mothers "at conception of a new embryo." These and other collateral assumptions, Edwards affirms, are held by "nearly all forms of reincarnationism," but with Stevenson "there is the additional implication that the memories and skills that the individual took over from the person who died and that are transmitted to the new regular body appear there for a relatively short time during childhood to disappear forever after." He avers, "If Stevenson's reports are evidence of reincarnation they must be evidence for the collateral assumptions just mentioned."

Here and elsewhere in his book, Edwards is setting up a strawman depiction of reincarnation to assail. His portrayal of reincarnation comes closest to the Theosophical version, which is atypical of traditional beliefs in reincarnation in many ways (Matlock, *Signs* 75–82). Theosophy promotes the idea that souls immigrate to Earth from other planets, but this is not a feature of Asian religious traditions. Buddhists believe that reincarnation occurs at conception, but Hindus hold that the soul may enter its new body at any point during gestation, and Druze assert that it moves immediately at death into the body of a child then being born. Buddhists generally maintain that karma determines the selection of parents, the Druze say that God chooses the parents, and animistic tribal peoples believe the choice is made by the individual.

Stevenson starts out with none of these assumptions, but looks to his data to tell him what reincarnation involves. Past-life memories fade by age eight in many of Stevenson's cases (Stevenson, *Children* 108), but not in all of them.

Edwards (256) asks which is more likely—his Theosophical concept of reincarnation, or "that Stevenson's children, their parents, or some of the other witnesses and informants are, intentionally or unintentionally, not telling the truth: that they are lying, or that their very fallible memories and powers of observations have led them to make false statements and bogus identifications." The choice is a false one, because Edwards' concept is not the only concept of the reincarnation process found in religious and occult traditions. Moreover, Stevenson's investigations were directed precisely at ascertaining whether deception, self-deception, or faulty memory could account for the case phenomena. He discovered deception and self-deception in a few instances (Stevenson, Pasricha, and Samararatne). Other researchers (Haraldsson and Matlock 255–60; Rivas) have documented similar processes in other cases. However, field investigations have ruled out deception and self-deception and by interviewing and reinterviewing multiple firsthand witnesses have determined that memory errors play a very small role in the cases and cannot account for the identification of the previous person in any of them.

Edwards gets into trouble when he tries to show how Stevenson has been duped by his informants. His first example (256–58) is the case of Jagdish Chandra, which was reported originally by K.K.N. Sahay in the 1920s, reinvestigated by Stevenson in the 1960s, and reported in the first volume of his *Cases of the Reincarnation Type* series in 1975 (CORT I, 144–75). Edwards appears not to have read the case report, but relies on remarks about it in a book review by J. Fraser Nicol. Jagdish Chandra was Sahay's son. Although Sahay made notes of his memories and published them in a newspaper in the course of verifying them, Nicol thinks Jagdish could have learned about the deceased person with whom he identified (Jai Gopal Pandey) from his parents or from a family servant. Edwards embraces Nicol's logic, adding that he believes Sahay himself to be "the guilty party," thus accusing Sahay of fraud and Stevenson of not having uncovered it. He sketches an elaborate scenario through which the case might have developed, even while admitting this to be wholly conjectural.

Had Edwards read Stevenson's case report, he might have been more cautious in endorsing Nicol's characterization of it. One of Nicol's reservations, echoed by Edwards, is that Jai Gopal's father did not credit the case. Nicol, however, did not note the reasons he might not have wanted to, something Stevenson (CORT I, 155–56) discusses at length. Jagdish recalled things that would have been embarrassing to this man, who therefore was strongly motivated to deny the case's legitimacy. Edwards would also have learned that Jagdish evinced an unusually strong behavioral identification with Jai Gopal and that this case is one of the exceptions to the rule about the fading of memories by late childhood. Jagdish, who was born in 1920, told Stevenson in 1969 that he still had clear memories of Jai Gopal's life (CORT I, 172).

Edwards (258–59) next considers another of Stevenson's cases that has come under fire, that of Sujith Lakmal Jayaratne (CORT II 235–80). Again, Edwards relies on a secondary treatment of the report (Moore 167–78). This is another case in which a written record was made before the previous person was identified, and Brooke Noel Moore tries to demolish it by means of hypotheticals. The previous person, Sami Fernando, was a colorful figure "whose name might well have been on the tongues of the local townsfolk" (174) and so have come to the attention of Sujith's family in a neighboring community, despite their denials of having heard of him before Sujith began narrating his memories. For both Moore (178) and Edwards (258–59) the decisive proof that something is wrong with the case is that Sujith was born barely six months after Sami's death. Their objection reveals the commitment to an a priori assumption about reincarnation (that it must come at conception) and lacks familiarity with Stevenson's case data. Cases with intermissions of under nine months are not uncommon (Matlock, *Signs* 180). Only if reincarnation necessarily occurs at conception would the possibility of a spirit ouster arise in such cases, and even if that did occur, it is not clear why it should imperil a reincarnation interpretation.

Edwards (259) refers more briefly to Leonard Angel's analysis of the Imad Elawar case (Stevenson, *Twenty Cases* 274–320). This is another case in which there was a record made (by Stevenson) of the subject's statements before verifications. However, because Imad's parents misconstrued some of the things Imad said, Stevenson initially recorded their confusions as his testimony, and Angel thinks this reveals Stevenson choosing what to credit and what not (Matlock, *Signs* 105–6). Later, Edwards (261) acknowledges a journal paper (Stevenson and Samararatne) in which Stevenson describes three new Sri Lankan cases with records made before verifications. "I concede that, on the face of it, these investigations are a significant improvement over earlier cases," he says. "However," he adds without elaboration, "they still have many gaping holes."

Edwards (259–60) introduces Ian Wilson's (21–22) observation that in many of Stevenson's Indian and Sri Lankan cases, the previous person lived in better circumstances than the case subject. For Wilson, and for Edwards, this suggests that the children are fantasizing better lives for themselves. This argument has become a skeptical favorite, but it doesn't work. To have had a previous life in better circumstances would mean a karmic demotion into the present life, perhaps not something Asian children would imagine and certainly not something their parents would invent for them or wish to encourage. Skeptics often allege that Stevenson's cases are shaped by cultural demands, but here they are projecting their own values onto the case subjects and their families.

Edwards (260) next takes up W.G. Roll's (197–99) contention that "linkages" between persons of the past and present lives can account for Stevenson's case subjects' acquisition of information about the past. Roll reached this conclusion on the basis of a study of seven published cases with written records made prior to verifications. In five (although perhaps in only four) of these seven cases, he noticed a "spatial proximity" of some sort between persons connected to the lives before the onset of the cases. Roll's sample size is small and the percentage of cases that do not conform to the pattern is large, besides which his hypothesis does not even attempt to cover the cases' behavioral and physical features (Matlock, "Past Life" 245–46).

Although Edwards (258 note 13) cites Matlock's "Past Life Memory Case Studies," he does not acknowledge Matlock's critique of Roll's study. Nor does he appear to realize that Roll was talking not primarily about "normal" avenues of communication (Roll accepts that Stevenson's investigations have mostly ruled those out), rather about the transfer of information by extrasensory means. Roll (199) did write that "the close connection between some of the children ... and the surviving relatives or friends of the deceased raises the question of sensory cues for some of Stevenson's cases." However, Edwards (260) erroneously states that in "all" of the cases the two lives passed in the same vicinity and quotes Roll as saying that this closeness "raises questions [sic] of sensory cues" explaining, "by which of course Roll means 'normal sources of information.'"

It would be tedious to proceed further through Edwards' chapter on Stevenson.

Fortunately, Matlock has addressed the rest of the material (stemming from the comments of C. T. K. Chari, D. Scott Rogo, and others) in "Past Life Memory Case Studies" and *Signs of Reincarnation*. Edwards evidently has not read any of Stevenson's case reports, apart from his paper on the three cases with written records made before verifications (Stevenson and Samararatne), and instead relies on the contributions of critics who have. Edwards has dutifully cataloged this commentary, and in so doing has performed the valuable service of bringing together the major criticisms of Stevenson's work in one place. The most striking aspect of this ensemble is its astonishing weakness. Again and again, we see the critics cherry-picking, distorting, resorting to hypothetical proposals and unfounded speculations. There is a strong contrast between this armchair exposition and Stevenson's painstakingly detailed reports of field investigations, but because his critics prefer to read and quote each other rather than perusing Stevenson's writing for themselves, newer generations of critics probably do not realize how wide of the mark many of their impressions of him are.

Research Findings: Patterns Across the Dataset

A common skeptical practice is to pick at individual cases, ignoring patterns across the entire dataset of cases studied and reported by Stevenson and his colleagues. When skeptics comment on patterns, it is usually to draw attention to what they consider indications of cultural shaping. Where changing sex between lives is believed possible, sex-change cases are found, but where it is believed impossible, few or no sex-change cases have come to light (Matlock, *Signs* 182–83). Skeptics (e.g., Augustine 27) view this as proof that the cases are contrived in response to cultural demands. This is an important issue. It seems unfair to set aside substantiated cases on such weak grounds, yet there must be an explanation for the relationship between belief and experience here and elsewhere. We will return to this problem after considering the various patterns that have emerged from the data.

In addition to culture-linked patterns, there are several patterns that Matlock ("Patterns"; *Signs* 177–83) identifies as universal or near-universal. Some universal and near-universal patterns relate to the case subject, whereas others concern the deceased person whose life the child recalls. The latter in particular make little sense under the premise that the cases are sociocultural constructs.

Among the near-universal factors related to the case subject is the subject's sex. Case subjects are predominantly male. Boys outnumber girls as subjects in Stevenson's collection by a two-to-one margin (63% to 37%). Boys predominate in all countries except Sri Lanka, where just over half (51%) are girls (Matlock, *Signs* 178). Most subjects start to speak of their memories between the ages of two and five, although some begin as early as eighteen months. The younger the child when first speaking of the previous life, the more developed the memories tend to be overall. Older children not only have less well-developed past-life memories, their initial memories are more likely to be triggered by something seen or heard (Matlock, *Signs* 178).

Most children stop speaking about the previous life after a few years, and their memories seem to have faded from their conscious awareness. Stevenson (*Children* 109) related the fading to the start of school, when children begin spending a large amount of time away from home and are confronted with a wealth of new stimuli. Edwards (262) considered it more likely that the children cease speaking about the previous lives "because they have become tired of the charade and now have better things to do." Stevenson's explanation does make sense psychologically, however, and in any event, as we have seen, the fading is not as universal as was once thought. In follow-up studies, Erlendur Haraldsson found that as many as 38 percent of subjects in Sri Lanka (Haraldsson 387) and 75 percent of subjects in Lebanon (Haraldsson and Abu-Izzeddin 987) retained some past-life memories at least into young adulthood, when they were re-interviewed.

Most children remember having died close to where they were born. Long-distance cases (with distances greater than 50 kilometers, or 31 miles, from the place of death to the place of birth) occur in larger countries such as India and the United States, but cases that cross international boundaries are unusual (Haraldsson and Matlock 229–35). According to Jim Tucker (*Return* 202), death and reincarnation occur in the same country in over 90 percent of Stevenson's cases.

One of the most important universal factors on the side of the previous person is the manner in which that person died. Violent deaths— by accident, murder, or suicide, during war, and so forth—are far more common than violent death in the general population during the same period everywhere cases have been studied. Violent deaths are associated with significantly shorter intermissions between lives (Matlock, *Signs* 179). Intermissions are especially short when deaths are by suicide (Haraldsson and Matlock 253). With natural deaths, such as by illness, the age at death makes a difference. The younger a person is when he dies naturally, the more likely his life is to be recalled later (Tucker, *Return* 201–2).

Premature deaths—by violence or illness—are lives cut short. Their abrupt ending might produce the sense of things left undone, an effect Stevenson termed "unfinished" or "continuing business." He noted some kind of continuing business in the great majority of his cases and suggested that this seemed to be a major factor in promoting past-life memory (Stevenson, *Children* 212). Another factor that has turned out to have a bearing on past-life memory is the previous person's mental qualities. In several cases, the previous persons were practiced meditators. This factor is most apparent with natural death. Many persons who died natural deaths at an advanced age were devoutly religious or had practiced meditation regularly (Matlock, *Signs* 206).

There are relatively few culture-linked features and none of the others are as clear-cut as sex change between lives. Median intermission length conforms in a general way to expectations about when reincarnation occurs. The median intermission length in Buddhist countries is longer than nine months, in line with the assumption that the reincarnating consciousness stream joins the body at conception, whereas among the Druze, the median is only eight months, far from immediate rebirth but closer than in Buddhism (Matlock, *Signs* 180–81). Globally, the median in Stevenson's cases is sixteen to eighteen months, but Western cases frequently have intermissions longer than this, perhaps due to the Western expectation of seeing loved ones again in heaven after death (Matlock, *Signs* 187). The median intermission of published American stranger cases is around thirty years (Matlock, *Signs* 186).

Western cases tend to be less well developed than Asian cases and many fewer are "solved"—that is, have an identified previous person. In Stevenson's collection in 1983, 80 percent of Burmese, 79 percent of Lebanese, and 77 percent of Indian cases were solved, in contrast to only 20 percent of American nontribal cases (Cook et al. 117). The low proportion of solved Western cases impacts other variables and skews the patterns in the data. There is cross-cultural variation in the relationship between the case subject and previous person (family, acquaintance, or stranger). Cases in family lines predominate in tribal societies, but are less common elsewhere. In India, the past and present families were related in 16 percent, acquainted in 41 percent, and complete strangers in 43 percent of the solved cases in Stevenson's collection (Matlock, *Signs* 181). In the United States, all but one solved case had a family connection and in the exceptional case, the previous person was a close friend of the mother (Stevenson, "American Children" 744). Stranger relationships were apparent in 80 percent of American cases, but because all those cases were unsolved, they are not reflected in the statistics.

Augustine (24) is right that in the great majority of Stevenson's cases, the two families had met before investigators arrived on the scene. Augustine interprets this to mean that there could have been an exchange of information about the previous persons prior to the investigation, even in stranger cases, but it is hard to see how this would account for the cases' universal and near-universal patterns. A study of cases with and without records made before the two families met and the child's memories were evaluated found that the two groups had about the same percentage of correct statements, although there were significantly more statements to check in the cases with written records (Schouten and Stevenson 505). From this it appears that the forgetting of pertinent information may be more important a factor than memory distortions in reincarnation cases.

Augustine (26) argues that the fact that the majority of Stevenson's cases come from places where reincarnation is taken for granted "suggests that cultural conditioning, not reincarnation, produces past-life memory claims." However, is it not possible that the cases not only suggested the belief in these places originally, but helped to preserve it as well? Western cases share the same universal and near-universal features as cases that develop elsewhere (Matlock, *Signs*; Stevenson, *European Cases*; Tucker, *Return*). It is only on a few variables, such as length of intermission, distance between locations of death and birth, and proportion of family vs. acquaintance and stranger cases (the last related to the number of solved cases), that Western cases differ significantly from those in the rest of the world (Matlock, "European Children").

The relation between beliefs and case characteristics is not as tight as many skeptics portray it as being (Matlock, *Signs* 183–85), yet for there to be any relationship at all requires explanation. Edwards (268–69) ridiculed Stevenson's suggestion that some of the compliance with cultural expectation came from carrying over into death the ideals of a given culture, but there is no obvious reason why this should not happen, and there is some suggestive evidence that it does (Matlock, *Signs* 187–89). An example is announcing dreams involving previous persons of an ethnic group different from the dreamer's. Before Ma Tin Aung Myo was born, her Burmese mother dreamed about a Japanese army cook she had befriended. Unlike usual Burmese announcing dreams, which come before a woman gets pregnant, these dreams occurred during the pregnancy, and rather than requesting permission to be reborn, as is typical of the Burmese, the cook declared his intention to do so (Stevenson, CORT IV 229–41). The intermission in this and other cases of Japanese soldiers killed and reborn in Burma was also much longer than the median for Burma, 129 months (10.8 years) as opposed to 21 months (1.7 years) (Stevenson and Keil 175).

Interpreting the Data: The Processual Soul Theory

If the case data cannot be explained as the result of cultural compliance, must they be taken as evidence for reincarnation? There are other possibilities to consider before we can reach this conclusion, although none are very satisfactory. Many people wonder about genetic memory, but it can be ruled out very easily. The autobiographical memory reported in reincarnation cases is not the sort of thing that can be passed down by heredity, but even if somehow it were to be, genetic memory would not account for cases in which there was no biological relationship between the subject and the previous person, nor for memories of lives in which no children were produced or for memories of events (such as deaths) that transpired after the last children were conceived (Matlock, *Signs* 118).

Spirit possession might be thought a plausible alternative to reincarnation, because it could help to explain the behavioral aspects of the cases as well as the memories. However, the possession would have to be transient and sporadic to account for the occasional upwelling of images the case subjects experience, and it is hard to see how possession would explain behavioral influences in the absence of conscious memories, as is sometimes seen. Nor could possession account for the birthmarks and congenital physical abnormalities that figure in many cases (Matlock, *Signs* 118; Stevenson, *Twenty Cases* 374–82).

C.T.K. Chari (314), W.G. Roll (199, 211), Stephen Braude and others have proposed that some apparent past-life memories might have been acquired via psi (ESP). Braude, a philosopher, has been particularly vocal about this possibility. In *Immortal Remains,* he maintains that behaviors, including skills, can be learned by psi, without supplying evidence that they can be picked up in that way. Braude suggests (181) that after they see birthmarks on a newborn baby, parents use their psi to locate a deceased person with scars matching the birthmarks, acquire information about his life, and transmit this to their child, shaping his behavioral repertoire in the process. Alternatively, someone in the previous family might psychically identify a newborn with birthmarks matching the deceased, then transfer data about that person to him or her. With a little ingenuity and the assumption that all one has to do is to wave a "magic wand" to produce memories, behaviors, and physical effects, it is possible to explain all reincarnation case phenomena in terms of a complex super-psi (Matlock, *Signs* 117).

Another problem with super-psi rationales is that past-life memory resembles present-life memory much more closely than it does psi. Many past-life memories are cued and most relate to the last months and days of previous life (a recency effect common in present-life memory). If years have passed since the previous life ended, children may find it easier to recognize living people in old photographs than as they currently appear, and the children may remark on changes made after their previous deaths. Psi tends to look to the present and future rather than to the past, and recipients of psi impressions, whether of the present, future, or past, do not confuse them with memories (Matlock, *Signs* 135–36).

Reincarnation is the most straightforward and parsimonious way of explaining the case data. It is the most obvious explanation for the data and intuitively the most logical, which no doubt is why people confronted with signs of reincarnation since the dawn of human society, seemingly, have reached that conclusion. However, reincarnation appears so improbable to modern Western culture, it will not do to espouse it simply because it is the most obvious explanation or because it is the only possibility left after all alternatives have been discarded. In order for reincarnation to be acceptable to Western science, there has to be a viable theory of how it works.

In *Reincarnation and Biology* (2: 2084–88), Stevenson proposed that consciousness is supported between lives by a subtle or astral body he termed a "psychophore." The psychophore, he thought, bore physical impressions (including wounds or scars) and acted as a "template" for the new body. Stevenson did not specify how consciousness moved from the psychophore to the new body. He may have conceived of the psychophore and physical body as isomorphic during embodied life, the consciousness stream shared between them.

Matlock (*Signs*) calls his own theory of the survival and reincarnation of consciousness the "processual soul theory" because it adheres to what philosophers call process metaphysics. The processual soul theory accounts for physical signs by supposing the reincarnating mind is directly responsible for them, through the exercise of psychokinesis (PK). This is not super-psi, but regular, simple psi, of the type involved in a variety of mind/body interactions, such as psychic healing and arguably the placebo effect (in which an inert substance has an effect that a person has been told it does) (Matlock, *Signs* 237). PK would allow the reincarnating mind to influence the formation of its new body without a psychophore as a template.

Because it doesn't introduce a new concept like a subtle body, the processual soul theory may be more acceptable to mainstream science than Stevenson's psychophore theory. However, the processual soul theory assigns a crucial role to PK, which also is controversial. The very idea that consciousness can exist independently of a body is dismissed by mainstream scientists to begin with, and until that issue is resolved, it seems unlikely that they will take the possibility of reincarnation seriously, regardless of the theoretical details. For parapsychologists, though, the processual soul theory provides a model of the reincarnation process alternative to Stevenson's psychophore.

Works Cited

Angel, Leonard. "Empirical Evidence of Reincarnation? Examining Stevenson's 'Most Impressive' Case." *Skeptical Inquirer*, vol. 18, no. 4, Sept.-Oct. 1994, pp. 481–87,

skepticalinquirer.org/1994/09/empirical-evidence-for-reincarnation-examining stevensons-most-impressive-case/. Accessed 31 Jan. 2021.
Augustine, Keith. "Introduction." *The Myth of an Afterlife: The Case Against Life after Death.* Edited by Michael Martin and Keith Augustine. Rowman and Littlefield, 2015, pp. 1–47.
Braude, Stephen E. *Immortal Remains: The Evidence for Life after Death.* Rowman and Littlefield, 2003.
Chari, C.T.K. "Reincarnation Research: Method and Interpretation." *Signet Handbook of Parapsychology.* Edited by Martin Ebon. NAL Books, 1978, pp. 313–24.
Cook, Emily Williams. "Research on Reincarnation-Type Cases: Present Status and Suggestions for Future Research." *Case Studies in Parapsychology: Papers Presented in Honor of Dr. Louisa E. Rhine at a Conference Held on November 12, 1983, at Bryan University Center, Duke University, Durham, North Carolina.* Edited by K. Ramakrishna Rao, McFarland, 1986, pp. 87–96.
Cook, Emily Williams, Satwant Pasricha, Godwin Samararatne, Win Maung, and Ian Stevenson, "A Review and Analysis of 'Unsolved' Cases of the Reincarnation Type. II: Comparison of Features of Solved and Unsolved cases. *Journal of the American Society for Psychical Research*, vol. 77, no. 2, 1983, pp. 115–135, med.virginia.edu/perceptual-studies/wpcontent/uploads/sites/360/2016/12/STE16.pdf. Accessed 31 Jan. 2021.
De Groot, Jan Jakob Maria. *The Religious System of China.* Vol. 4, Brill, 1901.
Diogenes Laertius. *Lives of Eminent Philosophers.* Edited by R.D. Hicks, www.perseus.tufts.edu/hopper/text?doc=Perseus:text:1999.01.0258. Accessed 31 Jan. 2021.
Edwards, Paul. *Reincarnation: A Critical Examination.* Prometheus Books, 1996.
Haraldsson, Erlendur. "Persistence of Past-Life Memories: Study of Adults Who Claimed in Their Childhood to Remember a Past Life." *Journal of Scientific Exploration*, vol. 19, 2008, pp. 385–393, www.researchgate.net/publication/255669556_Persistence_of_PastLife_Memories_Study_of_Adults_Who_Claimed_in_Their_Childhood_to_Remember_a_Past_Life. Accessed 31 Jan. 2021.
Haraldsson, Erlendur, and Majd Abu-Izzeddin. "Persistence of 'Past-Life' Memories in Adults Who, in their Childhood, Claimed Memories of a Past Life." *Journal of Nervous and Mental Disease*, vol. 200, 2012, pp. 985–89.
Haraldsson, Erlendur, and James G. Matlock. *I Saw a Light and Came Here: Children's Experiences of Reincarnation.* White Crow Books, 2017.
Hearn, Lafcadio. *Gleanings in Buddha-Fields: Studies of Hand and Soul in the Far East.* Houghton Mifflin, 1897.
Matlock, James G. "Announcing Dreams and Related Experiences." *Psi Encyclopedia.* Created 30 Jan. 2018, last updated 6 Apr. 2019. psi-encyclopedia.spr.ac.uk/articles/announcingdreams-and-related-experiences. Accessed 31 Jan. 2021.
_____. "European Children Who Recall Previous Lives." *Psi Encyclopedia.* Created 5 Aug. 2020, last updated 5 Aug. 2020, psi-encyclopedia.spr.ac.uk/articles/european-children-whorecall-previous-lives. Accessed 31 Jan. 2021.
_____. "Experimental Birthmarks and Birth Defects." *Psi Encyclopedia.* Created 12 June 2017, last updated 6 Apr. 2019. psi-encyclopedia.spr.ac.uk/articles/experimental-birthmarks-andbirth-defects. Accessed 11 Mar. 2021.
_____. "Past Life Memory Case Studies." *Advances in Parapsychological Research 6.* Edited by Stanley Krippner, McFarland, 1990, pp. 184–267.
_____. "Patterns in Reincarnation Cases." *Psi Encyclopedia.* Created 21 Feb. 2017, last updated 6 Apr. 2019. psi-encyclopedia.spr.ac.uk/articles/patterns-reincarnation-cases. Accessed 31 Jan. 2021.
_____. "Reincarnation Accounts Pre-1900." *Psi Encyclopedia.* Created: 24 July 2017; Last updated: 6 Apr. 2019. psi-encyclopedia.spr.ac.uk/articles/reincarnation-accounts-pre-1900. Accessed 31 Jan. 2021.
_____. *Signs of Reincarnation: Exploring Beliefs, Cases, and Theory.* Rowman and Littlefield, 2019.
Mills, Antonia, and Jim B. Tucker. "Past-life experiences." *Varieties of Anomalous Experience: Examining the Scientific Evidence.* 2nd ed., edited by Etzel Cardeña, Stephen J. Lynn, and Stanley Krippner, American Psychological Association, 2013, pp. 303–32.

Mills, Antonia, and Richard Slobodin, editors. *Amerindian Rebirth: Reincarnation Belief among North American Indians and Inuit.* University of Toronto Press, 1994.

Moore, Brooke Noel. *The Philosophical Possibilities Beyond Death.* Charles C. Thomas, 1981.

Nicol, J. Fraser. "Review of *Cases of the Reincarnation Type. Volume I. Ten Cases in India* by Ian Stevenson." *Parapsychology Review,* vol. 7, no. 5, 1976, pp. 12–15.

Pasricha, Satwant K. *Claims of Reincarnation: An Empirical Study of Cases in India.* Originally published by Harman Books, 1990, White Crow Books, 2019.

Philostratus the Athenian, *Vita Apollonii.* Carl Ludwig Kayser, editor, www.perseus.tufts.edu/hopper/text?doc=Perseus%3Atext%3A2008.01.0595%3Abook%3D3%3Achapter%3D24, Accessed 31 Jan. 2021.

Rivas, Titus. "Alfred Peacock? Reincarnation Fantasies about the *Titanic.*" *Journal of the Society for Psychical Research,* vol. 58, no. 1, 1991, pp. 10–15, www.titusrivas.nl/public/articles/read/655, Accessed 31 Jan. 2021.

Rogo, D. Scott. *The Search for Yesterday: A Critical Examination of the Evidence for Reincarnation.* Prentice-Hall, 1985.

Roll, W.G. "The Changing Perspective on Life after Death." *Advances in Parapsychological Research 3.* Edited by Stanley Krippner, Plenum, 1982, pp. 147–291.

Sahay, Kr. Kekai Nandan. *Reincarnation: Verified Cases of Rebirth after Death.* N.L. Gupta, [1927].

Schouten, Sybo, and Ian Stevenson. "Does the Socio-Psychological Hypothesis Explain Cases of the Reincarnation Type?" *Journal of Nervous and Mental Disease,* vol. 186, no. 8, 1998, pp. 504–6.

Shermer, Michael. *Heavens on Earth: The Scientific Search for the Afterlife, Immortality, and Utopia.* Henry Holt, 2018.

Stevenson, Ian. "American Children Who Claim to Remember Previous Lives." *Journal of Nervous and Mental Disease,* vol. 171, no. 12, 1983, pp. 742–48.

———. *Cases of the Reincarnation Type. Volume I: Ten Cases in India* [CORT I]. University Press of Virginia, 1975.

———. *Cases of the Reincarnation Type. Volume II: Ten Cases in Sri Lanka* [CORT II]. University Press of Virginia, 1977.

———. *Cases of the Reincarnation Type. Volume IV: Twelve Cases in Thailand and Burma* [CORT IV]. University Press of Virginia, 1983.

———. *Children Who Remember Previous Lives: A Question of Reincarnation.* Rev. ed., McFarland, 2001.

———. *European Cases of the Reincarnation Type.* McFarland, 2003.

———. "The Evidence for Survival from Claimed Memories of Former Incarnations. Part 1: Review of the Data." *Journal of the American Society for Psychical Research,* vol. 54, no. 2, April 1960, pp. 51–71.

———. "Reincarnation: Field Studies and Theoretical Issues." *Handbook of Parapsychology.* Edited by Benjamin B. Wolman, Van Nostrand Reinhold, 1977, pp. 631–63.

———. *Reincarnation and Biology: A Contribution to the Etiology of Birthmarks and Birth Defects.* Praeger, 1997. 2 vols.

———. *Twenty Cases Suggestive of Reincarnation.* 2nd ed., University Press of Virginia, 1974.

Stevenson, Ian, and [H. H.] Jürgen Keil. "Children of Myanmar Who Behave like Japanese Soldiers: A Possible Third Element in Personality." *Journal of Scientific Exploration,* vol. 19, no. 2, 2005, pp. 172–83.

Stevenson, Ian, S. [K.] Pasricha, and Godwin Samararatne. "Deception and Self-Deception in Cases of the Reincarnation Type: Seven Illustrative Cases in Asia." *Journal of the American Society for Psychical Research,* vol. 82, no. 1, 1981, pp. 1–31.

Stevenson, Ian, and Godwin Samararatne. "Three New Cases of the Reincarnation Type in Sri Lanka With [sic] Written Records Made Before [sic] Verifications." *Journal of Scientific Exploration,* vol. 2, no. 3, 1988, pp. 217–38, citeseerx.ist.psu.edu/viewdoc/download?doi=10.1.1.555.2888&rep=rep1&type=pdf. Accessed 31 Jan. 2021.

Sunderlal, R.B.S. "Cas apparents de réminiscences de vies antérieures." *Revue métapsychique,* vol. 4, no. 4, 1924, pp. 302–07.

Tucker, Jim B. *Life Before Life: A Scientific Investigation of Children's Memories of a Previous Life*. St. Martin's Press, 2005.
_____. *Return to Life: Extraordinary Cases of Children Who Remember Past Lives*. St. Martin's Press, 2013.
Tucker, Jim B., and H.H. Jürgen Keil. "Experimental Birthmarks: New Cases of an Asian Practice." *Journal of Scientific Exploration*, vol. 27, no. 3, 2013, pp. 269–82, journalofscientificexploration.org/index.php/jse/article/view/547. Accessed 31 Jan. 2021.
Tylor, Edward Burnett. *Primitive Culture: Researches into the Development of Mythology, Philosophy, Religion, Language, Art, and Custom*. 2nd ed., John Murray, 1877. 2 vols.
Wilson, Ian. *All in the Mind: Reincarnation, Hypnotic Regression, Stigmata, Multiple Personality, and Other Little-Understood Powers of the Mind*. Originally published as *Mind Out of Time? Reincarnation Investigated*. Victor Gollancz, 1981, Doubleday, 1982.
Wortabet, John. *Researches into the Religions of Syria*. James Nisbet, 1860.

An Overview of Research on Mediums

History and Cautions

STEPHEN J. PULLUM, CAROLE M. VAN CAMP, and WENDY DONLIN WASHINGTON

Introduction: The Fox Sisters

Although the practice of attempting to communicate with the dead dates back to ancient times, such as King Saul's visit with the dead prophet Samuel (1 Sam. 28:5–25; for discussion see Pullum, "Talking"), Spiritualism—the belief that the deceased can communicate with the living through another person known as a medium—began in this country in 1848. It was during this year when Maggie and Katie Fox, two girls around the ages of eight and six respectively, from Hydesville, New York, near Rochester, claimed that they could communicate with the deceased. What started as a joke on their gullible mother, these "communications" occurred through a series of rapping noises, which the spirits of the dead supposedly made in answer to questions posed to them by "sitters" during séances (Stuart 1–7; Weisberg 16–17). The girls started by making "rapping" noises at night by bumping an apple on a string against the floor of the room which they shared with their parents. One of the girls mimicked the raps by snapping her fingers, and the rapping copied her. After she snapped her fingers four times, four raps followed. If she stopped snapping her fingers, the sounds stopped momentarily (Kurtz 178).

The "spirit" knew a lot about the Foxes, their neighbors, and the many people who visited in order to experience the events (Davenport). For example, many people became convinced that the Fox house was haunted by the ghost of Charles Rosna, a traveling salesman who supposedly had been killed in the house five years before the Foxes moved in (Stuart 2-13; See also Weisberg 1-4, 24, 46, 56-58).

Under the oversight of their older sister Leah, eventually, the girls, now fifteen and thirteen, would take their show on the road, holding numerous séances for the public—for a fee. By this point, the girls had learned how to make loud knockings or rappings by cracking joints in their fingers, hips, knees, ankles, or toes. The well-known editor of *The New York Tribune* newspaper Horace Greeley (1811-1872), among other prominent citizens, once sat through a two-hour séance in a darkened room with the girls in order to learn more about "The Rochester Knockings." Although Greeley was not known for being overly critical of individuals' claims of the supernatural, this time he came away unimpressed, stating that "Spiritual communications" were "vague, unreal, shadowy, trivial.... To sit for two dreary, mortal hours in a darkened room, in a mixed company, waiting for someone's disembodied grandfather or aunt to tip a table or rap on a door," bemoaned Greeley, "is dull music at best; but to sit in vain is disgusting." In the final analysis, Greeley concluded, "I do not know that these 'communications' made through 'mediums' proceed from those who are said to be their authors, nor from the spirits of the departed at all" (Gaustad 380-81).

Others doubted the sisters' bona fides, with three professors from the Buffalo School of Medicine deciding that the sisters were making the noises by dislocating their knees. Adding further doubt, Maggie admitted that the rapping noises were fraudulent in a 147-page book (Davenport 87-93, 95). Maggie later took back her confession and explained that she had only made it for a large amount of money. However, she had already shown how she had made the rapping sounds (Davenport ch. 5).

On Sunday evening, October 21, 1888, after a forty-year career of successfully duping the public, the Fox sisters' methods of "communicating with the dead" came to light when Maggie appeared on stage in the theater of the New York Academy of Music. Nearby, her younger sister Katie sat in a viewing box approving of what Maggie was about to disclose. Before a crowd of between 2,000 to 3,000 people, some of whom were Spiritualists, some of whom were skeptics, not of few of whom were newspaper reporters, Maggie demonstrated with her feet how she was able to make rapping noises that had deceived people for many years. In fact, the sounds coming from her feet were so loud that they could be heard all over the auditorium. Three doctors came on stage to verify that the noises had indeed been made by the cracking of the sisters' ankles and other joints. The *New York Herald* newspaper reported Maggie as having confessed, "That I have been mainly instrumental in perpetrating the fraud of Spiritualism upon a too confiding public, many of you already know. It is the greatest sorrow of my life." As she continued with her physical demonstrations, Maggie clapped and danced around shouting, "It's a fraud! Spiritualism is a fraud from beginning to end! It's all a trick! There's no truth in it!" (qtd. in Stuart 299–300; see also Shepard 2: 1588, Stuart 1–7, 297–300; Weisberg 3, 241–246).

It should be added that the *Herald*, like other newspapers of the time, did not adhere to the journalistic standards of later times. For example, it devoted the equivalent of the front page to a deadly escape of animals from the Central Park Zoo, admitting at the article's end that it was a fabrication ("Awful Calamity"). Perhaps 9 November 1874 was a slow news day.

Maggie seems to have been easily led, first by her older sister Leah, whose persuasiveness may be shown by the fact that she married three times. Second, Maggie's confession may have been motivated by the Arctic explorer Elisha Kent Kane, her common-law husband, and by her conversion to Catholicism. Finally Spiritualists prevailed on her, then destitute and alcoholic, to retract her confession (Houdini 3–16). In spite of Maggie's public confession, many individuals who came to believe in Spiritualism as a result of the Fox sisters continued to believe in it. According to some reports, by 1855 adherents to this religion numbered in the millions (Shepard 2: 1588, Stuart 1–7; Weisberg 3, 241, 244).

More Historical Background

For the next twenty to thirty years following 1848, hundreds of people emerged on the heels of the Fox sisters, claiming that they, too, were able to communicate with the dead. Most of these individuals were women. This was not because women were somehow more "predisposed" to become a medium, "but because it provided relief from a narrow existence. Mediumship gave these women attention and, most important, freedom: freedom of movement and travel and freedom for outrageous behavior 'caused' by the spirits" (Guiley 359). Among the "outrageous behaviors" reported were swearing, drinking, and in some cases, engaging in illicit sexual activity. Several of these mediums charged for their services, but there were many who conducted séances for free (Guiley 359).

Mediumship fell into one of two categories—physical and mental. Physical mediums were those who claimed that they were able to conjure up the dead as evidenced by physical manifestations such as rappings, table tippings, and playing of musical instruments. There were also accounts of hands, fans, or other physical objects (known as apports) materializing during séances. It was reported that some mediums even levitated. Most individuals who fell into this category, however, were proven to be frauds (Carter, *Science and the Afterlife* 137–38).

Mental mediums, on the other hand, were those who claimed to be able to relay messages from the deceased. They could be categorized as either (1) clairvoyant (the most common type), in which the medium was awake and claimed to hear or see the deceased outside the normal range of senses or (2) trance, in which the medium would go into a dissociated state, where another entity known simply as a "control" would communicate with the living through the medium. Often while in a trance, mental mediums would vocalize what the "control" or other "drop-in" communicators—those unknown to either the medium or the sitter—had to say. These mediums were known as voice mediums because they would communicate information to sitters through speech, often in the same style characteristic of the deceased when alive. On other occasions, trance mediums would simply write down what the "control" wished to communicate. Sometimes mediums would do both. Ostensibly, trance mediums almost never remembered what they had communicated from the deceased once they came out of the trance (Carter, *Science and the Afterlife* 137–38).

Within a few years of the emergence of the Fox sisters in the United States, mediums began making their way across the ocean to England and other parts of Europe. One of the first was an American named Maria B. Hayden, who arrived in England in 1852 but stayed for only a year. Another renowned medium was Daniel Dunglas Home, discussed in Miller, "History," who, among others, also went to England in 1855 but returned shortly thereafter.

The Davenport Brothers

As Nickell reminds us, about the same time that the Fox sisters were providing séances for the public, another sibling team known as the Davenport brothers were also cashing in on false claims about the supernatural (19). First appearing on stage in 1855 at the ages of sixteen and fourteen, Ira Erastus Davenport (1839–1911) and his younger brother William Henry Davenport (1841–1877) were known primarily for operating in a 6-feet-wide by 2-feet-deep by 7-feet-tall closet that sat on stage on sawhorses. Within this "cabinet," as it would soon come to be called, which they took from show to show, many people thought that they were conjuring up the spirits of the deceased whose "spirit hands" played various musical instruments, gripped people sitting in the box with them, or twirled umbrellas while the Davenport brothers supposedly remained bound hand and foot in the box. Of course, all of this occurred in the dark, which made it difficult, if not impossible, to examine (Shepard 1: 377–79).

Advertisements of the Davenport brothers read,

> Musical instruments are made to play in the most extraordinary manner, and in the most profound and mysterious way. Human hands and arms become visible, and many other interesting experiments are presented, originating only with the Davenport brothers in the year 1855 and never produced with success by imitators. Sceptics [sic] are especially invited to be present and occupy front seats (qtd. in Haining 37).

Facing each other in a sitting position on opposite sides of the box, once the brothers were bound, two doors (one on the front of either side of the cabinet) were closed so that no one could see them as they would then proceed quickly to free themselves from the ropes. A third door in the center of the box had a diamond-shaped opening, allowing the audience to see inside. Once the two outer doors were opened again, audiences saw only the two brothers tied up as if they had been bound the entire time that audiences were watching musical instruments and other objects vaguely appear in the darkness to float in the air (Houdini 21-30).

Although they called their stage act a séance, neither brother publicly claimed to be a medium. Instead, they merely left that up to the imagination of their audiences, thousands of whom believed in Spiritualism because of the Davenport brothers. True-believing Spiritualists who often frequented their shows argued that what the Davenport brothers did was indeed proof positive that dead people often return to communicate with the living. However, like the Fox sisters, the Davenport brothers were not without their critics who believed they did what they did simply out of trickery. Moreover, at times, audiences did not take too kindly to being deceived. In fact, on a couple of occasions in England, onlookers stormed the stage and smashed their cabinets after the Davenport brothers refused to allow them to make sure their hands were tightly tied (Houdini 21-30).

After William Davenport's death in Australia in 1877, Ira stopped performing and returned to his native New York to retire. Before his death in 1911, however, he disclosed to the magician and escape artist Harry Houdini (1874-1926) how it was that they were able to untie themselves so quickly. He also confessed to Houdini that he and his brother had faked the whole notion that spirits could return from the dead to communicate with the living. By that point, though, thousands had already come to believe in spiritualism as a result of the Davenport brothers' shows (Houdini 26).

These and other mediums attracted much attention among the English, causing many to wonder about their veracity. What is ironic is that although Spiritualism began in the United States, the formal study of mediums and of paranormal activities associated with them actually began in England largely as a result of American mediums who had gone abroad (Shepard 1: 743, 773-78).

One of the first organizations to investigate mediums was the London Dialectical Society, which was formed in 1867. In 1871 it printed a controversial report that was generally favorable to Spiritualism and the question of survival (i.e., life after death), although there were those on the committee who wrote dissenting opinions. Some thirty-three individuals working across six subcommittees recorded the oral testimonies of thirty-one people who claimed to have witnessed paranormal activities during séances. The authors of the report concluded that the findings of the various subcommittees "substantially corroborate each other" (Shepard 1: 973). For example, witnesses reported hearing a variety of sounds in séances coming from walls, floors, or furniture.

Moreover, they claimed to have felt vibrations. Individuals also testified to being touched by the deceased. Additionally, they claimed that heavy objects would levitate without the help of external forces, and the deceased frequently gave correct answers to questions posed to them, answers which were supposedly known only to sitters (Shepard 1: 974).

The report, however, was not well received by various newspapers. According to Shepard, *The London Times,* for example, wrote that the report of the London Dialectical Society was "nothing more than a farrago [mixture] of impotent conclusions, garnished by a mass of the most monstrous rubbish it has ever been our misfortune to sit in judgment upon" (qtd. in Shepard 1: 974). In the final analysis, as a body, the London Dialectical Society merely kicked the can down the road, stating that "the subject is worthy of more serious attention and careful investigation than it has hitherto received" (qtd. in Shepard 1: 974).

A few years after the founding of the London Dialectical Society, The Society for Psychical Research (SPR) began on February 20, 1882. Shortly after the founding of the SPR in London, the American Society for Psychical Research (ASPR) was begun in Boston around 1885 to investigate paranormal phenomena in the U.S. Much of the research conducted by the ASPR on mediums in its early years was led by men such as William James, Richard Hodgson, and James Hyslop (1854–1920), long-time professor of logic and ethics at Columbia University, to mention a few (Shepard 1: 45).

Famous and Notable Cases

Although there are dozens of well-known mediums who have arisen since 1848, space will permit us to focus on only a couple. We have chosen these because they are two of the most popular mental mediums of all time who were heavily studied and considered legitimate by many researchers who have investigated the phenomenon of mediumship.

Leonora E. Piper

Leonora E. Piper (1859–1950), Boston housewife, is the best-known example of mental mediumship and the most famous medium of the nineteenth century to be studied on both sides of the Atlantic. (See Carter, *Science and the Afterlife*, 139–45, for a summary of Piper.) Like many mediums both then and now, Mrs. Piper had undergone an unusual childhood experience.

Around the age of eight, she supposedly was struck on the right side of her head before hearing a voice say, "Aunt Sara not dead, but with you still." Shortly afterwards she learned of the death of her aunt. Around the age of twenty-six, Piper visited a blind healing medium named J.R. Cocke. During her second visit, she went into a trance where she supposedly communicated correct information to one of the sitters in the séance, which reportedly came from a female Native American control named Chlorine. Not long thereafter, she began conducting her own séances, where she would go into a trance and pass along information to sitters from various controls such as George Washington, Abraham Lincoln, Henry Wadsworth Longfellow, Martin Luther, Cornelius Vanderbilt, and Johann Sebastian Bach, among others (Fodor 283–84). These controls soon gave way to a French doctor named "Phinuit," who, ironically, knew little about either French or medicine. He spoke in English with a French accent because, according to Piper, her sitters could not speak French. (It is interesting to note that Piper herself had studied French for two years.) Curiously, there was no record of Phinuit's existence even though Piper gave specific details about his life, which were easily traceable. In addition to taking on the accent and verbal mannerisms of the control, Piper often emulated her controls' physical idiosyncrasies (Douglas 110; Gardner 535; Gauld, "Discarnate Survival" 582).

After being introduced to her by his wife in 1885, William James began attending séances with Mrs. Piper and came away impressed with the information she gave him both from and about his deceased relatives. So impressed was James that, as part of his study, he sent some twenty-five other people to her for sittings under various pseudonyms. In spite of not knowing their real names reportedly, Piper's controls knew many of the sitters and gave them correct information about themselves. In time, James would refer to Mrs. Piper as his "own white crow," suggesting that she had abilities that ordinary individuals did not possess. In an often-quoted passage, James once wrote that if one wants to prove that not all crows are black, one only needs to find one white crow.

> My own white crow is Mrs. Piper. In the trances of this medium, I cannot resist the conviction that knowledge appears which she has never gained by the ordinary waking use of her eyes and ears and wits. What the source of this

knowledge may be I know not, and have not the glimmer of an explanatory suggestion to make; but from admitting the fact of such knowledge I can see no escape ... (James, *Will* 319).

After James' report to the SPR in 1886, Leonora was the first person to be paid a retainer by the SPR in order that she might devote herself exclusively to their research. To prevent her from getting information dishonestly, Leonora was shadowed by Richard Hodgson who, inter al., had her followed by detectives—just as SPR had done earlier in England—and opened her mail. Indeed, Hodgson would not meet with Leonora unless he covered his face so that she could not detect any expressions by which she could read his reactions. Despite all Hodgson's pains, he could detect no fraud by Leonora (Beloff 58–60; Carter, *Science and the Afterlife* 139–45; Gardner 535; See also Shepard 1: 1291–95; Gauld, "Discarnate Survival" 585).

Hodgson was a ruthless sceptic who was sent to Boston to take charge of the SPR investigation and who had ruined the reputations of Helena Petrovna Blavatsky (1831–1891), Russian-born medium and founder of Theosophy, and of the Italian medium Eusapia Palladino (1854–1918). When Piper returned to Boston from England, where investigators with the SPR could not decide if she received her information from the deceased or telepathically from sitters, Hodgson began a study of her in 1887 that lasted for close to eighteen years before he died of a heart attack at the age of fifty on 20 December 1905, following a game of handball (Beloff 58–60; Carter, *Science and the Afterlife* 139–45; Gardner 535; See also Shepard 1: 1291–95; Gauld, "Discarnate Survival" 585).

Leonora's case was particularly compelling not only for the level of surveillance that surrounded her, but also for the depth of the information she seemingly conveyed from the dead. In 1887, after his own personal sitting with Piper in which she reportedly gave him accurate information about himself, Hodgson arranged for some fifty other people to sit with her with similar results.

In time, Piper's control Phinuit would give way to another control named George Pelham (a slight variation of his real name Pellew), a Boston lawyer and good friend of Hodgson who had died in 1892. Pellew made a pact with Hodgson that he would contact Hodgson after death, if such a thing were possible. Pellew died at thirty-two and then, it appears, manifested himself in the automatic writing of Leonora Piper as "G.P." For five years Piper received messages which it seemed could only have come from Pellew himself, or at the very least from somebody who was strongly associated with Pellew, which Piper was not. "G.P." reportedly gave very accurate information both about Pellew and his friendship with Hodgson. Notably "G.P" "greeted" everybody whom Pellew had met in life (close to

30 people) in a room with 150 different sitters whom Hodgson brought and never greeted anybody whom Pellew had not met (of which there were 120 people) (Carter, *Science and the Afterlife* 139–45; Gardner 535–36; Gauld, "Discarnate Survival" 582–83, 585; see also Shepard 1: 1291–95).

This greatly impressed Hodgson and seemed decisive for him to become a true believer in Piper. In his report to the SPR in 1898, Hodgson maintained that he was convinced that the individuals who communicated through Mrs. Piper were individuals who survived death and were now communicating with the living (Carter, *Science and the Afterlife* 139–45; Gardner 535–36; Gauld, "Discarnate Survival" 582–83). Subsequently, Hodgson developed a strong belief in life after death, albeit in the scientifically argued idea of survivalism. Survivalists believed that life after death was probable, given the evidence before them. Spiritualists on the other hand believed emphatically in life after death as an article of faith and saw their mediumship as a mission whereby they could act as intermediaries—thereby "churches" and the like evolved around this missionary focus (Beloff 58).

Eight days after Hodgson's death, Mrs. Piper began relaying messages that purportedly came from him, now her new control. Because of this, William James started attending séances again with various sitters of Mrs. Piper as further study. After 75 sittings, which occurred over several years, James concluded in a 1909 report published in the *Proceedings of the American Society for Psychical Research*, Vol. III, that there was much evidence of "supernormal" knowledge and that Hodgson's personality showed through Mrs. Piper (Carter, *Science and the Afterlife* 145; Murphy 53–55; Shepard 1: 1294). In the final analysis, however, James wrote that he felt "an external will to communicate," doubted "that Mrs. Piper's dream-life, even equipped with 'telepathic' powers, accounts for all the result found ... [but] asked whether the will to communicate be Hodgson's ... or some mere spirit-counterfeit of Hodgson, ..." and remained uncertain, awaiting more facts (qtd. in Murphy and Ballou 209; See also James, *Essays* 359).

Given the conclusions of Hodgson, William James and even James Hyslop (who, after 12 sittings with Piper from 1898 to 1899, believed that he had been talking with his dead father, brother and uncles), what is ironic is that in an article in the *New York Herald* newspaper dated 20 October 1901 titled "I Am No Telephone to the Spirit World," Piper herself denied having any connections to the deceased:

> I must truthfully say that I do not believe that spirits of the dead have spoken through me when I have been in the trance state, as investigated by scientific men of Boston and Cambridge and those of the English Psychical Research Society, when I was taken to England to be studied. It may be that they have, but I do not affirm it (sec. 5, p. 1).

When asked if she were a Spiritualist (i.e., one who believes that the dead communicate with the living), she responded, "No, I have never considered myself one." When asked, "Have you never had any convincing proof of the possibility of spirit return?" she responded, "I cannot truthfully say that I have." Piper herself said, "When I read over the reports of the Society for Psychical Research it all seems to me that there is no evidence of sufficient scientific value to warrant acceptance of the spiritistic explanation" ("I Am," sec. 5, p. 1).

Instead, Piper attributed any correct information coming out of séances to an "unconscious expression of my subliminal self" or to telepathy (i.e., the transference of information in one person's mind to that of another). For example, Piper was reported saying that she knew of nothing which she said in trance which could not have come from her own mind, the mind of the "person in charge of the sitting," the minds of the sitters, or an absent living person's mind ("I Am," sec. 5, p. 2).

Reportedly upset with the *New York Herald's* advertisement of the article as a "confession," Piper forbade its publication. According to Fodor, she received a telegram from the *New York Herald*, which assured her that the word "confession" was used only for advertising purposes but would not appear in the article itself (286). It did, however. The newspaper characterized what she said as an "extraordinary confession—calm, dignified, profound" ("I Am," sec. 5, p. 2). As noted above, the *Herald* did not adhere to the stricter journalistic standards of today.

To complicate matters, in response to the *New York Herald*, five days later, on 25 October 1901, *The Boston Advertiser* quoted Piper as saying,

> I did not make any such statement as that published in the *New York Herald* to the effect that spirits of the departed do not control me.... My opinion is to-day as it was eighteen years ago. Spirits of the departed may have controlled me and they may not. I confess that I do not know. I have not changed.... I make no change in my relations (qtd. in Fodor 286).

Piper eventually retired from regular, public mediumship in 1911 shortly after an intense study by Dr. Granville Stanley Hall and his assistant Dr. Amy B. Tanner—although Piper did allow herself to be researched as late as 1927. Hall, former president of Clark University in Worcester, Massachusetts, who studied her on behalf of the American Society for Psychical Research, once said of her, "She is without question the most eminent American medium in this field" (Tanner and Hall xviii).

However, after 6 sessions with Piper during the spring of 1909, Hall and Tanner found no evidence of Piper being able to communicate with the dead. One of the strategies that they employed was to trick Piper into thinking that Hall and Richard Hodgson, her control, had actually been good friends in life even though the two had never met in person. Hall writes that Hodgson "surely was not all there," but "was not only fragmentary but incredibly stupid, oblivious, and changed ... in these sessions he always addressed me in the most familiar manner, had many totally false memories of former interviews with me and of discussions which never took place, and in a word seemed to feel just as intimate with me as Mrs. Piper in her normal state thought he used to" (Tanner and Hall xxi). Among other criticisms, Hall suggests that this "false recognition and spirit of camaraderie [from Hodgson] throughout [his sittings] was baffling" (Tanner and Hall xxi).

During her career as a professional medium, Piper was well known for her involvement in what was called cross-correspondences. She and a handful of other non-professional mediums who operated independently of each other in different parts of the world often claimed to receive automatic writings from various controls. These controls were usually deceased individuals from the Society for Psychical Research such as Edmund Gurney, Fred Myers, and Henry Sidgwick, who had all died by 1901. For about thirty years, these ladies would receive messages of a literary nature with esoteric allusions from classical Greek or Latin sources. These "correspondences" were supposedly beyond the intellectual abilities of the mediums themselves to concoct, with perhaps the exception of a Mrs. A.W. Verall, who was educated in the classics. Over time these cryptic writings were collected by a few third parties, who attempted to illustrate their connections to one another. Supposedly, these writings, when looked at as a whole, were evidence that the dead were trying to communicate with the living from beyond the grave, albeit in a rather esoteric manner (Beloff 12–13). Beloff points out that correspondences were "misconceived."

> For it demanded almost a lifetime of study combined with exceptional scholarly gifts in order to interpret and evaluate this huge body of material. And, even then, it allowed too much latitude to the ingenuity of the interpreter. Clearly, it was not by such recherché [rare] strategies as this that the bastions of skepticism would be stormed (13).

By all accounts, Mrs. Piper was believed to be an honest, sincere individual. Her integrity was never questioned by researchers (Carter, *Science and the Afterlife* 139–45; See also Shepard 1: 1291–95; Gauld, "Discarnate Survival" 585).

Gladys Osborne Leonard

Another very famous trance medium studied by the SPR was the English-born Gladys Osborne Leonard (1882–1968), who, like Piper, had seen visions as a child, which her parents frowned upon and tried to discourage her from discussing. At the age of twenty-four she reportedly saw a vision of her ailing mother in perfectly good health around the same time her mother had died (Leonard 20, 22–24).

Leonard's primary control was a young Hindu girl from India named "Feda," who, Leonard believed, died in childbirth in 1800 at the age of thirteen. "Feda" was supposedly the teenage wife of Leonard's great-great-grandfather William Hamilton. Although no record of "Feda" actually existed, family lore told of such a person. Feda urged the 32-year-old Leonard to become a full-time, professional medium in order to help people, who would soon undergo problems because "Something big and terrible is going to happen to the world" (Leonard 29–30, 52). This was a reference to the start of World War I, and Leonard would begin to hold private sittings for families who had lost loved ones during the war to help them deal with their grief.

After being recommended by a friend, physicist Sir Oliver Lodge and his wife went to Leonard for several sittings following the death of their 26-year-old son Raymond on 14 September 1915, during World War I. As a result of the publicity she received from Lodge in his book *Raymond or Life and Death* (1916), Leonard's popularity exploded. Leonard once remarked, "Looking back, I realize now ... how much I owe to [him].... [W]here would my work have been without Sir Oliver Lodge's help? I cannot imagine" (Leonard 59). Although Lodge was a physicist, he and his family openly avowed principles of Christianity, one of which affirmed that individuals live on following permanent physical death. Having already believed in survival and having lost a beloved son, Lodge, who was in a vulnerable position, became convinced that the things that Leonard was telling him (sometimes replete with table tippings) were actually being communicated to him from his deceased son Raymond (Lodge 105–24).

What really impressed Lodge, though, was Leonard's detailed reference to a picture that was taken of Raymond together with other officers in the British army in August of 1915, shortly before his death. Mrs. Lodge first learned of the photo on September 27 after a sitting with the British trance medium Alfred Vout Peters. On November 29, the Lodges eventually received a letter from a Mrs. Cheves who obtained several copies of the photograph from her son who was in the British army, asking the Lodges if they wanted one. The Lodges immediately wrote back that they did. In a sitting with Oliver Lodge on December 3, Mrs. Leonard described the photo to him in detail. It was not until December 7, however, that the Lodges actually received a copy of the picture from Mrs. Cheves and were able to verify what Mrs. Leonard had described in the photo only a few days earlier. This lent credence to Leonard's mediumship for the Lodges, even though it is likely that Leonard had long since seen a copy of the picture herself (Lodge, 105-24).

During her career as a medium, Mrs. Leonard was particularly known for two things: (1) book tests and (2) proxy sittings. During her book tests, in an attempt to convince her sitters that some deceased relative was communicating with them, Mrs. Leonard would refer to a book in the sitter's home, neither of which she had access to but which supposedly would be known by the deceased. Not only would she specify the book, but she would also indicate its location on the book shelf and the page number that contained information that reportedly would have some kind of subjective meaning to the sitter.

These book tests were studied by the Rev. Drayton Thomas (188?-1953), an active researcher for the SPR, who published his findings in two books: *Some New Evidence for Human Survival* (1922) and *Life Beyond Death with Evidence* (1928) (Shepard, 1: 209-10, 2: 1697; See also Douglas 152-53). As one can see from the above titles, Thomas believed that Leonard's book tests provided sufficient evidence that the dead can and do communicate with the living.

Another individual, Eleanor Sidgwick, wife of Henry, founder of SPR, and sister of Arthur Balfour, another founder, investigated Mrs. Leonard on behalf of the SPR, and was not so sure. After extensive study, she concluded that "many book tests and items of book tests are complete failures, and that apparent precision and fullness of detail in what the communicator says and confidence expressed by him that the test should be a good one, are no guarantee of success...." Out of 532 book tests she investigated from 34 sitters, she classified 92 as "successful" and 100 as "approximately successful." She concluded that 204 were "complete failures"; 40 were "nearly complete failures"; and 96 were "dubious." In other words, "taking the first two classes together we may say that about 36 per cent of the attempts were approximately successful." This means that 64 percent were not (Douglas 155).

In addition to book tests, Mrs. Leonard was also famous for conducting "proxy sittings," whereby individuals would sit with a medium as a substitute for someone else who wanted to communicate with a dead relative. Supposedly, this was done in order to avoid telepathy between the medium and the family member (Douglas 152).

Perhaps her most famous case involved the skeptic and professor of Greek Eric R. Dodds (1893-1979), who would eventually serve as President of the SPR from 1961 to 1963. Professor Dodds asked Drayton Thomas to serve as a proxy sitter for one of his friends, Mrs. Wilfred Lewis, who wanted to communicate with her deceased father, Frederic Macaulay, who had died on 20 May 1933. After 5 sittings which occurred during the summer of 1936 and the winter of 1937, Thomas argued that out of 124 statements made, 51 were "right," 12 were "good," 32 were "fair," and 29 were failures. Both Thomas, who already believed in life after death, and Mrs. Lewis were convinced that they had received information from her dead father. Moreover Dodds himself suggested, "It appears to me that the hypothesis of fraud, rational influence from disclosed facts, telepathy from the actual sitter, and coincidence cannot either singly or in combination account for the results obtained." This was because "only the barest information was supplied to sitter and medium and that through an indirect channel" (Carter, *Science and the Afterlife* 167; Douglas 153; Gauld, "Discarnate Survival" 588–89).

Research and Experiments

Recent studies on mediumship have reported positive results indicating that in some cases, mediums are receiving information directly from the deceased. At the forefront of such studies are Julie Beischel and others at the Windbridge Institute, who have designed systematic studies aimed at addressing common criticisms and concerns over mediumship.

However, many people today remain skeptical that mediums are actually able to communicate with the dead. There have been several alternative explanations for the alleged ability of some mediums to accurately report information about a dead individual and his or her relationship to the sitter. Controlled experiments can be used to eliminate these alternatives as explanations. In the following sections are presented a review and critique of the existing scientific literature that provides alternative explanations to the idea that the deceased are actually communicating with the living, including (1) cold readings, (2) using vague information that might be "true" about most individuals, (3) having prior knowledge about the individuals, and (4) telepathy between the sitter and the reader ("the living agent psi" hypothesis). These possibilities are examined in contrast to the survival hypothesis, which implies that the discarnate (i.e., deceased) is the actual source of the information being provided and that some people are able to communicate with those deceased individuals.

As has already been noted, scientific research into paranormal phenomena has been occurring at least since the late nineteenth century. In addition to the Society for Psychical Research (SPR), the Windbridge Institute for Applied Research in Human Potential is another organization that supports research into paranormal phenomena like mediumship. Both attempt to study mediums from a scientific perspective. The intent of this section is not to cover all research over the last 120-plus years but to describe the research in these organizations that has led to some "best practice" methods (for a more thorough review of the history of research in the area, see Carter, *Science and the Afterlife* or Schwartz). These approaches have been designed to eliminate alternative explanations for how mediums are reporting seemingly accurate information about the deceased. Most of these studies have sitters rating the quality of information provided by the medium about the deceased individual. The types of information provided by mediums vary and may include physical characteristics of the deceased while they were still alive; the manner in which the deceased died; specific facts about the deceased, like religion, occupation, and marriage status; what experience is like after death; and even occasionally what the deceased wishes to ask of the sitter.

One alternative explanation is that mediums are using cues from the sitter to make guesses about the characteristics of the deceased. This is known as cold reading. Cues can include the race, clothing, age, gender, religion, and nonverbal reactions of the sitters. For example, say that a medium meets a sitter named Daniella. The medium may be making generalizations from the way Daniella looks, the way she speaks, what she is wearing, and her name to infer that she is Hispanic. The medium guesses that there is a high likelihood that some deceased family members are Catholic. The medium says "I'm getting a sense that there is a presence here that wore a necklace with some sort of pendant, maybe a cross." Daniella then fills in some information with "Yes, yes that is my grandmother Elena." The medium can continue to use these cues to deduce more information from Daniella and build a reading that seems accurate.

To ensure that a medium is not using cold reading techniques to obtain information from a sitter or that the medium has some prior knowledge about the sitter, some research studies have used single-, double-, and triple- "blinding" procedures. In scientific research, "blinding" refers to withholding some information about the research procedures and design from participants (single-blind), or from the participant and the researcher interacting with a participant (double-blind), or from participant, researcher, and the evaluator of results (triple-blind). These blinding procedures are designed to reduce reactivity from the participant (e.g., the participant acting "as they are supposed to" or in socially conforming ways), and to reduce unintentional bias in the researcher. In medium studies, best practices suggested by researchers in the field include a special triple-blind as well: the blinding of the medium (Beischel 37–68). In research practice, this means that the medium must be separated from the sitter. If the medium is not seeing or talking directly to the sitter, then he or she cannot be reacting to cues to guess characteristics about the dead. Some studies have used a proxy (or stand-in) sitter, who is not the deceased's relative, but rather another individual, who presumably cannot cue the medium, as with Drayton Thomas. A screening procedure is used to select proxy sitters who believe in mediumship; they are then given a list of characteristics about the discarnate, which was originally provided by the real sitter (the relative) and simplified by the researcher. The medium is given the name of the sitter and the discarnate in order to perform the reading (Beischel 54).

Researchers have also addressed the alternative explanation that the sitter (rather than the deceased) is the source of the information (i.e., the living agent psi hypothesis). Separating the sitter and the medium is one way to deal with this telepathy (mind-reading) explanation, although distance would not necessarily prevent telepathy, which arguably is a form of nonlocal consciousness. Researchers also suggest giving the proxy sitter falsehoods along with the true facts (although the proxy sitter believes all the information is real). If the medium does not correct the falsehoods, this suggests that the source of the information is the sitter (Rock and Storm 579).

Another important aspect of the best-practice-research procedures is to provide the real sitter (that is, the deceased's relative) with pairs of readings from a medium, so the sitter may select from two readings the one that is most likely about his or her loved one. Initially, researchers look over the characteristics of multiple discarnates (based on the real sitter's descriptions). Researchers then pair two discarnates who are of the same gender, but who are otherwise very different (with regard to hair color, hobbies etc.). If, after the readings, the discarnates in the pair are too similar, the researchers may find another discarnate's reading, which is even more different from the target discarnate's. The real sitter then is given information from those two very different readings and is asked to select which of the two is most likely about his or her deceased loved one (Rock and Storm 374).

Criticism and Alternative Explanations

Weaknesses in the research on mediums include (1) how sitters are chosen, (2) the pairing procedure, (3) the rating scales used for sitters to rate the quality of the reading provided by the medium, and (4) the unfalsifiable nature of many of the explanations for incorrect readings. First, sitters are usually individuals who seek out and sign up for research involving mediums. They are usually only eligible to participate in the studies if they profess believing in the ability of some mediums to talk to the dead in the first place, and if they indicate that they have experienced some form of after-death communication. Obviously this population is very specialized. The biggest problem with using already-believers is *confirmation bias*, which is a well-studied cognitive phenomenon, in which people are likely to interpret information and evidence as confirming their preexisting beliefs (Irwin et al. 109).

Researchers have defended the use of this biased set of participants as necessary because using individuals, they say, who have no opinion, or a negative opinion of the ability of mediums, would deter the dead from wishing to participate in the reading. Using already believers is obviously more likely to yield positive results. But believers are also more likely than the general population to rate information provided by a medium as relevant and accurate. In addition, there is nothing to insure that the proxy sitter isn't cuing the medium with the information they were given, so it is still possible that a skilled medium may be using cold reading (Beischel 41). Relevant to the choice of participants is the "sheep-goat effect" (SGE) described by Gertrude Schmeidler ("Separating the Sheep" 46–49). She claimed that believers in psi unsurprisingly yield higher than chance results, but that unbelievers, more interestingly, score lower than chance. The pairing procedure is also problematic. Providing very different readings, one of a "distractor" discarnate who was physically and socially very different than the target discarnate and asking a sitter to pick one is essentially "stacking the deck" so that the sitter will select the correct reading. That is, sitters are already expecting one of the readings to be about their deceased person. Knowing this, they are likely to pick the reading that has some information that is relevant to this deceased individual. For example, a sitter may have had a tall father. Perhaps they pick the reading that mentions the deceased was tall, or they don't pick the reading that mentions the deceased was short. If both readings were about tall individuals, the sitter would have to rely on more specific (i.e., personal) information to choose the correct reading. In addition, it's possible that neither reading is particularly "correct." However, the sitter is asked to pick the one that is most relevant (if not totally accurate) (Beischel 59).

This problem overlaps with *how* the sitter is supposed to rate the quality of the readings. The most conservative method would be to only claim success in a reading if the sitter has rated the reading as an "obvious fit." The information would need to be 100 percent correct to earn this rating. However, most studies use less conservative reports from sitters. Often, a Likert scale is used, with numbers assigned to the quality of the fit ranging from 1 (no fit) to 5 (obvious fit) (e.g., Beischel 37–68). Only the lowest score of "no fit" would be interpreted as a failure of the reading. This means that all of the information was wrong, and no reasonable match could have been made. All higher ratings, however, would be considered at least partially correct and thereby support the notion that mediumship is real (Beischel 59).

In the Beischel study, blind sitters were asked to rate two readings, and were blind to which of the readings was supposed to reflect information from the deceased. Although sitters rated readings higher for the target discarnate (compared to the reading that was not for their discarnate/deceased relative), both readings rated between 2 and 3, which at best indicates "fit requiring more than minimal interpretation" (60). Although the difference in ratings was statistically significant, the reading for the discarnate was still not sufficiently clear to be rated an obvious fit, leaving room for confirmation bias to influence the results.

Whether in research or in private or public readings, mediums may provide a reading that is not an obvious fit, or they may not mention some rather obvious characteristics of the deceased. When this occurs, several explanations may be given to explain away this weakness. For example, individuals say that maybe the deceased no longer wishes to engage in certain behaviors (e.g., speak different languages, play instruments etc.). Maybe some information about their lives can't be remembered when they are dead. Maybe the medium's mind is filtering out information that is meaningless to them but would be meaningful to the sitter. Sometimes the deceased may communicate only spontaneously and thus are not available or willing when a planned reading is taking place (Beischel 37–68). Similarly, selecting a proxy sitter who already believes in mediumship is meant to make the deceased feel comfortable speaking with them because they may not wish to speak with someone who is skeptical.

These explanations are considered by many in the scientific community to be "ad-hoc" hypotheses, "adopted purely for the purpose of saving a theory from difficulty or refutation, but without any independent rationale" ("Ad hoc hypothesis"). Moreover, a hallmark of ad-hoc hypotheses is that there is no verifiable evidence to prove them. Indeed, they are explanations that make the primary hypothesis (that a medium is speaking to a deceased individual) unfalsifiable. For example, if a medium is speaking with a skeptical proxy sitter (one who may have doubts about life after death or the medium's skills), and the medium is not able to provide accurate information about the deceased, he or she may suggest that it is because the sitter is too skeptical for the deceased to wish to speak with them. Or perhaps it's because there is another non-believer involved in the reading. This makes it such that anyone who is skeptical (someone who waits for evidence before believing in a phenomenon) cannot really test mediums. Yet, a hallmark of good hypotheses is that they can be tested.

Saying that anyone who does not believe in mediums should not test mediums essentially makes the hypothesis that the deceased can communicate with the living untestable. The exception is that only true believers can be involved in the testing, yet as has been discussed already, true believers are biased in that they are looking for information to confirm their beliefs (confirmation bias), and they may disregard information that goes against their beliefs (Carroll).

An odd wrinkle on the issue of discarnates shunning skeptics is the Pauli Effect.

Wolfgang Pauli hypothesized the neutrino in 1930 and won the Nobel prize in physics in 1945. He also had the reputation of causing experimental failure by his mere presence, to the extent that Otto Stern (Nobel prize, physics 1943) would not allow Pauli in his lab. One can only imagine how this would apply to parapsychology, an interest Pauli shared with Carl Jung, his psychoanalyst ("Pauli," Ananthaswamy).

Critiques of the research vary depending on the premise under which the evaluator enters. Some approach the subject of mediumship already having accepted "the survival hypothesis"—that human consciousness survives after death, as many researchers in the nineteenth century did. These individuals will interpret the scientific evidence through the lens of those glasses, seeing differences in results between experiments as proving that we can actually contact the surviving consciousness.

Those who do not accept the survival hypothesis as a premise are viewing the evidence through different lenses and are much more skeptical. The evidence to support mediumship has to be so strong as to also confirm that there is individual survival after death. Both groups should remain skeptical when confronting any evidence but should be aware of their own biases in evaluating the evidence. No one is without bias, but one's bias should not determine the result of one's research.

Finally, the current "source of psi" debate is focused on whether mediums are getting their information from deceased persons, or from the sitter (through telepathy). The debate involves assuming that either some sort of life after death is real and allows for the deceased to speak with the living, or that sitters can relay messages (or have messages received by a medium) through telepathy, which would not imply survival of death. Just the same, both of these phenomena are rather extraordinary. David Hume thought that extraordinary claims require extraordinary evidence. Currently, many scientists remain skeptical of these phenomena, because the evidence is not sufficient. The research described above is impressively detailed, and often great care is taken to control for some alternative explanations. Unfortunately, there remains significant room for bias and false results.

Mediums in Popular Culture

Despite a lack of indisputable evidence that mediums are actually able to communicate with the deceased, there is an enormous interest in the phenomenon, and hundreds of millions of dollars per year are spent on the industry. (See, e.g., "Psychic Services in the United States.") Thousands of books are written on the subject, with some making best-seller lists (e.g., Kim Russo's *The Happy Medium*). Entire talk shows have been dedicated to showcasing readings by popular mediums, like John Edward's *Crossing Over*, James Van Praagh's *Beyond*, Teresa Caputo's *Long Island Medium*, and Tyler Henry's *Hollywood Medium*. Many other talk shows occasionally feature mediums, for example, *Dr. Oz*, *The Maury Povich Show*, *Dr. Phil*, and *Ellen*. The television series *Haunting Evidence*, *Ghost Whisperer* and several movies such as *Medium* have been inspired by famous contemporary mediums.

Watching readings on talk shows can be impressive. Mediums often choose an audience member or celebrity and do a reading, which produces information that would be considered correct by the sitter. Perhaps more often than not, these shows have been edited to highlight the instances in which the medium reported correct information, and when the sitter had the biggest emotional reactions. Many "misses" could have been edited out, and the result is that the medium looks highly accurate ("How Come"). However, it is important for viewers to not grant the same trust to mediumship on television programs as to scientific data collection. TV mediums are discussed in Pullum, "Talking," which is the next essay.

Conclusion

In the final analysis, mediums who claim to be able to communicate with the deceased are not likely to go out of existence any time soon. They have been with us in one form or another for thousands of years, and new ones appear to be cropping up all of the time. Moreover, for every medium in existence, hundreds, if not thousands, of people believe in them, perhaps largely because they already believe in life after death. So to believe that the deceased can communicate with the living is for many a very small ditch to jump. After all, goes the reasoning, if life goes on after physical death, who's to say that the dead can't return to talk with the living through a medium? This has been the conclusion of many researchers and writers for well over 150 years, despite the objections that others have raised.

Whether one believes that the deceased can communicate with the living through a medium (or through any other channel, for that matter), one thing is certain. The debate on this topic will likely continue to rage for centuries to come, even among academics. Unfortunately, it will, in all likelihood, continue to be the source of heated arguments, hurt feelings, and wounded relationships.

Works Cited

"Ad hoc hypothesis [sic]." *Oxford Reference,* www.oxfordreference.com/view/10.1093/oi/authority.20110803095351216. Accessed 25 July 2021.

Ananthaswamy, Anil. "When Quantum Physics Met Psychiatry." *Nature,* vol. 584, 26 Aug. 2020, pp. 513–14, doi: doi.org/10.1038/d41586-020-02456-5, www.nature.com/articles/d41586-020-02456-5. Accessed 7 Oct. 2021.

"Awful Calamity." *New York Herald,* 9 Nov. 1874, p. 3, www.rarenewspapers.com/view/583742? imagelist=1#full-images. Accessed 11 Mar. 2021.

Beischel, Julie. "Contemporary Methods Used in Laboratory-based [sic] Mediumship Research." *The Journal of Parapsychology,* vol. 71, 2007): pp. 37–68.

Beloff, John. "Historical Overview." Wolman, pp. 3–24.

Carroll, Robert Todd. "ad hoc hypothesis [sic]." *The Skeptic's Dictionary,* skepdic.com/adhoc.html. Accessed 7 Oct. 2021.

Carter, Chris. *Science and Psychic Phenomena: The Fall of the House of Skeptics.* Simon & Schuster, 2012.

———. *Science and the Afterlife Experience: Evidence for the Immortality of Consciousness.* Inner Traditions, 2012.

———. *Science and the Near-Death Experience: How Consciousness Survives Death.* Inner Traditions, 2010.

Davenport, Reuben Briggs. *The Death Blow to Spiritualism: Being the True Story of the Fox Sisters, as Revealed by Authority of Margaret Fox Kane and Catherine Fox Jencken.* D.W. Dillingham Co. Publishers. 1987.

Douglas, Alfred. *Extra-Sensory Powers: A Century of Psychical Research.* Overlook Press, 1977.

Fodor, Nandor. *Encyclopedia of Psychic Science.* University Books, 1966.

Gardner, Martin. "Mrs. Leonora Piper." *The Encyclopedia of the Paranormal.* Edited by Gordon Stein, Prometheus, 1996, pp. 534–39.

Gauld, Alan. "Discarnate Survival." Wolman pp. 577–630.

———. "Mrs. Piper." *Man, Myth, & Magic: An Illustrated Encyclopedia of the Supernatural.* Edited by Richard Cavendish. Marshal Cavendish, 1970, vol. 16. pp. 2199–2200.

Gaustad, Edwin S., editor. *A Documentary History of Religion in America to the Civil War.* Eerdmans, 1982.

Guiley, Rosemary Ellen. *Harper's Encyclopedia of Mystical and Paranormal Experience.* Harper, 1991.

Haining, Peter. *A Dictionary of Ghost Lore.* Prentice-Hall, 1984.

Hansel, C.E.M. *ESP: A Scientific Evaluation.* Charles Scribner's Sons, 1966.

Houdini, Harry. *A Magician Among* [sic] *the Spirits,* Harper and Bros., 1924.

"How Come TV Psychics Seem So Convincing?" *The Straight.* Nov. 18, 2003, www.straightdope.com/columns/read/2132/how-come-tv-psychics-seem-so-convincing. Accessed 5 Feb. 2021.

"I Am No Telephone To The [sic] Spirit World." *The New York Herald,* Sun. 20 Oct. 1901, sec. 5, pp. 1–3.

Irwin, Harvey J., Neil Dagnall, and Kenneth Drinkwater. "Paranormal Beliefs and Cognitive Processes Underlying the Formation of Delusions." *Australian Journal of Parapsychology,* vol. 12, no. 2, 2012, p. 107.

James, William. *Essays in Psychical Research*. Harvard University Press, 1986.
_____. *The Will to Believe*. Longmans, Green, and Co., 1910.
Kurtz, Paul, editor. "Spiritualists, Mediums and Psychics: Some Evidence of Fraud." *A Skeptic's Handbook of Parapsychology*. Prometheus Books, 1985, pp. 177–224.
Leonard, Gladys Osborne. *My Life in Two Worlds*. Cassell and Co., 1931.
Lodge, Oliver J. *Raymond or Life and Death*. George H. Doran, 1916.
Miller, Virginia. "The History of Parapsychology." In Shafer, *Probing Parapsychology*. McFarland.
Murphy, Gardner. "William James and Psychical Research." Wolman, pp. 48–55.
_____, and Robert O. Ballou, editors. *William James on Psychical Research*. Viking, 1960.
Nickell, Joe. "John Edward: Hustling the Bereaved." *Skeptical Inquirer* 25, no.6, Nov./Dec. 2001, pp. 19–22, skepticalinquirer.org/2001/11/john-edward-hustling-the-bereaved/. Accessed 6 Feb. 2021.
"The Pauli Effect, anecdotes [sic]." *ETH Zurich: ETH Library*, library.ethz.ch/en/locations-and-media/platforms/virtual-exhibitions/wolfgang-pauli-and-modern-physics/the-pauli-effect-anecdotes.html. Accessed 7 Oct. 2021.
"Psychic Services in the United States," IBISWORLD, www.clients1.ibisworld.com/reports/us/www.ibisworld.com/industry-statistics/market-size/psychic-services-united-states/. Accessed 11 Feb. 2021.
Pullum, Stephen J. "Talking to Your Dead Uncle Teddy: Probing the Validity and Persuasiveness of TV Mediums." In Shafer, *Probing Parapsychology*. McFarland.
Rinn, Joseph F. *Sixty Years of Psychical Research: Houdini and I Among* [sic] *the Spiritualists*. Truth Seeker, 1950.
Rock, Adam J., and L.C. Storm. "Testing Telepathy in the Medium/Proxy-sitter [sic] Dyad: A Protocol Focusing on the Source-of-psi [sic] Problem." *Journal of Scientific Exploration*, vol. 29, no. 4, Winter 2015, pp. 565–84.
Russo, Kim. *The Happy Medium: Life Lessons from the Other Side*. HarperCollins, 2016.
Schmeidler, Gertrude Raffel. "Separating the Sheep from the Goats." *Journal of the American Society for Psychical Research*, vol. 39, 1945, pp. 46–49.
Schwartz, Gary. *The Afterlife Experiments: Breakthrough Scientific Evidence of Life After* [sic] *Death*. Atria Books, 2002.
Shafer, Grant R., editor. *Probing Parapsychology: Essays on a Controversial Science*, McFarland.
Shepard, Leslie, editor. *Encyclopedia of Occultism & [sic] Parapsychology*. 3rd ed. Gale Research, 1991. 3 vols.
Society for Psychical Research, www.spr.ac.uk. Accessed 5 Feb. 2021.
Stein, Gordon. *The Sorcerer of Kings: The Case of Daniel Dunglas Home and William Crookes*. Prometheus Books, 1993.
Stuart, Nancy Rubin. *The Reluctant Spiritualist: The Life of Maggie Fox*. Harcourt, 2005.
Tanner, Amy E., and G. Stanley Hall. *Studies in Spiritism*. Appleton, 1910.
Thomas, Drayton. *Some New Evidence for Human Survival*. W. Collins Sons, 1922.
_____. *Life Beyond* [sic] *Death with Evidence*. W. Collins Sons, 1928.
Van Praagh, James. *Talking to Heaven: A Medium's Message of Life After* [sic] *Death*. Hodder Headline, 1998.
Washington, Peter. *Madame Blavatsky's Baboon: A History of the Mystics, Mediums, and Misfits Who Brought Spiritualism to America*. Schocken, 1995.
Weisberg, Barbara. *Talking to the Dead: Kate and Maggie Fox and the Rise of Spiritualism*. Harper, 2004.
Wolman, Benjamin B., editor. *Handbook of Parapsychology*. Van Nostrand Reinhold, 1977.

Talking to Your Dead Uncle Teddy
Probing the Validity and Persuasiveness of TV Mediums

STEPHEN J. PULLUM

Introduction

Mediums are individuals who claim that they can communicate with the dead. This idea is sometimes referred to as necromancy. Often contemporary mediums can be seen on television either standing before an audience or sitting across from an individual, providing them with information that a deceased loved one supposedly wants to share with the living through the medium. These sessions are called "readings." Occasionally mediums are referred to as *psychics*. However, these terms are not necessarily synonymous. Although all mediums are considered psychics, not all psychics are considered mediums. Well-known contemporary medium James Van Praagh suggests that while a medium is a psychic in that he or she is "very intuitive," a medium goes above and beyond a psychic. A medium (i.e., a person who goes between the spirit world and the material world) goes "to a higher level of ... frequency ... energy or dimension with their mind." According to Van Praagh, mediums pick up "feelings, visions, thoughts from the spirit world" and act as a "conduit" or "voice box" for spirits who wish to convey information to the living (Jako, "Talking to the Dead").

The practice of mediumship is a $2.3 billion industry ("Psychic Services"). Sometimes mediums will perform private readings, which can cost individuals anywhere from $650 to $850 a session. Moreover, collectively, mediums have written hundreds of books and have held untold numbers of seminars, which rake in thousands of dollars annually. James Van Praagh, for example, charges $50 to $150 a night to attend his events, depending on where one sits. Suffice it to say that mediumship is a thriving business with no signs of going away any time soon. According to a 2005 Gallup poll, seventy-five percent of all Americans reported believing in some form of the paranormal, which includes a wide range of phenomena such as extrasensory perception, haunted houses, and ghosts and spirits of the dead, to name a few. Specifically, twenty-one percent reported that "people can communicate mentally with someone who has died" (Moore 1–2).

Often individuals who watch mediums either on television or over the Internet want to know if there is any validity to their claims. The question, however, is not, "Is there life after death?" Rather, the question is, "If there is life after death, are the dead actually communicating with the living through these mediums?" This chapter attempts, in part, to address this inquiry and to elucidate many of the strategies that mediums employ in an attempt to persuade their audiences to believe in them. After providing a historical perspective (for a fuller history see Miller, "History"; Pullum et al., "Overview") and introducing the reader to several high-profile contemporary mediums, this chapter attempts to examine the above issues. Finally, the essay offers a theological critique of the practice of mediumship. A theological critique is important, in part, because many mediums claim to have a strong, Judeo-Christian upbringing. It seems only natural to examine what the Scriptures have to say about the topic of mediumship in light of this fact.

Historical Perspective

Although the practice of communicating with the dead—traditionally known as spiritualism—has existed in one form or another for centuries in various cultures, in the United States one can trace its roots back to 1848. It was founded on a hoax perpetrated by two young girls from Hydesville, New York (near Rochester), named Maggie and Katie Fox. Besides the Fox sisters, there have been hundreds of other mediums in the nineteenth and twentieth centuries who claimed that they could communicate with the deceased during a séance. Moreover, many of these individuals were studied for their veracity—often with mixed results—by both the Society for Psychical Research, which was founded in London in 1882 and the American Society for Psychical Research, which was founded in Boston in 1885 (Shepard, 2nd ed., 3: 1094–97; Shepard, 3rd ed., 2: 1543–45).

According to Carter, these mediums fell into one of two classifications: physical mediums and mental mediums. Physical mediums were those who were involved in physical acts such as table tippings, ectoplasm (i.e., a rubbery substance that supposedly emanated from the medium's body), apports (i.e., objects that materialized during a séance such as hands, flowers, pearls etc.) and even levitations as proof of their supernatural abilities to communicate with the deceased. Mental mediums, on the other hand, merely vocalized information, which they claimed was received from a sitter's dead relative or acquaintance (137–38).

Among some of the most well-known physical mediums were Daniel Dunglas Home (1833–1886), the Reverend William Stainton Moses (1839–1892), Eusapia Palladino (1854–1918), and Mina Stinson "Margery" Crandon (1888–1941), to name a few. Without doubt, two of the most popular mental mediums, who would often go into a trance when they supposedly communicated with the dead, were Leonora Piper (1857–1950) and Gladys Osborne Leonard (1882–1968) (Guiley, *Harper's Encyclopedia* 15, 266–67, 326–27, 445–46).

Contemporary TV Mediums

In addition to the above historical figures, there are a number of contemporary famous and notable media personalities who claim that they, too, can communicate with the dead. These individuals have frequently appeared on television either as hosts of their own shows or guests on others'.

Sylvia Browne

Born in Kansas City, Missouri, 19 October 1936, the same month and day as John Edward, to Bill and Celeste Shoemaker, Browne claims to come from a long line of psychics that date back over three hundred years. In fact, she attributes much of her psychic development to her grandmother Ada Coil, who, she claims, was also psychic. Browne suggests that as early as the age of three, she told her parents that she would have a baby sister by the time she was six, which happened. She reveals that at the age of five, at dinner one night, she saw the faces of both of her great-grandmothers melt away. They were both dead within two weeks afterward (Browne 3–4).

Perhaps the most significant event of her life, however, occurred around the age of eight when she tells that one night her bedroom began to glow with light. Out of the light stepped a tall, smiling, dark-haired woman who told her that she came from God and not to be afraid.

Browne later identified the figure as her "Spirit Guide," who was an Aztec-Incan woman named Iena. According to Browne, Iena had supposedly died in her native land of Colombia in the early 1500s. Browne would change Iena's name to Francine. She discloses that Francine would be her "constant companion, friend, adviser, teacher, confidant and protector" for the rest of her life (Browne 4).

As a young woman, Browne reports to have been raised "Catholic, Jewish, Episcopalian, and Lutheran, with an emphasis on Catholicism." In fact, for eighteen years, she was a Catholic schoolteacher. Believing that she had the gift of channeling, she recounts that crowds of fifteen to twenty people who gathered in living rooms for a reading would eventually grow to two or three hundred in town halls and churches. As her career progressed, she appeared on radio and television programs such as *The Montel Williams Show* and *Larry King Live*. Over time, she would stand before audiences of several thousands to perform her readings. In 1986, she founded the Society of Novus Spiritus ("New Spirit"), a "nondenominational" group, which was based on her Christian Gnosticism, with other religions blended in. The group's purpose was to worship a "benevolent God" and to reject guilt, sin, and retribution. Browne authored over fifty books, twenty-two of which made it onto the *New York Times* best-seller list. Sylvia Browne died in 2013 at the age of seventy-seven in San Jose, California (Browne 2–9).

James Van Praagh

James Van Praagh was born in Bayside, New York City on 23 August 1958. One of the most well-known mediums of our day, like other mediums, he has authored some twenty-five books, two of which have appeared on the *New York Times* best-seller list. Perhaps his most popular book was *Talking to Heaven* (1997), which sold over 600,000 copies hardcover ("Authors"; "James Van Praagh," Penguin).

Van Praagh was raised Catholic. He attended Sacred Heart grade school in New York City for eight years. At the age of fourteen, at the urging of his mother, he went away to prep school with a view of one day becoming a priest. Disgruntled with what he believed was an archaic belief system of the Catholic church, Van Praagh left (Eventually he would leave Catholicism altogether.) (Van Praagh 15–22).

He reveals that one of his earliest psychic experiences occurred when he was in the first grade. Out of nowhere, one day he walked up to his first-grade teacher and told her that her son John was going to be okay. Not realizing what on earth Van Praagh was referring to, his teacher became agitated with him. Van Praagh answered, "John was hit by a car, but he is okay. He just broke his leg." An hour later, his teacher was informed by the principal that her son had indeed just been in a car wreck (Van Praagh 4).

Van Praagh discloses how, as an 8-year-old altar boy, one night he asked God to prove to him that he existed. At that point, he claims that a wind blew through his room (even though the windows were closed), and he looked up to the ceiling where he saw a bright, pulsating light and a large, glowing hand coming down. This, he argues, was the answer to his prayers and "my first clairvoyant experience" (Van Praagh 7).

He spent the next three years in a New York City public school. From there he attended San Francisco State College (now San Francisco State University) where he majored in broadcasting, all the while dreaming of a career as a screenwriter (Van Praagh 15–22).

After graduating from college, Van Praagh moved to Los Angeles on 7 July 1982, to become a writer. There he met a medium named Brian Hurst, who told him, "The spirit people are telling me that one day you will give readings like this to other people. The spirits are planning to use you" (Van Praagh 22). Shortly thereafter, he quit his job at Paramount Studios and began reading people full time for a living.

Over the course of his career, Van Praagh has appeared on numerous television programs such as *Oprah, Larry King Live, Dr. Phil, 48 Hours,* and *The View,* to name a few. Van Praagh had his own television show from 2002 to 2003 named *Beyond with James Van Praagh*, which aired on the WB Network and closely resembled John Edward's program *Crossing Over*. He also helped produce CBS's *Ghost Whisperer,* a program about a young woman who believed she could communicate with the dead, which aired from January 2005 until January 2011. Nowadays, Van Praagh flies around the country holding seminars and giving readings in hotel conference rooms. He is one of the most well-known mediums of our time ("Who Is James").

Theresa Caputo

Known as the "Long Island Medium," Theresa Brigandi Caputo was born in Hicksville, New York, on 10 June 1966. She was raised a Catholic, a religion she continues to practice to this day. Her father was a public works supervisor for Nassau County, and her mother was a bookkeeper. She describes her family, which included her younger brother Michael, as the Long Island Italian version of *Leave It to Beaver* (Caputo, *There's* 1–2).

When Caputo was only four years old, she claims to have had her first encounter with the spirit world through frightening dreams. One recurring dream involved her watching a man from a second-floor window of her house pace up and down the sidewalk out front, calling out her name over and over again—"Theresa Brigandi, Theresa Brigandi, Theresa Brigandi." This dream horrified her at the time. She later came to believe that the man on the sidewalk was one of her spirit guides for that period of her life. Caputo also reveals how she frequently saw and heard a particular hobo in her dreams. Additionally, she confesses to have seen her great grandmother on her mother's side who had died four years before she was born standing at the foot of her bed and wearing a house dress. Describing her as short with dark hair, Caputo suggests, "I'd scream like a crazy person when I saw her too" (*There's* 3–4).

When Caputo was sixteen, she attended a psychic reading at her aunt's house. There, she claims to have felt the energy of "Nanny," her father's mother, who had recently died. While everyone else was sitting around the kitchen table with the psychic, Caputo was standing in the living room by the drapes conversing with her dead grandmother (Caputo, *There's* 8–9). It wasn't until the age of twenty-eight, however, that Caputo attended a meeting at her mother's house where she met Pat Longo, a "spiritual healer." A year later, Caputo was regularly attending Longo's weekly Wednesday night class when Longo told her, "You're a medium.... You have the ability to speak to dead people." As she continued attending Longo's classes, Caputo eventually began to channel messages from deceased relatives of her classmates. After taking on more and more of Longo's clients, Caputo's confidence grew to the point where she would channel information for strangers. According to Caputo, one of her first channelings occurred in Bed Bath & Beyond to a lady who had just lost her husband. After taking Longo's classes for five years, at the age of thirty-three, Caputo had gained enough confidence to begin receiving clients in her own home, which she continues to do to this day (Caputo, *There's* 14–23; Caputo, *You* ix-xi).

Nowadays she is the star of her own television program titled *The Long-Island Medium*, which airs each week on The Learning Channel. Her ex-husband Larry Caputo, eleven years her senior, whom she married in 1990, would often appear on the program with her. Caputo is author of two books: *There's More to Life Than This* (2013) and *You Can't Make This Stuff Up* (2014).

John Edward

Raised Catholic, John Edward McGee was born in Queens, New York, on 19 October 1969, the only child of Jack and Perinda ("Princess") McGee. Edward would eventually shorten his name to simply John Edward. His father, whom Edward describes as a "strong-willed Irishman," was a city cop. His mother, whom he similarly describes as a "strong-willed Italian," was a factory secretary and office manager. Edward's parents divorced when he was a teenager, and he and his mother moved to Long Island to live with his grandmother, who also believed in mediums (Edward 35–36).

According to Edward, his mother, who was always having "psychic house parties," introduced him to psychics at an early age. When he was only fifteen, for example, a psychic by the name of Lydia Clar came to his house to read his aunts and cousins. After being nagged by his cousin Roseann to let Clar read him, Edward relented. That evening Clar told him that he had "highly evolved spiritual guides" who were "ready to work with you" and that he eventually would become a famous psychic. Within a few weeks thereafter, he started reading people at psychic fairs on weekends and in psychic seminars held in hotel conference rooms (Edward 38–41).

Over time Edward would appear on various radio programs in and around New York City, all the while increasing his popularity. Eventually he would have his own syndicated television program on the Sci Fi Channel called *Crossing Over with John Edward*. The program would run from 2000 until 2004 and consisted of Edward "reading" various people in his audience, ostensibly channeling information from their dead relatives. Today Edward is a bestselling author and internationally known medium.

Tyler Henry

One of the youngest and newest mediums to burst onto the television scene is a twenty-something Californian named Tyler Henry Koelewyn (born 13 January 1996). Using simply the name Tyler Henry, his program *Hollywood Medium with Tyler Henry* first aired in January 2016, over the E! network. By his third episode, he had amassed over three million viewers (Wagmeister). He describes himself as a "Macaulay Culkin look-alike" (Henry 4) who reads for celebrities, the likes of which have included the Kardashians, the ex-NBA player John Salley, and singer, songwriter Bobby Brown, ex-husband of Whitney Houston, among others. Henry reveals how at the age of ten he experienced his first "knowingness" when one morning he woke up and felt the premonition that his maternal grandmother was about to pass away. As he and his mother were about to leave their house to visit his grandmother, Henry tells of how his mother received a phone call, telling her that her mother had just passed away. He claims that that night his grandmother appeared in his room at the foot of his bed to tell him what she had left for him as an inheritance (Henry 8–11).

By his eighteenth birthday, Henry was performing readings for individuals in his hometown of Hanford, California, and driving to Los Angeles on the weekends to conduct readings for celebrities (Henry 81–89). He began the fifth season of his television program *Hollywood Medium with Tyler Henry* in January 2020. He is also author of a book titled *Between Two Worlds: Lessons from the Other Side*.

Contemporary Criticisms

Many individuals today believe in the validity of mediums. However, there is a number of others who question their abilities to communicate with the dead. Among these is the well-known skeptic and self-proclaimed magician James Randi, head of the internationally known James Randi Educational Foundation. Perhaps Randi is best known for issuing his one-million-dollar challenge to any person or group of people who could demonstrate under agreed-upon scientifically controlled conditions their supernatural or paranormal powers. On the *Larry King Live* show on 3 September 2001, when asked by Larry King if she would accept his challenge, psychic Sylvia Browne agreed to allow Randi to test her ("Sylvia Browne Accepts"). However, Browne never followed up on her commitment, stating instead that she couldn't reach Randi, which, according to Randi, was ironic, given the fact that she was a psychic who should know this type of information (Randi). No psychic has collected on Randi's challenge. In 2015 the offer was discontinued (James Randi Educational Foundation; "James Randi and the One Million Dollar"). However, Randi himself has confirmed his own occasional dishonesty (Storr, "James Randi").

Sylvia Browne has had some dramatic failures. George Noory told Browne on his *Coast to Coast* radio show (2 January 2006), based on false information, that all but one of thirteen West Virginia coal miners had survived an accident and asked how she would feel if all the miners "might have all died." Browne replied, "No. I knew they were going to be found." When word came later in the show that all the miners were dead, Browne said that that is what she thought. Noory tried to give Browne an out, but her embarrassment was evident (Friedman, Belanger). On 26 February 2003, Browne told the parents of missing Shawn Hornbeck that their son was dead. In January 2007 Shawn was found alive (Belanger). In 2004 Browne told Louwana Miller on the *Montel Williams Show* that her missing daughter Amanda Berry was dead. Amanda was found alive on 6 May 2013, seven years after her mother died (Farberov; Yang et al.).

Asking Questions and Shifting Time

Another individual, however, has been successful at testing the powers of mediums. To verify the validity of psychic James Van Praagh, Miklos Jako, retired teacher and author of *Confronting Believers* (Infinity Publishing), was willing to fork over $700 of his own money for a twenty-minute private reading. During his "experiment," Jako asked Van Praagh a number of personal questions about Jako's family to determine how accurate Van Praagh would be. Jako chose Van Praagh because he believed Van Praagh was the most famous and successful of all psychics. He believed that if he could debunk Van Praagh, then he would have debunked the entire phenomenon of mediumship (Jako, "Talking").

Jako, who reported his meeting with Van Praagh on *YouTube*, identified several techniques that Van Praagh used. Jako says that mediums "ask a ton of questions and see what sticks" ("Talking"). Clients typically remember the hits and forget the misses. In fact, according to Jako, Van Praagh had 12 hits and 64 misses during his 20-minute reading with him—an 84 percent failure rate, "exceptionally poor," according to Jako ("Talking"). Besides employing warm readings and hot readings (which will be discussed in more detail momentarily), Jako also argues that Van Praagh often used the "time-shifting technique" ("Talking"). Here mediums ask a question and wait for the answer. As soon as they hear the answer, they assert that they just received this information from the deceased. In reality, mediums receive the information only after the client gives it to them, but this technique happens so quickly that the client is not even aware of what just occurred. Moreover, much of the information that Jako claims Van Praagh gave him was trivial, nothing really significant to Jako ("Talking").

Exploiting Grief While Relieving Guilt

In addition to the above criticisms by Jako, some have criticized mediums for playing off the grief of those who have lost loved ones (Nickell 19). Lewis suggests that many times audiences in crisis—those who are down and out or are hurting—often seek out charismatic leaders to help them overcome the heartache and struggles of their ordinary lives (96–99). This same principle can be applied to audiences of mediums.

Statistically, John Edward explains what he calls the 20–60–20 rule. Twenty percent of those who seek out mediums, according to Edward, are true believers. They are the credulous individuals who believe anything a medium tells them. The other 20 per cent are skeptics who do not believe that mediums can communicate with the dead at all. The rest are the 60 percent in the middle who do not know what to believe but are willing to keep an open mind. They have neither embraced mediums nor rejected them (Edward 103–04). Although the precise numbers of Edward's theory are open to debate, if Edward is correct, this means that at least 80 percent of those who experience a medium are ready, willing, and able to entertain at least the possibility that what mediums say is the truth.

Qualitatively, those who seek out readings from mediums are often individuals who are grieving over the loss of a loved one. These people often feel guilty for one reason or another after a relative has passed away. "Did I do enough to save her?" "Did I make the right decision to take her off life support?" or "Did I spend enough time with him?" are types of questions that the grieving might ask.

Mediums almost always tell a grieving audience member that his or her deceased loved one is okay, that he or she is in a better place, and that the living relative should not feel guilty for not having tried to do more to save the deceased relative's life. Never do mediums tell an individual that his or her deceased family member is in torment and that he or she is warning the client not to come there. The right discourse is what mediums seem to offer at just the right time (see, for example, "Psychic Medium"). For example, one might hear, "Your mother is saying that she forgives you" or "Your brother is saying that you shouldn't worry about the disagreement you two had before he suddenly passed." These quotations testify to the fact that many individuals find relief in what they hear from a medium.

Sylvia Browne suggests that when she first started reading people, she soon realized that she "could change and even save people's lives." Browne once confessed that she was interested in offering her "clients and friends" "comfort ... in times of trouble and despair" (8). Likewise, Theresa Caputo reveals that when she began as a medium, "I fully accepted my gift from God and devoted myself to helping others with my abilities" (*You* xi). Mediums are quick to point out that they are in business to help others feel good about themselves, not to make them feel worse.

During one of John Edward's readings, one woman who began dating another man shortly after her first husband had passed away heard Edward say, "I feel that there's going to be another wedding." He told the woman that her first husband was "giving you the green light." According to Edward, the deceased husband was telling the woman, "You should be allowed to be happy." Having the burden of guilt of marrying another man lifted from her shoulders, the woman responded, "I was so happy [to hear this]. It gave me such a peace, really to know that he [the deceased husband] was okay with that [her marrying another man]" ("John Edward").

After hearing Theresa Caputo tell a daughter that her deceased mother wanted to thank her for being able to "release her soul with dignity and grace" when she passed away, the daughter tearfully responded, "I feel relieved" ("Spirit in Paradise: The Son also Visits"). In another reading, Caputo told a woman who was feeling guilty over her brother's suicide that her brother was telling her that it was not her fault. When Caputo told the woman that her deceased brother said that he was the one who was being "selfish," the woman responded, "And I think that for me lifted a huge weight because I've come to realize that I can't take responsibility for the choices he made" ("Spirit in Paradise: Snowbird").

In her book *Questions from Earth, Answers from Heaven*, medium Char Margolis confesses, "I do try to be compassionate and understanding while being truthful. I give messages in a positive manner. And I really do care for every single person I read for. That can mean sometimes communicating what I get as gently as possible" (29). Similarly, James Van Praagh has asked his audiences to share his ideas with others who want to make contact with their deceased loved ones. "I do this for love," says Van Praagh, "for them [who've lost a loved one], to help them, so if you know of anyone that this could help service, please share this with them" (Jako, "Talking"). Audiences are naturally attracted to these kinds of attitudes. Good will toward an audience can take a speaker a long way toward persuading them.

In his *Rhetoric*, Aristotle says that there are three modes of persuasion: ethos, pathos, and logos. Ethos is the character of the speaker, including a friendly attitude. Pathos is the emotion of the audience, such as the emotional vulnerability detailed in the previous section. Logos is the argument which the speaker presents, including the numerous detailed examples which mediums provide. Of the three, ethos might very well be a speaker's single most potent form of persuasion (25). He argues that three things impact a speaker's ethos: "good sense, good moral character, and good will" (91). If this be the case, then mediums' ethos will be high with those who are hurting or feeling guilty, which would be pathos, because mediums have expressed nothing but good will toward those individuals. Ostensibly, they truly want to help others feel better.

In addition to good will, charisma (Lewis; sometimes referred to as dynamism) can contribute to a speaker's ethos. Audiences generally do not like boring speakers, and mediums are not boring. Never do mediums struggle for words. This is probably because they have had so much experience standing before large audiences. They know the routine and have built up a repertoire of things to say. Never is there hesitancy in their voices. Because mediums speak with such confidence, it is difficult for audiences to doubt them.

Providing Detailed Examples

One of the most compelling strategies that mediums employ is their use of examples. Examples not only illustrate the claim that mediums can communicate with the dead but also serve as "proof" of such claims. Mediums frequently cite example after example in hopes that at least one (if not all) persuades the audience that they can communicate with the deceased.

Mediums' supplying verifiable information to their clients would be a form of logos. For instance, in his best-selling book *Crossing Over*, in a reading typical of contemporary mediums, John Edward tells about an interview he had with Bill Falk, a journalist with the Long Island newspaper *Newsday* who, according to Edward, had written an "objective, open-minded, and genuinely inquisitive article" on communicating with the dead (59). As part of his research, Falk had Edward read a lawyer named Joan Cheever, a middle-aged woman who was the former managing editor of the *National Law Journal* and co-attorney for the convicted murderer Walter Key Williams, who was eventually executed by the state of Texas. Edward suggests that Falk picked Cheever for him to read because Falk was certain that Edward would know absolutely nothing about her, which may or may not have been correct (59).

As the reading unfolded, Edward claims that several of Cheever's relatives began to communicate with him. Then, Edward began asking Cheever a number of questions: "Is there someone around you who had a sudden passing?" Edward continued, "I'm getting a very sudden feeling. Is there someone whose actions led to their passing? It wasn't a suicide, but their actions brought about their own passing." Edward probed further: "Did that make headlines? Because he's showing me headlines. But it's not just the passing that put him in headlines." Edward then confessed to getting an M and an L. These were the initials of Walter William's parents Melba and Lucian. Edward then pointed out to Cheever that "You worked together on a project, on a team" with someone. "It's not like you just worked for the same company." Cheever acknowledged what he was saying. Then Edward said, "the spirit quickly acknowledged a Bob who worked in television," to which both Falk and Cheever reacted positively. Edward then followed with, "I got an 'H.'" Cheever affirmed it. "Does it sound like Hirsh?" asked Edward. Cheever's legal partner on the Williams case was Bob Hirshcorn (Edward 60–61).

Upon hearing her reading, according to Edward, Cheever was "stunned" and acknowledged that Edward was telling the truth. Edward continued to disclose how "the spirit told me that Joan [Cheever] was writing something." Cheever affirmed that she was writing a book about her experience with Williams. "He says, 'Make sure you get it right,'" continued Edward. At that point Cheever was "taken aback." Edward then asked, "Did this gentleman have feelings for you?" At first Cheever denied it. "Yes, he did," insisted Edward. Finally, Cheever "fessed up." According to Edward, Cheever was "100 percent convinced that was Walter" and that what Edward had read was correct (Edward 61).

Because examples like the one above are so full of specific information that Edward supposedly "got right," audiences are left believing that he must have supernatural powers. "Otherwise," one might ask, "how could Edward have known all of those details?" Moreover, it also doesn't hurt using a lawyer in the example because they are trained to be critical—hard to convince—but that is precisely what Edward claims he had done. And if Edwards could convince a lawyer, he must be legitimate, goes the reasoning.

Although true believers in mediums argue that the above types of examples prove that mediums are legitimate because they "get right" esoteric details that no one could seemingly know unless they had supernatural knowledge, why is it that mediums ask so many questions? Why should mediums have to ask, "Is there a J or a G or an R and an E in the name?" If the dead are conveying correct information to mediums, why do not mediums just assert it? Why should they have to ask for confirmation? When mediums ask questions such as, "Is your father dead?," it is often only after a person answers "yes" that the medium then tells the individual not to worry because he or she was not present at his or her father's passing. If the deceased relative really were communicating with a medium, why do mediums have to ask if the relative is dead in the first place?

Employing Cold, Medium, and Hot Readings

Historian of science Michael Shermer explains how it is that mediums often obtain correct information about a person's life, leaving the impression that they have supernatural abilities. According to Shermer, mediums may employ either a cold, warm, or hot reading. A cold reading occurs when a medium reads someone whom he or she has never seen before (hence the notion of "cold"). The medium observes a person's clothing, jewelry, tattoos, or other nonverbal cues such as facial expressions, body postures, vocal traits, or other subtle nuances to draw certain conclusions ("Michael Shermer"). According to *Wired* magazine, "The very best practitioners can pick up enough information in what seems like innocent, idle conversation to convince you that they know very specific things about you ('Medium')." And while many of the things mediums say are misses, audiences tend to remember only the hits. Critics also add that when a medium is on television, the misses have often been edited out to make it appear that the medium is correct all of the time ("How Come").

Mediums and true believers in mediums are quick to confess that they are never 100 percent correct. But they attribute this incorrectness to the fact that often the vibrations they receive from the dead are so fast that they frequently misinterpret them. Some mediums suggest that what they do is like hearing a foreign language that is being spoken so fast that they can't decode it. Such an explanation satisfies the true believer (Jako, "Talking").

Shermer and other critics explain that during warm readings, mediums take a shotgun approach by making general statements that might apply to almost anyone. For example, a medium might say, "I feel that there is someone here who has lost a loved one recently." Or they might reveal, "Someone in through here [pointing to a section of the audience] has recently made a large purchase" or "I'm feeling someone over here who has recently gone through some type of breakup." When mediums do this, contends Shermer, they are merely saying things that are true about virtually everyone and would be correct eighty to ninety percent of the time with an audience ("Michael Shermer").

Whenever individuals in an audience confirm these kinds of vague generalizations by mediums, this is called the Barnum or Forer Effect, named after the showman P.T. Barnum and the psychologist Bertram Forer. Forer found that individuals often believed that descriptions and generalizations that could apply to almost anyone were applicable specifically and solely to them (Kersner). In regard to mediums, individuals in an audience search their backgrounds to find something that might possibly—if not remotely—relate to what the medium is saying. While some audience members will let the medium languish when a medium offers up incorrect information, most audiences want so badly to help the medium succeed that they quickly respond in the affirmative to the slightest inkling of a connection.

A hot reading, which mediums deny doing, occurs when someone digs into a person's past for information. In other words, a medium researches another person and passes off the information that was researched as if he or she has just been told this by the deceased. Shermer suggests that "most psychics don't cheat like that" ("Michael Shermer"). The fact is, audiences really never know to what extent a medium has looked into a person's background prior to the reading or how much the medium already knew about the individual in the first place, even if he or she didn't investigate the person. According to Shermer, even if a medium hasn't engaged in hot readings, cold and warm readings alone are sufficient to leave audiences with the impression that they are clairvoyant ("Michael Shermer").

An interesting example of "hot reading" is Arthur Ford's (1896–1971) seance with Episcopal bishop James Pike. Alan Spraggett and William Rauscher, Ford's biographers, found Ford's files on Pike after Ford's death. These convinced Spraggett and Rauscher that Ford had researched Pike before convincing him that Ford had contacted Pike's son who had died by suicide (Spraggett).

Employing Star Power

In addition to the above rhetorical principles, mediums often employ star power to persuade others that they are legitimate, that they are indeed able to communicate with the dead. Perhaps this principle is no better seen than in Theresa Caputo's television program *Long Island Medium*. On this program, she has read for several celebrities: Susan Lucci, daytime soap opera star, actress Katie Lowes, along with her mother and aunt, and Jim Parsons (aka Sheldon on *The Big Bang Theory*) and his sister. Caputo told Lucci that her deceased grandmother was actually the one who protected her when she hit the windshield in a car wreck years ago and underwent four hours of surgery to remove slivers of glass from her eye. Afterwards, Lucci disclosed how wonderful she felt after learning this ("Celebrity Spirit").

Caputo told Katie Lowes, who appeared in the ABC series *Scandal*, and her mom and aunt that their dad Charlie (Lowes' granddad)—who died from Alzheimer's Disease—just turned to their deceased mother in the spirit world and kissed her on the cheek. In doing so, he reminded her of what a good job they did raising their daughters. The women were wiping away tears. Katie testified to how Caputo had helped bring "healing" and "closure" to their family ("Celebrity Spirit").

Jim Parsons began to cry profusely after he learned that his deceased father allegedly communicated through Caputo how proud he was of him because he did not give up on his dreams to become an actor. Afterward, Parsons testified, "She's [Caputo's] even more powerful than you suspect her to be." These testimonies are often given while very sentimental music, which is designed to evoke an emotional response from the television viewer, plays in the background ("Celebrity Spirit").

When mediums surround themselves with celebrities, either by claiming they've communicated with deceased celebrities, by featuring celebrities on their own programs, or by appearing themselves on celebrities' programs (e.g., *The Montel Williams Show*, *Larry King Live*, *Dr. Phil* etc.), audiences see them as legitimate. Moreover, the fact that mediums are on television at all—in and of itself—provides them a certain amount of credibility. This is especially true when viewers hear television hosts say things like "Every time she's here the audience goes crazy," as Montel Williams once said of Sylvia Browne, who, according to Williams "has made some amazing predictions" ("Sylvia Browne on Montel Williams"). On one occasion, Hoda Kotb, co-anchor for NBC's *Today Show*, introduced Tyler Henry this way: "With his uncanny ability to connect with those who have passed, twenty-year-old Tyler Henry has been blowing celebrities' minds off and on camera in his hit E! series *Hollywood Medium with*

Tyler Henry" ("Hollywood Medium Tyler Henry Has"). Critics want to know how TV celebrities and announcers are an authority on the legitimacy of mediums.

Unfortunately, when television announcers introduce a medium in the above fashion, unsuspecting viewers take it to be the truth. After all, if one is worthy enough to be on television, he or she must be legitimate. A medium's message is validated in the minds of the viewers simply because the medium has appeared on *Oprah, Anderson Cooper, Dr. Phil, Larry King*, or some similar program, all of which have credibility with many television viewers. In an interview with Katie Couric, actor Malcolm-Jamal Warner (who played Theo on *The Cosby Show* in the eighties) once commented on the reality of a black middle class in America. What he said then could easily be said now about the perceived legitimacy of television mediums: "But like everything else in life, it's not legitimized until it's on television" (*America Inside Out*).

What the Bible Says About Mediums

Even though there is not much mentioned in either the Hebrew Bible or New Testament about mediumship, it is important for people of faith to look at what the Bible has to say about this topic for three reasons. First, many mediums (a) believe in God, (b) believe that God gave them their "gift" and (c) are religious beings who come out of some tradition that claims to be biblically based. In some cases, mediums continue to practice to this day the faith in which they were raised. At the very least they are spiritually minded in large part because of their biblical upbringing. It seems logical, then, to examine what the Bible has to say about this subject.

Second, and perhaps more importantly, because mediums (and the people for whom they read) believe in an afterlife, something the New Testament clearly teaches, and because they also claim to have the gift of communicating with the dead, this becomes confusing for people of faith who may not know what to think. In fact, some people of faith may buy into what mediums teach because mediums present just enough biblical truth (e.g., that there is life after death) for them to also believe that mediums can communicate with the dead. If the Bible teaches that there is an afterlife, as mediums suggest, then who is to say that it does not also teach that the dead can communicate with the living?

When one examines the Scriptures closely, even though they may teach that there is an afterlife, there is little support for the idea that the dead can communicate with the living. In fact, the Bible teaches that communication with the dead is sinful (Jackson 1–6). In the Hebrew Bible, for example, the Israelites were warned by Moses not to dabble in the occult. Moses wrote, "There shall not be found among you any one ... who practices divination, a soothsayer, or an augur, or a sorcerer, or a medium, or a wizard, or a necromancer. For whoever does these things is an abomination to the Lord... (Deut. 18:10-12)." Elsewhere, God commanded, "Do not turn to mediums or wizards; do not seek them out, to be defiled by them: ..." (Lev. 19:31). To do so caused one to be "cut ... off from among his people" (Lev. 20:6; see also Isa. 8:19, Gal. 5:20 for other passages warning against such practices). Moses is not saying that individuals could actually communicate with the dead. Rather, he is merely issuing an injunction that one should not try to consult mediums in the first place.

The book of Ecclesiastes also has something to say about the subject: "For the living know they will die, but the dead know nothing.... Their love and their hate and their envy have already perished, and they have no more for ever any share in all that is done under the sun ... for there is no work or thought or knowledge or wisdom in Sheol, to which you are going" (9:5-6, 10). According to Jackson, these verses teach that once one passes away, he or she has no knowledge of anything at all and will never return to earth, unlike what mediums teach. Deane's *Pulpit Commentary* on *Ecclesiastes* says, "What passes upon the earth affects them [the dead] not; the knowledge of it reaches them no longer" (qtd. in Jackson 4).

Some biblical scholars believe that the above verses in Ecclesiastes rule out mediums only because they reject the idea of an afterlife, which rejection is also a contradiction of the New Testament. In *Understanding the Old Testament*, Anderson et al. argue, "Apparently [Ecclesiastes] was not governed by the covenant thinking of Israel's priests and prophets" (537). Pointing out that the word "Israel" appears only once in the book (1:12) to refer to the people under Solomon's reign, they suggest that individual destiny becomes acutely problematic when one is separated from a historical community, which gives one meaning. Ecclesiastes does not avoid the problem by preaching individual afterlife. There is nothing immortal in individuals, as there is none in animals (Eccles. 3: 18-22). The dead "all go to one place" (3:20). Hope ends with this life. "[A] living dog is better than a dead lion" (Eccles. 9: 4-5; Anderson et al. 537-38).

In addition to the above passages from the Hebrew Bible, the New Testament story of the rich man and Lazarus bears on the subject. Luke 16:19-31 tells how both of these men died. The rich man, who went to torment, begged Abraham to send Lazarus back to warn his five brothers so that they wouldn't wind up as he did. Abraham replied, "They have Moses and the Prophets; let them hear them," to which the rich man responded,

"No, father Abraham; but if some one goes to them from the dead, they will repent." Abraham answered, "If they do not hear Moses and the prophets, neither will they be convinced even if some one should rise from the dead." Jackson argues, "It is obvious that he could not get a message to [his brethren], otherwise he would not have requested that Lazarus be sent. It is likewise revealed that Lazarus was not permitted to make the journey back to earthly environs" (4). Although the text never explicitly says that Lazarus cannot return to earth, but merely that he would not be believed if he did, the inference is that if the rich man himself could have gone back, then he would not have had to ask for Lazarus to return to warn the rich man's brothers.

Some individuals counter with the story in the Old Testament of Saul conjuring up Samuel in the séance with the woman of Endor to prove that the dead can communicate with the living (1 Sam. 28: 11–15). In his commentary on 1 Samuel, for instance, McCarter believes that Samuel appeared by the effort of the medium. He suggests, "[T]he woman's efforts produce an apparition that turns out to be the shade of Samuel himself..." (422). Likewise May and Metzger contend, "Saul consults the spirit of Samuel through the witch (medium) of Endor..." (369 note).

Other commentaries, however, take a different stance. For example, the conservative *Wycliffe Bible Commentary* says that different commentators differ on whether the witch of Endor really communicated with the dead, was self-deluded, or was faking. According to this commentary, "ancient rabbis," Justin Martyr, Origen, and Augustine said that Samuel's ghost really appeared. Tertullian, Jerome, and "earlier orthodoxy" thought that the apparition was a "delusion." Almost all of "the more modern orthodox" exegetes write that Samuel really appeared, not by the witch's power, but at the command of God (Pfeiffer and Harrison 292).

Any commentator who says that it was a "delusion" which appeared to Saul ignores the literal text, which says, "When the woman saw Samuel" (verse 12), "Then Samuel said" (v. 15), "And Samuel said" (v. 16).

In response to the use of the witch of Endor as proof that the dead can talk to the living, in his book *The Gospel Versus Occultism*, Conley admits that Samuel really appeared. He adds that:

> [It] was God that caused him to do so, and not the witch, who was as surprised as anyone when Samuel actually appeared. She was so astonished and frightened she "cried with a loud voice." She was obviously set to deceive Saul into thinking she could communicate with Samuel, but when Samuel actually appeared, she knew God had done it and realized who Saul must be (25).

The conclusion that Conley draws is that this story should in no way be used to justify a practice that would be considered miraculous in our time—that of talking to the dead. Conservative critics suggest that the witch of Endor really had no power to conjure up the deceased, and that she admitted this when she shrieked with fear, totally surprised at what had happened. Moreover, when Samuel did appear, he did not talk to Saul through the woman. He talked to Saul directly. There was no mediumship occurring.

Although Samuel addresses Saul in the text, Saul apparently did not see Samuel because Saul asks the medium what she saw (vv. 13–14). Conley says that the medium shouted (v. 12) in surprise when Samuel appeared because, like all mediums, she was a faker. Against Conley, the text does not say why she shouted. Jewish tradition speculates that the medium expected Samuel to appear in a horizontal posture, and she shouted because he appears standing (Hirsch). This is supported by the fact that in v. 14 the Greek Bible has "orthion," meaning "upright," equivalent to Hebrew "zqp," while the Hebrew Bible has "zqn," meaning "old" (McCarter 419). Others say that she screamed because the appearance of Samuel meant that her client was Saul, or v. 12 originally said "And the woman saw *Saul* (May and Metzger 370n), which coheres with her complaint that Saul deceived her."

Theologians also point out that if it was God who made Samuel appear, why did he appear when the medium summoned him, rather than responding to Saul's previous, legitimate inquiries to God (v. 6)? Moreover, why did Samuel complain to Saul about bringing him up (v. 15) if God did it?

Ultimately, 1 Chr. 10:13–14 condemns Saul: "So Saul died for his unfaithfulness; he was unfaithful to the LORD in that he did not keep the commandment of the LORD, and also consulted a medium, seeking guidance, and did not seek guidance from the LORD...." This is consistent with other Biblical prohibitions on necromancy. Later Christian theology says that mediums cannot communicate with the dead, but, according to some theologians, the story of the witch of Endor, who calls back dead Samuel, who speaks to Saul, does not support such a conclusion.

Conclusion

The practice of mediums is big business in our day and age. However, it is controversial, to say the least. Many people are fascinated with their work and believe in them. Others are skeptical. Today's TV mediums, like many mediums of the past, are mental. They tell those in their audiences that audience members' deceased relatives are actually communicating through them, and this is very comforting to some.

When one realizes who the true believers really are and how mediums make them feel better after a reading, he or she has a better understanding of why they have become so successful. Mediums provide hope for individuals who have lost loved ones and are worried that they may never talk with them again. This goes a long way toward convincing others to accept them. Many people simply want to believe. These audience emotions are Aristotle's pathos. Coupled with the fact that mediums have high Aristotelian ethos through good will and charisma and employ numerous examples, which sometimes contain minute details to prove their clairvoyance, which are Aristotle's logos, it is difficult for viewers not to be impressed. Further, when mediums appear on television and surround themselves with celebrities, it becomes even more difficult for audiences not to believe. When examined against the Judeo-Christian scriptures, however, mediumship cannot be approved.

Spiritualists and mediums have been around for centuries. It is doubtful that they are going away any time soon. Although it would be impossible to wish them out of existence, critics have tried to curtail their popularity by pointing out many of their shortcomings in hopes that at the very least it will be more difficult for the unwary to be persuaded by them. In the final analysis, in spite of their good will and glib personalities, things are not always as mediums would have us to believe.

Works Cited

America Inside Out with Katie Couric. National Geographic Television. Spectrum Cable. Wilmington, NC. 18 Apr. 2018.
Anderson, Bernard W., Steven Bishop, and Judith H. Newman. *Understanding the Old Testament.* 5th ed., Pearson Prentice Hall, 2007.
Aristotle. *Rhetoric.* Translated by W. Rhys Roberts. The Modern Library, 1954.
"Authors similar [sic] to James Van Praagh." *Goodreads,* www.goodreads.com/author/similar/40330.JamesVan Praagh. Accessed 28 July 2021.
Belanger, Jeff. "When Psychics Go Bad." 11 February 2007. jeffbelanger.com/when-psychics go-bad/. Accessed 6 Feb. 2021.
Blackmore, S.J. "Review of *The Supernatural A-Z: The Truth and the Lies* by James Randi." *Journal of the Society for Psychical Research,* vol. 61, 1996, pp. 270–272.
Browne, Sylvia. *The Other Side and Back: A Psychic's Guide to Our World and Beyond.* Dutton, 1999.
Caputo, Theresa. *There's More to Life Than This: Healing Messages, Remarkable Stories, and Insight About the Other Side from the Long Island Medium.* Atria, 2013.
_____. *You Can't Make This Stuff Up: Life-Changing Lessons from Heaven.* Atria, 2014.
Carter, Chris. *Science and the Afterlife Experience: Evidence for the Immortality of Consciousness.* Inner Traditions, 2012.
"Celebrity Spirit." *Long Island Medium,* season 8, episode 1, The Learning Channel, 3 Jan. 2016.
Conley, Darrell. *The Gospel Versus Occultism.* Apologetics Press, 1997.
Edward, John. *Crossing Over: The Stories Behind the Stories.* Jodere, 2001.
Farberov, Snejana. "Celebrity psychic Sylvia Browne who wrongly predicted death of Ohio kidnapping victim Amanda Berry dies aged 77 [sic]." *Daily Mail,* 20 Nov. 2013, www.

dailymail.co.uk/news/article-2510966/Sylvia-Browne-wrongly-predicteddeath-Ohio kidnapping-victim-Amanda-Berry-passes-away-77.html. Accessed 6 Feb. 2021.
Finucane, R.C. *Appearances of the Dead: A Cultural History of Ghosts*. Prometheus Books, 1984.
Friedman, Roger. "TV Psychic Misses Mark on Miners." 5 Jan. 2006, www.foxnews.com/story/tv-psychic-misses-mark-on-miners, 5 Jan. 2006. Accessed 29 July 2021.
Gaustad, Edwin S., ed. *A Documentary History of Religion in America to the Civil War*. Eerdmans, 1982.
Guiley, Rosemary Ellen. *The Encyclopedia of Ghosts and Spirits*. Facts on File, 1992.
———. *Harper's Encyclopedia of Mystical & Paranormal Experience*. Harper, 1991.
Haining, Peter. *A Dictionary of Ghost Lore*. Prentice-Hall, 1984.
Henry, Tyler. *Between Two Worlds: Lessons from the Other Side*. Gallery, 2016.
Hirsch, Emil G. "Endor, the Witch of." Cyrus Adler et al., editors. *Jewish Encyclopedia*. Funk and Wagnalls, 1906. 12 vols., www.jewishencyclopedia.com/articles/5755-endor-thewitch-of. Accessed 19 Jan. 2022.
"Hollywood Medium Tyler Henry Has An [sic] Emotional Reading with Hoda." 9 Mar. 2016, *YouTube*, www.youtube.com/watch?v=L-t15dsvFH4. Accessed 6 Feb. 2021.
"'Hollywood Medium with Tyler Henry' [sic] Renewed for Season 4 by E!" *Deadline*. deadline.com/2018/08/hollywood-medium-with-tyler-henry-renewed-season-4-e-1202454219/. Accessed 6 Feb. 2021.
Houdini, Harry. *A Magician Among* [sic] *the Spirits*, Harper and Bros., 1924.
"How Come TV Psychics Seem So Convincing?" *The Straight Dope*. 18 Nov. 2003. www.straightdope.com/columns/read/2132/how-come-tv-psychics-seem-so-convincing. Accessed 6 Feb. 2021.
Jackson, Wayne. "Can the Living Talk To [sic] the Dead?" *Christian Courier*: pp. 1–6, www.christiancourier.com/articles/1503-can-the-living-communicate. Accessed 6 Feb. 2021.
Jako, Miklos. *Confronting Believers*. Infinity, 2005.
———. "Talking to the Dead: James Van Praagh Tested." *YouTube*, www.youtube.com/watch?v=b_1TtZ1tNww, 26 July 2013. Accessed 6 Feb. 2021.
———. "Van Praagh Tested: My Session with James Van Praagh." *You Tube*, www.youtube.com/watch?v=9Lt-GeXPR2Y. 7 July 2013. Accessed 6 Feb. 2021.
"James Randi and the One Million Dollar Paranormal Challenge." *YouTube*, www.youtube.com/watch?v=4Ja6ronAWsY. 23 May 2012. Accessed 6 Feb. 2021.
James Randi Educational Foundation, web.randi.org/. 11 Jan. 2018. Accessed 6 Feb. 2021.
"James Van Praagh," 9 News Exclusive. *YouTube*, www.youtube.com/watch?v=s6rZTrT4YXk. 14 Mar. 2014. Accessed 6 Feb. 2021.
"James Van Praagh." Penguin Random House, www.penguinrandomhouse.com/authors/31863/james-van-praagh/. Accessed 28 July 2021.
"John Edward Speaks to Lost Loved Ones." *Maury*. *YouTube*, www.youtube.com/watch?v=iERF6u_PigA. 28 Apr. 2009. Accessed 6 Feb. 2021.
Kersner, Kate. "Did that Astrologer Read You Right? That's the Forer Effect." *YouTube*. 20 March 2015, science.howstuffworks.com/life/inside-the-Mind/human-brain/forerefect.htm. Accessed 6 Feb. 2021.
Lewis, Todd V. "Charisma and Media Evangelists: An Explication and Model of Communication Influence." The Southern Communication Journal, vol. 54, Fall 1988, pp. 93–111.
Margolis, Char. *Questions from Earth, Answers from Heaven*. St. Martins, 1999.
May, Herbert G., and Bruce M. Metzger, editors. *The New Oxford Annotated Bible with the Apocrypha*. Oxford University, 1977.
McCarter, P. Kyle. *1 Samuel*. Anchor Bible. Vol. 8, Doubleday, 1980.
"The 'Medium' Is Not the Messenger." *Wired*. 9 Apr. 2012. www.wired.com/2012/04/opinion-randilimedium0409/. Accessed 6 Feb. 2021.
"Michael Shermer Debunks James Van Praagh and Psychics." *YouTube*. 12 Nov. 2007. www.youtube.com/watch?v=3Ax_VuNTcZw. Accessed 6 Feb. 2021.
Miller, Virginia. "The History of Parapsychology." In Shafer, *Probing Parapsychology*. McFarland.
Moore, David W. "Three in Four Americans Believe in Paranormal: Little Change from

Similar Results in 2001." *Gallup News Service,* news.gallup.com/poll/16915/three-fouramericans-Believe-paranormal.aspx. 16 June 2005. Accessed 6 Feb. 2021.
Nickell, Joe. "John Edward: Hustling the Bereaved." *Skeptical Inquirer* 25, no.6, Nov./Dec. 2001, pp. 19 -22, skepticalinquirer.org/2001/11/john-edward-hustling-the-bereaved/. Accessed 6 Feb. 2021.
Pfeiffer, Charles F., and Everett F. Harrison, editors. *The Wycliffe Bible Commentary.* Moody Press, 1962.
"Psychic Medium John Edward Help [sic] Bring Closure to Loved Ones." www.bing.com/videos/search?q=john+edwards+psychic&view=detail&mid=C8B414980EA085660963 C8B414980EA085660963&FORM=VIRE. 25 April 2018.
"Psychic Services in the United States." *IBISWORLD.* 31 Dec. 2019. www.ibisworld.com/industry-statistics/market-size/psychic-services-united-states/. Accessed 6 Feb. 2021.
Pullum, Stephen J., Carole M. Van Camp, and Wendy Donlin Washington. "An Overview of Research on Mediums: History and Cautions." In Shafer, *Probing Parapsychology.* McFarland.
Randi, James. "Homeopathy, Quackery, and Fraud." *TED Talk. YouTube,* www.youtube.com/watch?v=c0Z7KeNCi7g. 20 Apr. 2010. Accessed 6 Feb. 2021.
Shafer, Grant R., editor. *Probing Parapsychology: Essays on a Controversial Science.* McFarland.
Shepard, Leslie, editor. *Encyclopedia of Occultism & [sic] Parapsychology.* 2nd ed., Gale Research, 1984–1985. 3 vols.
Shepard, Leslie, editor. *Encyclopedia of Occultism & Parapsychology.* 3rd ed., Gale Research, 1991. 2 vols.
"Spirit in Paradise: Snowbird." *Long Island Medium,* season 8, episode 2, The Learning Channel, 30 Jan. 2016.
_____: "The Son also Visits." *Long Island Medium,* season 8, episode 3, The Learning Channel, 17 Jan. 2016.
Spraggett, Alan, reply by Martin Gardener. "A Spirited Exchange." *The New York Review of Books.* 1 Nov. 1973, www.nybooks.com/articles/1973/11/01/a-spirited-exchange/. Accessed 6 Feb. 2021.
Storr, W. *The Heretics: Adventures with the Enemies of Science.* Picador, 2013.
_____. "James Randi: Debunking the King of the Debunkers." *Metaphysics and Psychology,* www.soulask.com/james-randi-debunking-the-king-of-the-debunkers/. Accessed 6 Aug. 2020.
Stuart, Nancy Rubin. *The Reluctant Spiritualist: The Life of Maggie Fox.* Harcourt, 2005.
"Sylvia Browne Accepts $1 Million Challenge" *Larry King Live.* 3 Sep. 2001. *YouTube,* www.youtube.com/Watch?v=_vggBUJ0kE. 10 Oct. 2007. Accessed 6 Feb. 2021
"Sylvia Browne on Montel Williams Finalle [sic] Week." 14 May 2008. *YouTube,* www.youtube.com/watch?v=QvaTMLvRLRI. 10 Apr. 2015. Accessed 6 Feb.2021.
Van Praagh, James. *Talking to Heaven: A Medium's Message of Life After Death.* Dutton, 1997.
Wagmeister, Elizabeth. "E! Orders Two More Episodes of 'Hollywood Medium with Tyler Henry.'" *Variety,* 5 Feb. 2016, variety.com/2016/tv/news/hollywood-teen-medium-episode order-season-1-e-1201697888. Accessed 6 Feb. 2021.
Weisberg, Barbara. *Talking to the Dead: Kate and Maggie Fox and the Rise of Spiritualism.* Harper, 2004.
"Who Is James Van Praagh?" *James Van Praagh: Psychic Medium, Author & Master Teacher,* www.vanpraagh.com/about/. Accessed 28 July 2021.
Yang, Allie, Alexa Valiente, and Joseph Diaz. "Cleveland kidnapping survivors Amanda Berry, Gina DeJesus on journey from captivity to helping others [sic]...." *ABC News,* 1 Jan. 2020, abcnews.go.com/US/cleveland-kidnapping-survivors-amanda-berry-gina-dejesusjourney/story?id=67858538. Accessed 6 Feb. 2021.

Serpent-Handling as Near-Death Experience

Ralph W. Hood, Jr.

Introduction

It is often said that youth is wasted on the young, and perhaps it is. It is likely that only later in life do individuals reflect upon such grave questions as why they exist at all and perhaps more darkly why must they die. Some psychologists have even speculated that religion and science stand in opposition to one another on the issue of death. Many religions assure us that death is neither final, nor an end to life. Scientists on the other hand, are more likely to see life as a terminal illness with the ultimate prognosis of death. Of course, not all people of religious faith share a singular view of death, nor do all scientists share a pessimistic view of life. Still to question death is something few youth ponder. In a sense this may be wise. A little reflection reveals that in a curious sense death is, if not inevitable, certainly inconceivable.

Death in View

Consider for a second two extreme options regarding death. One is that death is an end, a termination of conscious awareness and as a famous philosopher once said, when one dies, one simply rots. Less bluntly, the body simply decays and with it any possibility of continued conscious awareness. This claim begs important assumptions that we shall address below. One is that consciousness is somehow intimately linked to if not caused by bodily processes. The other is that survival of bodily death is associated with a continued conscious awareness, perhaps in another dimension. These two assumptions seem to be at odds with one another. The latter is more likely to be associated with religious descriptions that vary widely and fascinate us with what remain various faith possibilities. Science, as we have suggested above, is more skeptical of any and all proposed religious possibilities. That is, until recently with the advent of studies of near-death experience (NDE).

A Thought Experiment

Now let us try a little thought experiment. Try to assume that death is an end, that you no longer exist. Try as you will it will not work. You cannot imagine what it is like not to be! Close your eyes and try. Likely what you will find is your current sense of what it is like to be alive, but with you absent. You have snuck in your presence as the observer of your absence and hence witness your own death. To do so, you must postulate your continued existence. If death is truly an end to consciousness you will not know it, either then or now. Only if death does not terminate consciousness will you know that, and to do so you must die! So, thinking about death perhaps is not something that youth should ponder, but with advancing age it seems a question many must. Are there any means psychologists have to suggest some answers?

Being Near Death Is Not Being Dead

Psychologists have known for many years now that some persons near death report experiences suggestive of what death might be like. Before we consider such experiences, we need to think a bit about being "near death." Medical experts have long puzzled over how to decide when one is "dead." Note a similar and currently controversial question, in the Western world at least, is how to decide when one is "alive." This is partly the issue involved in debates over abortion. At what point, if any, is willfully terminating a pregnancy taking a life? This is a complex issue, and we need not address it here. But if we cannot be sure or have varying opinions about when life begins, can we be any surer of when it ends? There are documented cases of what were once thought to be merely folk tales: coffins in the hills of Appalachia unearthed with scratch marks on the upper inside lid. We will discuss our own research on the intriguing Appalachian practice of serpent handling below as a provocative instance that may shed some light on NDE. Here we simply note that it would be foolish to think Appalachians ever intentionally buried their loved ones alive. More likely, quick burials of the recently deceased included those whose hearts had appeared to stop but continued to beat.

The spontaneous reversal of cardiac arrest without medical intervention is well established and commonly referred to as the Lazarus phenomena (Maleck et al.). Apparently upon burial some hearts spontaneously begin to beat again, but since already buried, we have the reality of the horror of scratch marks of the revived struggling to escape their dark fate. Today, mere heart stoppage, called "cardiac arrest" by physicians, is not considered "death," especially since hearts are routinely shocked, squeezed, and struck to beat again if medical or trained lay persons are available to act quickly. Thus, while surely not dead, those whose hearts have stopped might be termed "near death." What if we could study such persons and ask them what it was like when their hearts were stopped, and they were near death? Shortly we shall look at research in cardiac cases where heart stoppage was both documented, and patients reported what it was like to be so near death.

However, here we must simply state the obvious. People are only "dead" when there appears to be no technological means to revive them. So heart stoppage in and of itself is not death as it once was thought to be because we can routinely revive hearts. However, as noted above, if consciousness of being alive is linked to bodily processes, it appears that the heart is not the best pale to examine. Many now think it is the brain that is crucial.

It is well known that the brain is intimately involved in both our sense of being conscious and in our ability to be aware that we are conscious. Huge unanswered questions regarding the relationship between brain states and mental states are beyond the scope of what we can address here (see Greyson, "Near-Death Experiences," for review). However, it is clear that most experts would agree when someone's brain is not functioning, even if the rest of the person's body is functioning, that person is neither aware nor conscious of herself as existing.

Nitkin defines brain death as "Irreversible cessation of all functions of the entire brain, including the brain stem. A person who is brain dead is dead, with no chance of revival." She explains how brain death is diagnosed. A consultant performs a complete neurological examination to detect any evidence of brain or brainstem function, such as respiratory, pupillary, and gag reflexes. The tests must be done again at least 6 hours later to rule out temporary conditions, e.g., high drug doses or very cold temperatures (Nitkin). The fact that the exam must be repeated at least once indicates that the diagnosis is imprecise (Wijdicks). However, brain death, or "Death by Neurologic Criteria," is by definition irreversible (Lewis and Caplan).

In any case, for many, brain death is death itself. It is defined above as an irreversible loss of all brain function. Medical personnel, when unable to revive brains, accept this as an irreversible terminal event. The person is dead and their body should be buried or cremated. But then the question of cardiac arrest emerges here, when the brain is deprived of blood, and brain waves stop. In those rare cases when brains appear to be non-functioning, what if the person survives and what if they tell us about what they experienced, if indeed they experience anything at all when the brain is not functioning. We will return to this question a bit later. First, however, we need to look at two views that have influenced Western thought and continue to provide a tension between religious and scientific thought. There is no easier way to do this than to consider the great painting created from 1509 to 1511 by Italian Renaissance artist Raphael that hangs in the Apostolic Palace in the Vatican, called *The School of Athens*. Arthur Herman has written a wonderful text tracing the history of Western thought based upon the two central figures in this painting.

The School of Athens

In "The School of Athens" many Greek philosophers are represented, but we need only focus on the two central figures that are the focus of Herman's history. One is Plato with his hand held high and his finger pointing vertically to the heavens. The other is his most famous student, Aristotle, with his hand held forward and pointing horizontally parallel to the earth. Plato's vertical hand and Aristotle's horizontal hand are two options that suggest religion and science respectively. Let us consider the vertical first.

Plato is justly famous for articulating the views of his mentor, Socrates, and scholars struggle to determine how, if at all, one can distinguish the views of these two Greek philosophers. For our purposes, we need simply refer to a Platonic world view, a mixture of the thoughts of these two great thinkers in which the world revealed to us by sense is a forever changing kaleidoscope of change. As such, in the Platonic world view, the senses but dimly reflect an unchanging reality we cannot know directly. We are somehow trapped in our body and that essential part of us that can know reality directly (the soul) is released only upon death. Thus only by dying can we know truth. It is this claim, that upon death the soul is free to return to where it belongs and can only then know truth, which is one of the great ideas of the Western world. It is also one of the great sources of religious or spiritual modes of thought. In Plato's *Republic* (Book 10, 614d–621d) there is a report of a warrior, Er, who was slain in battle. Ten days after being slain, when the decayed corpses of the other slain were being collected, Er's corpse was found undecayed. He was brought home, and on the twelfth day, when placed upon his funeral pyre, he revived and told the astonished of his journey to another world and all that he saw there.

Many think from this story alone, the Platonic world view was created, best noted also in the *Republic* by Plato's famous allegory of the cave (Book 7, 514a–520c). Here Plato has Socrates argue that our existence in the world is like being trapped in a darkened cave, across the back of which a puppet show is flashed with figures of persons and animals cast as shadows on the wall. Humans born in the cave and chained so they cannot see anything but the shadows on the cave wall would mistake them for reality. If one could escape the cave and see the sun, he or she would at first be blinded by the light, but gradually come to know the truth that those trapped in the cave are kept from. One modern authority has likened Plato's cave to television or forms of digital media and the foolishness of believing what is on the screen (even "reality" TV) is real. For our purposes, the point is that for the Platonic world view, it is only upon death that we can truly know anything, for only then is the soul released from the body, the cave, within which it is trapped (Herman 17).

NDE: Exiting and Returning to the Cave

The phrase "near-death experience" (NDE) was coined in 1972 by John C. Lilly (147), whose remarkable career included attending medical school and leading the counterculture with Ram Dass, Timothy Leary, and Werner Erhard. Raymond Moody also attended medical school with the explicit intent of exploring the possible reality of Plato's allegory of the cave. His widely popular work *Life After Life* (1975) can be credited not only with popularizing the phrase NDE, but launching the field of empirical research on such experiences as well. Based largely upon persons who had suffered cardiac arrest and were resuscitated, Moody identified fifteen criteria common among NDEs. In a subsequent book, Moody added four additional criteria of NDEs. It is important to note that no experience reported by any of Moody's subjects fulfilled all nineteen criteria, to fit into which a condition need only include some symptoms, as in a syndrome (Jones). Consequently we can best use Moody's criteria as common descriptions of persons who have been resuscitated from cardiac arrest and other experiences from which they would likely have died without immediate medical intervention.

The most frequently cited descriptions of NDEs have been woven into a thematic narrative of a prototypical NDE. Not surprisingly, given Moody's longstanding interest in Plato, Moody's idealized experience reads like a modern version of the allegory of the cave. It includes the soul leaving the body, going through a dark tunnel, typically toward a luminous white light; a panoramic review of one's life where one's past "flashes before their eyes"; and then the return to one's body. As a consequence of surviving a NDE most persons report a great peace, a loss of any fear of death, and a sense that their return is mandated for some purpose to be completed before their final transition from an earthly life. In this sense they return to the cave (body) knowing what is certain, that it is but a temporary, not an ultimate home. Since most of Moody's data were collected in a medical setting with people suffering from cardiac arrest, an interesting common feature is that persons remember being officially pronounced dead! Other prominent medical doctors who have studied NDEs report this same official pronouncement, but of course this is precisely the issue skeptics deny. By definition, if the patient is revived, many critics would say it is because they were not dead.

Among medical doctors who empirically study NDEs, Bruce Greyson has been most open to the possibility that researchers should take the experience of being near, if not actually, dead seriously. Early in the then emerging field of NDE studies, he collected eighty criteria of NDEs culled from as many reports of NDEs as he could locate. He gradually reduced these items to 33. The 33-item scale was administered to 67 individuals, all describing NDEs (some more than one) that occurred from 9 months to 72 years before they completed this scale, which yielded a mean elapsed time, between the NDE and completion of the scale, of 17.9 years (Greyson, "Near Death Experience Scale" 371). Most NDEs occurred as a result of complications in surgery or childbirth, but also included were suicide attempts and sudden natural events such as anaphylactic reactions.

Using unspecified means, Greyson produced a final NDE scale somewhat different than the now classic paradigm of NDE that has become identified with Moody's prototypical narrative. Greyson's scale includes items familiar to NDE researchers and partisans, but in ways that are less doctrinaire. The scale consists of sixteen items, measuring cognitive, affective, paranormal, and transcendental dimensions, each with four items. His cognitive dimension includes the question, "Did scenes from your past come back to you?" His affective dimension notes such items as "Did you have a feeling of peace or pleasantness?" His paranormal dimension asks, "Did you seem to be aware of things going on elsewhere, as if by ESP?" Finally, his transcendental dimension asks such things as "Did you seem to enter some other, unearthly world?" (Greyson, "Near-Death Experience Scale," 372–73).

At this point in our understanding of NDE, it is best to view both Moody's criteria and Greyson's scale as providing a loose clustering of criteria, differentially reported by those who, in a crisis experience, in which death is an imminent possibility, become consciously aware of what they experience as another dimension. Below we will return to our own studies of NDE among Appalachian believers in the ritual of handling serpents. Our criteria and those of Moody and Greyson are best seen as taking Plato's cave allegory seriously precisely because NDE is taken so by those who have the experience. But what of those who deny any validity to any experiential claims of persons near death other than that they might be pleasant illusions in moments of crisis or a toxic psychosis of a brain starved for oxygen?

Science and the Horizontal View of Aristotle

Plato's most famous student, one who many think came to outshine his mentor in influence and importance, was Aristotle. In "The School of Athens," Raphael has him looking forward, beside his mentor, but with his own hand pointing firmly forward, horizontal to the earth. Here is the refusal to focus upon the heavens and instead the assertion that the only reality we are assured is what our senses reveal to us. For Aristotle, the changing images in the cave are less the faint shadows of a grander reality, than all simply the only reality we can know. The senses reveal change; hence it is change that is real. Rather than the soul being trapped in the body, the soul is the form of the ever-changing body. Look at older photos of yourself—how you have changed and yet remain confident that it is you who have changed!

This conundrum drives an immense body of philosophical and scientific speculation on how something can change and yet be that which is aware that it has changed. Yet as a physician's son, Aristotle distances himself from the speculation of his more spiritually oriented mentor, Plato. Aristotle ignores the heavens in favor of exploring the cave. Within the cave we are born, mature, decline and die. No immortal soul survives, and thus death is inevitable and with it a cessation of consciousness. As such, strictly biological understandings of NDE suggest that if consciousness is a product of physiological states, especially of the brain, changes in such states when near death have no real importance other than perhaps to aid us to pass quietly into oblivion. They have no evidential force for Plato's vertical reality, a world of pure form of which sense-based reality is but a faint copy of what only death can truly reveal. Aristotle's hand remains firmly horizontal, and he sees our inevitable fate as a brute fact. We are born within the cave and shall die within it. The hand pointing to the heavens reveals nothing of interest to science. There is nothing outside the cave.

An Impasse?

Thus, we have an impasse in the claims of persons and their NDEs. Regardless of the emotional power of their visions and the assurance that they have seen the "other side," a realm of life beyond death, scientists in the Aristotelian tradition remain confident that physiology can explain NDE as mere phantasms of a dying brain. The irony of purely scientific explanations of NDE is that they are completely "cave phenomena." For contemporary scientists in the Aristotelian tradition every aspect of NDE has likely explanations in the normal physiology of a dying body. Rodin (1980), himself a physician who had a profound positive NDE, wonderfully pleasant at the time, came to believe that it was but a toxic psychosis brought about by oxygen deprivation. Counterclaims of a body-based explanation of imagery and phenomena experienced near death have been made that discredit any ontological claims suggested by Plato's pointed finger. However, it appears that no single physiological factor is a necessary requirement for the many phenomena associated with NDEs articulated by Moody and Greyson (Greyson, "Near Death Experiences" 318).

Whatever the reality of the physiological facts, scientists are largely restricted to what persons report when they are near death. For instance, reporting an experience of near death is not necessarily to describe any fact about being irreversibly dead. Perhaps a cardiac arrest deprived the brain of oxygen, and the experience is more like a hallucination or a dream that can be dismissed as a toxic psychosis of a dying brain. While this possibility has prominent support, it also is problematic (see Greyson, "Near-Death Experiences," 333; Hood and Williamson, *Them That Believe* 175 for reviews). There is no need to review the range of such explanations here, for as we have noted above, if death is a termination of consciousness, we shall never experience it. Here we need but note a caution, the real issue is simply whether we look up or not. If we choose to consider Plato's allegory of the cave seriously, even in the more modern analogy to staring forever at a television screen, then understanding how the television set works (e.g., brain physiology) does not yield any information about whence the images and sounds arise (Strassman 38), except that we might learn that the television signal comes from somewhere else. Indeed, if NDEs come from somewhere else than the brain, Plato's approach looks better.

However, if we only gaze straight ahead, we cannot expect to see what is up!

A "Brain Dead" Doctor's View

In a recent bestselling book, neurosurgeon Eben Alexander (2012) describes his own NDE. Unlike other physicians such as Rodin noted above, Alexander became convinced that his experience had ontological validity (i.e., was true). It was not simply cardiac arrest or an oxygen depleted brain from which Alexander was resuscitated, but from *E. coli* meningitis which medically meant the issue was not with his heart but with his brain. What makes Alexander's case interesting is that he provides an example of a person who both knows about NDEs from a third- and from a first-person perspective.

As a neurosurgeon he heard countless patients recount their own experiences of being near death, which as a medical doctor he dismissed. His concern was only with repairing the body and not what was claimed to be experienced outside. "Brain death" is recognized worldwide, but lacks a global consensus on diagnostic criteria (Wijdicks), although the condition is defined as irreversible. However, after his own experience with meningitis, a medical condition that he believes rendered him "brain dead" and unconscious, Alexander became convinced that Plato, not Aristotle, has the greater truth. He also recognized that NDEs overlap with another area of paranormal psychology, out of body experience (OBE) among healthy living persons. What if the reports of NDEs are more like a travelogue than visionary imaginings of a dying brain? What if we could, however briefly, enter Plato's heaven before we died?

William James and Two Psychologies

Arguably William James was and remains America's greatest psychologist. Our defense for this claim is largely based upon two remarkable books by James that remain undisputable classics and are foundations for two psychologies whose views are as different as those of Plato and Aristotle. The first is his monumental *Principles of Psychology* (1890/1981) that sought to see how far psychology could go as a purely natural science. In this sense his gaze was that of Aristotle's horizontal arm, straight ahead. At the period of writing this book James was also one of the earliest presidents of the American Psychological Association (APA), established in 1892. However, after completing this work, James remained open to the gaze from Plato's upstretched hand. In his second indisputably classic text, *The Varieties of Religious Experience* (1902/1985) James abandoned the purely Aristotelian view and sought to explore experiences that today we are more likely to call spiritual, even paranormal.

Here it is important to note that William James was the only person to be twice president of the APA, once while exploring the natural scientific boundaries of psychology (1894), the other time after (1903) his wildly successful *Varieties of Religious Experience*. Further, unlike most early psychologists, James not only remained a member of the American Society for Psychical Research (ASPR) but served as its president (1896–1899). The simple fact is that William James then and now reminds us to take the report of spiritual experience seriously and to recognize that physiological descriptions of the body cannot simply replace the report of experiences that transcend the cave. James saw no contradiction between the facts of brain physiology and the claims of immortality.

We introduce this brief commentary on James only to indicate that the fact that much of contemporary psychology ignores the paranormal restricts too much what they study. It dismisses individuals' reports of their experience that psychologists have decided in advance are impossible. To appeal to *The School of Athens* a final time, they refuse to share a gaze in the direction of Plato.

If much of contemporary psychology has simply tried to expand only upon the limiting assumptions of Aristotle's horizontal view and James' merely provisional view in the *Principles*, there are exceptions, especially among psychologists who take reports of personal experience as not simply anecdotal evidence to be ignored, but as experience that has evidential significance.

While James was collecting rich descriptive material for the *Varieties*, geologist Albert Heim (1892), whose observation of time distortion may have influenced Einstein (Green), was studying persons like himself, who experienced life threatening falls while hiking in the Alps. He observed that, in his own experience and the majority of others he later interviewed, the anticipation of sudden death surprisingly did not elicit fear but rather intense feelings of peace and acceptance. With the Internet many follow in Heim's footsteps, seeking confirmation of their own experience by sharing it with others and in print journals such as *Anabiosis* (established in 1981, now called *Journal of Near-Death Studies*).

Nearness to Death: Psychological Not Medical

Following both James' and Heim's assumption that NDEs are much akin to OBEs, perhaps akin to travelogues, we propose Alexander's ("journey to heaven") over Rodin's ("toxic psychoses") view. Physiological correlates of NDEs must yield to the need for further explorations of what people actually experience in anticipation of death. It has long been noted that importance of religion correlates positively with depth of NDEs (Greyson, "Near-Death Experiences" 342–43).

Thus, whether or not one is "near" death is not simply a medical claim, but a psychological one as well. For those firmly influenced by Plato's pointing, all life is but a preparation for death. Since at least the Middle Ages many religious believers meditate or pray on their eventual physical death every day. This is captured in the Latin phrase, *memento mori* ("remember you must die"). We now can focus upon our own efforts to explore NDE among Appalachian serpent handlers for whom *memento mori* is a living reality among believers who arguably represent one of America's most unique religious traditions.

NDE Among Appalachian Serpent Handlers

In several publications my colleague W. Paul Williamson and I have argued for the relevance of the study of serpent handling believers to the study of NDEs. Much of this essay is a summary of these more detailed reports both of medically oriented research on NDE and of the relevance of serpent handling for the shaping of the content of NDE based upon specific religious commitments (Hood and Williamson, *Them That Believe* 2008). The fact that serpent handling occurs within a subculture in which death from the voluntary handling of poisonous serpents occurs assures that serpent handlers practice a ritual with a clear foreknowledge that they might be maimed or killed. In other words, the practice of their ritual places them near death, both in terms of a sense of the possibility of being bitten, and if bitten, the possibility of death.

Most handlers have seen loved ones maimed and killed. That few seek medical treatment for bites allows us to access a sample of persons whose NDEs are much more akin to early research in NDE such as Heim's with accidents from falls in the Alps noted above. Like Heim, and in the spirit of William James' *Varieties*, we seek to explore the descriptions of individuals who in high-risk settings have experienced the likelihood of death yet survived. Furthermore, our research materials, including interviews with handlers, are all archived at the Lupton Library at the University of Tennessee at Chattanooga.

A Brief Historical Context for Serpent Handling

The ritual of handling serpents emerged with the rise of the Pentecostal movement in America at the beginning of the twentieth century (Vile).

Seeking emotional criteria for evidence of the baptism of the Holy Ghost, appeals were made to a literal reading of the Bible, including the gospel of Mark 16:17–18: "And these signs shall follow them that believe. In my name.... They shall take up serpents; and if they drink any deadly thing, it shall not hurt them;...." Two other passages are relevant. Luke 10:19 says, "Behold, I have given you authority to tread upon serpents and scorpions, and over all the power of the enemy; and nothing shall hurt you." Acts 28:1–6 tells how St. Paul amazed the Maltese by surviving the bite of a deadly snake unharmed.

Early Pentecostal churches such as the Church of God endorsed the signs stated in Mark's gospel, known as "signs following believers" (16:17), including the handling of poisonous serpents. Scientific evidence of serpent striking behavior especially under conditions of voluntary handling is sparse. However, contrary to many expectations, over twenty-five years of continued field research with handlers reveals that the probability of being bitten is low and, over time, is largely a function of the frequency of handling. Thus, the initial appeal of the wonders of handling serpents without being bitten (evidence of the power of God to protect the handler) gradually gave way to the reality of more frequent bites, maiming, and deaths. Therefore, the churches that once endorsed the practice came to oppose it, while maintaining the other less problematic signs (glossolalia, laying on hands, and casting out demons). However, all over Appalachia the fiercely independent renegade churches continued the practice on into the present time. The frequency of handling as an established ritual has produced a continuous series of bites, maiming, and death among those who persist in the tradition (Hood and Williamson, *Them That Believe* 239–45).

Appalachian handlers usually use rattlesnakes (Vile). Rattlesnake bites are usually not fatal, but this statistic includes the majority of cases, which are medically treated. Severity of illness depends on the depth of the wound. Untreated victims risk severe organ damage, such as loss of parts of the intestine, or kidney failure, or death (Young and Yellayi).

The ultimate inability to predict serpent-striking behavior assures a wide range of perspectives on explaining why someone is bitten. Of interest here is the simple fact that all handlers are aware of and most have been witness to severe bites to fellow believers that have maimed some and killed others. Thus, when they are bitten they can both reasonably anticipate the severity of their wounds and realistically anticipate the likelihood that they will die. Our study took advantage of these facts in conducting interviews with thirteen handlers, all severely bitten, who anticipated maiming and death and yet survived, most without any medical treatment, to describe their experiences. Since most did not have medical treatment for their bites, we cannot document how clinically near death they were. However, our focus is not upon medical or biological indicators of being near death. Our approach is purely psychological. Everyone we interviewed clearly described an anticipation of imminent death, and many survived to bear witness of their faith with bodies maimed by a willingness to obey what they perceived to be the mandate to take up serpents in Mark 16:17–18 (Hood and Williamson, *Them That Believe* 178).

We asked all participants, "Can you think about the time you experienced what you thought was a fatal serpent bite and describe it for me in as much detail as possible?" For approximately thirty to sixty minutes, participants described their experiences from the moment of being struck through the hours that followed. They came from churches in Alabama, Georgia, Kentucky, Tennessee, and West Virginia. Ages of participants ranged from early twenties to early seventies. All were male, and nine were preachers in the tradition. The elapsed time from actual near-fatal bite to interview varied from four years to approximately thirty years. All interviews were videotaped with permission of the participants and are archived in the special collections of the Lupton library at the University of Tennessee at Chattanooga (Hood and Williamson, *Them That Believe* 178).

After collection, each of the thirteen interviews was transcribed verbatim to a protocol text for a thematic analysis of the NDEs based upon a hermeneutical technique focused upon understanding from the participant's own perspective. Protocols were analyzed by an interpretive group who, using the hermeneutic technique, examined them in terms of participant awareness and units of meaning with respect to the event of receiving what was thought to be a fatal serpent bite and the consequences leading to an anticipated death. Next the units of meaning were grouped together to form a series of themes that described the meaning of the experience of the NDE for the participant. After each protocol was analyzed for such themes, a comparison was made across all thirteen protocols to derive a general pattern of themes that emerged as consistent in describing the core meaning of the experience for participants. From this analysis, a global or generalized (nomothetic) description was derived that described the meaning in the experience of receiving a potentially fatal serpent bite while practicing one's faith and anticipating death as a consequence. This global description was presented to one of the research participants who indicated that it did in fact capture his basic experience of NDE. Thus, our research complements that described above by both Moody and Greyson in which we seek to use participants' first-hand reports as a template to describe what it is like to experience being near death. Some of the participants who described their NDEs to us subsequently went on to die from serpent bites (Hood and Williamson, *Them That Believe* 248–49).

Thematic Structure of NDE from Handling Serpents

Our methodology focused upon the phenomenology of being bit and deriving a consensually agreed (by researchers and participants) thematic structure that describes the meaning of NDE from a serpent bite in the participants' life world. Four themes emerged from the analysis, which we identify in the participants' own words as: (1) "It Hit Me"; (2) "Fear"/"Victory"; (3) "Suffering"; and (4) "Backtracking"/"Surrender." We will briefly discuss examples of each of these (Hood and Williamson, *Them That Believe* 178).

1. *"It 'Hit' Me"*: The first theme that emerged across all handler protocols was a description of the sudden, unanticipated recognition of being struck by the serpent in a way that differed from experiences of less serious bites encountered by participants who knew the bite would not be lethal. This bite was perceived as being more severe than others upon infliction. Instead of being "bit," most participants declared that they were "hit" by the serpent. For example, one participant said, he picked up a serpent and, "Then, bam! ... A little voice said, 'You're gonna die over this one'" (Hood and Williamson, *Them That Believe* 178–79).

Another participant was handling next to woman who also was handling when the unexpected happened: "I had my hand like that, and she [another handler] turned and when she did, it bit me on the arm. It struck me. I saw it and felt it at the same time, when it *hit* me.... I knew I was hurt. I knew it." Eleven of the thirteen participants had experienced multiple serpent bites over their histories as handlers. However, with some bites they knew the result could be fatal (Hood and Williamson, *Them That Believe* 180).

2. *"Fear"/"Victory"*: A second theme that emerged from the analysis was bipolar and began with an initial "fear" of dying from the bite that eventually gave way to what some described as "victory," or overcoming the fear of death. "It [death] was a possibility. I thought this could be the end of it. That is [sic] it might be the one that takes me on.... I really didn't know if I was going to live, or if I was going to die, but at that particular point when I felt the Lord move on me, I didn't care, because I figured either way I would be with him." (Hood and Williamson, *Them That Believe* 179). In describing the outcome of the bite, participants did not always move sequentially from fear to victory, but often oscillated between the two experiences on this continuum based on the degree to which they felt God moving on them (as described above). However, all described an awareness of victory

over the fear of death as the eventual outcome in processing their way through the experience. The overcoming of a fear of death appears as one of the most universal characteristics of NDE, whether in religious contexts as here or secular contexts such as Heim's skiers, or medical contexts such as with Moody's initial research of NDE (Hood and Williamson, *Them That Believe* 180).

3. *"Suffering"*: A third theme that emerged from our analysis of interviews was that of suffering. The experience of anticipated death among handlers was most often accompanied by an awareness of intense physical suffering. This is not surprising since among the well documented immediate proximate effects of serpent bite are pain, hemorrhage, swelling, breathing difficulty, temporary blindness, and periods of unconsciousness. All these characteristics of suffering were described in the experiences of our participants in varying degrees. Still, like other reports of NDEs, even with suffering there can be intense peace, as described by one participant: "I knew I was going out [going to die]. I couldn't talk. They kept praying and praying. I just told them to leave me alone. I was in the most beautiful place that I ever saw in my life" (Hood and Williamson, *Them That Believe* 180).

4. *"Backtracking/Life Review"*: Backtracking is linked to an eventual surrender to the outcome of the bite—whether survival (with likely maiming) or death. While panoramic life reviews have long been identified with NDEs, in serpent handlers they take the unique form of trying to understand the reason for being bit and seeking highly individualistic explanations for their bite, as illustrated in the following excerpt: "I just felt like I wanted to handle it, and I went to the box and got it [sic] and it bit.... You search your life.... See, you search yourself. How come?"

When anticipating death from a serpent bite, participants became aware first of reflecting over their life to search out reasons for the infliction, then of resolving any conflicts with God or others that came to mind, and finally of surrendering to the ultimate will of God and even to death (Hood and Williamson, *Them That Believe* 181).

A Global (Nomothetic) Description of NDEs from Serpent Bite

Together the above themes form a thematic structure that handlers who have survived bites accept as descriptive of their individual experiences. While we need not create a single master narrative for all NDEs, as with those researchers noted above, within more narrowly triggered specific NDEs there are what we will term global meanings. Within the geographically isolated and fairly restrictive theological boundaries of the serpent handlers, the themes described above interconnect to form a coherent narrative (Hood and Williamson, *Them That Believe* 182).

It can be summarized as follows. Near death by serpent bite involves a structure of meaning characterized by four independent themes. This structure involves a feeling of being (1) "hit" by the serpent in such a way that the strike is experienced as extremely serious, likely to maim or kill. The experience of overcoming (2) "fear" by "victory" is encountered first, by a sense of losing life in the face of doubt, and later as a confidence that whatever the outcome, it is God's will. Soon after envenomation, intense (3) "suffering" occurs in terms of pain, swelling, blurred or lost vision, breathing difficulties, and loss of consciousness in varying degrees. Anticipating death, the stricken believer (4) "backtracks" over his life, contemplating both the reason for and the finality of his bite. Fear of the anticipation of death may be relieved by visions of luminous places in which the believer is contented to remain. Ultimate victory is experienced in the eventual acceptance of both the serpent bite and its outcome as God's will for the obedient believer, whether it means full recovery, maiming, or death (Hood and Williamson, *Them That Believe* 182).

While this global meaning emerges from across all protocol texts of our interviews, we do not propose it either as a master narrative or as a full explication of understanding of NDEs from serpent bites in religious settings. It is, however, a useful heuristic summary that illuminates for the interested person the individual variations in the experience of being nearly fatally bit within a subculture that had over the years created a religious frame within which to understand the phenomenon.

Aftereffects of NDEs from Serpent Bites

Our research, like much of the NDE research, is heavily weighted toward the positive aftereffects of NDEs due to the problem of subject mortality. That is, by soliciting persons who had NDEs from serpent bites and remain within the tradition, those who left because of bites, or even entire churches that eliminated the ritual because of bites, are ignored. Thus, not surprisingly, among the thirteen survivors of serpent bites we interviewed, all subscribe to a common structure of meaning that emerges from the survival of their experience. The structure is simple and coherent. The survivors are resolute in that, by being obedient to the "Word," they simply affirm that surviving serpent handling is indeed among signs following believers; their beliefs are followed by practice of the signs of Mark 16:17–18, which include the commandment to take up serpents. It is simply an act of obedience that defines a tradition where, as many have said, the imperative to take up serpents does not include assurance that one will not be bit, although Mark 16:18 says, "...and they will pick up snakes in their hand and if they drink anything deadly, it will not hurt them, they will lay hands on the sick and they will be well." As one aged participant, claiming hundreds of bites in his long career, with body maimed, but his faith unyielding, put it:

> If [a serpent] bites you and takes you away from here.... That's the way I want to go anyhow.... I told them ... to have church when they put me away ... want to be rolled in here ... them [sic] have church over me, and handle serpents ... sing when they're wheeling me out, "I Won't Be Coming Back Anymore" (Hood and Williamson, *Them That Believe* 183).

Such resolution as this bespeaks the power that some find in a tradition that reckons the potential for maiming and death as but a small sacrifice for being obedient believers of their Lord and in the NDE knowing that they are simply leaving the cave, something that everyone influenced by Plato's upturned hand believes is not simply their fate, but their liberation.

Conclusion: Plato or Aristotle?

Our approach has been to place the anticipation of death from serpent bites within the larger context of research on NDE and to explore the way people narrate their experience.

Rather than seek a single, ideal master narrative of NDEs, the variation of these experiences, both across cultures and over time, suggests less uniformity than many have proposed. Neither are they to be uncritically accepted as evidence for an afterlife nor should they be dismissed as inadmissible evidence in a narrowly defined science. William James is our model for an open-minded acceptance of a variety of methods, each suited to a limited world of experience so that nothing of human experience is deemed dogmatically to be impossible. As medically oriented studies have failed to find a single unifying physiological explanation for all NDEs, our own position is that religious traditions also cannot be expected to yield a single master-narrative that transcends culture and history. What we can anticipate is collaborative work among diverse disciplines to piece together what clearly are varieties of NDEs and of their causes and consequences as well.

If we return to Raphael's "The School of Athens" painting we can note that there are over fifty persons represented, twenty-one variously and with some dispute identified. However, the two central figures, Aristotle and Plato, are indisputable and of these, Plato most assuredly has the most distinctive gesture, shared with no other figure in the painting. Only Plato has his hand held vertically, pointing to something. But what?

Scholars continue to dispute the meanings of the gestures of the figures in the classic Renaissance painting, but that they have some meaning is not disputed. There may be no definitive evidence possible for either Plato's or Aristotle's gaze and gesture, but surely we can choose which gaze to share. As for the meaning of the gestures, especially Plato's, our own view is clear. It links two deaths hundreds of years apart and both well documented.

In Friedrich von Hügel's masterful study of St. Catherine of Genoa, he notes that friends in attendance at her death in 1510, including Raphael, who was in the midst of his great painting, "The School of Athens," asked her if she wanted to speak. Unable to speak, she silently pointed with her right index finger towards the sky. "Her friends understood by this that she had to go and communicate in heaven" (Hügel 215). In 1999, preaching a revival at Sand Mountain, Alabama, a legendary serpent handler was struck and fatally bitten by a large rattlesnake. The handler was asked if he wanted help, but like St. Catherine of Genoa, the handler raised his hand and pointed to the heavens and simply said, "I'm going home" (Hood and Williamson, *Them That Believe* 263). In these two examples we think we have the meaning of the gesture Raphael meant to convey with the upright hand of Plato in "The School of Athens." It is also why the study of NDE remains so important. Whether in medical settings as noted by Moody, or in the aftermath of accidents as noted by Heim, or in religious settings as noted in our own research, the experiences of those near death may in fact be indicative of the meaning Raphael intended to convey with Plato's gesture, and of the reality which his philosophy suggests, and cannot be dismissed as merely an illusory by-product of dying.

Works Cited

Alexander, Eben. *Proof of Heaven: A Neurosurgeon's Journey into the Afterlife*. Simon & Schuster Paperbacks, 2012.

Green, J. Timothy. "Did a Near-Death Experience Inspire Einstein's Theory of Relativity?" *World of Lucid Dreaming*, www.world-of-lucid-dreaming.com/was-einstein-influenced-by-a-near-death-experience.html, 28 May 2020. Accessed 11 Feb. 2021.

Greyson, B. "The Near-Death Experience Scale: Construction, Reliability, and Validity." *Journal of Nervous and Mental Disease*, vol. 171, 1983, pp. 369–75.

———. "Near-Death Experiences." E. Cardeña, S.J. Lynn, and S. Krippner, editors. *Varieties of Anomalous Experience*, 2nd ed., American Psychological association, 2014, pp. 333–67.

Heim, Albert von St. Gallen "Notizen ueber den Tod durch Absturz," *Jahrbuch des Schweizer Alpenclub*, vol. 27, 1892, pp. 327–37.

Herman, Arthur. *The Cave and the Light: Plato versus Aristotle, and the Struggle for the Soul of Western Civilization.* Random House, 2013.
Hood, Ralph W., Jr., and W. Paul Williamson. "Ralph W. Hood and W. Paul Williamson field recordings, MS-074." University of Tennessee at Chattanooga Special Collections, findingaids.utc.edu/repositories/2/resources/109. Accessed 21 Mar. 2021.
———. *Them That Believe: The Power and Meaning of the Christian Serpent Handling Tradition.* University of California Press, 2008.
Hood-Williamson Research Archives for the Holiness Serpent Handling Sect of Appalachia. University of Tennessee at Chattanooga Lupton Library: University Archives (Special Collections), www.lib.utc.edu.
Hügel, F. von. *The Mystical Element of Religion: As Studied in Saint Catherine of Genoa and Her Friends.* Crossroad, 1923/1999.
James, W. *The Principles of Psychology.* Harvard University Press, 1890/1981.
———. *The Varieties of Religious Experience: A Study in Human Nature.* Harvard University Press, 1902/1985.
Jones, Kirtly Parker. "What Exactly Are Syndromes?" *The Scope*, University of Utah Health, 7 Dec. 2017, healthcare.utah.edu/the-scope/shows.php?shows=0_398izmir. Accessed 11 Feb. 2021.
Lewis, Ariane, and Arthur Caplan. "Response to a Trial on Reversal of Death by Neurologic Criteria." *Critical Care*, vol. 20, 2016, p. 377, www.ncbi.nlm.nih.gov/pmc/articles/PMC5118884/. Accessed 11 Feb. 2021.
Lilly, John C. *The Center of the Cyclone.* Random House, 1972.
Maleck, W. H., S.N. Piper, J. Triem, J. Boldt, and F.U. Zittel. "Unexpected Return of Spontaneous Circulation after Cessation of Resuscitation (Lazarus Phenomenon)." *Resuscitation*, vol. 39, 1998, pp. 125–128.
May, Herbert G., and Bruce M. Metzger, editors. *The New Oxford Annotated Bible with the Apocrypha.* Oxford University, 1977.
Moody, R.A. *Life after Life.* Mockingbird Books, 1975.
Nitkin, Karen. "The Challenges of Defining and Diagnosing Brain Death." *Johns Hopkins Medicine News and Publications*, 7 Nov. 2017, www.hopkinsmedicine.org/news/articles/the-challenges-of-defining-and-diagnosing-brain-death. Accessed 11 Feb. 2021.
Plato. *The Republic.* Trans. by Desmond Lee, Penguin, 1954.
Rodin, E.A. "The Reality of Near Death Experiences: A Personal Perspective." *The Journal of Nervous and Mental Disease*, vol. 168, 1980, pp. 259–263.
Strassman, R. "Endogenous Ketamine-Like Compounds and the NDE." *Journal of Near-Death Studies.* vol. 16, 1997, pp. 27–41.
Vile, John R. "Snake Handling." *The First Amendment Encyclopedia*, mtsu.edu/first-amendment/article/928/snake-handling, 27 May 2020. Accessed 19 Jan. 2022.
Wijdicks, E.F.M. "Brain Death Worldwide: Accepted Fact but No Global Consensus in Diagnostic Criteria." *Neurology*, vol.58, no. 1, Jan.2002, pp. 20–25, doi:10.1212/wnl.58.1.20.
Young, Becky, and Sirisha Yellayi. "Rattlesnake Bite." *Healthline*, www.healthline.com/health/rattlesnake-bite#timeline, 4 June 2020. Accessed 11 Feb. 2021.

Near-Death Experiences 1

History, Explanations, Anecdotes

Grant R. Shafer

Introduction

Apart from pain, death is our greatest fear. This makes evolutionary sense because dead organisms cannot reproduce. The desire for immortality follows from our fear of death. Interest in near-death experiences (NDEs), which seem to evidence life after death, should surprise no one.

What are near-death experiences? They can be distinguished from other phenomena, such as death-bed visions, although some observers would include any paranormal experience which occurs to a person whether actually in the process of dying or even in immediate danger of death, which would include death-bed visions. Ring and Valarino (229–39) even write of "quasiNDEs" in times of personal crisis. Holden ("Veridical Perception" 1–2) distinguishes "near-death *episodes* [italics Holden]—the physical circumstances of being near death" from "near-death *experiences*," which encompass the psychological experience of an alternate reality actually reported by only a minority of people who survive near-death episodes. Van Lommel et al. say, "Identical experiences to NDE, so-called fear-death experiences, are mainly reported after situations in which death seemed unavoidable: serious traffic accidents, mountaineering accidents, or isolation such as with shipwreck...." (2039) Sam Parnia, a critical care physician, prefers a narrow definition of NDEs, restricted to experiences during cardiac arrest. Parnia et al. ("Qualitative and Quantitative Study" 150) state "three criteria required to pronounce an individual dead (no cardiac output, no spontaneous respiratory effort ... fixed dilated pupils)."

We need here to distinguish three related heart ailments. Heart failure is when the heart cannot pump enough blood. It is different from heart attack. Heart attack is similar to stroke. Stroke happens when blood supply to the brain is stopped by a blocked or burst artery. Heart attack happens when an artery is blocked, and blood stops flowing to the heart, causing damage to the heart. Cardiac arrest is when the heart stops pumping properly with ventricular tachycardia (pulse too fast), ventricular fibrillation (disorganized pulse), and asystole (no pulse) (Sabom, *Light and Death* 54–55). This begins the process of death. Different parts of the body die in the absence of oxygen and other nutrients. When the brain is sufficiently damaged, we consider death irreversible.

Parnia (*What Happens,* 91–92) tells that the EEG (electroencephalogram) measures electrical activity from the cerebral cortex. EEG flatlines around ten seconds after the heart stops. Parnia ("Near Death Experiences" 8) says, "Studies in animals have demonstrated that an absence of cortical activity as measured by EEG correlates with an absence or reduction in activity of the deep brain structures as measured by in-dwelling electrodes…."

Parnia (*Erasing Death* 173) has proposed calling NDEs "actual-death experiences" (ADEs). Parnia has a broad definition of death. Death is a gradual process during which different parts of the body die at different times, beginning with cardiac arrest, which can now be reversed, and ending with death of bone cells (Parnia, *Erasing Death* 49, 81). Parnia (*Erasing Death* 49, 286) says that brain cells can survive eight hours after death. Parnia (*Erasing Death* 53–85) distinguishes between "reversible" and "irreversible" death and shows that what is reversible depends on the progress of medicine. Holden ("Veridical Perception" 187) explains, "…*reversible death* [emphasis Holden] refers to conditions such as prolonged cardiac and respiratory arrest from which a person, either spontaneously or as a result of other people's efforts, resuscitates and survives. *Irreversible death* [emphasis Holden] refers to the condition in which the dying process has advanced so far that resuscitation cannot occur…." Delacour (ix, 45, 212) claims that Konstantin Hossmann and Klaus Zuelch restored brain cells after more than 1 hour without blood in apes and cats. In 2019, Himanshu Bansal began attempting to reverse brain death, to harsh criticism by ethicists ("Non-randomized"; Muse).

Although John C. Lilly (147) first used the term "near-death experience" in 1972, Raymond A. Moody brought the phenomenon to popular awareness with the publication of *Life After Life* in 1975. Although Russell Noyes, Roy Kletti, Kenneth Ring, Bruce Greyson ("Near Death Experience Scale"), and others have produced slightly different lists of elements of NDEs, Moody's (10–102) will suffice for us. It included:

   1. ineffability, i.e., near-death experiencers (NDErs) have difficulty describing the experience,

2. hearing the news that one is dead,
3. feelings of peace and quiet,
4. annoying or pleasant noise,
5. the dark tunnel through which one travels,
6. the sense of traveling out of the body,
7. meeting others, known or unknown,
8. the being of light, often understood as God,
9. the incredibly fast review of one's life,
10. the border or limit, beyond which one cannot return to life (In Valentinian Gnosticism the lowest goddess, Sophia, tried to know the supreme god, the Abyss). This knowledge would have destroyed her. She was restrained and saved by the "boundary" (Greek "horos") between the divine and outer world (Rudolph 155, 320, Irenaeus bk. 1, ch. 2.2).
11. coming back to life, often unwillingly,
12. telling others, who generally don't want to hear,
13. effects on lives, generally positive, often paranormal,
14. new, generally positive, views of death,
15. corroboration of perceptions during NDEs, with which this essay will mostly deal.

A minority of NDEs are distressing. Nancy E. Bush "classified rarer, distressing types of NDE into (a) experiences phenomenologically like the blissful type but interpreted as terrifying; (b) reexperiences of nonexistence or eternal void; (c) experiences with blatant hellish imagery..." (qtd. in Greyson, "Near-Death Experiences" 337). Greyson ("Near-Death Experiences" 337) characterizes aftereffects of NDEs: "The aftereffects most often reported include increases in spiritual attitudes and interests; concern for others; appreciation of life; and decreases in fear of death, materialism, and competitiveness.... Near-death experients tend to see themselves as integral parts of a benevolent and purposeful universe, in which personal gain, particularly at others' expense, is counterproductive.... Although a less fearful attitude toward death has been associated with an increase in suicidal thoughts..., near-death experients paradoxically express stronger objections to suicide that do comparison samples, primarily on the basis of increased transpersonal or transcendental beliefs...." Van Lommel et al. (2042) write "Significant differences in answers to 13 of the 34 items in the life-change inventory between people with and without an NDE are shown in table 4. For instance, people who had NDE had a significant increase in belief in an afterlife and decrease in fear of death compared with people who had not had this experience." However, they add (2042), "All patients, including those who did not have NDE, had gone through a positive change and were more self assured, socially aware, and religious than before...." Ring (*Omega Project* 191) says that the effects of interest in NDEs may mimic the aftereffects of NDEs. Beverly Brodsky's account of her NDE (Ring and Valarino 236–39, 297–99) is particularly eloquent.

While many aftereffects of NDEs are positive, there are drawbacks. Greyson ("Near Death Experiences" 344–45) observes that many NDErs did not want to return to earthly life, suffer cognitive dissonance and disbelief from others, doubt their own sanity, find that the unconditional love which they espouse conflicts with mundane conditions and limitations of human relationships, and suffer much divorce. Bush ("Is 10 Years" 7) says that NDEs cause "long-term depression, broken relationships, disrupted career, feelings of severe alienation, an inability to function in the world, long years of struggling with the keen sense of altered reality. And those around NDErs are critical. Divorce appears to be a frequent aftereffect;...." Christian reports that 65 percent of NDErs divorce afterward, compared to 19 percent of controls.

NDEs show substantial consistency over time and across cultures. Greyson, ("Near Death Experiences" 338) observes that earlier beliefs influence NDEs, but meeting beings and realms are cross-cultural and that (358) "[t]he central features of NDEs are universal and have not been influenced by time. These have been observed throughout history and in different cultures. These notwithstanding, cultural influences have probably played a role in some NDEs' reported descriptions." Greyson ("Near-Death Experiences" 334) finds folklore and writings of NDEs in European, Middle Eastern, African, East Indian, East Asian, Pacific, and Native American traditions.

Holden et al. ("Field" 1–16) tell that NDEs are reported among native Americans, Pacific islanders, and Asians, in 95 percent of world cultures (Sheils 1978), e.g., by Henry Schoolcraft (1825) *Travels in the Central Portion of the Mississippi Valley,* David Livingstone (1872) *Adventures and Discoveries in the Interior of Africa,* Samuel Woodworth Cozzens (1873), *The Marvelous Country: Three Years in Arizona and New Mexico* (Holden et al., "Field" 2), Barrow (1848), Winslow (1868), Clarke (1878), Little (1881), Munck (1887), A.S. Wiltse (1889) *St. Louis Medical and Surgical Journal,* Mormons (Lundahl 1979, 1993–1994), and James Hyslop (1907, 1918) (Holden et al., "Field" 4).

Gregory Shushan (38) says, "The popular Western conception of the NDE may not be universal, though it encompasses particular sub-experiences which are." Shushan (42) recounts that medieval European and Zuni NDEs are inconsistent with their cultural ideas of afterlife. Shushan (46) also says that *The Tibetan Book of the Dead (Bardo Thodol)* parallels NDEs in that it says that the "'*Dharma-Kaya* [God or

Ultimate Reality] of Clear Light' will be experienced in whatever form will most comfort and calm the individual." Buddhists see the Buddha, Christians Jesus, Hindus the god of death, etc. Another parallel between *Bardo Thodol* and NDEs is "the natural sound of Reality, reverberating like a thousand thunders simultaneously sounding...." (Evans-Wentz 104; cf. "The Noise," Moody, 19–20). Shushan (165) suggests "that the NDE influenced conceptions of afterlife experience in ancient civilizations...." Kalweit (70 qtd. in Shushan 167) said "asked about the origins of their knowledge of the Beyond, the members of the various ['small-scale'] cultures say that they gained this knowledge from the experiences of those who have returned (i.e. [sic] NDErs) and from shamans...." Shushan studied afterlife concepts of five early civilizations: Old and Middle Kingdom Egypt, Sumerian and Old Babylonian Mesopotamia, Vedic India, pre-Buddhist China, and pre–Columbian Mesoamerica.

He found nine shared NDE elements: 1. Out of Body Experience/Ascent, 2. Corpse [of oneself] Encounter, 3. Darkness/Tunnel, 4. Deceased Relatives/Ancestors, 5. Presence or Being of Light, 6. Conduct Evaluation/Life Review, 7. Barriers/Obstacles, 8. Divinization /Oneness/Enlightenment, 9. Other Realm/Origin Point (Shushan 157–60). Shushan sees a two-way street: NDEs influence cultural ideas of death (165–74), which influence NDEs (195–99).

On the other hand, Jens Schlieter (185–92, 194–96, 202, 205, 209–10, 213–16, 221–22) maintains that near-death experiences and some of their parts (vision of God, judgment, the tunnel, or the life review) are bound up with European religion.

George Gallup and William Proctor did a large survey on NDEs in 1982. Fifteen percent of adult Americans had NDEs (198), which was 35 percent of those who had a near-death encounter (26), and 2 percent reported premonitions (32, 54–55, 201). Holden ("Veridical Perception" 185) says that 1 of 5 or 6 ND episodes include NDEs. Greyson ("Near-Death Experiences" 334) reported that only 10–20 percent of people close to death have NDEs and (338) "Retrospective studies of near-death experients have shown them collectively to be psychologically healthy individuals who do not differ from comparison groups in age, gender, race, religion, religiosity, or mental health...." Parnia (*Erasing Death* 173) says that five independent studies 2003–2013 say that 10–20 percent of resuscitated cardiac arrest patients have cognitive, mental experiences after death starts. Morse et al. ("Near-Death Experiences" 585) report that 4 of 7 child survivors of life-threatening illness which they studied had NDEs. "...Differences in estimates of frequency and uncertainty as to causes of this experience result from varying definitions of the phenomenon, and from inadequate methods of research"

(Greyson, "Incidence of Near-Death Experiences," qtd. in van Lommel et al. 2039–40).

One striking result from Gallup was that physicians and more so other scientists were more skeptical than the general public about life after death. Thirty-two percent of "physicians," (Gallup and Proctor 144) believed in afterlife. They are misleadingly labeled as "leading scientists (209)," a separate group in Gallup and Proctor's book. Gallup and Proctor say that they used "a small but representative sample of persons in the field of medicine, drawn at random from Marquis' *Who's Who in America*," but don't say whether they are only M.D.s and D.O.s or nurses, P.A.s and other medical staff (212). Sixteen percent of "leading scientists" (26, 144, 207), separated from medical workers by Gallup and Proctor, believe in afterlife. Again the authors used "a small but representative sample of persons in the field of science, drawn at random from Marquis' *Who's Who in America*," (209) but don't specify degrees or other qualifications. Scientific skepticism contrasts with public faith: 67 percent of the general public believes in afterlife (26, 183). However, Sabom (*Light and Death* 103) reports, "In a recent [27 Mar. 1997] USA Today poll, 75% of female and 63% of male physicians admitted to the use of prayer or meditation in treating themselves...."

Their prevalence and consistency suggest that NDEs are a psychological fact, perhaps explicable through Jungian psychology (Grosso). Thus we can discard the notion that NDEs are a hoax. Millions of Americans claim them. NDErs believe in their experiences, which are remarkably consistent across cultures. That leaves 2 possibilities, hallucinations caused by physical or psychological stress, or evidence of afterlife.

History

Here we will look back at historical phenomena related to NDEs. Purposeful burial of the dead, suggesting concern for afterlife, was practiced by Neanderthals, an extinct human species (Than). From Sumerian Inanna (3400 BCE) to Jesus (1 Pet. 3:19) gods and heroes have visited the dead and returned. In Egypt attempts revive the dead began with Olei En-ches around 2500 and ended when Ramses III outlawed them around 1250 BCE (Delacour 46–47). The Egyptian Book of the Dead instructed how to travel to a happy afterlife in 1550 BCE.

Ancient Greek mystery cults seem to have mimicked NDEs (Ustinova 119–23). In 375 BCE Plato (*Republic* 614a–621d) wrote that Er, a soldier from Pamphylia on the Mediterranean coast of Turkey, was killed in battle, was about to be cremated twelve days later, revived, and told an elaborate story of the afterlife. The ancient essayist and biographer Plutarch (c. 46–119, *Moralia* 563D–568A, 7: 269–299; see also van der Sluijs 223, 244–49, 251, who proposes also the story of Timarchus in *Moralia* 589F–593A, 7: 459–477, as a near-death experience) tells a story about Aridaeus, also known as Thespesius, a local ne'er-do-well who fell, hit his head, and went into a coma. During the time he was in the coma Aridaeus encountered his spirit guide. Through the instruction of his guide Aridaeus found the error of his ways and, while being instructed, he discovered alternate dimensions of consciousness. Fortunately, he returned from his astral travels just as the community was preparing to bury him. The consequence of this excursion was not only his profound report of discovery but a lifestyle transformed from being the local profligate to a moral exemplar.

The New Testament tells two stories of Lazarus. In Luke 16:19–31 (written c. 80 CE), Lazarus is a disabled beggar who lies at the porch of a high-living rich man, wanting to eat what falls from the rich man's table. Both men die, the beggar goes to heaven, and the rich man to hell. The rich man asks Abraham in heaven to send Lazarus with a drop of water to cool the rich man's tongue. Abraham replies that no one can pass the chasm between heaven and hell. The rich man asks Abraham to send Lazarus to warn the rich man's brothers about hell. Abraham replies that if the brothers do not believe the prophets, they will not believe someone who rises from the dead.

In John 11:1–44, 12:1–2, 9–11, 17 (written c. 90 CE), Jesus has a friend named Lazarus, with sisters Mary and Martha, who dies. Lazarus lies four days in the grave, and then Jesus raises him. The two stories are related, but how is in question. Luke 10:38–42 tells how Jesus visits the sisters Mary and Martha, but they are not related to Lazarus. The most important detail for us is that Lazarus is connected with a return from death in both stories.

The Buddhist Tsung-mi (780–841 CE) reported "…We read of dead persons who have revived and told about happenings in the world of the dead;…" (*On the Original Nature of Man*, qtd. in de Bary 183). The Tibetan Book of the Dead was composed between 750 and 1350 to teach Buddhists how to navigate the afterlife. *The Art of Dying* was published around 1415, probably in response to the Black Death, which killed nearly one third of Europeans between 1347 and 1352. The book advised Catholics on how to prepare for death, offering comfort and instruction on how to resist temptation.

Around 1740 Pierre-Jean du Monchaux, a French military doctor, wrote the first known medical report of near-death experiences (tome I, pp. 43–45). Albert von St. Gallen Heim (1849–1937), a geologist and mountain climber, had a near fatal fall. He wrote about survivors of such falls and other near-death episodes. Apart from the surprising calm which fallers experience, he noted that "time became greatly expanded" for the fallers (Heim). Because Albert Einstein remembered Heim's lectures, some speculate that he suggested to Einstein the relative nature of time (J. Green).

By the early 1970s an unprecedented increase of resuscitations caused the realization that death is not an instantaneous event but a gradual process (Holden et al., "Field" 3). In 1977–1978 Raymond Moody, John Audette, Kenneth Ring, Michael Sabom, and Bruce Greyson formed the Association for the Scientific Study of Near-Death Experiences, which became the International Association for Near-Death Studies in 1981. Also in 1981 began *Anabiosis: Journal for Near Death Studies*, which became the *Journal of Near-Death Studies* in 1987 (Holden et al., "Field" 4).

Research was first restricted to retrospective studies, which use "convenience samples," people who consent *after* their being close to death to be interviewed. On the other hand, in prospective research, the investigators have data about the subject's encounter with death *prior* to and during the experience. Prospective research is usually done in hospitals. Over periods of months or years the investigators interview all consenting patients who underwent certain medical conditions: resuscitation from an episode involving cardiac and respiratory arrest. Thus the medical condition has been observed and recorded, "and the sample is more complete." It includes everyone who "survived the first moments of physical death" and consents "to be interviewed." (Holden et al., "Field" 6).

"The general idea of prospective investigation of AVP ['apparently nonphysical veridical NDE perception'] is to make present continuously a controlled perceptual stimulus, knowable only to a material NDEr...." (Holden, "Veridical Perception" 203). From 1979 to 2009 there were 42 retrospective U.S. studies on 2500 NDErs, and 10 prospective North American and European prospective studies on 270 NDErs (Holden et al., "Field" 7) "The 'gold standard' of research, involving random assignment of participants to experimental and control conditions, is not currently feasible in the study of NDEs .... (Holden et al., 'Field' 7)." *Flatliners,* a 1990 movie, was about such a study. In practice NDEs are unpredictable (Holden et al., "Field" 10). Kenneth Ring 1980 introduced the Weighted Core Experience Index in 1980, and Greyson the NDE Scale in 1983, "...A later Rasch statistical analysis of the NDE Scale showed the NDE to be a cohesive, unitary phenomenon (Lange, Greyson, and Houran 2004), of which NDEr's [sic] descriptions did not change over a 20 [sic] -year period (Greyson 2007)...." (Holden et al., "Field" 11). Correlates of NDEs include cultural, psychological, and physiological factors, which are important for predictability and controllability. Research on aftereffects is hindered by sample bias (Holden et al., "Field" 12).

Holden et al. ("Field" 16) cite Kelly (2007) that NDEs include reports of information which NDErs would seem unable to acquire through their physical senses ("veridical experiences"), some under close medical observation and others by the blind. However, they concede that it is difficult to rule out "sensory leakage, lucky guesses, and after-the-fact errors in reconstructing the event." While ghost stories, seances, children's past life memories, and deathbed visions hint at survival of death, NDEs promise more rigor and perhaps control in research.

Explanations

French (1) classified explanations of NDEs into three broad groups: 1. spiritual, i.e., that NDEs are really experiences of afterlife, 2. psychological, 3. physiological.

Some psychological explanations are as follows. R. Noyes, R. Kletti propose depersonalization, that faced with the prospect of death, as in other intolerably stressful situations, the self suppresses its own concerns (Greyson, "Near Death Experiences" 339). Irwin, Ring, Dalenberg, and Paulson propose dissociation, a similar process in which the self withdraws emotionally from events, feelings, or environment. Dissociation is not necessarily disordered (Greyson, "Near Death Experiences" 339–40). Ring and Irwin found more childhood trauma among NDErs (Greyson, "Near Death Experiences" 338, 340). Ring also stresses psychological absorption, the ability to "focus one's attention on imaginative or selected sensory experiences to the exclusion of other events in the external environment (Greyson, 'Near Death Experiences' 340)." Wilson and Barber found that "strong investment in fantasy life, vivid hallucinatory ability, intense sensory experience, and excellent eidetic memory," hypnotic responsiveness, and hypnosis all produce experience like NDEs, which are on the whole adaptive (Greyson, "Near Death Experiences" 341).

In 1930 Oskar Pfister provided the inspiration for the expectancy model of NDEs. He theorized that NDEs are manufactured in the psyche, reacting to the fear of a death which is known to be close. Experients draw on their own memories and traditions to construct a script to defend them from death. Greyson ("Near Death Experiences" 347) objects: "Another flaw of this model can be found in children's accounts of NDEs. These are similar to adults,' and this despite children being less affected by religious or cultural influences about death." NDEs differ from cultural norms. Subjects' accounts often differed from their own "religious and personal expectations regarding death (Greyson, 'Near Death Experiences' 347)." Finally, although the word "near-death experience" was first used in 1972 and the phenomenon first defined in 1975, recent stories of NDEs are essentially like those told before 1975 except for more common mention of a tunnel (Greyson, "Near Death Experiences" 347).

Carl Sagan (1979) suggested that near death experiences could be a reliving of the experience of birth. Greyson ("Near Death Experiences" 347–48) counters that reports of leaving the body through a tunnel are equally frequent among subjects who were born by cesarean section and natural birth. Also, he claims that newborns do not possess "the visual acuity, spatial stability of their visual images, mental alertness, and cortical coding capacity to register memories of the birth experience." Against Greyson and supporting Sagan, there is evidence of memories of birth. Ring and Valarino tell of NDEs recalled from ages seven years to birth itself, such as how 7-year-old Kristle drowned and saw medical staff's efforts to revive her and her family's activities at home (100–01, 104–13), with veridical details, such as being suckled as a newborn by a mother's friend (114–17). Chamberlain (*Consciousness* 34; "Expanding Boundaries") also documents birth memories with veridical details.

Greyson ("Near Death Experiences" 347–48) cites Grof (1975) and Grosso (1983), who suggest that NDEs draw on Jungian archetypes. Irwin and Watt (171–72) criticize them for explaining one unknown with another unknown.

Sabom (*Light* 61–62, 77) cites research (Lown et al., 1978, Lown et al., 1976, Reich and Gold, 1983) indicating that the "serenity" of NDEs may be a natural life-saving adaptation.

Greyson ("Near Death Experiences" 342) relates NDEs to post-traumatic stress disorder (PTSD) and frames them as a religious/spiritual problem (342–43) rather than mental illness (344). Greyson ("Near Death Experiences" 338) says, "Retrospective studies of near-death experients have shown them collectively to be psychologically healthy individuals who do not differ from comparison groups in age, gender, race, religion, religiosity, or mental health…." This undermines purely psychological explanations.

Physiological explanations suggest that NDEs may simply be hallucinations produced by the brain, which malfunctions in cardiac arrest. Low blood oxygen levels (hypoxia or anoxia) may induce hallucinations and hence might account for NDEs. Low oxygen levels sometimes come before death, and NDEs are like loss of consciousness from G-force, as when fighter pilots undergo fast and strong acceleration which drains blood from the brain. But "distress and agitation" typify hypoxic hallucinations, which are unlike near death experiences, which are generally pleasant (Greyson, "Near Death Experiences" 348).

Some propose that hypercapnia, abnormally high carbon dioxide levels, accounts for NDEs. But NDEs are found both with high as well as low concentration of carbon dioxide (Greyson, "Near Death Experiences" 348).

Greyson ("Near Death Experiences" 349) says that NDEs could be caused by chemicals, e.g., endorphins, other endogenous peptide opioids, serotonin, glutamate, endopsychosins, N-methyl-D-aspartate, muscarinic and adenocorticotropic hormones, and enkephalins, or by metabolic or cerebral malfunctions in the dying, as suggested by S. Blackmore (1993). However, intoxicated NDEs are bizarre and confused like hallucinations (Greyson, "Near Death Experiences" 335), and "findings suggest that drug- or metabolically induced delirium in fact inhibits NDEs or at least interferes with their later recall" (Greyson "Near Death Experiences" 348–49). Further, hallucinations cloud thinking, frighten, irritate, and cause idiosyncratic visions unlike relatively consistent NDEs. Fever, anoxia, and drugs likewise decrease the occurrence of NDEs (349). Osis and Haraldsson agree that medical conditions, such drug- or disease-induced hallucinations, inhibit rather than foster NDEs (156–157).

Neuroanatomical models suggest that NDEs come from various areas of the brain, i.e., the limbic system, the hippocampus, the left temporal lobe, Reissen's fiber in the central canal of the spinal cord, the prefrontal cortex, or the right temporal lobe. Although the models are untested, any or all of them could explain NDEs and how they are expressed and interpreted (Greyson, "Near Death Experiences" 349).

Blanke and Dieguez (2009) suggest a model with two kinds of NDEs.

    1. NDEs from mostly right-hemisphere brain damage manifest out of body experiences, movement, and silence.
    2. NDEs from mostly left-hemisphere brain damage manifest meeting with spirits, sounds, but no movement.

The two types approximate Sabom's (1982) autoscopic and transcendental NDEs (Greyson, "Near Death Experiences" 357).

Granqvist et al. (2005) say that "[s]ensed presence and mystical experiences are predicted by suggestibility, not by the application of transcranial weak complex magnetic fields" (1–6). They did not validate Persinger's (234) suggestion that NDEs are caused "by electrical stimulation of deep, mesiobasal temporal lobe structures (Greyson, 'Near Death Experiences' 349)." Temporal lobe stimulation seldom causes OBEs, but when it does, there are bizarre body images, inaccurate perceptions, and memories are frightful and not long retained. As to explaining NDEs as dreams, REM is prevented in situations which produce NDEs (Greyson, "Near Death Experiences" 350).

Multifactorial neurophysical explanations such as from Saavedra-Aguilar, Gomez-Jeria (1989) and Blackmore (1993) attribute NDEs to interaction of the temporal lobe, hypoxia, psychological stress, neurotransmitters, the visual cortex, the hippocampus, memory, and language (Greyson, "Near Death Experiences" 351).

Sabom (*Recollections*) rules out eleven naturalistic explanations of NDEs.

> 1. *Semiconscious perception.* In non-emergency or elective cardioversion, a thirty-minute procedure which is used to treat arrhythmias, an intravenous line in the arm renders the patient unconscious. One or more electrical shocks are applied through two paddles, one on the chest and the other on the back, or both on the chest. The shock lasts less than a second and stops and resets the heart rhythm. Usually patients wake up quickly and don't remember the shock. Semiconscious elective cardioversion patients report pain, but cardioversion NDErs report no pain in their NDEs (154–55), some NDErs distinguished talk heard while semiconscious from later visions (155–56), and some NDErs reported their experience from a time when they were alone (156).
> 2. *Conscious fabrication.* NDErs received little reward for reports, researchers were skeptical, NDErs were reluctant to report, and NDEs appeared to change the lives of NDErs (157), NDErs were ignorant of NDEs, made reports different from others, and supplied veridical details (158–59).
> 3. *Subconscious fabrication.* One patient had several ND episodes but only one NDE, and one patient had multiple different NDEs (159–60).
> 4. *Depersonalization.* NDEs differ from experience of ND episodes (163). Sabom's assertion here is undermined by the fact that NDEs, or experiences almost identical to NDEs, also occur in situations spread along the range from strong emotional experiences without danger or fear of death, to so-called "fear-death" experiences, to conscious deathbed visions, up to cardiac arrest.
> 5. *Autoscopic hallucinations* center on the physical body and interaction of the self and its double, seem unreal, and often involve negative emotions (164–65).
> 6. *Dreams.* By contrast NDEs seem real (165–66).
> 7. *Prior expectation.* By contrast NDEs tend to surprise experients (166–69).
> 8. *Drug induced delusion or hallucination* is "highly variable and idiosyncratic," unlike NDEs, which are mutually similar (168). One patient did report an "NDE" about a time bomb in a restaurant with their friends (168–69). Patients tend to differentiate their hallucinations from their NDEs (169–171).

9. *Endorphins.* B-endorphin causes painlessness lasting 22–73 hours (Lancet 19 January 1980), but in NDEs painlessness occurs only in the NDE itself. B-endorphin causes somnolence in contrast to NDE hyper alertness (171–173).

10. *Temporal lobe seizure* causes distorted perceptions, negative emotions, smells and tastes, reliving random single events, and automatic obtrusive thoughts crowding the mind (173–74).

11. *Altered states of consciousness.* Hypoxia causes impaired function unlike the lucidity of NDEs. Hypercarbia is like NDEs except for visions with color displays like stained glass windows, animated fantasy objects, compulsion to solve math puzzles and enigmas, seeing multiples, and shapeless and objectless horror (174–178). Inadequately anesthetized patients report pain, hear medical workers, which is reported in NDEs, dream of coworkers, and have no visuals. Hypnotic regression recovers things heard but not seen (178–80).

Osis and Haraldsson generally concur with Sabom. Neither hallucinogenic drugs, brain impairment, nephritis, nor hallucinogenic illnesses statistically significantly affected NDEs nor lucid awareness. They say that their observations contradicted the "sick-brain" theory:

> ... [P]atients who had hallucinogenic maladies saw apparitions three times less [than] those ... who were free of such impairments. Patients with the above-mentioned hallucinogenic troubles also reacted much less with religious emotions (13 percent) [than] the other patients ... if the medical factors had any influence on seeing apparitions, they tended to suppress rather than generate visions that are suggestive of an afterlife (157).

Parnia (*What Happens* 92–94) discusses the following: (1) Some suggest that NDEs do not occur during cardiac arrest, but before or after. However, some NDErs describe events in the middle of cardiac arrest, when memory is usually lost. (2) Others say that NDEs are due to undetected brain activity. But such activity would not likely be conscious. (3) NDEs arise from quantum processes. (4) Consciousness may be independent of the brain as Plato and Descartes thought (110). These issues will be more fully discussed in Shafer, "Theoretical Criticisms."

Greyson, ("Near Death Experiences" 335–36) remarks the "perception that one's thinking is faster and more lucid than usual at a time when the brain is physiologically impaired," R. Noyes and D. Slymen "hyperalertness elements, such as vivid and rapid thought and sharper vision and hearing" (Greyson, "Near Death Experiences" 336), which are surprising in a malfunctioning brain. Parnia (*What Happens* 92–94) comments that NDErs report clear lucid thought at a time of brain dysfunction.

Sabom (*Recollections* 184) adds, "The details of these perceptions [by cardiac arrest patients in the Atlanta Study] were found to be accurate in all instances where corroborating evidence was available. Moreover, there appeared to be no plausible explanation for the accuracy of these observations involving the usual physical senses...."

The presence or lack of consciousness is also problematic. Robson said in 1969, "One must therefore conclude that there is as yet no practical means of measurement of the depth of anaesthesia within the range required today" (788). Citing Robson, Sabom said in 1982, "no generally acceptable medical or scientific definition of unconsciousness had been proposed which could consistently be verified using objective scientific techniques. Anesthesiologists, using all the clinical skills and technology (including electroencephalography) at their disposal, are often unable to determine accurately the level of awareness (or consciousness) of closely monitored patients under general anesthesia... (*Recollections* 7)." The nature of consciousness is so important for the understanding of NDE, and such a philosophical crux, that I discuss it in Shafer, "Theoretical Criticism."

Paranormal Aspects

We have already touched on NDEs which include reports of perceptions by the experients which are very difficult to explain naturalistically. In the following, we will look at the variety of paranormal reports about NDEs.

Jean-Baptiste Delacour writes of revivals of people apparently dead. He claims that Mrs. Francis Leslie was apparently dead in the morning, and doctors started her autopsy around midday. Her body was unusually warm, so that she received an adrenal injection. She regained consciousness after half an hour, told of her NDE and reluctance to return to life, and died after twelve hours. A. Winstel proposed a natural explanation (Delacour 29–37). Penka Naidenova was clinically dead for 120 minutes, then walked and talked (Delacour 97–101). Serge Lama's NDE included recall of a past life (Delacour, 105–08). In Russia, a man was found hanged, and a Prof. Bruchanenko revived him. The hanged man reported an NDE but died four days later (Delacour 131–335). Fred Phillips was executed in the electric chair. He was revived, purportedly by Robert E. Cornish, a student of George Washington Crile, and reported an NDE (Delacour 143–53). Mrs. Theresa Laffield emerged from a three-week coma and reported no NDE. However, after Prof. Johns of Whitechapel administered an "injection to induce an artificial hypnosis," Laffield told of the life of her father John Clavel, and more interestingly, of the unrelated Philomene Carter

(Delacour 157–63). William Cannon told about his past-life regression of a "band of light.... In the seventh life he floated or soared as if he had wings, as if for him the force of gravity no longer existed. By contrast, moreover, all previous existences had been marked by the same struggles with suffering and care that are familiar in all daily lives..." (Delacour 164). Mrs. Sidney Beale asked Helen Aintree to ask Beale's dead husband where his life insurance policy was, and Beale found it where Aintree said it would be (Delacour 190).

These stories would be important if true, but Delacour's lack of critical thinking is shown by his wasting pp. 191–94 on Arthur Ford, whose literary executor, Canon William V. Rauscher, and biographer, Allen Spraggett, discovered extensive files of newspaper clippings and other sources which Ford used to "reveal" information to his victims (Blau; Spraggett). Some might excuse Delacour because the German version of his book appeared in 1973, when Rauscher and Spraggett revealed their findings but continued to champion Ford's psychic ability, and the American version a year later.

Further, apart from the positive psychological aftereffects of NDEs, NDErs report paranormal abilities. Ring and Valarino (1998) report healings and abnormally "hot hands" (218–19). Ring personally endorses healers Barbara Harris Whitfield (219) and Helen Nelson but concedes that there has "not yet been any rigorous and systemic study (220)." Howard Mickel, professor emeritus of religious studies at Wichita State University, told how Ralph Duncan had terminal leukemia, had an NDE, and was healed (224–25). Margot Grey was dying from surgical complications, had an NDE, and was healed (138, 225). Ring's friend "Steve" said that a woman acquaintance said that she was blind, had an NDE, and her sight was restored (225–26). Stella had terminal cancer, had an NDE, was cured, and healed others (226). Kathy Hayward had terminal Hodgkin's disease, had an NDE, and survived (226–27). Ring (*Omega Project* 109–10) reports that Beryl Hendricks found a golf-ball sized tumor, which disappeared after her NDE/CE IV ("Close Encounter of the Fourth Kind," i.e., alien abduction). Ring thought that NDEs and CE IVs might be the same thing seen from different perspectives (*Omega Project* passim). Sabom (*Light* 105–06; Helene, 1984) tells of eight gravely ill patients anomalously healed after NDEs, including a man admitted with burns over 60 percent of his body, comatose, pronounced dead, who had an NDE and recovered without scars, although the stories were not medically verified.

Ring and Valarino (221) say that NDErs report more electric malfunctions (Sutherland, *Transformed* 128–29). Ring personally witnessed "Stella" shutting off classroom lights (Ring and Valarino 222). Knittweis

(224) reported that 4 of 7 NDErs which he studied reported electrical anomalies. The 7 NDErs as a group had readings of electrical activity "just short of" statistically significantly higher than 10 controls, who reported no NDEs nor electrical anomalies. Three NDErs claiming healing abilities and 1 studying healing had significantly higher readings than controls. These 4 had also reported electrical anomalies.

Veridical Perceptions

Moreover, NDErs report details of the experience which are true and difficult to explain given the circumstances, such as no apparent brain activity. Many have speculated that these "veridical perceptions" prove that consciousness is not a brain process, and that consciousness survives death. Holden ("Veridical Perception" 185–86) defines veridical perception as visual, auditory, kinesthetic, olfactory, etc., which someone relates as happening during their NDE and which is verified as agreeing with "material consensus reality." Holden includes any verified NDE perception even if it might be through normal sensory or cognitive means. "Apparently nonphysical veridical NDE perception" (AVP) includes "veridical perceptions that, considering the positions and/or conditions of their physical bodies during the near-death episodes, apparently could not have been the result of normal sensory processes or logical inference—nor, therefore, brain mediation—either before, during, or after those episodes...." Holden ("Veridical Perception" 195–96) studied 107 AVP anecdotes in 39 publications and found 8 percent of "material" and 11 percent of "transmaterial cases involved even some error," 38 percent of material and 33 percent of transmaterial cases were completely accurate.

Groth-Marnot (105) recounts telepathy, precognition, meeting unknown dead relatives (Barrett,1926, Cobb, 1877, 1882, Hyslop, 1907), and that 39 percent of NDEers claim ESP, and 21 percent are the subject of other people's psychic experience (107). Groth concedes "...However, proving that the NDE occurred during the time of the flat EEG is nearly impossible as well as there being extreme difficulty in proving that there was not some form of unmeasured electrical activity somewhere in the brain which might have produced the NDE" (113). He rightly observes that where the parapsychologist sees survival of death or telepathy, the traditional scientist sees skillful guessing and researcher bias (114).

Osis and Haraldsson are instructive because their study was done in India, offering a transcultural perspective. They write that a patient appeared dead. When he came to, he said that he was taken away by white clad messengers to a beautiful place. A man with an account book told the messengers that they had taken the wrong man and to take the man back. Because of the beauty of the place the patient did not desire to leave. According to the nurse, another patient with the same name was in the hospital. When the first patient was revived, the other man expired (*At the Hour* 153). Osis and Haraldsson report other cases where a patient was escorted to another world due to an error of the "other world bureaucracy." "Indian Christians, a clergyman, and a teacher" were some of the patients "taken away," but "error cases" of this sort were not reported by Americans (*At the Hour* 153).

A woman suffering from pneumonia had lost consciousness and nearly died. Her report showed "[t]ypical Indian concerns. She thought that she was in heaven, which had many houses, one unfinished. She inquired whose it was." The messenger answered, "It is for you, but it is not entirely finished because you have not yet completed your days in the world. You should arrange for your son's marriage. Your day shall come after the birth of your grandson." She in fact died after the birth of her grandson (*At the Hour* 156). It is also significant that although reincarnation is generally presumed in Indian thought, it does not play a large part in the NDEs reported by Osis and Haraldsson.

Precognition is another paranormal claim associated with NDEs. Ring ("Precognitive and Prophetic Visions") describes the "personal flashforward" (PFF), a life review extended to future events, in one case a prediction of the Three Mile Island nuclear accident, in another, of the Mt. St. Helen's eruption (Ring, "Precognitive and Prophetic Visions" 55, 57–58; Groth 110). Lundahl ("Otherworld") reports that NDErs sometimes appear to see their own true future.

Gallup and Proctor (32, 54, 172, 178) discovered that about 2 percent, or approximately 500,000 Americans, experienced an NDE premonition. Schwaninger et al. say, "One [9 % of their subjects] reported visualizing scenes from the future..." (223–24). Sabom (*Light* 162) reports of his 1994 Atlanta Study of 160 patients, 47 NDErs and 113 controls, that 55 percent of conservative Christian NDErs, 46 percent of liberal Christian NDErs, 67 percent of non–Christian theist NDErs, and 21 percent of controls reported precognition.

Ring ("Precognitive and Prophetic Visions") writes that PFFs often are remembered only when fulfilled (49), which casts doubt on them because they could be nothing but deja vu elaborated by a false memory. The most dramatic example is that "Belle" claimed that in her 1971 NDE she was shown Raymond Moody's photo and told that she would meet him. On Halloween 1975 Moody's son came to her door (Ring, "Precognitive and Prophetic Visions" 52–54). Ring ("Prophetic Visions in 1988" 4, 9–10, 12–14, 17) observes that many NDErs predicted catastrophe for 1988, which appears to be a projection of angst about social changes, as Cohn (1970) observed of medieval radicals.

The following are veridical perceptions reported in NDEs. Ring and Valarino (100–01) tell that 7-year-old Kristle drowned and saw medical staff working on her and details of her family's home life. Ring (*Omega Project* 100) tells that a wounded unconscious GI in Vietnam saw a scar atop an attending sergeant's head. Ring and Lawrence (225–26) and Ring and Valarino (65–67) tell that Kimberly Clark, personally well-known to Ring, said that "Maria," a migrant worker, was on a floor lower than the worn shoe on the third-floor ledge of a Seattle hospital when she saw the shoe. Ring and Lawrence (226–27) tell how Kathy (Ring and Valarino 67, "Cathy" Milne) Milne told of a patient who saw a red shoe on the roof of a hospital in Hartford, Connecticut, another resuscitated patient in Hartford remembered Joyce Harmon's plaid shoe laces (Ring and Lawrence 227), and a third remembered Sue Saunder's yellow smock (227–28).

Parnia (*Erasing Death* 225–228) repeats Tom Aufderheide's anecdote that his cardiac arrest patient remembered Aufderheide's feeling abandoned and eating his patient's lunch, with similar stories of Douglas Chamberlain, Richard Mansfield and others. Lawrence (*Death* 43–44, 48) writes that "Heather" correctly described the build and hair of a consulting doctor previously unknown to her. Lawrence (*Death* 167) recounts three "Peak in Darien" experiences: Vi Horton met a previously unknown brother ("Turning Point"), another woman saw a previously unknown sister (Callanan and Kelley; "1997" on Lawrence 167 is erroneous, and "2012" is the date in "References," p. 225), and Eben Alexander (2012) saw a previously unknown sister. Morse et al. ("Childhood" 1111) reported that 3 child patients remembered intraoperative events. Parnia (*What Happens* 79–81) recounts how Joan La Rovere reported her patient's memory of medical personnel talking during the patient's resuscitation.

Ring and Cooper ("Near-Death") report visual perception in OBEs and NDEs of the blind. They (126) cite (Kirtley, 1975) that (1) there are no visual images in the dreams of the congenitally blind; (2) individuals blinded before the age of 5 also tend not to have visual imagery; (3) those who become sightless between the ages of 5 and 7 may or may not retain visual imagery; and (4) most persons who lose their sight after age 7 do retain visual imagery, although its clarity tends to fade with time. In addition, various researchers have found that hearing tends to be the primary sense involved in dreams of the blind, with tactile and kinesthetic elements next.

Some examples follow. In 1991 Nancy was permanently blinded in surgery. She "saw" Leon, her lover, and Dick, the father of her child (Ring and Cooper, "Near Death" 122-24, *Mindsight* 109-20). Ring and Cooper (*Mindsight*, "Authors Advisory" 1-9) tell of unreliable cases. For example, Larry Dossey admitted to Ring (Ring and Cooper, *Mindsight* 158-60, 174-75) that Dossey (1989) fabricated the story of how blind "Sarah" had a dramatic visual perception. It was better documented that "Pat" threw up in "Irene's" presence, "Cheryl" observed it in an OBE (out of body experience), and "Pat" confirmed it (Ring and Cooper, *Mindsight* 103-05). Blind "Frank" saw in an OBE a tie which his friend bought for him, although some details could not be corroborated (105-07). Another case involved an OBE in which a husband reported dirty dishes in the sink, which was corroborated by and greatly annoyed his wife (108-09). There was more than 1 report of sights from the ceiling of hospital rooms, such as dust on the upper side of light fixtures (*Mindsight* 158-60, 174-75).

Sabom (*Recollections*) describes his study of 57 coronary patients. Twenty-five controls, with similar background to 32 NDErs, were admitted to a coronary care unit and had no NDE. Twenty-three controls described CPR, 20 with major errors, e.g., mouth to mouth resuscitation, wooden throat paddles, blows to the back, opening the chest cavity, hitting the solar plexus, and straddling the patient. Three controls gave limited descriptions without major error (*Recollections* 84-86), 32 NDEr survivors of nonsurgical crisis claimed to see their own resuscitation, 26 only gave a general description of resuscitation without major error, but 6 correctly recalled specific details. Holden, ("Veridical Perception" 201-02) says that resuscitated patients who did not see their bodies in an OBE thought that they had been defibrillated although they had not.

Sabom (*Recollections* 99-105) says that Case 4, Mr. S., I-32, described technical details such as the preselect needle and separate charge needle on the defibrillator, lidocaine pushes, and labeled watt-seconds. He claimed no prior knowledge, seemed honest, and the autoscopic details appeared too specific to be from general knowledge (114). Mr. S was unlikely to have learned the details from hospital staff, because Mr. S' report was taken before he had had much opportunity to get details from staff (114). Generally, NDErs' visual reports were accurate but did not fit well with likely staff conversation and included elements outside NDErs' likely visual field (115).

Beauregard et al. say that, from 2002 to 2012 in prospective studies in the Netherlands, UK, and U.S., about15 percent of survivors claimed consciousness during cardiac arrest. Beauregard et al. find this "intriguing" given the "interruption" of blood flow to the brain. EEG shows no brain activity after 10 to 20 seconds, "and the patient is deeply comatose." Therefore remembered "clear and lucid mental experiences" are "not expected."

Beauregard et al. report that in one such case the heart surgery patient Ms. J.S. could not see the equipment " behind the head section of the operating table" as she rolled into the operating room. J.S. reported an OBE during the operation in which she saw a nurse give instruments to the surgeon and anesthesia and echography machines behind her head, despite general anesthesia and her eyes taped shut. Her surgeon verified her descriptions of the nurse and equipment but whether J. S.' OBE happened during 15 minutes of cardiac arrest cannot be ascertained. Despite this uncertainty about when the NDE occurred, Ms. J. S.' account is difficult to explain naturalistically.

Cook et al. presented 14 cases containing "enhanced mentation," OBE, and ESP (377). In 2 other papers, they had remarked the "importance of normal or even enhanced mentation accompanying such severe physiological impairment" (379). They also refer to Osis and McCormick's (1980) study in which a visual target could be seen only from one line of sight, and the experimental subject was adept at self-induced OBEs. The subject was successful in describing the target. Osis and McCormick surmised that this was during OBE, rather than by clairvoyance (Cook et al. 381).

Osis and McCormick's report is extremely important. If true, it suggests that OBEs really include ESP, and that NDEs may show that consciousness is not a brain process. Tart also reports that a "selected" experimental subject correctly recalled a 5-digit number target purportedly seen during an OBE ("Psychophysiological Study" 17). We will recall these cases when we discuss the failure of all but 1 NDEr to report targets in multiple prospective studies.

"Peak in Darien" experiences, named by Cobbe (1877, 1882) after the discovery of the Pacific Ocean, also suggest disembodied consciousness, in which a dying person claims to have seen a recently dead person, whose death the dying person could not have known through the senses. Cook et al. (382) reference Barrett, 1926, pp. 10-26; Callanan & Kelley, 1992, pp. 86-87, 93-94; Crookall, 1960/1966, pp. 21-22; Gurney & Myers, 1889, pp. 459-460; Hyslop, 1908, pp. 88-89; Myers, 1903, ii, pp. 339-342; Osis & Haraldsson, 1977/1986, p. 166; Ring, 1980, p. 208; Sidgwick, 1885, pp. 92-93. A.T. Baird (81-96) reports 13 cases where a dying person learned that other acquaintances were dead.

Cook et al. continue that Sir Alexander Ogston saw a previously unknown Boer War surgeon die in different part of the hospital (Cook et al. 383). In World War I a British Dr. X saw activities beyond a hill after his plane crashed (383-85). W.A. Laufmann flew out of a hospital during an OBE and met his friend Milton Blose (385). Celia Green (1968) reports that a bedridden woman described another bed-ridden woman around a corner (Cook et al. 385-86). Mrs. R.M. saw her daughter from the hospital in a gift shop and heard her read a card (386). The Rev. L. J. Bertrand (c. 1850) was hypothermic and saw distant activities of associates (386–87). W. Martin (reported by the London Sunday *Express* 26 May 1935) observed his parents 12 miles away, the death of a neighbor, and stillbirth of her daughter (387–88), "Linda McKnight" saw a Christmas tree and sheets drying outside her hospital (388–90), "Jean Morrow" saw her mother smoking in the waiting room (390–91), "Jennifer Edwards" saw parents 1/2 mile away (391–92), "Peggy Raso" heard talk 50 feet away (392–95), Stefan von Jankovich saw and heard details which occurred during his unconsciousness after an auto accident (395–98), and "Rose Heath" learned of her cousin's death and saw his uniform (398–99). During his unconsciousness Al Sullivan saw one of his doctors "flapping his arms," a post-scrub mannerism confirmed by colleagues (399). This is similar to a report by Lawrence (*In a World* 119–20) discussed in my next essay (Shafer, "Near-Death Experiences 2").

Conclusion

We have seen that NDEs are difficult to define because (1) very similar experiences happen in situations where death is not near or even in question, (2) advancing medical technology makes death difficult to define, and (3) consciousness, which is inseparable from any experience, can be observed directly only by the conscious subject. I have thrown a broad net in this essay. After rehearsing some different definitions of NDEs and death, we have covered the history of NDEs, which goes probably back to the origin of humans, and materialist explanations of NDEs, which have not been quite successful, and many anecdotes of NDEs and related phenomena. The careful reader will have many questions, and especially will wonder whether NDEs are merely psychological reactions to the shut-down of the body, the brain, and perhaps of consciousness itself, or whether NDEs are evidence that consciousness survives death. We shall see in the next essay that more rigorous studies have not given a definite answer, but the evidence somewhat favors the survival hypothesis, despite the falsification of materialism which that implies.

Works Cited

Alexander, Eben. *Proof of Heaven: A Neurosurgeon's Journey into the Afterlife*. Simon & Schuster, 2012.
Baird, A.T. *One Hundred Cases for Survival after Death*. Ackerman, 1944.
Barrett, W.F. *Death-Bed Visions*. Methuen, 1926.
Beauregard, Mario, É.L. St.-Pierre, G. Rayburn, and P. Demers. "Conscious Mental Activity during a Deep Hypothermic Cardiocirculatory Arrest?" *Resuscitation*, vol. 83, 2012,

p. e19, www.resuscitationjournal.com/article/S0300-9572(11)00575-2/pdf. Accessed 15 Feb. 2021.

Blackmore, Susan. *Dying to Live: Science and the Near-Death Experience*. Prometheus, 1993.

Blanke, Olaf, and Sebastian Dieguez. "Leaving Life and Body Behind" S. Laureys, G. Tononi, editors. *The Neurology of Consciousness*. Academic Press/Elsevier, 2009, pp. 303–25.

Blau, Eleanor. "Cheating in Pike's Seance Is Alleged." *New York Times*, 11 Mar. 1973, www.nytimes.com/1973/03/11/archives/cheating-in-pikes-seance-is-alleged. Accessed 21 Feb. 2021.

Bush, Nancy Evans. *Dancing Past the Dark: Distressing Near-Death Experiences*. Nancy Evans Bush, 2012.

———. "Is Ten Years a Life Review?" *Journal of Near-Death Studies*, vol. 10, 1991, pp. 5–9. Accessed 21 Feb. 2021.

Callanan, M., P. Kelley. *Final Gifts: Understanding the Special Awareness, Needs, and Communication of the Dying*. Simon & Schuster, 2012.

Cardena, Etzel., Steven Jay Lynn, and Stanley Krippner, editors. *Varieties of Anomalous Experience: Examining the Scientific Evidence*. 2nd ed., American Psychological Association, 2014.

Chamberlain, David., *Consciousness at Birth: A Review of the Empirical Evidence*. Chamberlain Publications, 1983.

———. "The Expanding Boundaries of Memory." *ReVision*, vol. 12, 1990, pp. 11–20.

Christian, Sandra Rozan. "Marital Satisfaction and Stability Following a Near-Death Experience of One of the Marital Partners." University of North Texas dissertation, 2005, digital.library.unt.edu/ark:/67531/metadc4893/m1/?page=3. Accessed 21 Feb. 2021.

Clark, Kimberly. "Clinical interventions with Near-Death Experiencers." Bruce Greyson, Charles P. Flynn, editors. *The Near-Death Experience: Problems, Prospects, Perspectives*. Charles C. Thomas, 1984, pp. 242–55.

Cobbe, Frances Power. "The Peak-in Darien: The Riddle of Death." *Littel's Living Age and New Quarterly Review*, vol. 134, 1877, pp. 374–379.

———. *Peak in Darien*. Williams and Norgate, 1882.

Cohn, Norman. *The Pursuit of the Millennium: Revolutionary Millenarians and Mystical Anarchists of the Middle Ages*, rev. ed., Oxford University Press, 1970.

Cook, Emily Williams, Bruce Greyson, and Ian Stevenson. "Do Any Near-Death Experiences Provide Evidence for the Survival of Human Personality after Death? Relevant Features and Illustrative Case Reports." *Journal of Scientific Exploration*, vol. 12, 1998, pp. 377–406, med.virginia.edu/perceptual-studies/wp-content/uploads/sites/360/2017/01/STE46_Do-Near-Death-Experiences-Provide-Evidence-for-Survival-of-Human-Personality.pdf. Accessed 15 Feb. 2021.

De Bary, William Theodore, editor. *The Buddhist Tradition in India, China, and Japan*. Random House, 1969.

Delacour, Jean-Baptiste. *Glimpses of the Beyond: The Extraordinary Experiences of People Who Have Crossed the Brink of Death and Returned*. Trans. by E.B. Garside from *Aus dem Jenseits Zurueck*. Econ Verlag, 1973, Delacorte Press, 1974.

Dossey, Larry. *Recovering the Soul*. Bantam, 1989.

Du Monchaux, Pierre-Jean. *Anecdotes de médecine ou choix de faits singuliers qui ont rapport à l'anatomie, la pharmacie, l'histoire naturelle, et auxquelles on a joint des anecdotes concernant les médecins les plus célèbres*. Lille, J.B. Henry, 1766. (N.b. The Hathi Trust online edition of *Anecdotes* (Paris?: s.n., 1762) from Universidad Complutense de Madrid skips pp. 61–64 and does not include the passage on NDEs.), www.google.com/books/edition/Anecdotes_de_médecine/u4yAEahRmNIC?hl=en&gbpv=1&dq=Anecdotes+de+médecine+ou+choix+de+faits+singuliers+qui+ont+ %09rapport+à+l'anatomie,+la+pharmacie,+l'histoire+naturelle,+et+auxquelles+on+a+joint+%09des+%09anecdotes+concernant+les+médecins+les+plus+célèbres&printsec=frontcover. Accessed 16 Feb. 2021.

Evans-Wentz, W.Y. *The Tibetan Book of the Dead*. 3rd. ed., Oxford University Press, 1960.

French, Christopher C. "Near-Death Experiences in Cardiac Arrest Survivors." *Progress in Brain Research*, vol. 150, 1 Jan. 2005, pp. 351–67, www.newdualism.org/nde-papers/French/French-The%20Boundaries%20of%20Consciousness%20Neurobiology%20and%20Neuropathology_2006--351.pdf. Accessed 21 Feb. 2021.

Gallup, George, and William Proctor. *Adventures in Immortality: A Look Beyond the Threshold of Death*. McGraw-Hill, 1982.

Granqvist, P., M. Fredrickson, P. Untge, A. Hagenfeldt, S. Valind, D. Larhammar, and M. Larson. "Sensed Presence and Mystical Experiences Are Predicted by Suggestibility, Not by the Application of Transcranial Weak Complex Magnetic Fields." *Neuroscience Letters*, vol. 379, 2005, pp. 1–6, www.researchgate.net/publication/7887692_Sensed_presence_and_mystical_experiences_are_predicted_by_suggestibility_not_by_the_application_of_transcranial_weak_complex_magnetic_fields. Accessed 16 Feb. 2021.

Green, Celia. *Out-of-the-Body Experiences*. Hamish Hamilton, 1968.

Green, J. Timothy. "Did a Near-Death Experience Inspire Einstein's Theory of Relativity?" *World of Lucid Dreaming*, www.google.com/search?client=safari&rls=en&q=www.world-oflucid-+dreaming.com/was-+einstein-+influenced-by-a-near-deathexperience.html.&ie=UTF-8&oe=UTF-8. Accessed 16 Feb. 2021.

Greyson, Bruce. "Biological Aspects of Near-Death Experiences." *Perspectives in Biology and Medicine*, vol. 42, 1998, pp. 14–32, med.virginia.edu/perceptual-studies/wp-content/uploads/sites/360/2017/01/NDE32_biological-Aspects-of-NDEs.pdf. Accessed 16 Feb. 2021.

_____. "The Incidence of Near-Death Experiences." *Medical Psychiatry*, vol. 1, Dec. 1998, pp. 92–99.

_____. "The Near-Death Experience Scale: Construction, Reliability, and Validity." *Journal of Nervous and Mental Disease*, vol. 171, 1983, pp. 369–75, www.researchgate.net/publication/16345325_The_neardeath_experience_scale_Construction_reliability_and_validity. Accessed 21 Feb. 2021.

_____. "Near-Death Experiences." Cardena et al., *Varieties*, pp. 333–67.

Greyson, Bruce, Emily Williams Kelly, and Edward F. Kelly. "Explanatory Models for Near-Death Experiences." Holden et al., *Handbook*, pp. 213–234.

Grof, S. *Realms of the Human Unconscious*. Viking, 1975.

Grosso, M. "Jung, Parapsychology, and the Near-Death Experience: Toward a Transpersonal Paradigm." *Anabiosis: The Journal of Near-Death Studies*, vol. 3, 1983, pp. 3–38, digital.library.unt.edu/ark:/67531/metadc1051969/m1/1/. Accessed 21 Feb. 2021.

Groth-Marnot, Gary. "Paranormal Phenomena and the Near-Death Experience." George K. Zollschan, John F. Schumacher, Greg F. Walsh, editors. *Exploring the Paranormal: Perspectives on Belief and Experience*. Prism Press, Unity Press, 1989, pp. 105–16.

Heim, Albert von St. Gallen. "Notizen ueber den Tod durch Absturz." *Jahrbuch des Schweizer Alpenclub*, vol. 27, 1892, pp. 327–337, docplayer.org/151674194-Jahrbuch-des-schweizer-alpenclub-notizen-ueber-den-tod-durch-absturz-heim-albert-bern-1892-zentralbibliothek-zuerich.html. Accessed 20 Feb. 2021.

Helene, Nina. *An Exploratory Study of the Near-Death Encounters of Christians*. diss. Boston University, 1984.

Holden, Janice Miner. "Veridical Perception in Near-Death Experiences." Holden et al. *Handbook*, pp. 185–212.

_____. "Visual Perception during the Naturalistic Near-Death Out-of-Body Experience. *Journal of Near-Death Studies*, vol. 7, 1988, pp. 107–120, digital.library.unt.edu/ark:/67531/metadc799004/m1/. Accessed 21 Feb. 2021.

_____, Bruce Greyson, and Debbie James. "The Field of Near-Death Studies: Past, Present, and Future," Holden et al., *Handbook*, pp. 1–16.

_____, editors. *The Handbook of Near-Death Experiences: Thirty Years of Investigation*. Praeger/ABC-CLIO, 2009.

Holden, Janice Miner, Jeffrey Long, and B. Jason McLurg. "Characteristics of Western NDErs." Holden et al., *Handbook*, pp. 109–34.

Hyslop, James H. "Visions of the Dying." *Journal of the American Society for Psychical Research*, vol. 1, 1907, pp. 45–55.

Irenaeus. *Adversus Haereses,* vol. 1, Ante-Nicene Christian Library, A. Cleveland Coxe, James Donaldson, Alexander Roberts, editors, T. and T. Clark, 1867–73. 24 vols., www.newadvent.org/fathers/0103102.htm. Accessed 7 Nov. 2020.

Irwin, Harvey J., and Caroline A. Watt. *An Introduction to Parapsychology.* 5th ed., McFarland, 2007.

Kalweit, H. *Dreamtime and Inner Space: The World of the Shaman.* Shambhala, 1984; trans. 1988.

Knittweis, Jim W. "Electrical Sensitivity of Near-Death Experiencers." *Journal of Near-Death Studies,* vol. 15, no. 3, Spring 1997, pp. 223–25, digital.library.unt.edu/ark:/67531/metadc799307/?q=knittweis. Accessed 15 Feb. 2021.

Lawrence, Madelaine. *In a World of Their Own: Experiencing Unconsciousness.* Praeger, 1997.

———. *The Death View Revolution: A Guide to Transpersonal Experiences Surrounding Death.* White Crow, 2014.

Lilly, John C. *The Center of the Cyclone: An Autobiography of Inner Space.* Julian Press, 1972.

Lown, Bernard, Regis DeSilva, and Richard Lenson. "Roles of Psychologic Stress and Autonomic Nervous System Changes in Provocation of Ventricular Premature Complexes." *The American Journal of Cardiology,* vol. 41, 1978, pp. 979–95.

Lown, Bernard, John Temte, Peter Reich, et al. "Basis for Recurring Ventricular Fibrillation in the Absence of Coronary Heart Disease and Its Management." *The New England Journal of Medicine,* vol. 294, no. 12, 1976, pp. 623–29.

Lundahl, Craig R. "Mormon Near-Death Experiences." *Free Inquiry in Creative Sociology,* vol. 7, 1979, pp. 101–07.

———. "Otherworld Personal Future Revelations in Near-Death Experiences." *Journal of Near- Death Studies,* vol. 11, no. 3, Spring 1993, pp. 171–79, www.newdualism.org/nde-papers/Lundahl/Lundahl-Journal%20of%20Near-Death%20Studies_1993-11-171-179.pdf, Accessed 15 Feb. 2021.

Moody, Raymond A., Jr. *Life after Life: The Investigation of a Phenomenon—Survival of Bodily Death,* preface by Melvin Morse, foreword by Elisabeth Kuebler-Ross. HarperCollins, 1975, 2001.

Morse, M., P. Castillo, D. Venecia, J. Milstein, and D.C. Tyler. "Childhood Near-Death Experiences." *American Journal of Diseases of Children,* vol. 140, 1986, pp. 1110–14, www.researchgate.net/publication/20135245_Childhood_Near-Death_Experiences. Accessed 15 Feb. 2021.

Morse, M., D. Conner, D. Tyler, "Near-Death Experiences in a Pediatric Population." *American Journal of Diseases of Children,* vol. 139, 1985, pp. 585–600.

Muse, Queen. "Philly-Based Bioquark Wants a Shot at Bringing the Dead Back to Life." *Philadelphia,* 25 July 2019, www.phillymag.com/healthcare-news/2019/07/25/bioquark-brain-dead-reanima-project-ira-pastor/. Accessed 3 Aug. 2021.

"Non-randomized, Open-labeled, Interventional, Single Group, Proof of Concept Study With [sic] Multi-modality Approach in Cases of Brain Death Due to Traumatic Brain Injury Having Diffuse Axonal Injury." U.S. National Library of Medicine, clinicaltrials.gov/ct2/show/NCT02742857? term=bioquark&rank=1. Accessed 3 Aug. 2021.

Osis, Karlis, and Erlendur Haraldsson. *At the Hour of Death,* rev. ed., introduction by Elisabeth Kubler-Ross. White Crow, 2012.

Osis, Karlis, and D. McCormick. "Kinetic effects at the ostensible location of an out-of-body projection during perceptual testing. " *Journal of the American Society for Psychical Research,* vol. 74, 1980, 319.

Parnia, Sam. *Erasing Death: The Science That Is Rewriting the Boundaries between Life and Death.* With Josh Young, HarperCollins, 2013.

———. "Near Death Experiences in Cardiac Arrest: Visions of a Dying Brain or Visions of a New Science of Consciousness." *Resuscitation,* vol. 52, 2002, pp. 5–11.

———. *What Happens When We Die.* Hay House, 2006.

Parnia, Sam, D.G. Waller, R. Yeates, and P. Fenwick. "A Qualitative and Quantitative Study of the Incidence, Features and Aetiology of Near Death Experiences in Cardiac Arrest

Survivors." *Resuscitation*, vol. 48, no. 2, 2001, pp. 149–56, www.horizonresearch.org/ndearticle_1_.pdf. Accessed 12 Feb. 2021.
Persinger, M.A. "Modern Neuroscience and Near-Death Experiences." *Journal of Near-Death Studies*, vol. 7, 1989, pp. 233–39, www.newdualism.org/nde-papers/Persinger/Persinger-Journal%20of%20Near-Death%20Studies_1989-7-233-239.pdf. Accessed 20 Feb. 2021.
Pfister, Oskar. "Shockdenken [sic] und shockfantasien bei hoechster todesgefahr," *Zeitschrift fuer Psychoanalyse*, vol. 16, 1930, pp. 430–55.
Plato. *The Republic*. Trans. by Desmond Lee, Penguin, 2007.
Plutarch. *Moralia in Fifteen Volumes*. Trans. by Phillip H. De Lacey and Benedict Einarson, Harvard University Press, William Heinemann, 1959, archive.org/stream/moraliainfiftee07plut#page/268/mode/2up. Accessed 16 Feb. 2021.
Reich, P., P. Gold, "Interruption of Recurrent Ventricular Fibrillation by Psychiatric Intervention," *General Hospital Psychiatry*, vol. 5, 1983, pp. 255–57.
Ring, Kenneth. "Amazing Grace: The Near-Death Experience as Compensatory Gift." *Journal of Near-Death Studies*, vol. 10, 1991, pp. 11–39, www.newdualism.org/nde-papers/Ring/Ring-Journal%20of%20Near-Death%20Studies_1991-10-11-39.pdf. Accessed 20 Feb. 2021.
_____. *Heading toward Omega*. William Morrow, 1984.
_____. *Life at Death: A Scientific Investigation of the Near-Death Experience*. Coward, McCann, and Geoghegan, 1980.
_____. *The Omega Project*. William Morrow, 1992.
_____. "Precognitive and Prophetic Visions in Near Death Experiences." *Anabiosis*, vol. 2, 1982, pp. 47–74, digital.library.unt.edu/ark:/67531/metadc1051996/m2/1/high_res_d/-vol2-no1-47.pdf. Accessed 20 Feb. 2021.
_____. "Prophetic Visions in 1988: A Critical Reappraisal." *Journal of Near-Death Studies*, vol. 7, 1988, pp. 4–18, digital.library.unt.edu/ark:/67531/metadc798876/m1/1/. Accessed 21 Feb. 2021.
_____, and Sharon Cooper. *Mindsight: Near-Death and Out-of-Body Experiences in the Blind*. William James Center for Consciousness Studies, 1999.
_____. "Near-Death and Out-of-Body Experiences in the Blind: A Study of Apparent Eyeless Vision." *Journal of Near-Death Studies*, vol. 16, no. 12, 1997, pp. 101–47, digital.library.unt.edu/ark:/67531/metadc799333/m2/1/high_res_d/vol16-no2-101.pdf. Accessed 21 Feb. 2021.
Ring, Kenneth, and Madelaine Lawrence. "Further Evidence for Veridical Perception during Near-Death Experiences." *Journal of Near-Death Studies*, vol. 11, 1993, pp. 223–29, www.researchgate.net/publication/226754118_Further_evidence_for_veridical_perception_during_near-death_experiences/link/0fcfd513923c05c0e5000000/download. Accessed 15 Feb. 2021.
Ring, Kenneth, and Evelyn Elsaesser Valarino. *Lessons from the Light: What We Can Learn from the Near-Death Experience*. Insight, 1998.
Robson, J.G. "Measurement of Depth of Anaesthesia." *British Journal of Anaesthesia*, vol. 41, no. 9, 1969, pp. 785–88.
Rudolph, Kurt. *Gnosis*. HarperSanFrancisco [sic], 1984.
Saavedra-Aguilar, Juan C., and Juan S. Gomez-Jeria. "A Neurobiological Model for Near-Death Experiences." *Journal of Near-Death Studies*, vol. 7, no. 4, 1989, pp. 205–22.
Sabom, Michael B. *Light and Death: One Doctor's Fascinating Account of Near-Death Experiences*. Zondervan Publishing House, 1998.
_____. *Recollections of Death: A Medical Investigation*. Harper and Row, 1982.
Sagan, Carl. *Broca's Brain: Reflections on the Romance of Science*. Random House, 1979.
Schlieter, Jens. *What Is It Like to Be Dead: Near-Death Experiences, Christianity, and the Occult*. Oxford University Press, 2108.
Schwaninger, J., P.R. Eisenberg, K.B. Schechtman, et al. "A Prospective Analysis of Near-Death Experiences in Cardiac Arrest Patients." *Journal of Near-Death Studies*, 2002, vol. 20, pp. 215–32, www.researchgate.net/publication/225101914_A_Prospective_Analysis_of_Near-Death_Experiences_in_Cardiac_Arrest_Patients. Accessed 15 Feb. 2021.

Shafer, Grant R. "Near-Death Experiences 2: More Rigorous Studies." In Shafer, *Probing Parapsychology*.

_____. "Theoretical Criticism of Psychic Research." Shafer, *Probing Parapsychology*.

_____, editor. *Probing Parapsychology: Essays on a Controversial Science*. McFarland.

Shushan, Gregory. *Conceptions of the Afterlife in Early Civilizations: Universalism, Constructivism and Near-Death Experience*. Bloomsbury, 2010.

Spraggett, Alan, reply by Martin Gardener. "A Spirited Exchange." *The New York Review of Books*. 1 Nov. 1973, www.nybooks.com/articles/1973/11/01/a-spirited-exchange/. Accessed 6 Feb. 2021.

Sutherland, Cherie. "'Trailing Clouds of Glory': The Near-Death Experiences of Western Children and Teens." Holden et al., *Handbook* pp. 87–108.

_____. *Transformed by the Light: Life after Near-Death Experiences*. Bantam, 1992.

Tart, Charles T. "A Second Psychophysiological Study of Out-of-the-Body Experiences in a Gifted Subject." International Journal of Parapsychology, vol. 9, 1967, pp. 251–58, s3.amazonaws.com/cttart/articles/april2013articles/Second+Psychophysiological+Study+of+Out-of-Body+Experiences+in+a+Gifted+Subject.pdf. Accessed 20 Feb.2021.

_____. "A Psychophysiological Study of Out-of-the-Body Experiences in a Selected Subject." *Journal of the American Society for Psychic Research*, vol. 62, 1968, pp. 3–27, s3.amazonaws.com/cttart/articles/april2013articles/Psychophysiological+-Study+of+Out+of+The+Body+Experiences+in+a+Selected+Subjec t+(2).pdf. Accessed 20 Feb. 2021.

Than, Ker. "Neanderthal Burials Confirmed as Ancient Ritual." *National Geographic*, 16 Dec. 2013, www.nationalgeographic.com/news/2013/12/131216-la-chapelle-neanderthal-burials-graves/. Accessed 16 Feb. 2021.

"Turning Point--Life after Death: Personal Experiences." ABC television, aired 1995. www.youtube.com/watch?v=PZywS7ZKbS8 retrieved 6/6/2014. Accessed 30 Aug. 2021.

Ustinova, Yulia. "To Live in Joy and Die with Hope: Experiential Aspects of Ancient Greek Mystery Rites." *Bulletin of the Institute of Classical Studies*, vol. 56, no. 2, 2013, pp. 105–23, www-jstor-org.ezproxy.emich.edu/stable/44254135?seq=17#metadata_info_tab_contents. Accessed 16 Feb. 2021.

Van der Sluijs, Marinus. "Three Ancient Reports of Near-Death Experiences: Bremmer Revisited." *Journal of Near-Death Studies*, vol. 24. no. 4, Summer 2009, pp. 223–53, mythopedia.info/vanderSluijs-JNDS27.pdf. Accessed 16 Feb. 2021.

Van Lommel, Pim. "About the Continuity of Our Consciousness." *Advances in Experimental Medicine and Biology*, vol. 550, 2004, pp. 115–32, pimvanlommel.nl/wp-content/uploads/2017/11/About-the-Continuity-of-ourconsciousness.pdf. Accessed 16 Feb. 2021.

_____, Ruud van Wees, Vincent Meyers, and Ingrid Elfferich. "Near-Death Experience in Survivors of Cardiac Arrest: A Prospective Study in the Netherlands." *The Lancet*, vol. 358, no. 9298, 15 Dec. 2001, pp. 2039–45, pimvanlommel.nl/wpcontent/uploads/2017/10/Pim- van-Lommel-Lancet-artikel-near-death-experience.pdf. Accessed 12 Feb. 2021.

Near-Death Experiences 2
More Rigorous Studies
Grant R. Shafer

My previous essay included more general consideration of NDEs: their history, mostly materialistic explanations of them, their apparently paranormal aspects, and veridical perceptions, all mostly anecdotal material. This essay deals with more rigorous scientific studies, i.e., retrospective study of the case of Pam Reynolds, prospective studies, reasons why they failed to provide irrefutable evidence that NDEs are more than psychological phenomena, and my conclusion as to the ontological status of NDEs.

Pamela Reynolds Lowery

The previous cases are anecdotal. In contrast, the case of Pam Reynolds is perhaps the best-documented and the most controversial NDE. Sabom (*Light* 37–51, 184–90) gives the most complete account of the case. Ms. Reynolds suffered a giant basilar artery aneurysm in 1991. Two carotid arteries support the front half of the brain, and the basilar artery supports the back. An aneurysm is a weakening or ballooning of an artery. Rupture of a cerebral aneurysm causes hemorrhage with disability or death.

Robert F. Spetzler, director of the Barrow Neurological Institute, performed a hypothermic cardiac arrest, or "standstill" to remove the aneurysm. In "standstill" body temperature is lowered to 60°F, blood drained from the head, and flat brain waves are induced to protect the brain during the procedure (Sabom, *Light* 37).

Ms. Reynolds' eyes were taped shut (Sabom, *Light* 38), yet she "saw" that her head was not completely shaved but not that it was cut, and that the Midas Rex bone saw was like an electric toothbrush with interchangeable blades in a case like those for socket wrenches (41), she remembered the heart-lung machine, respirator, but did not recognize many tools (42). Despite one ear plugged and the other with a speaker emitting 100 dB clicks (volume of outboard motor, power lawn mower, motorcycle, farm tractor, jackhammer, garbage truck) (39), Ms. Reynolds heard the bone saw, talk about her blood vessels being too small, and "Hotel California" playing in the background (43, 47). Medical reports corroborate these details (48).

As planned, her cardiac arrest was completed, her brain waves flatlined, and 20 minutes later her brain was considered totally shut down (Sabom, *Light* 43). This conclusion was based on her flat spontaneous EEG, which signifies no cortical function, absence of brain-stem auditory evoked potentials (BAEPs=brain-stem auditory evoked responses, BAERs), read from the EEG, in response to 100 dB clicks, which indicated no brain stem function, and exsanguination of the brain, which meant no brain function at all (49). Sabom does not mention another test of Ms. Reynolds' brain function, SSEP, somatosensory evoked potential, which involves placing an electrode usually on the arm or leg to stimulate the nerves and electrodes on the spine or scalp to record reception of the signal. In a general description of the "standstill" procedure, Spetzler (868) includes SSEPs as a standard practice.

Spetzler et al. say,

> Baseline evoked potential recordings [BAEP/Rs and SSEPs, Spetzler et al. 868] are made during this preparatory phase prior to the incision.... The exposure proceeds during the early cooling stages.... It is at this point in the procedure that the surgeon decides whether the aneurysm can be clipped primarily or whether circulatory arrest is required... (Spetzler et al. 870).

Thus anesthesia is administered and monitored prior to opening the skull, but exsanguination follows only if necessitated by the form of the aneurysm revealed by the opening.

Ms. Reynolds reported later that during the operation she saw her late grandmother, uncle, aunt, and beings of light, her relatives fed her, her grandmother sent her back, and her uncle pushed her back into her body, which looked "like a train wreck" (Sabom, *Light* 44–46).

Of course, Ms. Reynolds' report should not be taken at face value, and some have argued that nothing paranormal occurred. Holden says that the "crux" of the analyses of Blackmore (1993), Woerlee (2004), and Augustine (2006) is that the AVPs [apparently nonphysical veridical NDE perceptions] were actually acquired through the physical senses and the operations of the still-working brain ("Veridical Perception" 198).

Gerald Woerlee (2011) is the most outspoken proponent of a materialistic explanation of the Pam Reynolds case, i.e., that she heard or imagined her perceptions without any paranormal process. Woerlee says that "a disembodied conscious mind" which goes through solid concrete will not be affected by sound waves in air, and thus cannot hear. Casinos and blind and deaf people disprove telepathy and clairvoyance. Therefore, OBErs hear only through their physical sense of hearing (7).

In response to Woerlee, Ms. Reynolds did not claim to have passed through any floors. Woerlee's objection is irrelevant to Ms. Reynolds' case. Stuart Hameroff rightly responds that sounds which are not observed in brain monitoring are unlikely to be consciously heard, that consciousness without sense organs is not less mysterious than consciousness with sense organs, and that such non-local consciousness should not be blocked by physical objects. Hameroff explains this through the theory which he proposed with Roger Penrose, that consciousness originates at the quantum level ("Response" 27–28; "Quantum").

Whether or not Hameroff's and Penrose's theory is correct, Woerlee begs the question by insisting that paranormal hearing requires interaction with sound waves. If extrasensory perception, which is what is in question here, required such interaction, it would not be extrasensory. Woerlee likewise begs the question by asserting that casinos, blind, and deaf people prove that ESP does not exist. We have seen in particular that blind people do report paranormal sight, documented by Ring and Cooper (*Mindsight*, "Near-Death"), recounted in my previous essay (Shafer, "Near-Death Experiences 1").

Woerlee says that the 100-dB clicks of BAEP used to monitor Ms. Reynolds' consciousness would not interfere with hearing. He calculates that only 1/100 sec was occupied by the clicks (8). He says (8) "The duration of the BAEPs induced by these clicking sounds is clearly indicated in Figure 2 of the same article [Spetzler et al. 869]: they last no more than 12 milliseconds."

Woerlee's article contains a number of minor errors. On p. 4 he says that BAEP involves "100 dB clicking sounds applied to both ears," which agrees with Spetzler et al. (869) that the clicks are delivered by "ear speakers" (note the plural) and that BAEPs are recorded for both ears (Fig. 2), which Spetzler confirmed in an interview about Pam Reynolds (Broome qtd. in Holden, "Veridical Perception" 199). However, Worelee gives incorrect references to one ear on pp. 9 and 19. Woerlee says (9), "At a rate of 11.3 clicks per second, this means these clicking sounds generated brainstem activity lasting a total time equal to 11.3 × 12 = 124,6 [sic] milliseconds = 0.1246 seconds of brainstem activity per second." On p. 8 he misspells Peter Raudzens' name. On p. 15 he writes ungrammatically "all drugs used during anesthesia ... have *an* identical dosebrain effects...."

It appears that sometimes Woerlee's materialist convictions also get the better of his common sense. On p. 14 he claims that draping makes it impossible for an anesthesiologist to detect patient movement. On p. 18 he confidently asserts, "There is no muscular mechanism or physical possibility by which such a two foot jump—or even a one millimeter jump, for that matter—could occur as a result of an electrical shock applied to the chest...."

Woerlee's reasoning is opaque and his calculations are erroneous. He says (8), "What this all means is that at a rate of 11.3 clicks per second, a total time equal to 11.3×100 [μsec]= 11,300 μsec = 11.3 milliseconds per second was occupied by these clicking sounds." In fact, $11.3 \times 100 = 1130$, not 11,300. Is "100" a misprint for "1000," sloppy proofreading? 11.3×12 also does not equal 124.6 msec as miscalculated by Woerlee, but 135.6 msec. Although this miscalculation does not destroy Woerlee's argument, it shows carelessness. Woerlee also does not explain why he chose 11.3 rather than any other number between 11 and 33 allowed in BAEP (Spetzler et al. 869). Did he misread the range 11 to 33 as 11.3?

More to the point, I calculate, based on Woerlee's and Spetzler's figures, 11 to 33 clicks/sec multiplied by 12 msec/click equals 0.132 to 0.396 sec/sec. Based on his arithmetical error Woerlee (9) asserts that only 12.46 percent of Ms. Reynolds' hearing was taken by the clicks, in contradiction of his statement on the previous page (8) that the clicks took "little more than" 1/100, 1 percent, of a second. Against Woerlee's arithmetical failures, I calculate that between 13.2 percent to more than 39.6 percent of each second was filled with the clicks. Woerlee here underestimates the duration of the clicks by factors between 1.06 and 3.17 (p. 9) and between 13.2 and 39.6 (p. 8). The clicks actually occupied roughly between 1/8 and 2/5 of the time. Woerlee's contention, based on miscalculation, that normal hearing would allow Ms. Reynolds to ignore loud clicks of such duration, is not credible.

If Ms. Reynolds was hearing normally, besides not reporting the clicks, why didn't she report the pain of having her skull opened? She did report the sound of the bone saw and the sight of medical equipment and her head half shaved, despite the tape over her eyes.

Semiconscious elective cardioversion patients do hear medical workers but report pain and have no visuals (Sabom, *Recollections* 154–55, 178–80). Woerlee cites one study (Artusio 1954) that gaseous anesthetics allow consciousness while removing pain. Sabom (*Recollections*) also asserts that cardioversion NDErs report no pain in their NDEs (154–55), and some NDErs distinguished talk heard while semiconscious from later visions (155–56). If Ms. Reynolds' hearing of conversation and music was semiconscious, it is a little odd that she reported no pain and extremely odd that she reported no clicks. These facts cast doubt on the contention that her hearing was normal.

Despite Woerlee's opaque reasoning and erroneous calculations, the correct time might be adequate for Ms. Reynolds to hear noise, conversation, and music over the 100-dB clicking sounds applied to one ear (Woerlee 7, 9) as well as the continuous 40-dB white noise applied to the other ear. But again, one wonders why she did not report the loud clicking.

Woerlee is correct when he observes that (12) Ms. Reynolds' auditory perceptions appear to have occurred when she was only under general anesthesia, not cardiac arrest, and that (7) some patients are aware under this condition. He continues (13), "The proof of this effect was revealed in Sabom's (1998) account where he stated that Reynolds' EEG flattened only after her heart arrested: 'As Pam's heart arrested, her brain waves flattened into complete electrocerebral silence. Brain-stem function weakened as the clicks from the ear speakers produced lower and lower spikes on the monitoring electrogram (43).'"

This EEG activity indicates a lack of burst suppression, "burst" being a unique electroencephalogram (EEG) pattern commonly seen in cases of severely reduced brain activity such as overdose of general anesthesia (Liang et al. 1). Anesthesia is used in hypothermic bypass to induce burst suppression in order to reduce oxygen metabolism by the brain, which protects it from injury. Hameroff does not agree that the lack of burst suppression indicates consciousness: "…in addition, the lack of EEG burst suppression by the barbiturates prior to bypass and hypothermia is surprising—and worrisome. But burst suppression is not necessary for adequate anesthetic depth … ('Response' 27)."

Woerlee (9–10) says also that the earphones used would not prevent hearing noise, speech, and music. For example, he says, "Regardless of the sound excluding properties of earphones, no earphone or earplug blocks bone conduction of sound through the bones of the skull. All this information means that Reynolds would hear bone conduction of sounds above a level of 40–50 decibels (Woerlee 10)." Spetzler says "…The contralateral ear is masked to prevent boneconducted acoustic crossover…." (869), which seems to contradict Woerlee.

Sabom tells, "Pam stated that she did not hear or perceive anything prior to her out-of-body experience, and that this experience began with hearing the bone saw. At this point in the operation, she had been under anesthesia for about 90 minutes…" (*Light* 185). One wonders why she did not hear anything until this point if she heard afterward through normal channels.

Holden mentions the possibility that Ms. Reynolds was underanesthetized and responds by pointing out that her brain was monitored in 3 different ways (SSEP, BAEP, and spontaneous EEG). BAEP included 90–100-dB clicks ("louder than a whistling teakettle and as loud as a lawn mower or a subway when a train is going through it") 11–33 times per second. Holden questions whether one could correctly hear a normal 60-dB conversation over the clicks coming from molded earphones molded to one's ears. Holden also asks why, if Ms. Reynolds heard normally, she never mentioned the clicks to Sabom (Holden, "Veridical Perception" 198–99).

Woerlee says, "they were no more than an ignored background noise." (9) Again, since the clicks took up between 13.2 percent and 39.6 percent of each second, as I calculate against Woerlee's inconsistent and incorrect calculations of 1 percent and 12.46 percent, normal hearing should have made Ms. Reynolds aware of them.

Further, Woerlee is incorrect when he says (14), " The only clinical measures of consciousness were pulse rate, blood pressure, and the BAEP, none of which are [sic] individually reliable," following Sabom in omitting SSEP. As Holden indicates, 3 separate tests, SSEP, BAEP, and spontaneous EEG, satisfied Spetzler that Ms. Reynolds was unconscious. Spetzler et al. say, "With this technique, intraoperative monitoring includes recording the spontaneous electroencephalographic (EEG) activity, somatosensory evoked potentials (SSEP's) [sic], and brain-stem auditory evoked potentials (BAEP's) [sic]" (868).

Spetzler himself later said that it was "inconceivable" that, despite "clicking modules in each ear," Ms. Reynolds heard "through normal auditory pathways" (Broome qtd. in Holden, "Veridical Perception" 199).

Even granting that Ms. Reynolds heard normally, it remains to be explained how she accurately "saw" the procedure with her eyes taped shut, that her head was not completely shaved and that there were the Midas Rex bone saw, the heart-lung machine, and the respirator (Sabom, *Light* 38, 41–42). Sabom asked her, "Were there any details that you had not seen before"? She answered, "The saw thing that I hated the sound of looked like an electric toothbrush and it had a dent in it, a groove at the top where the saw appeared to go into the handle, but it didn't…. And the saw had interchangeable blades, too, but these blades were in what looked like a socket wrench case…" (*Light* 186). That Sabom's question was about things which Ms. Reynolds had not seen before undermines the contention that Ms. Reynolds imagined the Midas Rex saw from prior knowledge.

Holden ("Veridical Perception" 187) cites Sabom that Ms. Reynolds saw "the interchangeable saw blades in a socket-wrench-type case," but that ("Veridical Perception" 193, Sabom, *Light* 41, 187) she misplaced a groove on the saw. Since eyewitness memory is notoriously unreliable, the fact that Ms. Reynolds remembered correctly the blades in their case outweighs fact that she remembered incorrectly a groove. Skeptics usually say of correct perceptions of medical details by NDErs that the veridical perceptions are imagined from prior knowledge perhaps gained from television. Do patients really remember so well details of television?

Woerlee and other skeptics have raised valid questions about the paranormality of the Pam Reynolds case, but their arguments that her perceptions were entirely natural are not convincing. Even if Ms. Reynolds heard the saw, the conversation, and the song normally before and after her brain was shut down, which is doubtful, given her not mentioning the long, loud BAEP clicks, her accurate vision of her head half-shaved and the bone saw are not adequately explained. Woerlee's illogical argument against the possibility of nonlocal consciousness shows his presupposition that the Reynolds case cannot be paranormal. His mechanical, grammatical, logical, and factual errors show his unsurprising failure to take the case seriously, and his miscalculation of the duration of the clicks is particularly careless and important. The Pam Reynolds case is a serious challenge to materialist explanations of consciousness.

Prospective studies

Retrospective studies, like that of Pam Reynolds, find NDErs by soliciting a more or less broad sample of the public, which is thus self-selected, and whose NDEs may be long past. On the other hand, Holden says, "The general idea of prospective investigation of AVP is to make present continuously a controlled perceptual stimulus [usually a visual target], knowable only to a material NDEr..." ("Veridical Perception" 203). Prospective studies prepare to survey survivors of cardiac arrest as soon as possible after their NDEs, usually before they leave the hospital.

Pim van Lommel et al. (2001) prospectively studied NDEs without visual targets among 344 cardiac arrest patients who had been successfully resuscitated in 10 Netherlands hospitals. Van Lommel et al. say that 62 subjects (18%) reported NDEs. Forty-one (12%) reported a core experience. Van Lommel et al. add that similar experiences are claimed by patients with "serious but not immediately life-threatening diseases," with depression, and without apparent reason in completely awake persons. Deathbed visions are like NDES and happen in dying patients. Experiences identical to NDEs, "fear-death experiences," happen when death seems imminent as in traffic accidents, mountaineering, or "isolation such as with shipwreck" (2039).

Van Lommel et al. "defined clinical death as a period of unconsciousness" because of inadequate blood provided to the brain due to insufficient blood circulation and respiration (2040). Patients not claiming NDEs were controls for patient NDErs, and psychological (e.g., fear before CPR), demographic (e.g., age, sex), medical (e.g., more than 1 cardiopulmonary resuscitation) and pharmacological data were compared between the 2 groups. The work also included a longitudinal study where the 2 groups (those who had had an NDE and those who had not had one) were compared at 2 and 8 years, for life changes (Van Lommel et al. 2039–40, 2042).

Van Lommel tells of what is called a "Peak in Darien" experience, apparently during the 2001 study. A CA (cardiac arrest) patient reported that he saw, along with his dead grandmother, an unknown man " who had looked at me lovingly." Ten years later, on her deathbed his mother admitted that the patient was conceived in an adulterous relationship. His biological father was Jewish and murdered in the Holocaust. The patient said that the picture which his mother showed him was of the man whom the patient had seen in his NDE (5).

Van Lommel et al. also recorded the following anecdote from coronary care nurse of an out of body experience (OBE) with veridical perception. An ambulance delivered a cyanotic, comatose man discovered in a meadow. Staff gave him artificial respiration, heart massage, and defibrillation. Intubation necessitated removing his upper denture, which was placed on the "crash car." Next meeting the nurse more than a week later, the patient said, " Oh, that nurse knows where my dentures are." He described the "crash car" and specified that the nurse put his plate in the crash car drawer. The nurse was very surprised that the man remembered her and what she did with his denture because he had been in "deep coma" receiving CPR. The patient claimed an OBE, described in accurate detail the appearance and activity of the medical staff working on him and the hospital room in which it took place. He had feared that the staff would stop CPR and allow him to die, which cohered with the fact that the staff "had been very negative about the patient's prognosis...." His efforts to communicate were desperate but unsuccessful (2041).

Schwaninger et al. (2002) also did not place visual targets but interviewed cardiac arrest survivors according to Ring's (*Life* 265–70) schedule and evaluated their responses with Greyson's ("Near-Death Experience Scale") scale. They write of paranormal claims and a "Peak in Darien" experience. No one reported ESP (Schwaninger et al. 221).

Schwaninger et al. write:
One (9 percent) reported visualizing scenes from the future, and one (9 percent) reported scenes from her past (223–24).

More NDErs than nonNDErs reported increases in telepathic ability, but those differences were not statistically significant (227).

One patient in this study reported meeting in her NDE a deceased brother whom she had not previously known ("Peak in Darien experience"). The existence of this sibling was subsequently verified by her parents (230).

There have been 7 studies, by Holden (1990), Lawrence (1997), Parnia

(2001, 2014, 2019), Greyson (2006), and Sartori (2008), to record OBE perceptions prospectively by putting unusual images in places to be viewed by NDErs, such as in a ceiling corner of a hospital room. None were seen by experients, although Parnia et al. ("Abstract"; Kesteven) report that 1 subject heard an auditory target. Let's look at some details from these 7 studies.

Holden and Joesten ("Near Death Veridicality" 50–51) report that only 2 resuscitations occurred in their 6-month study in 1990. The patients were unavailable to be interviewed. Visual targets were placed so as to be visible only "looking down from the ceiling" on holders, but the holders were disturbed by nurses and visitors and fell off the walls (46–47, 50).

Lawrence ("In a World" 158) hid an electric sign in Hartford Hospital for NDErs to read, but only 3 patients reported OBEs, and only their early stages, and no patient had a full NDE (159). However, NDEr "Louis" saw his late mother in brown, which his aunts later said was her favorite color. He reported a doctor flapping his arms, which was in fact the doctor's habit. Louis also saw a gaunt boy. Louis' dead mother said that the boy would be back later. In fact the boy later had a tumor (119–20; in personal communication (23 October 2019) Lawrence told GRS that she did not know if the boy died).

Parnia et al. (2001) report that at Southampton General Hospital in England 11.1 percent of 63 cardiac arrest survivors reported memories, the majority of which had NDE features ("Qualitative and Quantitative Study" 149). Parnia et al. intended to evaluate "prospectively the possible veridical nature of out of body experiences." They hung boards from the ceilings which "had various figures" which could not be seen at floor level. In the year of the study "63 patients survived and were interviewed," of whom 56 (88.8%) remembered nothing from when they were unconscious. The other 7 survivors' (11.1%) memories were evaluated with the Greyson NDE scale. By this standard 4 patients (6.3%) had NDEs. The remaining 3 patients (4.8%) did not fulfill the criteria for NDE. Interestingly, however, 2 (3.2%) out of those three reported some features of a NDE (e.g., feelings of peace or seeing dead family members) but not enough to fulfill the Greyson criteria. One subject (1.6%) reported memory but no characteristics of NDE ("Qualitative and Quantitative Study" 151). Parnia et al. could not test whether OBEs included veridical perceptions because no patient reported OBEs ("Qualitative and Quantitative Study" 152).

The following assessment by Parnia et al. is significant. They say that the NDEs were unlike "confusional hallucinations ... highly structured, narrative, easily recalled, and clear...." They add, "The data suggests that in this cardiac arrest model, the NDE arises during unconsciousness." There is a terminological problem here. NDEs are conscious experiences.

It is almost an oxymoron to say that a conscious experience occurs during unconsciousness. It would be better to say that the NDE may have occurred when consciousness could not be detected externally. Parnia et al. are also surprised by the occurrence and remembrance of "[c]omplex experiences such as are reported in the NDE" in the "dysfunctional" brain of a "deeply comatose patient" because "the cerebral structures which underpin subjective experience and memory must be severely impaired" without oxygen ("Qualitative and Quantitative Study" 154).

Parnia et al. continue that unconscious patients would not be expected to have subjective experience, as with 88.8 percent of patients, or at most a confusional state if partial brain function is continued. Even an inundation of neurotransmitters should not produce "clear, lucid remembered experiences." This is confirmed because cardiac arrest first terminates cortical function and then brainstem function ("Qualitative and Quantitative Study" 154).

However (as Woerlee said of Pam Reynolds), perhaps the reported experiences happen "during the loss of, or on regaining, consciousness" ("Qualitative and Quantitative Study" 154). Parnia et al. argue against that. No patients' accounts suggested that NDE arose as consciousness faded or returned. During CA loss of brain function is speeded up. The EEG manifests changes within a few seconds, consequently the passage from consciousness to unconsciousness is swift, and it seems immediate to patients. Experiences which happen while consciousness is returning are confusional. NDEs of Parnia et al.'s patients were not so. Parnia et al. concede that more data is needed to "confirm the timing of the experience." Parnia et al. call for " a multi-centre trial" to gather a sufficient prospective sample. This would allow a necessarily detailed examination of "psychological (including out of body experiences) and physiological aspects of the experience" ("Qualitative and Quantitative Study" 154–55).

Parnia et al. ("Qualitative and Quantitative Study" 154) showed the difficulty of physiological explanations of NDEs because they are characterized as "highly structured, narrative, easily recalled, and clear," which is not what one would expect in the various brain dysfunctions which are adduced to explain them. They are also relatively consistent in their content. Further, NDEs seem to take place when the patient is "unconscious" as determined by external signs. But NDEs are rare, 6.3 percent of cardiac arrest survivors in this study. OBEs are even rarer, none in this study, so that no one saw the visual targets (Parnia et al., "Qualitative and Quantitative Study" 154–55).

Greyson et al. ("Failure" 85) interviewed 52 patients in whom cardiac arrest was induced to install implantable cardioverter/defibrillators (ICDs). ICDs "monitor the patient's heartbeat and automatically detect cardiac arrest and administer an electrical shock to return the heart to normal rhythm" (Greyson et al., "Failure" 85). Greyson et al. responded to Blackmore's question about when NDEs occurred (Broome, 2002) by including a time display in the animated targets (Holden, "Veridical Perception" 210). None of the subjects had a near-death experience or out-of-body experience (Greyson et al., "Failure" 85).

Sartori et al. reported OBE, veridical perception, "Peak in Darien" experience, and unexplained healing in an NDE at Morriston Hospital in Swansea, South Wales. A 60-year-old male suffered blood poisoning and multiple organ failure following emergency bowel surgery which rendered him unconscious (Sartori et al. 71). The patient did not see the visual target placed for the prospective study (Sartori et al. 74). Details of the principal author's final interview with the patient follow.

The patient did not look in the direction of the visual target during his NDE but at Sartori, his physician, and "2 or 3 others" (Sartori et al. 74). He appeared to be unconscious and saw his mother-in-law, whom he had never met in life ("Peak in Darien") and later recognized from photos. He had not spoken of his mother-in-law before, didn't know or care much who she was during his NDE, but afterward identified her from photographs (75). The patient wondered why he saw his mother-in-law and not his own mother. He did see his father (Sartori et al. 74).

Had the patient seen photographs of his mother-in-law before his NDE? If so, seeing his mother-in-law could be mere imagination, enabled by unconscious memory of her pictures, especially since he knew that she was dead, although why he would imagine the mother-in-law rather than his own mother is unclear. The patient also "said that he didn't know who she was at the time, but later recognized her from photos" (Sartori et al. 75), so that it is again unclear why he would imagine her.

The patient distinguished his NDE from hallucinations caused by patient-controlled morphine (Sartori et al. 76), which coheres with Sabom (*Recollections* 169–171). The patient also reported veridically a physiotherapist peeking from behind a curtain, an eye exam, and cleaning of his mouth (Sartori et al. 78–79).

Most dramatically, the patient had congenital cerebral palsy with a claw-like contracture of the right hand which prevented his opening it. The hospital had previously made a splint for the paralyzed hand, which did not help. "It was documented in the patient's medical admission notes that he had cerebral palsy with a right spastic hemiparesis," i.e., his right side was weakened by muscular contraction. Following the NDE, the patient could open his right hand, which the physiotherapist said should have required an operation (Sartori et al. 77, 82–83). The patient also showed improvement in his congenital hemiplegic limp (69).

Parnia et al. ("Qualitative and Quantitative Study" 155) called for " a multi-centre trial" to study NDEs. Parnia and 30 co-authors conducted the AWARE study with 330 survivors of 2060 cardiac arrests, 1000 visual targets in 15 hospitals, in 3 countries, over 4 years (2008–2012) (Parnia et al., "AWARE" 1799–1802). No patient reported seeing the visual targets. Parnia says that the AWARE study placed targets for 10 percent of hospital beds (*Erasing Death* 234), but 50 percent of cardiac arrests were not near targets (236). Only 0.1 percent of cardiac arrest survivors had OBEs (256).

Parnia et al. say that because only 2 percent of patients had explicit memory of VA (visual awareness), using images objectively to test specific reports detailing VA was unsuccessful. However, 1 verified case of VA suggests that consciousness persists after the first 20 to 30 seconds after CA, the period in which some brain electrical activity remains. This represents a measurable time of consciousness after the brain usually becomes isoelectric (flat EEG) ("AWARE"1803). That is, the patient reported conscious experience while his brain showed no activity.

Parnia (*Erasing Death* 255) reports also that a 51-year-old woman saw a nurse whom she recognized later, but no target was near. He says that consciousness seems to have remained 3 to 5 minutes into the time when the brain usually stops working and cortical activity ends. The patient's memory agreed with true and documented events, which made hallucination or illusion unlikely (Parnia, "Understanding the Cognitive Experience" 68).

Parnia et al. continue that they contacted 2 patients "for in-depth interviews to verify their experiences against documented CA events." 1 could not be interviewed because of illness. The other was a 57-year-old man, "Mr. A." He remembered looking at activities from a corner of the ceiling. His description of people, sounds, and activities from his resuscitation were verified from his medical records and corroborated his accounts in detail (Parnia et al., "AWARE" 1802; Parnia, *Erasing Death* 251–254).

Particularly important was his description of an automated external defibrillator (AED). Current AED algorithms indicate that when he heard recorded prompts from the AED, it probably was during up to 3 minutes of consciousness during CA and CPR (Parnia et al., "AWARE" 1802; see also Parnia, *Erasing Death* 251–254). "Mr. A" continued remembering the period before CA in Recollection #1. He answered the nurse and felt strong pressure but not pain on his groin. Then he "blanked out." Next he heard an automated voice saying, "shock the patient, shock the patient.'" He saw a woman "up in (the) corner of the room ... beckoning me." He thought, "I can't get up there." He felt that the woman knew him, was trustworthy, and "there for a reason" which he didn't know. Immediately he was "up there, looking down," Despite his vision from the operating table being obstructed by a blue drape (Parnia, *Erasing Death* 251–54) he looked at himself, the nurse, and a bald man whose face was not visible.

Mr. A's statements that he was "looking down at me [himself]" (Parnia, "Aware," Table 2, Category 5 recollections, Recollection # 1, p. 1803) and that "I could see my body" (Category 5 recollections, Recollection # 2, p. 1803) conflict with Parnia's assertion that "our study suggests that VA and veridical perception during CA are dissimilar to autoscopy since patients did not describe seeing their own double ('AWARE' 1803–04)."

Mr. A continued that the bald man "was quite a chunky fella" wearing blue scrubs and a blue hat. The following day his NDE "Mr. A" recognized the man in blue when he visited. Medical records corroborated the use of the AED, the medical team during CA, and the role of the man in blue (Parnia et al., "AWARE" 1803).

In another interview (Recollection #2) Mr. A remembered the nurse saying, "dial 444 cardiac arrest" and his fear. He looked down from the ceiling at a nurse whom he recognized only later. He saw his body and "everything at once," his blood pressure being taken, a physician putting something down Mr. A.'s throat, a "nurse pumping on [his] chest, ... blood gases and blood sugar levels being taken (Parnia, 'AWARE' 1803)." No target was near, and he did not report seeing one (Parnia, *Erasing Death* 251–54).

Recollection #2 is different from Recollection #1 in that Mr. A does not mention the woman beckoning up in the corner of the room. Does this discrepancy mean that Mr. A. fabricated the story? Perhaps his memory changed as he recovered from his CA. This case is extremely interesting because the patient had accurate memories apparently during his cardiac arrest, although "EEG flatlines around ten seconds after the heart stops" Parnia (*What Happens* 92), so that the experience appears to have occurred in the absence of brain activity.

However, Chawla et al., Grigg et al., Wetzel et al., Borjigin et al., and Parnia (qtd. in "Research Claims"; *Erasing Death* 170) suggest that brain activity and even consciousness may persist during CPR, without cerebral blood flow, without blood pressure, with flatlined EEG, even after otherwise diagnosed brain death. Even so, the lucid consciousness characteristic of NDE is surprising in such conditions of brain dysfunction, which usually allow confusional mentation at best (Greyson, "Near Death Experiences" 335–36; Sabom, *Recollections* 156–80; Parnia, *What Happens* 92–94).

Parnia (*What Happens* 1) remarks on this paradox that NDErs remember clear lucid thought during brain dysfunction. Parnia (*What Happens* 2) responds to the suggestion that NDE does not occur during cardiac arrest with the assertion that some NDErs describe events in the middle of cardiac arrest, when memory is usually lost. In 2006 Parnia (*What Happens* 3) met the suggestion that NDEs arise from undetected brain activity by observing that such activity is unlikely to be conscious. In 2002, Parnia also said, "...Studies in animals have demonstrated that an absence of cortical activity as measured by EEG correlates with an absence or reduction in activity of the deep brain structures as measured by in-dwelling electrodes..." ("Near Death Experiences" 8).

This appears to contradict what Parnia said in 2018 to the *NZ Herald*, that brain activity can persist hours after cardiac arrest, and CPR enables consciousness ("Research Claims"). Parnia (*What Happens* 77–79) also relates how colleague Richard Mansfield reported that his patient remembered details from when he was asystolic (EEG flatlined, neither abnormal nor normal electrical activity). Beauregard et al. (1) write, "During the last decade, prospective studies conducted in the Netherlands, United Kingdom, and United States have revealed that approximately 15% of cardiac arrest survivors report conscious mental activity while their hearts are stopped." But if NDEs occur only with brain function, they presumably are not paranormal.

Van Lommel also points out that NDE and veridical perceptions, with remarkable mental clarity, appear to happen when the brain is normally incapable of such functions. He mentions his own study (van Lommel et al.) and those of other researchers (Greyson, "Incidence"; Parnia et al., "Qualitative and Quantitative Study") of subjects diagnosed as clinically dead. This means VF (ventricular fibrillation) on the ECG (electrocardiogram), total absence of electrical activity of the cerebral cortex (flat EEG), with inactivity of the brainstem, evidenced by the loss of the corneal and gag reflexes, and fixed and dilated pupils. But NDErs in such states of brain dysfunction, or no function, claim lucid awareness, in which cognition, emotion, self-awareness, and childhood memories remained, as well as OBE. Van Lommel concludes based on corroborated OBEs, such as the dentures in the cart, the NDE must occur during when consciousness cannot be detected from outside, as by EEG, and not in the first or last seconds of consciousness detected from outside ("About the Continuity" 7).

Given the size of the AWARE study, including 31 authors, 330 survivors of 2060 cardiac arrests, 1000 visual targets in 15 hospitals, in 3 countries, over 4 years (Parnia et al., "AWARE" 1799–1802), the results are rather disappointing. Only "9 of 101 patients (9%) had experiences compatible with NDE's" (Parnia et al., "AWARE" 1802). None saw the visual targets, which is not surprising because they were not in rooms with targets, although one ("Mr. A") did have veridical perception without apparent brain activity (Parnia et al., "AWARE" 1802).

Parnia began AWARE II, "A Multi-Centre Observational Study of the

Relationship between the Quality of Brain Resuscitation and Consciousness, Neurological, Functional and Cognitive Outcomes following Cardiac Arrest," a prospective study, on 1 August 2014, set the finish of the study for 31 May 2017, and planned for 900–1500 subjects. AWARE II seems to have been held up when Parnia went from the University of Southampton in the UK to the Stony Brook School of Medicine in New York, then to the New York University Medical Center, but AWARE II continued, with 12 sites in the study and new sites in the UK and the U.S. anticipated for 2018. A new end date was set for 2020 ("Wehrstein").

Some results of AWARE II are now available. AWARE II presented images and sounds on a tablet computer during CPR. Forty-four patients of 465 (9%) survived cardiac arrest. Twenty-one were interviewed. Four (19%) had memories such as positive emotions, perceptions of relatives and others suggesting external awareness such as conversations of others and medication given. One accurately remembered the audio stimuli, but none remembered the visual stimuli (Parnia et al., "Abstract"). The patient who remembered reported "two beeps from a machine that made a noise at three-minute intervals." This allowed researchers to record how long that person's experience lasted (Kesteven and Summerson). Other memories were typical of NDE: joy and peace, vision of light, a tunnel, life review, and survivors felt positively changed (Parnia et al., "Abstract").

Parnia is now the Principal Investigator at the Parnia Lab, NYU Grossman School of Medicine. The National Institutes of Health (NIH) has recognized a little-known phenomenon among advanced dementia patients designated "terminal" or "paradoxical lucidity" (PL), surprising mental lucidity and speech, particularly near death. PL also is associated with deathbed visions (Bering) and similar to NDEs, and NIH has become interested in Parnia Lab's NDE research ("New Studies"). Parnia says, "The common unresolved question for both of these areas of research is how do you have lucidity at a time when the brain is assumed to not be functioning? A major subgroup of people who go through this have had advanced end-stage dementia and maybe have had no lucidity for years" (qtd. in "New Studies").

Parnia has a 5-year grant from the National Institute on Aging with which he plans to formulate the first-ever definition and measurement scale for PL. "The Parnia Lab has pioneered the use of noninvasive brain monitoring of regional cerebral oxygenation (rSO2) using near infrared spectroscopy, and of end-tidal carbon dioxide (ETCO2) as sensitive physiological markers of circulation quality and perfusion to the brain and vital organs during CPR" ("New Studies").

What do we have from these prospective studies? "[F]rom sources before 1975, systematic studies, and peer reviewed reports," no more than

150 AVPs were investigated, a small minority at all erroneous, the great majority involving evidence of accurate AVPs, but five hospital studies (Holden, Lawrence, Parnia, Greyson, Sartori) yielded no AVP, according to Holden ("Veridical Perception" 209–10). That is disputable. Lawrence (*In a World* 119–20) reported 3 corroborated paranormal visions of "Louis," and Sartori et al. (74–75, 82–83) a patient with corroborated "Peak in Darien" and anomalous healing. The AWARE study also provided 2 AVPs: the woman who saw the unknown nurse, and the man who heard the AED prompts (Parnia, *Erasing Death* 240–55; Parnia et al., "AWARE").

However, the results of AWARE II are also disappointing. Of 465 cardiac arrest patients, only 1 correctly described the audio, and none the visual. Could this be similar to Pam Reynolds' hearing, which Woerlee argues was natural? Although only 1 subject in prospective NDE studies reported perceiving a target, Tart ("Second," "Psychophysiological") reported, and Osis and McCormick are said to have reported, that their OBErs correctly reported visual targets, but I could not read Osis and McCormick's study because of COVID-19 library restrictions (Cook et al. 381).

The biggest problem in AWARE II was the diminishing sample size. AWARE II was to include 900 to 1500 subjects. From the 456 cardiac arrests actually available were only 44 survivors, of whom 21 were interviewed. One might think that Parnia has turned to paradoxical lucidity because of the lack of results in NDE research. Even so, on 9 July 2020 Parnia announced "a study of consiousness [sic] during deep hypothermic circulatory arrest," the operation which Pam Reynolds survived (Parnia, "I am pleased").

Rationalizing Failure

Greyson said of the failure of patients to report visual targets that only 5 poorly funded studies had investigated veridical NDE as of 2007. The 5 studies reported only 12 NDEs with OBE, 8 from Sartori (2004), 4 by Parnia et al. (2001), and 0 from Holden and Joesten (1990), Madelaine Lawrence (1997), or Greyson et al. (2006). Twelve NDEs with OBE is a very small sample ("Comments" 242).

Subjects were not entirely cooperative. Holden ("Veridical Perception" 205) says that a slight majority of NDErs said that they would attend to details extraneous to their bodies. Sartori et al.'s (74) NDEr is an example of the minority. Parnia also rationalizes patient failure to see the targets, "…Finally, we would have to address the question of why people having out-of-body experiences (assuming they are even real) would even look at the images we put up (rather than focusing on the doctors working on them)" (*Erasing Death* 231). Holden says, "...In all studies of this kind [Holden, Joesten 1990; Lawrence 1996, 1997; Parnia et al. 2001; Sartori 2004], the researchers reported problems with the staff and/or visitors looking at the targets and, thus, compromising the masked research protocol..." ("Veridical Perception" 205).

Nevertheless some accounts are impressive. Holden says that in AVP (apparently nonphysical veridical NDE perception), NDErs claim veridical perceptions which, because of the placement and situation of their bodies during the experiences, seemingly could not have resulted from "normal sensory processes or logical inference—nor, therefore, brain mediation—either before—during, or after those episodes..." ("Veridical Perception" 186). We have seen above that Holden ("Veridical Perception" 209) is too negative about AVPs in prospective studies, omitting those reported by Lawrence and Sartori et al.

Perhaps the most significant rationale for the failure of patients in prospective studies to report perceiving targets is that few cardiac arrest patients survive, less than 6 percent out of hospital, and 24 percent in hospital ("Cardiac Survival"; cf. "American Heart"), and the majority of survivors remember nothing. Parnia et al. interviewed 140 of 330 survivors of 2060 cardiac arrests, and of the 140 interviewed, 85 reported no memories at all (Parnia et al., "AWARE" 1801–02). The AWARE researchers installed targets for 10 percent of hospital beds (Parnia, *Erasing Death* 234), and 50 percent of cardiac arrests were not near targets (236).

Conclusion

Near-death experiences have been reported in many cultures from antiquity to the present. By the 1970s, the advance of resuscitation technology caused them to be more often reported. The stereotypical cross-cultural and cross-temporal nature of the reports and reluctance of the experients to report demonstrate that NDEs are a genuine psychological phenomenon, not attention-seeking fraud.

Given that, are they merely the last gasp of the dying brain? We have seen that this explanation is not entirely adequate, as Sabom (*Recollections* 154–80) argued persuasively. From a materialist standpoint, the occurrence of lucid conscious experience during brain malfunction, or even no apparent function, is a conundrum. There is sufficiently abundant anecdotal evidence to justify asking whether NDEs falsify materialist explanations of consciousness and provide evidence of the survival of the self after death.

Although doctrinaire materialists such as Gerald Woerlee and James

Alcock object to the idea that consciousness may be more than a brain process, quantum mechanics, as understood by Bohr, Schroedinger, and Wigner, et al., undermines the common sense on which materialism depends, and physics seems to require consciousness as a necessary factor along with matter, energy, space, and time. I further discuss theoretical objections to NDEs in Shafer, "Theoretical Criticism of Psychical Research."

Despite anecdotal evidence and theoretical justification, efforts to prove extrasensory perception in NDEs have been unsuccessful. Although Tart ("Second," "Psychophysiological") and Osis and McCormack claim that subjects have correctly described hidden targets in OBEs, and Parnia et al. that 1 subject did so for an auditory target in an NDE ("Abstract"), so far no NDEr has reported seeing a visual target in a prospective study. We have seen a number of explanations for this failure. Nevertheless we are left, even in prospective studies, with reports of veridical perceptions, in a sense more anecdotes, which might be explained materialistically, if tendentiously. Skeptics maintain that this kind of failure of research to provide irrefutable proof of paranormal phenomena proves that they do not exist. But absence of proof is not proof of absence. It is difficult to believe that the mass of anecdotes of ESP in NDEs is totally false. Future research may give us proof of the irreducible nature of consciousness, already hinted in quantum mechanics.

Works Cited

American Heart Association News. "CPR Is Key to Survival of Sudden Cardiac Arrest," www.heart.org/en/news/2018/07/12/cpr-is-key-to-survival-of-sudden-cardiac- arrest. Accessed 9 Aug. 2021.

Artusio, J.F. "Di-Ethyl Ether Analgesia: A Detailed Description of the First Stage of Ether Anesthesia in Man." *Journal of Pharmacology and Experimental Therapeutics*, vol. 111, 1954, pp. 343–48.

Barrett, W.F. *Death-Bed Visions*. Methuen, 1926.

Beauregard, Mario, É.L. St.-Pierre, G. Rayburn, P. Demers. "Conscious Mental Activity during a Deep Hypothermic Cardiocirculatory Arrest?" *Resuscitation*, vol. 83, 2012, p. e19, www.resuscitationjournal.com/article/S0300-9572(11)00575-2/pdf. Accessed 15 Feb. 2021.

Bering, Jesse. "One Last Goodbye: The Strange Case of Terminal Lucidity." *Scientific American*, 25 Nov. 2014, blogs.scientificamerican.com/bering-in-mind/one-last-goodbye-thestrange-case-of-terminal-lucidity/. Accessed 27 Feb. 2021.

Borjigin, J., U. Lee, T. Liu, et al. "Surge of Neurophysiological Coherence and Connectivity in the Dying Brain." *Proceedings of the National Academy of Sciences of the United States of America*, 2013, vol. 110, pp. 14432–7.1, www.pnas.org/content/110/35/14432. Accessed 15 Feb. 2021.

Broome, K., producer. *The Day I Died: The Mind, the Brain, and Near-Death Experiences* [Motion picture]. Films for the Humanities and Sciences, 2002.

Cardena, Etzel., Steven Jay Lynn, and Stanley Krippner, editors, *Varieties of Anomalous Experience: Examining the Scientific Evidence*. 2nd ed., American Psychological Association, 2014.

"Cardiac Survival Rates Around 6 Percent for Those Occurring Outside of a Hospital, Says IOM Report." News Release. National Academies of Sciences, Engineering, Medicine. www.nationalacademies.org/news/2015/06/cardiac-survival-rates-around-6percent-for-those-occurring-outside-of-a-hospital-says-iom-report. Accessed 9 Aug. 2021.

Chawla, L. S., S. Akst, C. Junker, B. Jacobs, and M.G. Seneff. "Surges of Electroencephalogram Activity at the Time of Death: A Case Series." *Journal of Palliative Medicine*, vol. 12 no. 12, 2009, pp. 1095–1100, liebertpub.com/doi/10.1089/jpm.2009.0159? url_ver=Z39.88-2003&rfr_id=ori%3Arid%3Acrossref.org&rfr_dat=cr_pub+ +0pubmed&. Accessed 12 Nov. 2020.

Cobbe, Frances Power. "The Peak-in Darien: The Riddle of Death," *Littel's Living Age and New Quarterly Review*, vol. 134, 1877, pp. 374–379.

_____. *Peak in Darien*, London: Williams and Norgate, 1882.

Cook, Emily Williams, Bruce Greyson, and Ian Stevenson. "Do Any Near-Death Experiences Provide Evidence for the Survival of Human Personality after Death? Relevant Features and Illustrative Case Reports," *Journal of Scientific Exploration*, vol. 12, 1998, pp. 377–406, https://med.virginia.edu/perceptual-studies/wp-content/uploads/sites/360/2017/01/STE46_Do-Near-Death-Experiences-Provide-Evidence-for-Survival-of- Human-Personality.pdf. Accessed 15 Feb. 2021.

Greyson, Bruce. "Comments on 'Does Paranormal Perception Occur in Near-Death Experiences?'" *Journal of Near-Death Studies*, vol 25, no. 4, 2007, pp. 237–44, med.virginia.edu/perceptual-studies/wp-content/uploads/sites/360/2017/01/NDE50-Augustine-1-JNDS.pdf. Accessed 20 Feb. 2021.

_____. "Incidence and Correlates of Near-Death Experiences in a Cardiac Care Unit." *General Hospital Psychiatry*, vol. 25, 2003, pp. 269–276.

_____. "The Near-Death Experience Scale: Construction, Reliability, and Validity." *Journal of Nervous and Mental Disease*, vol. 171, 1983, pp. 369–75, www.researchgate.net/publication/16345325_The_neardeath_experience_scale_Construction_reliability_and_validity. Accessed 21 Feb. 2021.

_____. "Near-Death Experiences." Cardena et al., *Varieties*, pp. 333–67.

_____, J.M. Holden, and J.P. Mounsey. "Failure to Elicit Near-Death Experiences in Induced Cardiac Arrest." *Journal of Near-Death Studies*, vol. 25, 2006, pp. 85–98, med.virginia.edu/perceptual-studies/wp-content/uploads/sites/360/2017/01/NDE47.pdf. Accessed 20 Feb. 2021.

Grigg, Madeline, et al. "Electroencephalographic Activity after Brain Death." *Archives of Neurology*, vol. 44, Sep. 1987, pp. 948–54.

Hameroff, Stuart. "Quantum Computation in Brain Microtubules? The Penrose–Hameroff 'Orch OR' Model of Consciousness." *Philosophical Transactions of the Royal Society of London A*, vol. 356, 1998, pp. 1869–1896, downloaded from rsta.royalsocietypublishing.org/ on March 6, 2015, www.quantumconsciousness.org/sites/default/files/1998%20Hameroff%20Quantum%20Computation%20in%20Brain%20Microtubules%20The%20Penrose%20Hameroff%20Orch%20OR%20model%20of%20consciousness%20%20Royal%20Society.pdf. Accessed 28 Feb. 2021.

_____. "Response to 'Could Pam Reynolds Hear?'" *Journal of Near-Death Studies*, vol. 30, no. 1, Fall 2011, pp. 26–28, digital.library.unt.edu/ark:/67531/metadc461724/m1/3/. Accessed 21 Feb. 2021.

Holden, Janice Miner. "Veridical Perception in Near-Death Experiences." Holden et al. *Handbook*. pp. 185–212.

_____, Bruce Greyson, Debbie James, editors. *The Handbook of Near-Death Experiences: Thirty Years of Investigation*. Praeger/ABC-CLIO, 2009.

Holden, Janice Miner, and L. Joesten. "Near-Death Veridicality Research in the Hospital Setting: Problems and Promise." *Journal of Near-Death Studies*, vol. 9, 1990, pp. 45–54, www.researchgate.net/publication/226626373_Neardeath_veridicality_research_in_the_hospital_setting_Problems_and_promise. Accessed 20 Feb. 2021.

Hyslop, James H. "Visions of the Dying." *Journal of the American Society for Psychical Research*, vol. 1, 1907, pp. 45–55.

Kesteven, Sophie, and Isabelle Summerson. "Some people can recall their near-death experience. Dr. Sam Parnia is trying to understand how." *ABC Radio National*, 6 Sep. 2021, abc.net.au/news/2021-09-07/recalled-near-death-experiences-scientific-research-sam-parnia/100374154. Accessed 21 Jan. 2022.

Lawrence, Madelaine. *In a World of Their Own: Experiencing Unconsciousness*. Praeger, 1997.

Liang, Zhenhu, Yinghua Wang, Yongshao Ren, Duan Li, Logan Voss, Jamie Sleigh, and Xiaoli Li, "Detection of Burst Suppression Patterns in EEG Using Recurrence Rate." *The Scientific World Journal*, vol. 2014, 2014 p. 1, downloads.hindawi.com/journals/tswj/2014/295070.pdf. Accessed 16 Feb. 2021.

"New Studies Explore End-of-Life Cognitive Thought & Improved Cardiopulmonary Resuscitation Methods." *NYU Langone Health News Hub*, 22 Dec. 2021, nyulangone.org/news/new-studies-explore-end-life-cognitive-thought-improved-cardiopulmonaryresuscitation-methods. Accessed 27 Feb. 2021.

Osis, Karlis, and McCormick, D. "Kinetic effects at the ostensible location of an out-of-body projection during perceptual testing." *Journal of the American Society for Psychical Research*, vol. 74, 1980, 319.

Parnia, Sam. *Erasing Death: The Science That Is Rewriting the Boundaries between Life and Death*. With Josh Young, HarperCollins, 2013.

———. "I am pleased to mention that we officially launched a study of consiousness [sic] during deep hypothermic circulatory arrest and recruited our first participant." @SamParniaMDPhD. 9:08 p.m., Jul 9, 2020, twitter.com/SamParniaMDPhD/status/1281394731273117696. Accessed 27 Feb. 2021.

———. "Near Death Experiences in Cardiac Arrest: Visions of a Dying Brain or Visions of a New Science of Consciousness." *Resuscitation*, vol. 52, 2002, pp. 5–11.

———. "Understanding the Cognitive Experience of Death and the Near-Death Experience." *QJM: An International Journal of Medicine*. vol. 110, no. 2, Feb. 2017, pp. 67–69, watermark.silver.com. Accessed 16 Feb. 2021.

———. *What Happens When We Die*. Hay House, 2006.

———, Tara Keshavarz, Meghan McMullin, and Tori Williams. "Abstract 387: Awareness and Cognitive Activity During Cardiac Arrest." *Circulation*, vol. 140, 11 Nov. 2019, p. A387, www.ahajournals.org/doi/10.1161/circ.140.suppl_2.387. Accessed 27 Feb. 2021.

Parnia, Sam, Ken Spearpoint, Gabriele de Vos, Peter Fenwick, Diana Goldberg, Jie Yang, Jiawen Zhu, Katie Baker, and Hayley Killingback et al. "AWARE—AWAreness during REsuscitation—A Prospective Study." *Resuscitation*, vol. 85, no. 12, 2014, pp. 1799–1805, med.virginia.edu/perceptual-studies/wpcontent/uploads/ sites/360/2017/01/NDE74-AWARE-Resus-2.pdf. Accessed 9 Aug. 2021

Parnia, Sam, D.G. Waller, R. Yeates, and P. Fenwick. "A Qualitative and Quantitative Study of the Incidence, Features and Aetiology of Near Death Experiences in Cardiac Arrest Survivors." *Resuscitation*, vol. 48, no. 2, 2001, pp. 149–56, www.horizonresearch.org/ndearticle_1_.pdf. Accessed 12 Feb. 2021.

"Research Claims Brain Still Functions after Death so You'll Be Aware of Everything." *New Zealand Herald*, 25 Nov. 2018, www.nzherald.co.nz/lifestyle/news/article.cfm?c_id=6&objectid=12165852. Accessed 15 Feb. 2021.

Ring, Kenneth. *Life at Death: A Scientific Investigation of the Near-Death Experience*. Coward, McCann, and Geoghegan, 1980.

———, and Sharon Cooper. *Mindsight: Near-Death and Out-of-Body Experiences in the Blind*. William James Center for Consciousness Studies, 1999.

———. "Near-Death and Out-of-Body Experiences in the Blind: A Study of Apparent Eyeless Vision." *Journal of Near-Death Studies*, vol. 16, no. 12, 1997, pp. 101–47, digital.library.unt.edu/ark:/67531/metadc799333/m2/1/high_res_d/vol16-no2-101.pdf. Accessed 21 Feb. 2021.

Sabom, Michael B. *Light and Death: One Doctor's Fascinating Account of Near-Death Experiences*. Zondervan Publishing House, 1998.

———. *Recollections of Death: A Medical Investigation*. Harper and Row, 1982.

Sartori, Penny. *The Near-Death Experiences of Hospitalized Intensive Care Patients: A Five Year Clinical Study*. The Edwin Mellen Press, 2008.

_____. "Touching The [sic] Light." *Nursing Standard*, vol. 23, no. 11, 19–25 Nov. 2008, pp. 26–27.

_____, Paul Badham, and Peter Fenwick. "A Prospectively Studied Near-Death Experience with Corroborated Out-of-Body Perceptions and Unexplained Healing." *Journal of Near-Death Studies*, vol. 25, 2006, pp. 69–84, www.iands.es/bibliografia/Sartori_Fenwick.pdf. Accessed 20 Feb. 2021.

Schwaninger, J., P.R. Eisenberg, K.B. Schechtman, et al. "A Prospective Analysis of Near-Death Experiences in Cardiac Arrest Patients." *Journal of Near-Death Studies*, 2002, vol. 20, pp. 215–32, www.researchgate.net/publication/225101914_A_Prospective_Analysis_of_Near-Death_Experiences_in_Cardiac_Arrest_Patients. Accessed 15 Feb. 2021.

Shafer, Grant R. "Extrasensory Perception: Telepathy, Clairvoyance, Precognition, and Retrocognition." In Shafer, *Probing Parapsychology*. McFarland.

_____. "Near-Death Experiences 1: History, Explanations, Anecdotes." In Shafer, *Probing Parapsychology*. McFarland.

_____. "Theoretical Criticism of Psychic Research." In Shafer, *Probing Parapsychology*. McFarland.

_____, editor. *Probing Parapsychology: Essays on a Controversial Science*. McFarland.

Spetzler, R. F., M.N. Hadley, D. Rigamonti, L.P. Carter, P.A. Raudzens, S.A. Shedd, and E. Wilkerson. "Aneurysms of the Basilar Artery Treated with Circulatory Arrest, Hypothermia, and Barbiturate Cerebral Protection." *Journal of Neurosurgery*, vol. 68, 1988, pp. 868–78, pdfs.semanticscholar.org/af1a/7b0c7620d4d1586e8b0192deba5d6cf0d59b.pdf?_ga=2.20060410.375739845.1613506114–2131473436.1613068587. Accessed 16 Feb. 2021.

Tart, Charles T. "A Second Psychophysiological Study of Out-of-the-Body Experiences in a Gifted Subject." *International Journal of Parapsychology*, vol. 9, 1967, pp. 251–58, s3.amazonaws.com/cttart/articles/april2013articles/Second+Psychophysiological+Study+of+-Out-of-Body+Experiences+in+a+Gifted+Subject.pdf. Accessed 20 Feb. 2021.

_____. "A Psychophysiological Study of Out-of-the-Body Experiences in a Selected Subject." *Journal of the American Society for Psychical Research*, vol. 62, 1968, pp. 3–27, s3.amazonaws.com/cttart/articles/april2013articles/Psychophysiological+-Study+of+Out+of+The+Body+Experiences+in+a+Selected+Subjec t+(2).pdf. Accessed 20 Feb. 2021.

Van Lommel, Pim. "About the Continuity of Our Consciousness." *Advances in Experimental Medicine and Biology*, vol. 550, 2004, pp. 115–32, pimvanlommel.nl/wp-content/uploads/2017/11/About-the-Continuity-of-ourconsciousness.pdf. Accessed 16 Feb. 2021.

Van Lommel, Pim, Ruud van Wees, Vincent Meyers, and Ingrid Elfferich. "Near-Death Experience in Survivors of Cardiac Arrest: A Prospective Study in the Netherlands." *The Lancet*, vol. 358, no. 9298, 15 Dec. 2001, pp. 2039–45, pimvanlommel.nl/wp-content/uploads/2017/10/Pim-van-Lommel-Lancet-artikel-near- death-experience.pdf. Accessed 12 Feb. 2021.

Wehrstein, K.M. "AWARE NDE Study," *Psi Encyclopedia*, psi-encyclopedia.spr.ac.uk/articles/aware-nde-study#AWARE_II. Accessed 23 Nov. 2019.

Wetzel, R. C., et al. "Hemodynamic Responses in Brain Dead Organ Donor Patients." *Anesthesia and Analgesia*, vol. 64, 1985, pp. 125–28, journals.lww.com/anesthesia-analgesia/Abstract/1985/02000/Hemodynamic_Responses_in_Brain_Dead_Organ_Donor_.5.aspx. Accessed 15 Feb. 2021.

Woerlee, Gerald M. "Could Pam Reynolds Hear? A New Investigation into the Possibility of Hearing During [sic] this Famous Near-Death Experience." *Journal of Near-Death Studies*, vol. 30, no.1, Fall 2011, pp. 3–25, digital.library.unt.edu/ark:/67531/metadc461684/m1/. Accessed 21 Feb. 2021.

Revising Our Concepts About Reality
The Challenge of Consciousness

DEAN RADIN

Scientific concepts about the nature of the universe radically evolved over the course of the twentieth century. Advancements in many disciplines, from physics to psychology, caused major revisions in how most educated people thought about themselves and their place in the universe, and in their understanding of the physical "fabric of reality."

Science will continue to evolve in the twenty-first century, with some of the most revolutionary advancements stimulated by the study of consciousness. Today's key questions about consciousness include (a) How can the physical brain account for nonphysical "qualia" (subjective experience)? and (b) How does evidence for exceptional cognitive skills and non-local forms of awareness influence our understanding of the mind-brain relationship? Question (a) has been called the "hard problem" of consciousness. Question (b) is what might be called the "harder problem" of consciousness, because it not only questions the neuroscience dogma that the mind is solely a product of brain activity, but it also challenges the set of assumptions that underlies modern science itself—the doctrine called materialism.

After Kuhn's account of the "structure of scientific revolutions," it is better appreciated that anomalies encountered within a discipline are strenuously resisted by the status quo, often to the point where evidence supporting the existence of the anomalies is viewed as chronically insufficient, or worse, it is labeled "pseudoscience." An anonymous paper of Lord Rayleigh, who formulated the Rayleigh-Jeans law, on paradoxes of electrodynamics, was rejected as that of a "paradoxer" (Kuhn 153 note 10). Eventually, evidence improves and accumulates until it becomes overwhelming and forces a paradigm shift. As anomalies associated with consciousness are better understood, there is a real possibility that by the turn of the twenty-second century the materialistic foundations of science will experience a meta-paradigm shift. Rather than being viewed as fundamental, materialism may be reframed as a special case of a more comprehensive worldview, one that views consciousness as fundamental. The scientific, technological, and sociological reverberations of such an ideological shift could dwarf all previous advancements in human knowledge.

Introduction

In April 1900, William Thomson, the Right Honorable Lord Kelvin gave a lecture to the Royal Society. In it, the prominent British physicist confidently stated that physics was so successful that it was essentially complete, except for "two clouds" (Kelvin 1). The two clouds would come to be known as the "luminiferous ether" (Kelvin 2) and the "ultraviolet catastrophe." Since Christian Huygens (1629–1695), light was thought to consist of waves in the luminiferous ether. By 1887 Michelson and Morley had shown that the ether did not exist. The ultraviolet catastrophe was the violation of the Rayleigh-Jeans law by the observed quantity of energy emitted at high frequencies from a black body. The phrase was coined by Ehrenfest in 1911 (Ehrenfest 92). Both clouds referred to anomalies that did not fit the predominant view of what is now called classical physics, and both clouds were assumed to be problems that would eventually be solved by minor tweaks to existing theories.

Eight months after Kelvin's lecture, German physicist Max Planck presented a new idea at a meeting of the German Physical Society held in Berlin (Planck). Planck's idea resolved the cloud of the ultraviolet catastrophe and founded quantum theory. Einstein explained away the cloud of luminferous ether in 1905 in proposing special relativity (Einstein).

This unexpected turn of events, one of many found in the history of science, serves to remind us why small clouds on the horizon are worthy of very close attention. Sometimes those clouds dissipate after slight revisions to existing ideas. But sometimes they are puzzles that persist for decades or centuries. In such cases, the solutions may stimulate paradigm shifts and usher in startlingly new concepts, technologies, and even new forms of civilization. Over the course of the twentieth century, Lord Kelvin's two clouds transformed the Western world from the industrial age into the atomic and information ages.

Today we are faced with two other very persistent clouds, commonly known as qualia and quanta. The first cloud has been a mystery throughout history. The second arose as a consequence of Planck's idea. "Qualia" refers to the nature of subjective experience and "quanta" to the fact that quantum objects (some much smaller than atoms) are exquisitely sensitive to being observed. Both clouds raise questions about the nature and role of consciousness in the physical world, and both are major challenges to the scientific paradigm of reductive materialism—the assumption that everything, including mind, consists of matter and energy, and that any system, regardless of how complex, can be completely understood by reducing it into its elementary physical components.

Some neuroscientists insist that qualia is a non-problem because consciousness is an illusory side effect of brain processing (Churchland, 1986; Crick, 1994). Others propose that any physical system as complex as the brain will spontaneously develop conscious awareness (through some as-yet unknown process) (Tegmark, 2015). Some physicists believe that the quantum observer effect (closely related to the "quantum measurement problem") is also a nonproblem, because consciousness plays no role in physics, or that the problem is already solved by concepts like decoherence (Schlosshauer, 2007).

Like Lord Kelvin, many scientists today undoubtedly assume that these two "consciousness clouds" will eventually be understood in conventional terms. I believe that that sentiment is wrong. These two clouds have stubbornly resisted orthodox explanations, and instead of wispy puffs fading away in the light of existing theories, qualia and quanta presage paradigmatic superstorms. They are also the leading edge of a host of related clouds, each more challenging than the last (Schwartz, 2010). This includes the phenomena of genius, savants, near-death experiences, mediumship, cases of reincarnation, and laboratory studies of psychic phenomena. All of these phenomena stretch the materialist "brain equals mind" assumption because they suggest that the mind is not inextricably limited to the operations of the physical brain.

Genius

No one who studies the lives and works of Mozart, da Vinci, Copernicus, Shakespeare, Einstein, or mathematician Srinivasa Ramanujan can doubt that genius is real, if rare. Of the estimated one hundred billion humans who have ever lived, every now and then someone comes along whose talent is so prodigious that it literally shapes the future course of civilization.

The challenge presented by genius is to imagine how the mind, viewed solely as an aspect of brain processing, could generate world-changing mathematical theorems, breakthrough scientific ideas, hypercreative inventions, masterwork books and musical compositions, etc., apparently arising out of the blue, often unbidden, and fully formed (Schwartz, 2010; Heilman, 2016).

If such ideas arose once in a person's lifetime, perhaps we might dismiss them as a fluke. But true genius is a persistent fount of paradigm-shattering creativity that defies our understanding of mindless electrochemical activity in a brain that is strictly limited to ideas it has already absorbed (Lingg and Frank, 1973; "Srinivasa").

Savants

Autistic savants have few to no social skills, often seem cognitively impaired, and yet they can display supernormal capacities of memory, musical talent, artistic talent, or lightning-fast mathematical calculations (Dossey, 2012; Cowan and Frith, 2009; Welling, 1994). The Academy Award-winning 1988 movie *Rain Man* was based partially on the life of savant Kim Peek, who among other things could correctly and instantly recall every word of the estimated 12,000 books he had read. Psychiatrists Darold Treffert and Daniel Christenson ("Inside" 108), discussing autistic savants, wrote that "Kim Peek possesses one of the most extraordinary memories ever recorded. Until we can explain his abilities, we cannot pretend to understand human cognition."

Treffert also described the case of Leslie Lemke, who "is blind, severely cognitively impaired and has cerebral palsy. Yet he played back Tchaikovsky's Piano Concerto No. 1 flawlessly after hearing it for the first time at age 14" (Treffert, *Islands* xiii). If one were to test normally healthy pianists who had not previously heard this concerto, it is safe to say that precisely none of them would be able to do this. Treffert goes on to describe the strange phenomenon of "acquired savants," in which, as the result of an accident or other acquired brain dysfunction, a normal person suddenly gains savant skills (*Islands* xv, xvii, 7–8, 11–12, 26, 38, 59–60, 193–203, 220–22). And then there are the completely astonishing cases of "sudden savants," in which apparently normal people spontaneously gain savant skills, for no known reason (Treffert, *Islands* xv-xvi).

How the brains of autistic savants work is a major problem for the neurosciences, and perhaps at some point their skills might be explainable via conventional concepts. But how similar skills can arise in acquired or sudden savants remains a baffling mystery.

Psychic Phenomena

Despite there being no broadly accepted explanations for the talents of genius and savants, they are so rare that they are easy to set aside in favor of understanding "ordinary" people. This is why commonly reported psychic phenomena, like telepathy, clairvoyance, precognition, and psychokinesis, are important to consider. These experiences have been reported by ordinary people throughout history, across all cultures, and at all levels of educational experience. And rather than having to rely on astonishing anecdotes for evidence, in this domain a wealth of strictly controlled experimental studies can be found in the peer reviewed scientific literature (Radin, 1997, 2006, 2013, 2018).

Scientific studies of psychic abilities began in the late 1800s. By the 1950s, the accumulated evidence had convinced many academics who had paid attention to the relevant literature. By the second decade of the twenty-first century, the weight of the empirical evidence was overwhelming to all but the most entrenched skeptics. Today, this topic is still regarded as controversial, but not because empirical data are lacking. Rather, the implications of these phenomena are so difficult to accommodate within a materialistic paradigm that critics find it easier to imagine that the evidence must be flawed in some unspecified way, or they insist on a suitable explanation first, before they will even look at the data.

It is beyond the scope of this article to do justice to the wealth of available evidence, but to illustrate the kind of evidence that is available, we will briefly review one type of telepathy experiment.

Testing for Telepathy

Telepathy involves the experience of gaining an impression about another person's experience, intentions, thoughts, or emotions without the use of the ordinary senses, and without regard to spatial distance or shielding. One of the most successful protocols for testing telepathy in the laboratory is called the ganzfeld method (meaning "whole field" in German). In this experiment, a "receiver" of telepathic information has a halved ping-pong ball placed over each eye, the face is illuminated by a soft red light, and white noise is played over headphones. This state of mild, unpatterned sensory stimulus induces a dream-like reverie, which is thought to be conducive to sensing telepathic impressions. While in this state, the receiver is asked to be open to any ideas or feelings gained while holding a distant "sender" in mind.

To conduct the experiment, you randomly select one photo out of a pool of four photos, where each image depicts a real object or scene with a clearly identifiable theme, and where the colors, shapes, and content of the four photos are as different from one other as possible. You give the selected photo to a "sender"—who is strictly isolated from the "receiver"—and ask him or her to mentally send that photo to the receiver. Note that the use of quoted words here emphasizes that these terms are descriptive only; they do not suggest underlying mechanisms.

The sender now mentally "transmits" the contents of the target photo to the receiver for twenty minutes. During that time, the receiver is relaxing in the ganzfeld state. After the sending period, the receiver—still strictly isolated from the sender—is taken out of the ganzfeld state and shown all four photos, one being the chosen target along with the three non-chosen decoys.

If telepathy does not exist, then the chances of the receiver correctly selecting the actual target in this design is one in four, or 25 percent. If telepathy does exist, and the experiment followed the strict isolation protocols, then the "hit rate" would be higher than 25 percent. Because chance is 25 percent in a single trial, performing this test just once would not provide confidence that telepathy did or did not exist. But what if the same test were independently performed by dozens of laboratories around the world for nearly a half century, and during that time nearly 4,000 such tests were performed? The statistical power provided by that many trials would then provide strong evidence either in favor of, or against, the existence of telepathy.

Meta-Analysis

A meta-analysis is a quantitative statistical method for combining the results of numerous experiments based on similar designs. It provides a way to tell if the effects studied in an experiment are repeatable, and whether those effects are attributable to chance. Meta-analysis is used in virtually all of the experimental sciences today, especially in the psychological, social, and medical domains because effects in those areas tend to be highly variable, so it is not possible to establish repeatability in a single experiment.

From 1974 to 2018, dozens of authors published 117 articles describing the results of their ganzfeld experiments. Meta-analyses of these studies were conducted seven times, spanning different time scales (Honorton, 1985; Bem and Honorton, 1994; Milton and Wiseman, 1999; Storm and Ertel, 2001; Bem, Palmer, and Broughton, 2001; Storm, Tressoldi, and Di Risio, 2010; Storm and Tressoldi, 2020). Each of these seven meta-analyses resulted in independently significant outcomes in favor of telepathy.

This means that repeatable telepathic effects have been observed by dozens of independent investigators around the world for nearly a half-century. Considering all known ganzfeld tests using four targets, some 3,885 tests were reported, resulting in 1,188 hits, for an overall hit rate of 30.6 percent (Storm and Tressoldi, in press version, p. 17 of 28 pp.). Five percent over the chance rate of 25 percent may not seem very impressive, but from a statistical perspective the overall result is associated with odds against chance above ten thousand trillion to one (Storm and Tressoldi, in press version, p. 17 of 28 pp.).

One critique often used to discount this result is that some ganzfeld experiments probably failed, which discouraged the investigators from reporting their study. Such "selective reporting" would indeed bias the overall result to make it seem stronger than it really was. However, critics who have studied the relevant literature in detail have agreed that selective reporting cannot eliminate the overall positive results. In addition, meta-analytical estimates of the number of presumed unreported "failed" experiments that would be required to nullify the known results confirms that that explanation is implausible (Storm and Tressoldi, in press version, p. 8 of 28 pp.).

Other critiques have questioned whether there might be flaws in the experimental design that would allow the receiver to somehow gain information about the target. Over the years, as critics suggested potential loopholes, each potential flaw was systematically eliminated and yet the same results continued to be observed. After nearly fifty years of such critiques, skeptics familiar with these studies admit that they can no longer identify any plausible explanations other than telepathy for these results. Even skeptics who explicitly disavow belief in any sort of telepathic phenomena, but nevertheless conducted this experiment themselves, obtained the same results as found in the meta-analyses (Delgado-Romero and Howard 298, 300).

Conclusion

If the paradigm of reductive materialism does not easily accommodate the challenges presented by the existence of genius, savants, telepathy (and many more examples that could have been mentioned), then what alternative paradigm might we consider? In a nutshell, a viable approach is the philosophical idea of *idealism*, i.e., that consciousness is fundamental. Fleshing out this proposal in detail would take more space than is available for this article, so I will simply point out that most of the physicists who founded quantum theory were idealists, and yet their worldview did not prevent them from developing the most successful physical theory in history. Their achievements demonstrate that science can advance perfectly well, even when based on a very different set of assumptions about the nature of reality.

And unlike materialism, from an idealistic perspective the various anomalies associated with consciousness are far easier to accommodate, because in idealism consciousness is not constrained by physical concepts like space, time, matter, or energy. If consciousness is not limited by such physical laws, then it is plausible that it is also not limited to gaining information only through the ordinary physical senses, nor is it limited to the operations of the brain. This in turn opens the door to understanding a whole host of subjective experiences. Despite the undeniable success of materialism as an ideology for understanding the physical world, the empirical and historical facts are that "anomalous" experiences do happen, even in controlled laboratory experiments. Thus, it is no longer a matter of whether materialism will be supplanted by a more comprehensive worldview, but when.

This essay is based on a speech I gave at the Second International Conference on Science and God, a virtual meeting on April 21, 2021, published in the conference proceedings. Copyright © 2021 Hyo Jeong International Foundation for the Unity of the Sciences (HJIFUS) Press, and republished here with permission of HJIFUS Press.

Works Cited

Bem, D. J., and C. Honorton. "Does Psi Exist? Replicable Evidence for an Anomalous Process of Information Transfer." *Psychological Bulletin*, vol. 115, 1994, pp. 4–18.
Bem, D. J., J. Palmer, and R.S. Broughton. "Updating the Ganzfeld Database: A Victim of Its Own Success?" *Journal of Parapsychology*, vol. 65, 2001, pp. 207–18.
Churchland, P.S. *Neurophilosophy: Toward a Unified Science of the Mind-Brain*. MIT Press, 1986.
Cowan, R., and C. Frith. "Do Calendrical Savants Use Calculation to Answer Date Questions? A Functional Magnetic Resonance Imaging Study." *Philosophical Transactions of the Royal Society B Biological Sciences*, vol. 364, no. 1522, 2009. pp. 1417–24.
Crick, F. *The Astonishing Hypothesis: The Scientific Search for the Soul*. Touchstone, 1994.
Delgado-Romero, E. A., and G.S. Howard. "Finding and Correcting Flawed Research Literatures." *The Humanistic Psychologist*, vol. 33, no. 4, 2005, pp. 293–303. doi.org/10.1207/s15473333thp3304_5, https://pdf4pro.com/fullscreen/finding-and-correcting-flawed-research-literatures-5b1093.html. Accessed 15 May 2021.
Dossey, L. "Fractals and the Mind." *Explore* (NY), vol. 8, no. 4, 2012, pp. 213–17.
Ehrenfest, Paul. "Welche Zuege der Lichtquantenhypothese spielen in der Theorie der Waermestrahlen eine wesentliche Rolle?"*Annalen der Physik*, vol. 341, no. 11, 1911, pp. 91–118, zenodo.org/record/1424215#.YG0fIy1h23V. Accessed 6 Apr. 2021.
Einstein, Albert. "Zur Elektrodynamik bewegter Koerper." *Annalen der Physik*, vol. 17, 1905, pp. 891–921.
Heilman, K.M. "Jews, Creativity and the Genius of Disobedience." *Journal of Religion and Health*, vol. 55, 2016, pp. 341–49.

Honorton, C. "Meta-Analysis of Psi Ganzfeld Research: A Response to Hyman." *Journal of Parapsychology,* vol. 49, 1985, pp. 51–92.

Kelvin, R.H.L. "I. Nineteenth [sic] Century Clouds over the Dynamical Theory of Heat and Light." *Philosophical Magazine,* Series 6, vol. 2, no. 7, 1901, pp. 1–40, doi:10.1080/14786440109462664, zenodo.org/record/1865998#.YG4pVS1h23U. Accessed 7 Apr. 2021.

Kuhn, Thomas S. *The Structure of Scientific Revolutions,* 3rd ed., University of Chicago Press, 1996.

Lingg, A. M., and H. Frank. *Mozart, Genius of Harmony.* Kennikat Press, 1973.

Marsa, Linda. "Extraordinary Minds: The Link between Savantism and Autism." *Spectrum.* 13 Jan. 2016, www.spectrumnews.org/features/deep-dive/extraordinary-minds-the-link-between-savantism-and-autism/. Accessed 6 Apr. 2021.

Milton, J., and R. Wiseman. "Does Psi Exist? Lack of Replication of an Anomalous Process of Information Transfer." *Psychological Bulletin,* vol. 125, 1999, pp. 387–91.

Planck, M. "On the Law of Distribution of Energy in the Normal Spectrum." *Annalen der Physik,* vol. 4, 1901, pp. 553–63.

Radin, Dean I. *The Conscious Universe.* HarperOne, 1997.

———. *Entangled Minds.* Simon & Schuster, 2006.

———. *Real Magic.* Penguin Random House, 2018.

———. *Supernormal.* Random House, 2013.

Schlosshauer, M.A. *Decoherence and the Quantum-to-Classical Transition.* Springer, 2007.

Schwartz, S. "Nonlocality and Exceptional Experiences: A Study of Genius, Religious Epiphany, and the Psychic." *Explore,* vol. 6, 2010, pp. 227–36.

"Srinivasa Aiyangar Ramanujan." *MacTutor,* mathshistory.st-andrews.ac.uk/Biographies/Ramanujan/. Accessed 11 Apr. 2021.

Storm, L., and S. Ertel. "Does Psi Exist? Comments on Milton and Wiseman's (1999) Meta-Analysis of Ganzfeld Research." *Psychological Bulletin,* vol. 127, 2001, pp. 424–33.

Storm, L., and P.E. Tressoldi. "Meta-Analysis of Free-response Studies, 2009–2018: Assessing the Noise Reduction Model Ten Years On." *Journal of the Society for Psychical Research,* vol. 84 no. 4, 2020, pp. 193–219; in press *Journal of the Society for Psychical Research,* 28 pp., psyarxiv.com/3d7at/. Accessed 12 May 2012.

Storm, L., P.E. Tressoldi, and L. Di Risio. "Meta-Analysis of Free-Response Studies, 1992–2008: Assessing the Noise Reduction Model in Parapsychology." *Psychological Bulletin,* vol. 136, no. 4, 2010, pp. 471–85.

Tegmark, M. "Consciousness as a State of Matter." *Chaos, Solitons, and Fractals,* vol. 76, 2015, pp. 238–70.

Treffert, Darold. "Savant Syndrome 2013: Myths and Realities." *SSM Health.* 25 Apr. 2017, www.agnesian.com/blog/savant-syndrome-2013-myths-and-realities. Accessed 6 Apr. 2021.

Treffert, Darold A. *Islands of Genius: The Bountiful Mind of the Autistic, Acquired, and Sudden Savant.* Jessica Kingsley Publishers, 2010.

———, and Daniel D. Christenson. "Inside the Mind of a Savant." *Scientific American,* vol. 293, no. 6, Dec. 2005/June 2006, pp. 108–113.

Tressoldi, P.E., and L. Storm. "Stage 2 Registered Report: Anomalous Perception in a Ganzfeld Condition—A Meta-analysis of More than 40 Years Investigation. 2021 [version 1; peer review: awaiting peer review]." *F1000Research,* 10:234, doi.org/10.12688/f1000research.51746.1. f1000research.com/articles/10-234. Accessed 13 May 2021.

Tressoldi, P. E., L. Storm, and D. Radin. "Extrasensory Perception and Quantum Models of Cognition." *NeuroQuantology,* vol. 8 no. 4, Supplement 1, December 2010, S81–87, www.researchgate.net/publication/215514293_Extrasensory_Perception_and_Quantum_Models_of_Cognition. Accessed 11 Apr. 2021.

Welling, H. "Prime Number Identification in Idiots [sic] Savants: Can They Calculate Them?" *Journal of Autism and Developmental Disorders,* vol. 24, no. 2, 1994, pp. 199–207.

Theoretical Criticism of Psychical Research

Grant R. Shafer

My other essays in this volume, one on ESP and two on NDEs, necessarily raise objections to parapsychological research. Objections are both empirical and theoretical. Empirical objections have been met in my essays on ESP and NDEs. This essay deals with theoretical objections to psi ("parapsychological psychic phenomena or powers" [*Merriam* 942]). The greatest of these is the philosophy of materialism, the idea that "the world is entirely composed of matter…" ("Materialism"). "Physicalism" has to some extent replaced the term "materialism" in philosophy because physics has shown that matter is equivalent to forces and energy ("Materialism"). Physicalism is the idea that "the real world is nothing more than the physical world" ("Physicalism"). Physicalism denies the independent existence of "abstract objects such as possibilities, universals or numbers and … mental events and states…" ("Physicalism"). Physicalism is not only weak in dealing with abstracts, but also with "many everyday objects such as chairs, tables, money, and colours [sic], …" ("Physicalism"). Given the dependence of physics on mathematics, the problem of the existence of numbers for physicalism is obvious. Another question for physicalism is the importance of possibility in quantum mechanics.

In order to discuss things not directly described by physics, physicalists say that things not amenable to description by physics "supervene" on the facts of physics ("Physicalism"). For example, mental properties, such as emotions, presuppose physical properties, such as electrochemical events in the brain. However, to succeed philosophically, supervenience needs to explain in more detail how the mental relates to the physical, which it has not yet done. Consequently supervenience "inherits rather than solves the problems of understanding the various areas" ("Supervenience").

Critics also object that psi contradicts what is known about physics and has no theoretical justification. J. Rhine did not think that ESP could be explained physically, especially because he thought that there was no adherence to the inverse square law, but Roll and Pratt proposed that poltergeist phenomena exhibited a decay function of distance (J. Rhine, "Extrasensory Perception" 169; Roll and Joines).

As an example of physicalist views, James E. Alcock (1981) (qtd. in Irwin and Watt 83) says, "If psi exists, science as we know it cannot." These objections ignore the way in which the theories of relativity and quantum mechanics have suggested unexpected connections in time and space and other revisions of materialism which could permit psi. What is true in Alcock's claim is that scientists will need to reimagine science if psi exists, but science is supposed to be a self-correcting endeavor rather than a permanent and fixed body of knowledge. New information must be integrated within the system.

Reber and Alcock argue that psi cannot exist because it violates "four fundamental principles of science":

1. *Causality*. Reber and Alcock say that no causal mechanism for psi has been proposed, and that claimed results are incoherent. Reber and Alcock ignore multiple physical theories of psi, discussed below, most prominently Hameroff and Penrose's Orchestrated Objective Reduction (Orch-OR) theory, which explains consciousness as a quantum process in the microtubules of living cells (Hameroff and Penrose). Niels Bohr thought that quantum mechanics violated causality (Faye). As to incoherent results, psi doesn't need to operate in exactly the same way in every situation in order to exist. To prove that not all crows are black, all one needs is William James' "one white crow" (James 319), not a complete theory.

2. *Time's arrow* rules out precognition, presumably because it would mean information moving from future to past. It is ironic that Reber and Alcock invoke Richard Feynman on this point because Feynman proposed that the positron is an electron moving backward in time (Feynman 749). Another problem with "time's arrow" is the delayed choice double-slit experiment, discussed later in this essay.

3. *Thermodynamics* likewise disproves precognition because it would need energy to pass from the future to the past. Feynman's theory of the positron again undermines Reber and Alcock. Bohr also thought that quantum mechanics violated the first law of thermodynamics, i.e., conservation of energy (Faye).

4. The *inverse square law* renders telepathy impossible. Against this Pratt and Roll proposed that recurrent spontaneous psychokinesis

(RSPK), better known as poltergeist phenomena, exhibits a decay function dependent on distance (Roll and Joines).

Reber and Alcock assure us that 2 anonymous physicists confirmed their interpretation of quantum mechanics. One was chosen by the authors and the other by the editor of *Skeptical Inquirer*. In court, both sides get a say in choosing the jury. Reber and Alcock's choice of a physicist is hardly objective, nor does *Skeptical Inquirer* impress one as objective about anything paranormal. That the authors' and editor's sample of physicists is not impartial is confirmed by the numerous physicists, such as Schroedinger, Heisenberg, Eugene Wigner (172), and Penrose, all Nobelists, whom quantum mechanics convinced of the necessity of considering consciousness as part of physics.

H. I. Brown writes of the contradiction of classical mechanics by relativity, that classical mechanics for a low velocity situation is not a special case of relativistic physics. "For dynamical problems Newtonian and relativistic dynamics never give the same results...." Newtonian mechanics is used in place of relativity "for a certain range of cases and a permissible margin of error, [because] the difference between the quantitative results supplied by the two theories can be ignored so that we might as well use the simpler equation of classical mechanics" (qtd. in Edge and Morris 308).

Reber and Alcock's error was also anticipated by J.H.M. Whiteman, who said that generally all scientists know that relativity and the quantum mechanics have revolutionized the world. However, most think "in very much the same way as before...." Physicists young and old "use formulas and techniques with hardly any realization of the acute conceptual difficulties raised by them...." They imagine a nineteenth-century cosmos, "grafting the quantum formulas onto a classical foundation," and are untroubled when conflicts arise (731).

Despite philosophical problems, scientists generally presume a physicalist framework for explaining the phenomena with which they deal. That is almost always correct and has greatly improved human life. However, explaining consciousness physically is extremely difficult. Consequently, some phenomena, particularly those studied in parapsychology, and consciousness itself, might not have exclusively physical causes.

Assuming that consciousness is only a brain product, an exclusively physical phenomenon, how would that work? Parnia (*What Happens*) rehearses a number of physicalist theories of consciousness:

    1. It is from specific patterns of activity within networks of brain cell connections; similarly

    2. "Synchronized and rhythmic electrical activity in networks of brain cells leads to conscious awareness and the binding of conscious

experience [how different sensations and thought are experienced as one thing]." Francis Crick and Christof Koch say that such action, "40 Hertz oscillation," makes consciousness (Parnia, *What Happens* 112–13, 117).

3. Neurons and their chemical connections are the fundamental units of information in the brain, and consciousness arises when a critical level of computational complexity is reached in the neural networks (112–13).

Susan Greenfield says that consciousness is from groups of synapses, and the largest group determines consciousness (Parnia, *What Happens* 113–14). Daniel Dennett counterintuitively calls consciousness an illusion and imagines that many networks and global activity create a virtual "captain of the crew," and information becomes conscious if its neurons are mobilized by competing, cooperative, collateral activities (Parnia, *What Happens* 118). Hans Flohr thinks that consciousness depends on NMDA (N-methyl-D-aspartate) receptors, Gerald Edelman and Giulio Tononi that perceptual areas interact with memory, value, and planning areas to cause consciousness (Parnia, *What Happens* 119). Surgeon Bahram Elahi says that consciousness is a subtle form of matter (Parnia, *What Happens* 124–125, *Erasing Death* 173, 176).

The phenomenon of NDE, which may occur when the brain is not working, challenges physicalist theories of consciousness. However, some research suggests that brain activity continues long enough after cardiac arrest to account for NDEs. Chawla et al. report, "In each case [of 7 observed], loss of blood pressure, as monitored by indwelling arterial line, was followed by a decline in BIS/PSI [bispectral index/Patient State Index], which uses EEG to 'reflect the level of consciousness/effect of anesthesia' activity followed by a transient spike in BIS/PSI activity that approached levels normally associated with consciousness." Parnia (*Erasing Death* 170) says that a few seconds before death, there is a passing surge of electrical activity, probably explained by inflow of calcium to neurons, but Myles and Cairo (2004) claimed that such surges might be false readings. Grigg et al. (1987) reported that 20 percent of patients at Loyola University Medical Center had active EEGs up to 7 days after otherwise diagnosed brain death. R.C. Wetzel et al. (1985) reported that organ donors had increased blood pressure and pulse as organs were removed. Borjigin et al. present "evidence [EEGs] of highly organized brain activity and neurophysiologic features consistent with conscious processing at near-death ... after cessation of cerebral blood flow" in rats and conclude that NDEs can be explained physically.

Parnia (qtd. in "Research Claims") asserted that the brain's cerebral cortex, known as the "thinking part," also slows down and flatlines, but the brain cells can still be active hours after the heart stopped. "Performing CPR on someone whose heart has stopped will send around fifty per cent of what blood it needs to the brain, which Dr. Parnia says is enough to kick-start its functions...[Parnia] added: 'If you manage to restart the heart, which is what CPR attempts to do, you'll gradually start to get the brain functioning again. The longer you're doing CPR, those brain cell death pathways are still happening—they're just happening at a slightly slower rate.'" Finally, neurology is very good at correlating brain states with mental states, although, for example, attempts to have computers read functional magnetic resonance imaging (fMRI) to reproduce what people see or imagine have had limited success (Hutson; Turner).

For Parnia, four questions remain. (1) How does brain activity make consciousness? (2) How do spatially distributed brain activities combine into a unitary sense (the "binding problem")? Apparently Crick and Koch's theory has not convinced Parnia. (3) How does the preconscious become conscious? (4) What gives the sense of free will (*What Happens* 120–21)?

Further, Greyson ("Near Death Experiences" 351–52) says: "Correlating a brain state with an experience does not necessarily imply that brain states cause the experience; the brain state may alternatively allow access to or simply reflect the experience...." Persinger, K. Jansen (1997), Jourdan (1994), and Strassman (1997) agree (Greyson, "Near Death Experiences" 352). It could be that mental states cause brain states rather than vice versa, as Nobelist neuroscientist John Eccles thinks (Parnia, *What Happens* 123–24, *Erasing Death* 193).

Van Lommel (7–8) denies that evidence exists for how the brain could make consciousness. He alludes without documentation also to research suggesting that awareness of stimuli precedes neurological processing. Presumably he means work done by Dean Radin ("Electrodermal presentiments") and Dick Bierman, among others. Van Lommel (7–8) also mentions Benjamin Libet's "delay-and-antedating hypothesis, of a delay in cerebral production combined with a subjective antedating of a conscious sensory experience," although Libet says that the "hypothesis does not provide a formally definitive contradiction of monist-identity theory (of the mind-brain relationship), ..." (1), which would make consciousness nothing but a brain process.

Van Lommel elaborates that in response to attempts to simulate consciousness using artificial intelligence, Penrose says that algorithms cannot simulate reasoning, and Simon Berkovitch and Herms Romijn insist that the brain is not capable of the quantity of operations, 1024 per second, needed to support our thoughts (8).

Examples of physical speculations about the operation of psi follow.

This presents a terminological problem. We have already considered some physicalist theories of consciousness. However, some explanations of consciousness in terms of relativity and quantum physics are incompatible with physicalism because they assert that consciousness is as irreducible as physical factors such as space-time, and matter-energy.

Albert Einstein complained that quantum mechanics included "spooky action at a distance" (*Born* 158). Schmeidler theorized that 2 objects widely separated in 3-dimensional space could be very close in 4-dimensional space due to "topological folding," as one can fold a sheet or towel to place any 2 points next to each other (Xiong 308). Bosonic string theory allows 26-dimensional space (Englert et al. 315). Tart, Puthoff, and May proposed 8-dimensional space in 1979. One problem with this is that string theory is unproven and conflicts with inflation, the most convincing model for the Big Bang (Xiong 308; Foster). Also, Xiong (309) says without documentation that the inverse-square law of gravity is increased by an exponent of 1 with each dimension beyond 3, becoming inverse-cube with 4 dimensions, inverse-4th-power with 5 dimensions, etc. This would limit the range of physical communication in higher-dimensional spaces.

Gardner Murphy, Bob Toben, Fred Wolf, and J.L. Friedman proposed "wormholes" as explanations for psi phenomena, but Robert L. Morris objected that although a message could enter a wormhole, it probably could not emerge (Xiong 309).

Kurt Goedel suggested that time turned back on itself like lines of longitude on the globe, which Stephen Hawking elaborated as "imaginary time," and J.R. Gott suggested that colliding universes could create "closed time loops," which parapsychologists used to explain precognition ("Watch Stephen"; Xiong 309–10). To explain precognition H. Adrian C. Dobbs and I.F. Shishkin also borrowed Richard Feynman's view of antimatter as matter moving backward in time, but antimatter is rare in our universe. Shishkin, Martin Ruderfer, and Dobbs appealed to Gerald Feinberg's faster-than-light tachyons to explain ESP, but, again, they have not been shown to exist (Xiong 310, Chari 812, 814; Beichler, "To Be," 45–46, "Search," 42–43). Ruderfer also suggested the neutrino, "a practically massless particle traveling with nearly the speed of light," which has been detected (Chari 811), as a carrier of psi. Feinberg himself proposed that both sound and electromagnetism are "time symmetrical," so that the "retarded wave" goes forward in time, but a symmetrical "promoting wave" goes backward in time. Critics say that the brain is electromagnetically too weak to produce the "promoting wave," and it has not been found (Xiong 310).

The previous theories might be compatible with physicalism. The following are more difficult to integrate. In 1982 Alain Aspect discovered that entangled electron pairs which have been separated affect each other instantaneously regardless of distance. Physicist David Bohm interprets Aspect's discovery to mean that there is no objective reality, but that the universe is a gigantic hologram. A hologram is produced by shining a laser on an object, shining a second laser onto the reflection of the first, and photographing their interference. Although the resulting image is unrecognizable in ordinary light, when lit by a laser, it exhibits a 3-dimensional image of the object. Further, however the image is divided, the fragment contains the whole image. Every part is a complete copy, containing all the information of the whole. Thus everything in a holographic universe would be fundamentally connected to everything else (Xiong 311–12).

Karl Pribram suggests that the brain is a hologram. Pribram found that regardless of what part of a rat's brain he removed, the remainder of the rat's brain could still perform complex tasks which it had learned before the removal. Pribram could not explain this until he learned of holograms. He theorizes that memories are not in single neurons or small groups of neurons, "but in patterns of nerve impulses that crisscross the entire brain in the same way that patterns of laser light crisscross the entire area of a piece of film containing a holographic image" (Xiong 313).

Non-physicalist explanations of consciousness have an intuitive appeal, which should be obvious given their prevalence in religion and folklore. Some say that consciousness is an irreducible thing like mass or gravity. David Chalmers agrees that consciousness is irreducible, but that it is a brain product (Parnia, *What Happens* 123), which seems a contradiction. Chalmers also suggests that consciousness may be as fundamental as space, time, or mass, i.e., "every system might be conscious at some level... [and] wherever information is being processed, there is some consciousness..., [but] we need to connect this fundamental with the other fundamentals...(Lillie)." Penrose and Hameroff say that at the quantum level, in the microtubules where consciousness resides, 2 (actually multiple) possibilities exist for any event at the same time, while at the classical level either 1 or the other must exist (Parnia, *Erasing Death* 191). Coming from the opposite direction, John Eccles argued on the basis of free will that mind is independent from and controls the brain, which mediates between consciousness and the world outside (Parnia, *What Happens* 123–24, *Erasing Death* 193).

Erwin Schroedinger's equation graphed a wave of probabilities for multiple positions of subatomic particles. However, such particles are observed in only 1 of the predicted positions. This led to the "Copenhagen explanation," i.e., that an observer is needed to "collapse" the probabilities into a single actuality. Helmut Schmidt, Richard Mattuck, Douglas

M. Stokes, Dean Radin, and physicist Evan Harris Walker have connected this to parapsychology (Xiong 311). Carl Friedrich von Weizaecker, who explained solar nuclear fusion and planet formation, and John Louis von Neumann, a pioneer of computer science, said that Schroedinger's equation complicates "traditional theories of mind-body dualism" (Chari 813). However, Schroedinger himself suggested in 1952 that each possible outcome actually occurs, causing multiple universes to branch off with each quantum event, resulting in an unimaginable number of universes (Deutsch 310). There is also the theory that quantum events cause multiple minds to branch off (Zeh). The last 2 explanations eliminate consciousness as the cause of the wave's collapse, as does the idea of "decoherence," that it is interaction with the environment rather than with a conscious observer, which causes the wave function to collapse (Ball, "Universe").

The founders of quantum mechanics did not espouse these physicalist explanations. Nineteen thirty-two Nobel laureate in physics Werner Heisenberg (50, 52) said of Schroedinger's equation, "...This looks as if we had introduced an element of subjectivism into the theory, as if we meant to say: what happens depends on our way of observing it or on the fact that we observe it.... Now this is a very strange result, since it seems to indicate that observation plays a decisive role in the event and the reality varies, depending on whether we observe it or not...." Schroedinger (40) himself is bolder, reversing his 1952 suggestion, "And then on the other hand, we say that consciousness is that by which this world first becomes manifest, by which indeed we can quite calmly say, it first becomes present; that the world *consists* [emphasis Schroedinger] of the elements of consciousness...." This should recall George Berkeley, "Their [of unthinking things] esse [to be] is percipi [to be perceived]..." (24). Schroedinger, Weizaecker, and Wigner linked the quantum-mechanical problem of the observer to Indian mysticism (Schroedinger, "The Vedantic Vision," *My View*; Chari 813, "Eugene").

Walker assumes that brain processes depend on quantum indeterminacy, and the brain becomes an REG (random event generator) controlled by the subject's will. However, if an REG is controlled by another entity, it would not be random. Walker adds, "...Since quantum effects are nonlocal in space and time, precognition and long-distance ESP follow (Rush, 'Physical and Quasi-Physical Theories' 289)." Schmidt devised a mathematical model which represents the experimenter as a computer and REG and assumes that psi stems from quantum indeterminacy (Rush, "Physical and Quasi-Physical Theories" 289–90). This suggests PK (psychokinesis). Hameroff and Penrose also see consciousness as a quantum event.

Van Lommel ventures into dangerous territory for a non-physicist:

Quantum physics has completely overturned the existing view of our material, manifest world, the so-called real-space. It tells us that particles ... can be described by a quantum mechanical wave function.... The experiment of Aspect [Aspect et al., "Experimental Test"; Aspect et al., "Experimental Realization." See a simple explanation separate from accompanying technical details in Myrvold, "Bell's Theorem,"], based on Bell's theorem [Bell], has established *non-locality* in quantum mechanics (*non-local interconnectedness*) [emphasis PvL]. Non-locality happens because all events are interrelated and influence each other (Van Lommel 8–9).

Einstein et al. (1935) objected to the interpretation of quantum mechanics in which reality is essentially a question of chance. There are two versions of his dictum that God doesn't play dice, one to Max Born in December 1926 and the other to Paul Epstein "before November 1945" (Baggot, Christie's). Bell formulated Einstein's objection as a theorem. Aspect et al. experimentally disproved Bell's Theorem and consequently Einstein's objection. Douglas Snyder (2002) proposed an experiment to solve the Einstein-Podolsky-Rosen reservation about the completeness of quantum mechanics, but it seems to have been obviated by Aspect et al.

Van Lommel goes in deeper, saying,

"Phase-space is an invisible, non-local, higher-dimensional space consisting of *fields of probability* ..." [emphasis PvL], in which past and "future" are indeterminate. Matter is absent, and "neither measurements nor observations are possible." The act of observation instantly turns probability into actuality. The wave function collapses. Penrose calls this "objective reduction." Observation is impossible without changing the thing observed. "... [O]nly *subjectivity* [emphasis PvL] remains ... " (Van Lommel 9).

Phase space is a combination of classical and quantum mechanics. "In classical mechanics, phase space is the space of all possible states [positions and velocities] of a physical system; ...(Tao)." In quantum mechanics only 1 of the pair, position or velocity, can be known, never both. What were points in classical phase space are wave functions of probability in quantum mechanical phase space (Tao). Van Lommel is correct in that quantum mechanical phase space is a realm of probability rather than certainty.

Steve Volk, who worked on *Erasing Death* (203) with Parnia, reports on the Hameroff-Penrose theory of consciousness, i.e., "orchestrated objective reduction," or Orch-OR. A patient under anesthesia shows mostly ordinary brain operation except for being unconscious. "Neurons keep firing, and even pain signals travel their normal routes ... but the patient feels no pain." Hameroff thinks that the microtubule is decisive in anesthesia and consciousness. Microtubules are important parts of the cell skeleton in all cells with a nucleus. They work in cell division, movement of the cell in its environment, and movement of parts within the cell. Hameroff points out that the paramecium lacks a central nervous system. Brain and nerve cells are absent, "but it swims around, finds food, finds a mate and avoids danger. It seems to make choices, and it definitely seems to process information.... In what part of the paramecium does this crude kind of cognition take place?" (qtd. in Volk 12) Hameroff thought that it was in the paramecium's microtubules (Hameroff, "Quantum" 1877).

Rod Eckenhoff, University of Pennsylvania researcher, found that anesthetics bind to tubulin proteins in tadpoles. If a microtubule-stabilizing drug was given, the anesthetic effects were reversed (Volk 23). Anirban Bandyopadhyay says that "the microtubule was mimicking a semiconductor..." (Volk 28). Jack Tuszynski's work suggests that microtubules conduct electricity and might be "memristors," which would operate like transistors, but different from transistors, they would preserve data (Volk 30–31).

Parnia (*Erasing Death* 192; *What Happens* 122–23) counters that microtubules exist outside the brain, that drugs damage microtubules but do not affect consciousness, and that quantum events in microtubules explain computation but not consciousness itself. However, Liester hypothesized cellular memory in organ transplant recipients, of which microtubules could be the vehicle. (See also Jay for a simpler treatment of the issue.)

Possibly the most decisive evidence of consciousness as an irreducible element in physics is the delayed choice quantum eraser experiment, first performed in 2000 (Kim et al.). It is an elaboration of the double-slit experiment of Thomas Young in 1801, which demonstrated that light behaves as waves. When a sub-atomic particle passes through one slit onto a screen, it forms a single band fading toward the edges. When it passes through two slits simultaneously, it forms an interference pattern of multiple bands (Ball, "Two Slits").

If one places a detector at one slit to determine if the particle traverses it, the interference pattern disappears, even if the detector is placed between the slit and the screen so as to detect the particle or wave *after* it passes through the slit. One would expect the pattern to be determined at the slits. Because the pattern is determined *after* the particle or wave traverses the slit, some physicists think that reversal of time is involved, but others disagree (Ball, "Two Slits").

Where consciousness may operate is when the experimenter destroys the detector reading before looking at it. In that case, the interference pattern reappears. Although one would expect the operation of the detector permanently to eliminate the interference pattern, the pattern reappears if the detector reading is destroyed without the conscious observer looking at it (Ball, "Two Slits"). Some physicists follow Schroedinger, Heisenberg,

Wigner, and Penrose in seeing the consciousness of the observer as decisive here. Others such as Sean Carroll disagree, likewise Lawrence Krauss, who said to Hameroff, "From a physics perspective, everything you said is nonsense (Volk 1)." Physicists sharply disagree on the role of consciousness. Therefore physics cannot presently rule out psi and even seems to require it.

Skeptics rightly may object that research has not unambiguously confirmed expectations of psychic phenomena based in physics. Ken Ring responded to Holden's pessimism about exciting NDE anecdotes and disappointing hospital studies, which fit the common pattern of promising psi research which is not replicated. His personal communication to Holden of 6 Sep. 2006 invokes the Jungian Trickster as governing NDE and quotes Einstein, "God is subtle, but not malicious" (Holden, "Veridical Perception" 210–11).

James E. Kennedy elaborates on the Trickster with an anecdote of tragic coincidence. He cites John Beloff that psi research is a "succession of false dawns and frustrated hopes." In innovative research, almost all early reports claim significance, and researchers believe that it is a breakthrough has occurred. But subsequent research frustrates these hopes, and time has not increased the evidence for psi (Kennedy 2).

Kennedy narrates:

> One noteworthy study was a NIH grant to investigate glioblastoma multiforme, a very rare, highly lethal brain tumor. In the early stages of the study, the primary investigator, Elisabeth Targ [daughter of psychic researcher Russell Targ and the niece of chess champion Bobby Fischer], unexpectedly was diagnosed with the rare cancer she was investigating and died from the condition at age 40 during the study.... The study was completed by the co-experimenter Andrew J. Freinkel, but ... [a]pparently ... was not successful...(2–3).

Kennedy (6) concludes that psi research will be applied to war, and the Trickster will not allow it. One need only remember Project Stargate, the Pentagon's effort to harness ESP (Shafer, "Extrasensory Perception").

Andres Ruzo tells a similar story with a happier ending. In his work as a geologist, he went into the jungles of Peru in search of the legendary "Boiling River," potentially a source of geothermal power. When only he, of his 8-member team, was tormented by bugs despite all his efforts, the local shaman, Maestro Juan Flores, told him that the jungle was protecting itself from the development which Ruzo would bring. Flores invited Ruzo to a ceremony, after which he was free of bugs. They found the Boiling River, but at some cost to his career, Ruzo decided to oppose development until the place could be protected (Ruzo). A good story, but is it true?

A more rigorous account of this kind of thing is provided by Suzanne

Simard, a professor of forest ecology at the University of British Columbia. She reports that plants communicate with each other with volatile organic compounds and root fungi, which form networks between trees resembling the neural networks of our brains. For example, when one plant is injured, it sends a warning to other plants, even of other species ("Trees"). Nothing paranormal is required here, but such unexpected integration of apparently unconscious organisms justifies careful consideration of the paranormal.

Irwin and Watt speculated about a "definitive experiment" and "cumulative evidence" for, and "logical status" of, psi (57–61). Theoretical objections to psi are weak, based on the problematic philosophy of materialism/physicalism. Great physicists claim that consciousness is a necessary part of quantum mechanics, although other physicists disagree. This makes the "logical status" of psi, appropriating Irwin and Watt's language, strong.

Research in the form of meta-analyses of ganzfeld (Radin, "Revising") coheres with the mass of anecdote to approximate Irwin and Watt's "definitive experiment" and "cumulative evidence" respectively. My tentative conclusion is that psi exists, although it is relatively weak, as is gravity compared with electromagnetism. This is good news for most people, who have always believed in the supernatural in the form of religion, which has given cohesion to society and hope to the individual.

Works Cited

Aspect, A., Dalibard, J., and Roger, G., "Experimental Test of Bell's Inequalities Using Time- Varying Analyzers." *Physical Review Letters*, vol. 49, 1982, pp. 1804–1807, journals.aps.org/prl/pdf/10.1103/PhysRevLett.49.1804. Accessed 16 Feb. 2021.

Aspect, A., Grangier, P., and Roger, G. "Experimental Realization of Einstein-Podolsky-Rosen-Bohm *Gedankenexperiment*: A New violation of Bell's Inequalities," *Physical Review Letters*, 49, 1982, pp. 91–94, journals.aps.org/prl/pdf/10.1103/PhysRevLett.49.91. Accessed 16 Feb. 2021.

Baggott, Jim. "What Einstein Meant by 'God does not play dice.'" *Britannica*. britannica.com/story/what-einstein-meant-by-god-does-not-play-dice. Accessed 20 Aug. 2021.

Ball, Philip. "Two Slits and One Hell of a Quantum Conundrum." *Nature*, vol. 560, no. 165, 7 Aug. 2018, doi: https://doi.org/10.1038/d41586-018-05892-6, www.nature.com/articles/d41586-018-05892-6. Accessed 4 Mar. 2021.

———. "The Universe Is Always Looking." *The Atlantic*. 20 Oct. 2018, theatlantic.com/science/archive/2018/10/beyond-weird-decoherence-quantum-weirdness-schrodingers-cat/573448/. Accessed 7 Sep. 2021.

Beichler, James E. "The Search for Spock! Developing the Theoretical Basis of Psi." *Yggdrasil: The Journal of Paraphysics*, vol. 1, no. 3, Spring 1998, pp. 304–74. academia.edu/8000877/The_Search_for_Spock_Developing_the_ Theoretical_Basis_of_Psi. Accessed 30 Jan. 2021.

———. "To Be or Not to Be! A Paraphysics for the New Millennium." *Journal of Scientific Exploration*, vol. 15, no. 1, 2001, pp. 33–56, citeseerx.ist.psu.edu/viewdoc/download?doi=10.1.1.462.8993&rep=rep1&type=pdf. Accessed 30 Jan. 2021.

Bell, J.S. "On the Einstein-Podolsky-Rosen Paradox." *Physics*, vol. 1, 1964, pp. 195–200, cds.cern.ch/record/111654/files/vol1p195-200_001.pdf. Accessed 16 Feb. 2021.

Berkeley, George. *A Treatise Concerning the Principles of Human Knowledge*. Edited by Kenneth Winkler, Hackett, 1982

Bierman, Dick J. "FMRI-Meditation Study of Presentiment: The Role of 'Coherence' in Retrocausal Processes." Paper presented at the symposium of the Bial Foundation, Porto, Portugal, Mar. 2008, uniamsterdam.nl/D.J.Bierman/PUBS/2010/JoP_74_pp273_299_CIRTS_proof.pdf. Accessed 2 Mar. 2021.

Blackburn, Simon, editor. *The Oxford Dictionary of Philosophy*. Oxford University Press, 1996.

Borjigin, J., U. Lee, and T. Liu, et al. "Surge of Neurophysiological Coherence and Connectivity in the Dying Brain." *Proceedings of the National Academy of Sciences of the United States of America*, 2013, vol. 110, pp. 14432–7.1. pnas.org/content/110/35/14432. Accessed 15 Feb. 2021.

The Born-Einstein Letters: Correspondence between Max and Hedwig Born and Albert Einstein 1916–1955. Commentaries by Max Born, trans. by Irene Born, introduction by Werner Heisenberg, foreword by Bertrand Russell, Macmillan, 1971.

Cardena, Etzel., Steven Jay Lynn, and Stanley Krippner, editors. *Varieties of Anomalous Experience: Examining the Scientific Evidence*. 2nd ed., American Psychological Association, 2014.

Carroll, Sean. "The Notorious Delayed-Choice Quantum Eraser." *Sean Carroll: In Truth, Only Atoms and the Void*, preposterousuniverse.com/blog/2019/09/21/the-notorious-delayed-choice-quantum-eraser/. Accessed 19 Sep. 2021.

Chari, C.T.K. "Some Generalized Theories and Models of Psi: A Critical Evaluation." Wolman et al., pp. 803–22.

Chawla, L. S., S. Akst, C. Junker, B. Jacobs, and M.G. Seneff. "Surges of Electroencephalogram Activity at the Time of Death: A Case Series." *Journal of Palliative Medicine*, vol. 12, no. 12, 2009, pp. 1095–1100, liebertpub.com/doi/10.1089/jpm.2009.0159?url_ver=Z39.88-2003&rfr_id=ori%3Arid%3Acrossref.org&rfr_dat=cr_pub++0pubmed&. Accessed 12 Nov. 2020.

Christie's. "2019, Live Auction 17037, Fine Printed Books & Manuscripts Including Americana," christies.com/lot/lot-6210431/?intObjectID=6210431&lid=1. Accessed 20 Aug. 2021.

Deutsch, David Elieser. *The Beginning of Infinity: Explanations That Transform the World*, Gildan, 2011, archive.org/details/beginningofinfin0000deut. Accessed 30 Jan. 2021.

Edge, Hoyt L., Robert L. Morris. "Psi and Science." Edge et al., pp. 295–324.

Edge, Hoyt L., Robert L. Morris, Joseph L. Rush, and John A. Palmer. *Foundations of Parapsychology: Exploring the Boundaries of Human Capability*. Foreword by Theodore Xenophon Barber, Routledge and Kegan Paul, 1986.

Einstein, Albert, Boris Podolsky, and Nathan Rosen. "Can Quantum-Mechanical Description of Physical Reality Be Considered Complete?" *Physical Review*, vol. 47, 15 May 1935, pp. 777–80, journals.aps.org/pr/pdf/10.1103/PhysRev.47.777. Accessed Sep. 2021.

Englert, F., H. Nicolai, and A.N. Schellekens. "Superstrings from 26 [sic] Dimensions." *Nuclear Physics B*, vol. 274, no. 2, September 1986, pp. 315–348, DOI: 10.1016/0550-3213(86)90288-9, researchgate.net/publication/222438338_Superstrings_from_26_dimensionscds.cern.ch/record/166328/files/198604011.pdf. Accessed 30 Jan. 2021.

"Eugene Paul Wigner." *New World Encyclopedia*, newworldencyclopedia.org/entry/Eugene_P._Wigner. Accessed 19 Sep. 2021.

Faye, Jan. "Copenhagen Interpretation of Quantum Mechanics." Zalta, *Stanford Encyclopedia of Philosophy*, plato.stanford.edu/entries/qm-copenhagen/. Accessed 29 Jan. 2021.

Feynman, R.P. "The Theory of Positrons." *Physical Review*, vol. 76, no. 6, 15 Sep. 1949, pp. 749–759, authors.library.caltech.edu/3520/1/FEYpr49b.pdf. Accessed 29 Jan. 2021.

Foster, Brendan. "Will String Theory Finally Be Put to the Experimental Test?" *Scientific American*, 25 Mar. 2020, scientificamerican.com/article/will-string-theory-finally-be-put-to-the- experimental-test/. Accessed 16 Sep. 2021.

Greyson, Bruce. "Near-Death Experiences." Cardena et al., *Varieties*, pp. 333–67.

Grigg, Madeline, et al. "Electroencephalographic Activity after Brain Death." *Archives of Neurology*, vol. 44, Sep. 1987, pp. 948–54.

Hameroff, Stuart. "Quantum Computation in Brain Microtubules? The Penrose–Hameroff 'Orch OR' Model of Consciousness." Philosophical Transactions of the Royal Society of London A, vol. 356, 1998, pp. 1869–1896, downloaded from rsta.royalsocietypublishing.org/ on March 6, 2015, quantumconsciousness.org/sites/default/files/1998%20Hameroff%20Quantum%20Computation%20in%20Brain%20Microtubules%20The%20Penrose%20Hameroff%20Orch%20OR%20model%20of%20consciousness%20%20Royal%20Society.pdf. Accessed 28 Feb. 2021.

Hameroff, S. R., and R. Penrose. "Consciousness in the Universe: An Updated Review of the 'Orch OR' Theory." R.R. Poznanski, J.A. Tuszynski and T.E. Feinberg, editors. *Biophysics of Consciousness: A Foundational Approach*. World Scientific, 2016, pp. 517–630, galileocommission.org/wp-content/uploads/2019/02/Hameroff-Penrose-2016-Consciousness-In-The-Universe-An-Updated-Review-Of-The-Orch-Or-Theory.pdf. Accessed 29 Jan. 2021.

Heisenberg, Werner. *Physics and Philosophy: The Revolution in Modern Science*, Harper, 1958.

Holden, Janice Miner. "Veridical Perception in Near-Death Experiences." Holden et al., *Handbook* pp. 185–212.

_____, Bruce Greyson, and Debbie James, editors. *The Handbook of Near-Death Experiences: Thirty Years of Investigation*. Praeger/ABC-CLIO, 2009.

Hutson, Matthew. "This 'mind-reading' algorithm can decode the pictures in your head." *Science*, 18 Jan. 2018, sciencemag.org/news/2018/01/mind-reading-algorithm-can-decode-pictures-your-head. Accessed 19 Aug. 2021.

Irwin, Harvey J., and Caroline A. Watt, *An Introduction to Parapsychology*, 5th ed., McFarland, 2007.

James, William. *The Will to Believe*. Longmans, Green, and Co., 1910.

Jansen, K.L.R. "Response to Commentaries on 'The Ketamine model of the Near-Death Experience....'" *Journal of Near-Death Studies*, vol. 16, 1997, pp. 79–95, researchgate.net/publication/227251559_Response_to_Commentaries_on_The_Ketamine_Model_of_the_Near-Death_Experience. Accessed 20 Feb. 2021.

Jay, Kaitlyn. "Organ transplants: a change of heart in more ways than one?" University of Melbourne, 15 Oct. 2016, blogs.unimelb.edu.au/sciencecommunication/2016/10/15/organ-transplants-a-change-ofheart-in more-ways-than-one/. Accessed 28 Feb. 2021.

Jourdan, J.-P. "Near-Death and Transcendental Experiences." *Journal of Near-Death Studies*, vol. 12, 1994, pp. 177–200, digital.library.unt.edu/ark:/67531/metadc799081/m1/. Accessed 21 Feb. 2021.

Kennedy, James E. "Coming to Terms with the Trickster." Paper presented at the Trickster Theory Panel at the 2016 Combined Convention of the Parapsychological Association (59th) and Society for Scientific Exploration (35th) in Boulder, Colorado, 2016, jeksite.org/psi/trickster_panel_paper.pdf. Accessed 16 Feb. 2021.

Kim, Yoon-Ho, R. Yu, S.P. Kulik, Y.H. Shih, and Marlan O. Scully. "A Delayed Choice Quantum Eraser." *Physical Review Letters*, vol. 84, 2000, pp. 1–5, DOI: 10.1103/PhysRevLett.84.1, arxiv.org/abs/quant-ph/9903047, Accessed 14 Aug. 2021.

Libet, Benjamin. "Subjective Antedating of a Sensory Experience and Mind-Brain Theories: Reply to Honderich." *Journal of Theoretical Biology*, vol. 114, no. 4, 21 June 1985, pp. 563–70. doi: 10.1016/s0022-5193(85)80043-6. PMID: 4021506, The Determinism and Freedom Philosophy Website, ucl.ac.uk/~uctytho/Libethimself.html. Accessed 2 Mar. 2021.

Liester, Mitchell B. "Personality Changes Following Heart Transplantation: The Role of Cellular Memory." *Medical Hypotheses*, vol. 135, Feb. 2020, researchgate.net/publication/336987446_Personality_Changes_Following_Heart_Transplantation_The_Role_of_Cellular_Memory. Accessed 28 Feb. 2021.

Lillie, Ben. "The hard problem of consciousness: David Chalmers at TED2014." TED Blog, 19 Mar. 2014, blog.ted.com/the-hard-problem-of-consciousness-david-chalmers-at-ed2014/. Accessed 11 Nov. 2020.

"Materialism." Blackburn, p. 233.

Merriam-Webster's Collegiate Dictionary, 10th ed., Merriam-Webster, Inc., 1996.
Myles, P. S., S. Cairo. "Artifact in the Bispectral Index in a Patient with Severe Ischemic Brain Injury." *Anesthesia and Analgesia*, vol. 98, 2004, pp. 706–07, journals.lww.com/anesthesiaanalgesia/Fulltext/2004/03000/Artifact_in_the_Bispectral_Index_in_a_Patient_with.27.aspx. Accessed 15 Feb. 2021.
Myrvold, Wayne, Marco Genovese, and Abner Shimony. "Bell's Theorem," Zalta, *Stanford Encyclopedia of Philosophy*, plato.stanford.edu/entries/bell-theorem/#Bib. Accessed 4 Nov. 2019.
Parnia, Sam. *Erasing Death: The Science That Is Rewriting the Boundaries between Life and Death*. With Josh Young, HarperCollins, 2013.
―――. *What Happens When We Die*. Hay House, 2006.
Persinger, M.A. "Modern Neuroscience and Near-Death Experiences." *Journal of Near-Death Studies*, vol. 7, 1989, pp. 233–39, newdualism.org/nde-papers/Persinger/Persinger-Journal%20of%20Near-Death%20Studies_1989-7-233-239.pdf. Accessed 20 Feb. 2021.
Radin, Dean. "Electrodermal presentiments of future emotions." *Journal of Scientific Exploration*, vol. 18, no. 2, June 2004, pp. 253–273, researchgate.net/publication/279770368_Electrodermal_presentiments_of_future_emotions. Accessed 2 Mar. 2021.
―――. "Revising Our Concepts about Reality: The Challenge of Consciousness." In Shafer, *Probing Parapsychology*. McFarland.
Reber, Arthur S., and James E. Alcock. "Why Parapsychological Claims Cannot Be True." *Skeptical Inquirer*. Vol. 43 no.4, Jul./Aug. 2019, skepticalinquirer.org/ 2019/07/why-parapsychological-claims-cannot-be-true/. Accessed 29 Jan. 2021.
Rejdak, Zdenek, editor. *Telepatie a Jasnovidnost*. Prague: Svoboda, 1970, antikvariat-delta.cz/Telepatie-a-jasnovidnost-d1462.htm. Accessed 30 Jan. 2021.
"Research Claims Brain Still Functions after Death so You'll Be Aware of Everything." *NZ Herald*, 25 Nov. 2018, nzherald.co.nz/lifestyle/news/article.cfm?c_id=6&objectid=12165852. Accessed 15 Feb. 2021.
Rhine, Joseph Banks. "Extrasensory Perception." Wolman et al., pp. 163–74.
Roll, William, and William T. Joines. "RSPK and Consciousness." *Journal of Parapsychology*, vol. 77, no. 2, 2013, pp. 192–211, search-proquest-com.ezproxy.emich.edu/docview/1537381275/fulltext/3C909BC7129D42D9PQ/1?accountid=10650. Accessed 30 Jan. 2021.
Rush, Joseph H. "Physical and Quasi-Physical Theories of Psi." Edge et al., pp. 276–92.
Ruzo, Andres. "Boiling River." "Shangri La." *Snap Judgment*, #712, wnyc.org/story/boilingriver-snap-712-shangri-la/. Accessed 3 March 2021.
Schroedinger, Erwin. *My View of the World*. Cambridge University Press, 1964.
Shafer, Grant R. "Extrasensory Perception: Telepathy, Clairvoyance, Precognition, and Retrocognition." In Shafer, *Probing Parapsychology*.
―――, editor. *Probing Parapsychology: Essays on a Controversial Science*. McFarland.
Shishkin, I.F. "O fyzikalni podstate telepatie." Rejdak, pp. 71–78.
Snyder, Douglas M. "On the Quantum Mechanical Wave Function as a Link Between [sic] Cognition and the Physical World: A Role for Psychology," *The Journal of Mind and Behavior*, Vol. 16, No. 2, Spring 1995, pp. 151–79, cds.cern.ch/record/569426/files/ext-2002-058.pdf. Accessed 8 Sep. 2021.
Strassman, R. "Endogenous Ketamine–like Compounds and the NDE: If So, So What?" *Journal of Near-Death Studies*, vol. 16, 1997, pp. 27–41, researchgate.net/publication/251220135_Endogenous_Ketamine-Like_Compounds_and_the_NDE_If_So_So_What. Accessed 20 Feb. 2021.
"Supervenience." Blackburn, p. 368.
Tao, Terence. "Phase Space." Department of Mathematics, UCLA, math.ucla.edu/~tao/preprints/phase_space.pdf. Accessed 9 Aug. 2021.
"Trees Talk To Each Other. 'Mother Tree' Ecologist Hears Lessons For People, Too [sic]." *Fresh Air*. NPR, 4 May 2021, npr.org/programs/fresh-air/2021/05/04/993507176/fresh-air-for-may-4-2021-mother-tree-ecologist-suzanne-simard. Accessed 15 Sep. 2021.
Turner, Karen. "This new device can visualize your thoughts (sort of)." *Washington Post*, 29 June 2016, washingtonpost.com/news/innovations/wp/2016/06/29/this-new-device-can-visualize-your-thoughts-sort-of/. Accessed 19 Aug. 2021.

Van Lommel, Pim. "About the Continuity of Our Consciousness." *Advances in Experimental Medicine and Biology*, vol. 550, 2004, pp. 115–32, pimvanlommel.nl/wp-content/uploads/2017/11/About-the-Continuity-of-ourconsciousness.pdf. Accessed 16 Feb. 2021.

Volk, Steve. "Can Quantum Physics Explain Consciousness? One Scientist Thinks It Might." *Discover*, 1 Mar. 2018, discovermagazine.com/the-sciences/can- quantum-physics-explain-consciousness-one-scientist-thinks-it-might. Accessed 28 Feb. 2021.

"Watch Stephen Hawking Casually Explain What Existed Before The [sic] Big Bang." *Science Alert*, 5 Mar. 2018, sciencealert.com/stephen-hawking-explains-what-was-around-before-the-big-bang. Accessed 30 Jan. 2021.

Wetzel et al. R.C. "Hemodynamic Responses in Brain Dead Organ Donor Patients." *Anesthesia and Analgesia*, vol. 64, 1985, pp. 125–28, journals.lww.com/anesthesia-analgesia/Abstract/1985/02000/Hemodynamic_Responses_in_Brain_Dead_Organ_Donor.5.aspx. Accessed 15 Feb. 2021.

Whiteman, J.H.M. "Parapsychology and Physics," Wolman et al., pp. 730–56.

Wigner, Eugene P. "Remarks on the Mind-Body Question." *Symmetries and Reflections*. Indiana University Press, 1967, pp. 171–84, archive.org/stream/symmetriesreflec0000wign#page/n11/mode/2up. Accessed 30 Jan. 2021.

Wolman, Benjamin B., Laura A. Dale, Gertrude Raffel Schmeidler, and Montague Ullman, editors. *Handbook of Parapsychology*. Van Nostrand Reinhold, 1977.

Xiong, Jesse Hong. *The Outline of Parapsychology*, rev. ed., University Press of America, 2010.

Zalta, Edward M., editor. *Stanford Encyclopedia of Philosophy*, rev. 2019, plato.stanford.edu. Accessed 8 Sep. 2021.

Zeh, H. Dieter. "On the Interpretation of Measurement in Quantum Theory." *Foundations of Physics*, vol. 1, no. 1, Mar. 1970, pp. 69–76, rzuser.unihd.de/~as3/FP70.pdf. Accessed 30 Jan. 2021.

Conclusion

Jay Harold Ellens

This volume is articulate, comprehensive, and readable. Quite obviously you have noticed that by now. A great word of thanks goes to each of the professionally skilled authors. They have taken us through all the sources, freshets, streams, and rivers of the parapsychological quest. The flood plain of the human mind and spirit is mapped out in most of its contours by our book. Fields of fascinating new experience and vision have been laid out for us scientifically. A couple of decades ago this territory was known to most of us only by rumor and speculation.

Now we have the evidence, cartography, and picture of this important psychospiritual space. The ground for skepticism regarding this field of research is shrinking rapidly. Science is gaining on the skeptics and reductionists who would explain away all this important human experience as myth, hallucination, or mental illness. By means of careful testing, analysis, and debate, our scientific understanding of our universe is continually evolving. Critical thinking is required at every step if we are to maximize the responsible science of parapsychology and minimize false and unwarranted conclusions.

We must be both cautious and circumspect, on the one hand, and on the other hand, open to the world of previously suspect but now clearly genuinely certified experience in this field. Curt Ducasse (2) observes and cautions that there is as much prejudice, naïveté, and intellectual dishonesty in the criticism of the skeptics of parapsychology as there can sometimes be on the part of those who research and promote this field.

Humans took parapsychological experiences seriously prior to the Industrial Revolution. They considered them a natural part of life and lived in terms of the insights they gave them, and the psychospiritual illumination they gained from those experiences. Since the dominance of empirical science in Western culture, starting in the early eighteenth century, the entire world of paranormal experiences has been viewed with suspicion. That suspicion excluded from serious scientific inquiry at least half of the world of human reality. The world of the positivists who developed a seemingly unlimited, exciting, and productive empirical system of research, gave that new revolutionary science an authoritative reputation. From it developed what came to be called the modern world.

Starting in the late 1950s some pushback to that rich scientific system began to raise its head, questioning to what extent empirical science could be trusted to handle the full range of human knowledge and concern. The twentieth century proved, with its two world wars and its uses of atomic science, to have used its scientific prowess to create the most violent century in history. This called into question the purpose and warrant of empirical science, and its roughshod deprecation of proper ethical claims.

That led many to feel that empirical science, for all its superior achievements in medicine and productive industry, was deficient on two fronts. It produced overwhelming destructive potentials for humankind, and it virtually neglected the entire world of human psychospirituality. It was able to tell us all about the material world, but virtually ignored that other half of the human experience. It left almost totally unexplored the world that could not be weighed and measured in the laboratory.

Modern science created good refrigerators and cars but left most of the issues of the human affect and spirit unexplored. It was not open to exploring the truth and reality of the human experience of the world of the ethereal and paranormal. However, those psychospiritual experiences proved to be as real to those to whom they revealed themselves as the empirical fact that water freezes at 32 degrees Fahrenheit at sea level. We might weigh and measure this world of reality and its individual phenomena in the classroom or laboratory only with difficulty, but that does not rule out its existence and demonstrable authenticity. It turns out that the world of psychospiritual facts and experiences can be definitively explored by the scientific method of phenomenological research and heuristic analysis. Parapsychology lies in this postmodern arena. It is now referred to as the world of postmodern science.

There is now an enormous reservoir of data on the reality of parapsychological experiences. These events happen in most human lives. We are beginning to gain ground in the analysis of the data, discerning the similarities and differences of the various human reports of parapsychological experiences. Soon the patterns, categories, and quality of these experiences will be increasingly evident to us scientifically. By means of that phenomenological data it is becoming increasingly possible to formulate more and more hypotheses regarding what the data means. Already, as this volume demonstrates, much progress has been made in this enterprise during the last two decades. When we have had a chance to test these hypotheses thoroughly, we will be able to determine what laws of normal human function are evident in what we have called the paranormal world of human experience.

The skeptics are still living in the world view of two hundred years ago when classical empirical science was assumed to be the only road to truth, ruling out the truths of parapsychology. That discarded over half of the human experience of the wide world of reality. Along with the parapsychological was also the casualty of the sacred and all things transcendent. The fear that if the parapsychological is true, the empirical methodology must be false, was in itself a false assumption. Truth is truth wherever we find it and however we find it.

Phenomenological science with its heuristic conclusions is as equally scientific as is the world of empirical science. In fact, what we discover phenomenologically is in the end also empirical. It produces the evidence and testimony of the reality of the parapsychological experience, as surely as the evidence of the ballistic impact of an artillery shell. It is the quality of the research and the evidence it produces that determines the reality and the truth.

Darwin's scientific handmaiden, Thomas Huxley, is said to have advised that we should handle facts like excited children, without prejudice or preconceived ideas, and excitedly explore where the facts lead us (Letter to Charles Kingsley 23 Sep. 1860). Then we will be open to learn what they mean and what kind of world they will reveal to us.

Works Cited

Ducasse, Curt. *Paranormal Science and Life after Death*. Charles C. Thomas, 1959.
Huxley, Thomas Henry, and Leonard Huxley. *Life and Letters of Thomas Henry Huxley Volume 1*. Project Gutenberg, gutenberg.org/ebooks/5084. Accessed 21 Sep. 2021.

Epilogue

Grant R. Shafer

At the end of our examination of parapsychology, what have we learned? The experiences which are the subject of parapsychology go back to the beginning of our species, to extinct humans such as the Neanderthals, perhaps even to our animal ancestors (Than). Scientific study of psi goes back to Francis Bacon (1561–1626), one of the founders of modern science, although intensive research began in the late nineteenth century, as Darwinism weakened religion.

Throughout the history of parapsychology many thinkers have denied its legitimacy because it might contradict materialism, if parapsychology proves that mind is not a product of matter. Although materialism is a useful working hypothesis in most of science, there are four reasons to question it as a total description of reality.

First, it is demoralizing. The idea that we are the product of unconscious, random physical processes which eventually will totally destroy us as individuals, if not as a species, is difficult for most people to live with, even if it is true.

Second, throughout history people have had lots of experiences which they understand as showing a side of reality not acknowledged by materialism. While these experiences might be entirely explicable within materialism, that is unlikely given materialism's inability to deal with even everyday reality ("Physicalism").

Third, similarly, there is not a cogent materialistic account of consciousness. Although states of mind are usually correlated with brain states, parapsychological data suggests that there are exceptions, and the jump from unconsciousness to consciousness is intuitively as abrupt as that from nothing to something.

Fourth, materialism has been compromised by the physics of the last century. Albert Einstein (1897–1955) demonstrated that matter, energy, time, space, and velocity shape each other, rather than matter and energy moving in a fixed framework of time and space, as Newton theorized. Quantum mechanics in the form of Schroedinger's wave equation presented us with two alternatives: that our universe is one of an inconceivable number; or that the observer causes one of many possible subatomic outcomes to happen. The second is embraced by physicists such as Heisenberg (1901–1976), Schroedinger (1877–1961), Weizaecker (1919–2007), and Wigner (1902–1995), who consider consciousness as a cause as well as an effect of physical processes.

The classic double-slit experiment, first performed by Thomas Young in 1801, presents serious problems for materialism. Even 1 particle apparently passes through both slits yielding an interference pattern, as would a water wave. If 1 slit is blocked, as the particle passes through the other slit, it shows up on the screen as a single band (as if it is an image of the slit; Ball).

If a detector is placed even between 1 slit and the screen, the interference pattern disappears. One would think that whether a single band or an interference pattern would appear was determined at the slits, but after the particle traverses the slits, the interference pattern can be replaced with a single band by placing a detecting device. Further, if the detector reading is destroyed before an observer sees it, the interference pattern returns. Weizaecker and Wigner thought that it was the "act of noticing," not the "physical act of measurement" which determined the result (Ball).

Although there is no irrefutable theoretical objection to psi as a real force in the world, experimental verification has been ambiguous. The history of parapsychology is characterized by impressive experimental results which are not replicated. The skeptical explanation is obvious. The initial studies were flawed by inadequate method or even fraud. I cannot exclude this possibility. A second explanation is related to the sheep-goat effect observed by Schmeidler, i.e., the belief of the former experimenter enabled psi, while the unbelief of the latter inhibited it. Even if this effect exists, as an explanation it can justify charlatans when their deceptions fail. A third explanation comes from Ring, who went further by saying that psi may be manipulated by something like the Jungian Trickster, which enables early success and causes later failure (Holden 210–11).

God, or the Devil, is in the details. What do the details of our book indicate? Stanley Krippner and Everton Maraldi cite Cardena's meta-analysis of psi research, Dean Radin cites a multitude of meta-analyses of ganzfeld, the former two researchers call for more research, and the latter two conclude that parapsychology has already produced convincing evidence that psi exists. V.G. Miller's history includes that of fraud and concludes that further research is needed. My own essay on ESP makes me think that it does exist, but that psi is a weak force in nature. Dr. Miller also presents persuasive cases of PK, although there is evidence of a physical process. James Matlock's treatment of reincarnation also suggests that it is real. Steve Pullum, Carole Van Camp, and Wendy Donlin argue against the veracity of mediums, but some of them are difficult to explain, such as Daniel Home. Ralph Hood shares some of his own work on snake handling as a near-death experience, but argues for the reality of the transcendent on philosophical rather than empirical grounds.

My own reading of research on near-death experiences suggests that consciousness may not be a brain process and may survive death. The most reasonable conclusion from the evidence in this book is that psi is analogous to the weak and strong nuclear forces and gravity, much weaker than electromagnetism, but real nonetheless, and that consciousness is an irreducible factor in nature like mass, energy, time, and space. Even if psi is relatively weak, we should perhaps consider whether this is a case in which "God has chosen the foolish things of the world to shame the wise, and God has chosen the weak things of the world to shame the strong, and God has chosen the low-born of the world and things of no account and things which do not exist to destroy the things which do exist..." (1 Cor. 1:27–28).

Works Cited

Bacon, Francis. *Sylva Sylvarum: A Natural History in Ten Centuries*, William Lee, 1658, pars. 939–97, pp. 205–18, archive.org/stream/sylvasylvarumo00baco?ref=ol#page/210/mode/2up. Accessed 10 September 2021.

Ball, Philip. "Two slits and one hell of a quantum conundrum." *Nature*, 7 Aug. 2018, nature.com/articles/d41586-018-05892-6. Accessed 4 Mar. 2021.

Blackburn, Simon, editor. *The Oxford Dictionary of Philosophy*. Oxford University Press, 1996.

Cardena, Etzel "The experimental evidence for parapsychological phenomena: A Review." *American Psychologist*, vol. 73, no. 5, July 2018, pp. 663–677, DOI: 10.1037/amp0000236. Accessed 4 Mar. 2021.

Holden, Janice Miner. "Veridical Perception in Near-Death Experiences." Janice Miner Holden, Bruce Greyson, and Debbie James, editors. *The Handbook of Near-Death Experiences: Thirty Years of Investigation*. Praeger/ABC-CLIO, 2009, pp. 185–212.

Schmeidler, Gertrude Raffel. "Separating the Sheep from the Goats." *Journal of the American Society for Psychical Research*, vol. 39, 1945, pp. 47–49.

Than, Ker. "Neanderthal Burials Confirmed as Ancient Ritual." *National Geographic*, 16 Dec. 2013, nationalgeographic.com/news/2013/12/131216-la-chapelle-neanderthal-burials-graves/. Accessed 16 Feb. 2021.

About the Contributors

Wendy **Donlin Washington** is an associate professor in the Psychology Department at the University of North Carolina, Wilmington. She holds a doctorate in experimental psychology from Auburn University. She has published research in behavior analysis, and teaches courses in behavior analysis, research methods, and science and pseudoscience.

Jay Harold **Ellens** (1932–2018) was an Army chaplain, retiring as colonel, and a civilian pastor. He received Ph.Ds. from Wayne State University and the University of Michigan. He wrote nearly two hundred books, most connecting spirituality with health. He was the founding editor of the *Journal of Psychology and Christianity*, the director of the Christian Association of Psychological Studies, and a professor at the Ecumenical Theological Seminary of Detroit.

Ralph W. **Hood, Jr.**, is a professor of psychology, the A. Martin Distinguished Professor of religious studies, and an Alumni Association Distinguished Professor at the University of Tennessee at Chattanooga. He is a coeditor of *Research in the Social Scientific Study of Religion* and the editor-in-chief of *Psychology and Religion*. He has been the president of Division 36 of the American Psychological Association and recipient of its William James award.

Stanley **Krippner**, Ph.D., is an affiliated distinguished professor of the California Institute of Integral Studies. He has received lifetime achievement awards from the Parapsychological Association, the International Association for the Study of Dreams, and the Society for Humanistic Psychology. He is a Fellow of the American Psychological Association, which granted him its 2002 Award for Distinguished Contributions to the International Development of Psychology.

Everton **Maraldi** is a professor of the post-graduate program in religious studies at the Pontifical Catholic University of São Paulo, Brazil. He has master's and doctorate degrees in social psychology from the Institute of Psychology of the University of São Paulo, Brazil. He is a member of the board of directors for the Parapsychological Association, and was a postdoctoral research fellow at Coventry University and the University of Oxford. His research interests are religious experiences, altered states of consciousness, dissociation, spirituality and health.

James G. **Matlock** is a Research Fellow with the Parapsychology Foundation, Inc. He holds a Ph.D. in anthropology but has devoted his career to parapsychology. He has contributed numerous articles to the Society for Psychical Research's online *Psi Encyclopedia*. He is coauthor, with Erlendur Haraldsson, of *I Saw a Light and Came Here: Children's Experiences of Reincarnation* (2016), and author of *Signs of Reincarnation: Exploring Beliefs, Cases, and Theory* (2019).

V.G. **Miller** is a research fellow with the Centre for Public and Contextual Theology, Charles Sturt University, Canberra. She received her doctorate at Murdoch University in the area of Old Testament studies. She is the author of *Grace: Free, Costly or Cheap?* (2012) and *A King and a Fool? The Succession Narrative as a Satire* (2019). She was the Crawford Miller visiting scholar at St. Cross College, Oxford, in 2019.

Stephen J. **Pullum** has taught since 1988 at the University of North Carolina, Wilmington, was the associate dean of the College of Arts and Sciences, and is a professor of communication studies. He received his MA in communication from the University of Tennessee and Ph.D. in communication from Indiana University. He wrote *"Foul Demons, Come Out!" The Rhetoric of Twentieth-Century American Faith Healing* (1999) and *Faith Healers and the Bible: What Scripture Really Says* (2015).

Dean **Radin** is a chief scientist at the Institute of Noetic Science and an associated distinguished professor at the California Institute of Integral Studies. He has a Ph.D. in psychology from the University of Illinois. He has worked at Bell Labs, Princeton University, University of Edinburgh, and SRI International. He has given over 600 talks and authored over 300 articles, 48 book chapters, and 6 books translated into 15 languages, including *The Conscious Universe*, *Entangled Minds*, *Supernormal*, and *Real Magic*.

Grant R. **Shafer** was educated at Wayne State University, Harvard University, and the University of Michigan, where he received a Ph.D. in near Eastern studies. He has taught at the University of Michigan, Siena Heights University, Eastern Michigan University, Washtenaw Community College, and Henry Ford College. He has published on Roman history, Islam, Buddhism, and early Christianity.

Carole M. **Van Camp** is an associate professor in the psychology department at the University of North Carolina, Wilmington. She holds a doctorate in school psychology from Louisiana State University. She has published research in applied behavior analysis, and teaches courses in behavior analysis, research methods, and science and pseudoscience.

Index

Aberfan, Wales 51–52
ad hoc 12, 113
afterlife 3, 4, 11, 12, 21–23, 30–32, 34, 35, 40, 78–205; *see also* survival
Aksakof, Alexander N. 63
Alcock, James E. 13, 201–202, 216, 217
Alexander, Eben 148, 176
alien abduction 173; *see also* extraterrestrial
American Civil War 40
American Society for Psychical Research 26, 101, 104, 119, 149
Ammon de Marteville, Countess Maria Louise 48
anecdotes 8, 18, 59, 174, 179, 185, 192, 201, 202, 210, 225, 226; *see also* experiment; spontaneous cases
anesthetics 20, 171, 172, 178, 186–89, 218, 223, 224
animals 19, 20, 45, 98, 134, 144, 160, 166, 198, 218, 221, 234
anomalous 7, 8, 9, 11, 13, 79, 206, 213
Apollonius of Tyana 46, 48, 49, 81
Appalachia 141, 146, 150, 151
apparently nonphysical veridical NDE perception (AVP) 166, 174, 186, 191, 200, 201
apparitions 11, 24, 42, 82, 171; *see also* ghosts; hauntings
apportation 64, 98, 120; *see also* materializations; physical mediumship
Aristotle 128, 143, 146–48, 156–57
Army Security Agency 29, 46, 50, 90, 107, 207
The Art of Dying 165
Aspect, Alain 220, 221, 223; *see also* quantum entanglement
astral projection 18, 92, 165; *see also* out-of-body experiences (OBEs)
astrology 20, 50
audio stimuli 199, 200; *see also* AWARE II
August Wilhelm, Prince of Prussia 48

Augustine, Keith 87, 89, 186
auras 24, 45
authentication 40, 42, 43, 44, 53, 54, 55, 58, 59, 232
autism 209
automated external defibrillator (AED) 196, 200; *see also* resuscitation
automatic writing 24, 99
autoscopy 31, 169, 170, 177, 197; *see also* out-of-body-experience
AWARE 196–98, 200
AWARE II 198–200

Bacon, Francis 39, 47, 48, 51, 54, 234
Balfour, Arthur 22
Bansal, Himanshu 160
Barnum, P.T. 131
Barrett, William 40
Beauregard, Mario 177, 178, 198
being of light 161–63, 181, 186; *see also* God
Beischel, Julie 109–13
Bell, John 223
Beloff, John 26, 32, 225
Bender, Hans 70
Bergquist, Lars 48
Berkeley, George 222
bias 7–9, 39, 44, 46, 49, 50, 55, 58, 74, 110, 112, 114, 166, 174, 212
Bible 18–19, 34, 46, 54, 119, 133–37, 151, 155–56
birth 82, 88–90, 107, 145, 168, 175, 179
birthmark 31, 79, 80, 81, 83, 91
Blackmore, Susan 168, 186, 194
Blake, William 33
blind people 46, 102, 144, 154, 167, 173, 176–177, 187, 209
blinding in research 29, 44, 110, 113; *see also* masked designs
Bohr, Niels 202, 216
bone conduction 189
bone saw, Midas Rex 186, 188–91

239

book tests 108
brain 142, 143, 146–148, 168, 169, 171, 174, 178, 179, 186, 187, 189, 191, 196–99, 201, 206, 208, 209, 213, 217–26, 236; death 142, 143, 146–48, 160, 197, 218; hemispheres 45, 169
brain waves 47, 57, 143, 185, 186, 189; see also electroencephalogram/ph (EEG)
brainstem 142, 186, 187, 189, 190, 194, 198; auditory evoked potentials/responses (BAEP/R) 186, 187, 189–91
Braud, William G. 45, 46
Braude, Stephen 91
"Bridey Murphy" (Virginia Tighe) 31
Brodsky, Beverly 162
Browne, Sylvia 120–21, 125, 127, 132
Browning, Robert Barrett 22
Buddhism 84, 89, 162–63, 165, 238; see also Eastern religions; India; Tibet
burial 141–43, 164, 165
Burma 89, 90
burst suppression 189
Bush, Nancy E. 161, 162

Caputo, Teresa 115, 122–23, 127, 132
Cardena, Etzel 12–14, 235
cardiac arrest (CA) 142–148, 159–60, 166, 168, 171, 172, 177, 186, 189, 191–201, 218
cardiopulmonary resuscitation (CPR) 177, 191, 192, 196–99, 219; see also resuscitation
cards 18, 24, 26, 28, 35, 39, 40–44, 47, 55–56
Carroll, Sean 225
Catherine de Medicis, Queen of France 50
Catholic 121, 122
causality 4, 216
cave, allegory of the 144–47
cave paintings 19
Cayce, Edgar 53
Central Intelligence Agency (CIA) 27, 49
cerebral cortex 160, 168, 186, 194, 196, 198, 218
cerebral palsy 195, 209
Chalmers, David 221
Chandra, Jagdish 84–85
Chari, C.T.K. 86, 91
Charles, Duke of Burgundy 48
children 11, 27, 31, 40, 66, 68, 70, 78–91, 102, 107, 123, 163, 167, 168, 177, 198, 233, 238
China 20–21, 27–28, 50, 67–68, 81, 163, 165
Chopin, Frederic 33
clairvoyance 4, 10, 11, 17, 23, 35, 38, 39, 41, 44, 48, 49, 56, 99, 187, 210
clinical death 18, 31, 152, 191, 198

coins 74
cold reading 109, 110, 112, 130, 131; see also hot reading; warm reading
coma 165, 172, 173, 177, 192, 194
computers 43–45, 49, 52, 199, 219, 222
Conan Doyle, Arthur 23
confirmation bias 55, 112–14
consciousness 11, 14, 32, 33, 34, 35, 43, 58, 74 , 78, 79, 92, 140–43, 146, 147, 171, 172, 174, 177–79, 187, 189–91, 193–202, 206–25, 234, 235, 236
conservation of energy 216
control in experiment 8, 12, 33 40, 41, 76, 109, 114, 125, 162, 166, 167, 174, 177, 191, 192, 210, 213
control in seance 99, 102–7
Cook, Emily Williams 178
Coover, John 40–41
Copperfield, David 64
correlation and causation 219
Crick, Francis 218, 219
criticism 11–14, 53–58, 65, 67, 75, 79, 82–87, 100, 109, 111–15, 125–36, 147, 190–91, 202, 210, 212, 216, 225, 231, 232, 235; see also skeptic
Croesus 9
Crookes, William 22, 64
cross correspondences 106
cryptomnesia 30
culture 86, 87, 89, 90, 162, 163, 164, 166, 167, 201, 210, 225
Curran, Pearl 25, 33, 25

Dalton, John 4
Daniel 50
Darwin, Charles 4, 233, 234
Davenport, William and Ira 99–100
death-bed visions 159, 167, 191, 199
decay function 69, 217
decline effects 44, 46, 55, 73–74
decoherence 208, 222
Delacour, Jean-Baptiste 160, 172–73
delayed choice double-slit/quantum eraser experiment 216, 224; see also positron; time symmetry
Delphic oracle 9
dementia 199
Democritus of Abdera 4
Dennett Daniel 218
denture 192, 198
depersonalization 167, 170
Descartes, Rene 171
dice 18, 28, 73, 223
Dieppe raid 53; see also world wars
dimensions 145, 220, 221, 223
dissociation 12, 55, 99, 167
distress 7, 8, 24

Index 241

divining 29–30, 38, 45
Dixon, Jeane L. Pinkert 51, 58
Dodds, Eric R. 108, 109
Domitian 46, 48
Dossey, Larry 177
double-slit experiment 216, 224, 235
dreams 7, 18, 28, 33, 40, 42, 45, 47, 52, 57, 79, 80, 147, 170
Druze 81–82, 84, 89
dualism 11, 222
Du Monchaux, Pierre-Jean 165

Eastern religions 4; *see also* Buddhism; Hinduism; India; Tibet
Ecclesiastes 134
ectoplasm 119–120; *see also* materialization; physical mediumship
Edward, John 58, 115, 120, 122–24, 126, 127, 129, 130
Edwards, Paul 79, 83–88, 90
Einstein, Albert 149, 166, 207, 208, 220, 223, 225, 234
electrocardiogram (ECG) 198
electroencephalogram/graph (EEG) 28, 47, 59, 143, 160, 174, 177, 186, 189, 190, 194, 196–98, 218; *see also* brain waves
electromagnetism 30, 34, 47, 59, 75, 220, 226, 236; *see also* magnetism
Elisha 19, 46
Ellens, Dan vi
Ellens, Grace Kortman v
Ellens, Jay Harold v, vi, 3, 5, 237
empirical 8, 13, 17, 33, 53, 59, 144, 145–47, 149, 151, 210, 213, 215, 231–33, 236; *see also* experiment
enhanced mentation 178; *see also* hyperalertness; lucidity
environment 3, 47, 224
Epicurus 4
Er 143, 165–66
ether, luminiferous 207
ethos 128, 137
experiment 4, 8, 11–14, 18, 24–27, 35, 38–45, 47–49, 51, 53, 55–59, 64–67, 72–76, 100, 109, 114, 125, 141, 166, 178, 208, 210–13, 218, 222–25, 232, 233, 235; *see also* empirical
experimenter psi 39, 44, 45, 222
exsanguination 186
extrasensory perception (ESP) 3, 10, 11, 17, 26–28, 38–62, 91, 119, 174, 187, 192, 202, 215, 216, 220, 222, 225, 235; *see also* clairvoyance; telepathy
extra-terrestrial 65; *see also* alien abduction
extremely low frequency (ELF) radiation 47

failure 50, 51, 54, 57, 58, 108, 109, 112, 114, 125, 126, 156, 178, 185, 188, 200–2, 212, 236
falsifiability 13, 14, 54, 67, 179, 201, 114
fear 136, 145, 149, 153–55, 159, 161, 167, 191, 192, 197, 233
fear-death experiences 159, 170, 191
Feynman, Richard 216, 220
Fischer, Oskar v, 26, 38, 51
flapping arms 179, 193; *see also* Louis; Sullivan, Al
Flatliners 166
forced choice 43, 44; *see also* free-response
Ford, Arthur 131, 173; *see also* Pike, James
Forer Effect 131
Fox, Katie 21, 39–40, 96–100, 119
Fox, Leah 21, 39–40, 96–100, 119
Fox, Maggie 21, 39–40, 96–100, 119
Franklin, Benjamin 20
fraud 10, 13, 21, 22, 25, 26, 30, 34, 43, 44, 45, 51, 53, 56–59, 63, 65–69, 71–72, 75, 79, 84, 97–100, 109, 135, 177, 201, 235
free-response 28, 43, 44; *see also* forced choice
free will 219, 221
Freud, Sigmund 20, 25
Fukurai, Tomokichi 71-72

Gallup, George 119, 163, 164, 175
ganzfeld 28, 45, 57–59, 210–12, 226, 235; *see also* telepathy
Geller, Uri 18, 58, 64–65, 76
gender 28, 87, 89, 98, 110, 111, 152, 163, 168, 191
general ESP (GESP) 39, 41
genius 208–10, 212
ghosts 4, 24, 39, 42, 58, 119, 135–36, 167; *see also* apparitions; hauntings
Gnosticism 121, 161
God vi, 34, 84, 120–22, 127, 133–36, 151, 153–55, 161–63, 223, 225, 235, 236; *see also* being of light
Goedel, Kurt 220
gospel 50, 135, 151
Gospel of Thomas 3
gravity 59, 173, 220, 221, 226, 236
Greeley, Horace 97
Greyson, Bruce 145–147, 152, 161–63, 166–69, 171, 192–95, 200, 219
Gurney, Edmund 18, 22, 24, 40, 43, 52, 106

hallucination 18, 24, 31, 40, 42, 75, 76, 147, 157, 164, 167–71, 193, 195, 196 , 231
Hameroff, Stuart 187, 189, 216, 221–25
Hansel, Charles Edward Mark 48, 49, 56, 57–59

242 Index

Hanussen, Eric Jan 51
Haraldsson, Erlundur 55, 88, 169, 171, 174–75, 238
haruspicy 19, 50
hauntings 11, 68, 119; *see also* apparitions; ghosts
Hawking, Stephen 220
healing 29, 34, 35, 58, 92, 102, 123, 132, 173–74, 195, 200; *see also* medical science
Hebrew Bible 133–35; *see also* Old Testament
Heim, Albert von St. Gallen 149, 150, 154, 157, 165
Heisenberg, Werner 217, 222, 224, 235
Henry, Tyler 115, 132, 133
Henry II, King of France 50
Herodotus 9
Hinduism 84, 107, 163; *see also* Eastern religions; India
history 1, 3, 4, 9, 17–43, 50, 96, 110, 119, 143, 159, 162, 164–67, 179, 185, 207, 208, 210, 213, 232, 234, 235
Hitler, Adolf 51
Hodgson, Richard 22, 101, 103–6
Holden, Janice Miner 159, 160, 162, 163, 167, 174, 177, 186, 189, 190, 192, 193, 200, 201, 225
hologram 221
Holt, Henry 63
Holy Alliance 48
Home, Daniel Dunglas 21–22, 64, 99, 120, 236
Homer 81
Honorton, Charles 28, 43, 45, 46, 57, 58
Hood, Ralph W., Jr. 140, 236, 237
hot reading 126, 130, 131; *see also* cold reading; warm reading
"Hotel California" 186
Houdini, Harry 58, 100
Hume, David 53, 59, 114
Hyman, Raymond 57
hyperalertness 32, 171, 178; *see also* enhanced mentation; lucidity
hypnosis 17, 19, 20, 28, 30, 31, 34, 40, 45, 47, 76, 79, 167, 171, 172; *see also* mesmerism
hypothermic cardiac arrest 185, 189, 200; *see also* standstill
Hyslop, James 25, 101, 104, 162

idealism 143, 144, 212, 222
imaginary time 220
India 80, 83, 86, 88, 89, 107, 162, 163, 174–75, 222; *see also* Eastern religions, Buddhism, Hinduism
International Association for Near-Death Studies 166

intoxication 45, 72, 169
inverse square law 216, 220
Irenaeus 161
Irwin, Harvey J. 5, 13, 45, 46, 53, 58, 167, 168, 226

Jahn, Robert G. 49
Jako, Miklos 125–26
James, William 23, 101–4, 148–50, 156, 216
Japan 71–72, 81, 90
Jayaratne, Sujith Lakma 85
Jesus 3, 50, 53, 54, 163–65
Jung, Carl Gustav 20, 32, 53, 70–71, 114, 164, 168, 225, 235
Jupiter 49

Kant, Immanuel 48
karma 84, 86
Katsugoro 81
Kelvin, William Thomson (1st Baron) 207, 208
Kennedy, J.E. 57, 58, 225
King, Larry 121, 122, 125, 132, 133
King, Stephen 73
Kletti, Roy 160, 167
Krause, Lawrence 225
Krippner, Stanley vi, 3, 7, 27, 28, 43, 47, 57, 235, 237
Kuhn, Thomas S. 206
Kulagina, Nina 66, 67, 70, 75

Lawrence, Madelaine vi, 176, 179, 192, 193, 200, 201
Lazarus 134–35, 142, 165
Lebanon 88, 89
Leonard, Gladys Osborne 106–9, 120
Lepanto 48
Leucippus of Miletus 4
levitation 18, 21, 22, 63, 64, 98, 101, 120; *see also* physical mediumship
Levy, W.J. 56
Libet, Benjamin 52, 219
life review 32, 145, 154, 155, 161, 163
Likert scale 112
Lilly, John C. 144, 160
Lincoln, Abraham 46, 51, 102
living agent psi 105, 109, 111
Lodge, Oliver 22, 107–8
logos 128–137
London Dialectical Society 101
Louis 193; *see also* flapping arms; Sullivan, Al
Louis XI, King of France 48
Louisa Ulrika, Queen of Sweden 48
lucidity 171, 178, 194, 197–201; paradoxical/terminal 199, 200; *see also* enhanced mentation; hyperalertness

magic 19, 39, 57, 63, 65, 91, 100, 125, 238
magnetism 14, 20, 21, 24, 56, 169, 219; *see also* electromagnetism
Maraldi, Everton 235, 237
Martians 50
masked designs 12, 201; *see also* blinding in research
materialism 3, 4, 58, 59, 92, 140, 161, 179, 185, 187, 188, 191, 201, 202, 206–8, 210, 213, 215–17, 225, 232, 234, 235; *see also* physicalism
materialization 10, 63–65, 98, 120; *see also* apportation; ectoplasm; physical mediumship
Matlock, James G. 78, 79, 86, 236–38
May, Edwin C. 49, 220
McCormick, D. 178, 182, 200, 202, 204
McGraw, Philip Calvin 122, 132, 133
McMoneagle, Joseph 50
medical science 20, 31, 34, 66, 67, 82, 92, 97, 141, 142, 144, 145, 147–52, 154, 156, 57, 160, 162, 164–69, 171–173, 176, 179, 186, 188, 190–92, 194–97, 199, 211, 218, 232; *see also* healing
meditation 45, 89, 150, 164
mediums 3, 10, 12, 21, 23, 25–27, 40, 45, 63, 64, 71, 82, 96–139, 208, 236
memory 7, 8, 11, 30, 42–44, 64, 78–91, 99, 106, 113, 126, 130, 145, 150, 166–71, 175–77, 186, 190, 192–99, 201, 209, 218, 221, 224, 225
Mendel, Gregor 56
mental illness 8, 13, 69, 70, 146, 147, 162, 163, 168, 231
mental mediumship; 98, 99, 101, 102, 120, 136; *see also* physical mediumship
mesmerism 19–21, 24, 30, 34; *see also* hypnosis
meta-analysis 12, 46, 58, 59, 211–12, 226, 235
methodology 8, 11, 13, 14, 26, 28, 29, 33, 38, 41–46, 54, 56, 57, 82, 83, 110, 112, 153, 156, 164, 210, 211, 232, 233, 235, 237, 238
Michelson-Morley experiment 207
micro-kinesis 18, 73–75
microtubules 216, 221, 223, 224
Milholen, Layla vi
Miller, V.G. vi, 3, 9, 10, 235–37
monism 11, 219
Moody, Raymond A. 31, 144–47, 152, 154, 157, 160, 166, 175
Morse, Melvin L. 163, 176
Moses 134, 135
Moses, William Stainton 23, 120
Mt. St. Helens 175
Mozart, Wolfgang 33, 208
multiple minds 222

multiple universes 220, 222, 235
musical instruments 21, 22, 64, 98–100
Myers, Frederick W.H. 22, 24, 40, 106

N-methyl-D-aspartate 169, 218
USS *Nautilus* 47
Neanderthals 164, 234
near-death episodes 159, 163, 165, 174
near-death experiences (NDEs) 3, 4, 11, 17, 18, 31–32, 34, 35, 50, 140–205, 208, 215, 218, 219, 236; aftereffects 161–62, 173, 199; criteria 144–46, 152–53, 160–63, 193; distressing 161
necromancy 118, 134
neural networks 217, 218, 226
neutrino 220
New Testament 4, 133, 134
New York *Herald* 97, 98, 104–105
New Zealand *Herald* 198
Newton, Isaac 4, 217, 235
nonlocal/non-local 11, 111, 187, 191, 206, 222, 223
Noory, George 125
Nostradamus 50
Noyes, Russell 160, 167, 171
nuclear forces 59, 236

observer 32, 141, 208, 221–225, 235
Old Testament 51, 135, 238; *see also* Hebrew Bible
Orchestrated Objective Reduction (Orch-OR) 216, 223
Osis, Karlis 169, 171, 174–75, 178, 200, 202
Ouija board 25
out-of-body experiences (OBEs) 10, 17, 18, 31, 50, 144, 148, 161, 163, 169, 173, 176–78, 186, 187, 189, 191–97, 198, 200; *see also* astral projection; autoscopy

pain 20, 30, 154, 155, 159, 170, 188, 196, 223
pairing 111, 112
Palladino, Eusapia 63, 103, 120
Palmer, John A. 39, 45, 46, 54–56
paranormal 1, 9, 13, 20, 26, 30, 34, 35, 82, 100, 101, 109, 119, 149, 159, 172, 185, 187, 191, 198, 200, 202, 225, 232
parapsychology, definition of 8–9
Parnia, Sam 159, 160, 163, 171, 176, 192–202, 217–19, 223, 224
past life regression 11, 17, 22, 30, 31, 53; *see also* reincarnation
pathos 128, 137
Pauli, Wofgang 114
Peak in Darien 176, 178, 192, 195, 200
Pearce, Hubert E. 52, 56, 59
Penrose, Roger 187, 216, 217, 219, 221–23, 225

Pentecostalism 151
Persinger, M.A. 169, 219
Pfister, Oskar 167
phase-space 223
philosophy 3, 12, 13, 22, 23, 32–33, 40, 52, 53, 58, 80, 91, 92, 140, 143, 146, 157, 172, 206–230, 236; *see also* theory
physical mediumship 10, 21, 23, 98, 119, 120; *see also* apportation; ectoplasm; levitation; mental mediumship; psychokinesis (PK)
physicalism 11, 58, 92, 215–17, 220, 221, 222, 225, 234; *see also* materialism
physics 4, 32, 53, 58, 59, 75, 202, 206, 207, 212–13, 217, 219, 225, 232, 235, 236; classical 207, 217, 221, 223, 233
Pike, James 131; *see also* Ford, Arthur
Piper, Leonora E. 102–6, 120
Pius V, Pope St. 48
Planck, Max 207
plants 47, 226
Plato 143–50, 156–57, 164, 171
Plutarch 165
Podmore, Frank 22, 24
poltergeist 11, 23, 68–71, 216–17; *see also* psychokinesis (PK); recurrent spontaneous psycho-kinesis (RSPK)
position effects 46
positron 216; *see also* delayed choice double-slit/quantum eraser experiment; time symmetry
possession 79, 91, 105
post traumatic stress disorder (PTSD) 168
Praise, Felicia 67
Pratt, Joseph Gaither 47, 56, 59, 68–69, 216
precognition 10, 17, 18, 23, 26, 29, 33, 38, 39, 41, 44, 45, 50–52, 56, 75, 174, 175, 192, 210, 216, 220, 222
prior knowledge 109
process 8, 9, 11–13, 26, 32, 43, 54, 55, 71, 74, 84, 140, 142, 167, 171, 174, 178, 187, 201, 202, 208, 216, 218, 219, 221, 222, 234–36; *see also* authentication
processual soul theory 90–92
prodigies 81, 208
prospective studies 166, 177, 185, 191–202; *see also* retrospective studies
proxy sittings 108, 110–113
psi 9, 11, 13, 14, 17, 26, 29, 30, 32, 34, 35, 43, 45, 53, 54, 58, 59, 73, 91, 92, 112, 210–12, 215, 216, 219, 220, 222, 225, 231–36
psi hitting (ψH) 46, 55; *see also* sheep-goat effect (SGE)
psi missing (ψM) 27, 46, 55, 57; *see also* sheep-goat effect (SGE)

psychokinesis (PK) 3, 4, 10, 11, 17, 18, 26, 29, 39, 44, 45, 52, 54, 63–77, 92, 210, 217, 222, 236; *see also* poltergeist; recurrent spontaneous psycho-kinesis (RSPK)
psychophore 92; *see also* astral projection
Pullum, Stephen J. 10, 21, 34, 236, 237
Puthoff, Harold E. 27, 43, 47, 49, 76, 220
pyrokinesis 63, 72, 73; *see also* spontaneous ignition
Pythagoras 81

qi gong 20, 21
qualia 206–8
quantum entanglement 221; *see also* Aspect, Alain
quantum mechanics 4, 14, 32, 59, 75, 171, 187, 202, 207, 208, 212–13, 215–17, 220–24, 226, 235

Race, Victor 20, 34, 35
Radin, Dean 52, 54, 58, 219, 222, 235, 238
radionics 30
Rain Man 209
Randi, James 58, 65, 125
random event generator (REG) 39, 43, 54, 56, 57, 222
random number generator 75
random number tables 42, 44, 45, 57
Raphael Sanzio da Urbino 143, 146, 156, 157
Rayleigh, John William Strutt (3rd Baron) 206, 207
reading 44, 50, 79, 111–13, 115, 118, 121–27, 129–31, 137, 151, 174, 218, 224, 235, 236; *see also* cold reading; hot reading; warm reading
recurrent spontaneous psycho-kinesis (RSPK) *see* poltergeist; psychokinesis (PK)
reincarnation 3, 11, 12, 17, 30–31, 78–95, 167, 208; *see also* past life regression
Rejdak, Zdenek 66
relativity 4, 59, 207, 216, 217, 220
religion 4, 8, 9, 12, 18, 19, 21, 32, 81, 84, 89, 98, 110, 121, 122, 133, 140, 141, 143, 150, 154, 156, 167, 168, 173, 221, 225
remote viewing 11, 28–29, 38, 49–50
replicability 13, 27, 35, 46, 47, 54, 55, 75, 211, 212, 225, 235
resuscitation 31, 142, 144, 160, 166, 176, 177, 191–99, 201, 219; *see also* cardioplumonanry resuscitation (CPR)
retrocognition 11, 17, 33, 38, 44, 53, 192
retrospective studies 163, 166, 168, 185, 191; *see also* prospective studies
Reynolds (Lowery), Pamela 185–91, 194, 200

Index   245

Rhine, Joseph Banks 18, 24–26, 35, 38, 41, 43–47, 52, 53, 55–57, 64, 73, 74, 216
Rhine, Louisa Ella 7, 14, 43, 44, 52, 55
Richet, Charles 25, 40
Ring, Kenneth 31, 159, 160, 162, 166–68, 173, 175–78, 187, 192, 225, 235
Roll, William 68–69, 86, 91, 216
Russia 47, 49, 63, 66, 163, 172; *see also* Soviet Union
Ruzo, Andres 225

Sabom, Michael B. 164, 166, 168–73, 175, 177, 185, 188–90, 195, 201
Sagan, Carl 168
Sahay, K.K.N. 83–84
St. Catherine of Genoa 157
Samaritan woman 53
Samona, Alexandrina 82
Samuel, prophet of Israel 19, 34, 96, 135–36
Sannwald, J.E. 42, 52
Sartori, Penny 193, 195, 200, 201
Saul, King of Israel 19, 34, 96, 135–36
savants 208–10, 212
Schaberl, Annemarie 68, 70
Schlieter, Jens vi, 163
Schmeidler, Gertrude Raffel 26–27, 44, 45, 112, 220, 235
Schmidt, Helmut 29, 43, 44, 56, 57, 74–75, 221, 222
The School of Athens 143, 146, 149, 156–57
Schroedinger, Erwin 4, 32, 52, 58, 202, 217, 221, 222, 224, 235; *see also* wave equation
Schwaninger, J. 175, 192
seance 19, 21–22, 40, 64, 96–102, 104, 105, 119, 120, 135, 167
semiconductors 224
Sergeyev, Genady 66, 75
Serios, Ted 72
serpent handling 140–158, 236
Shafer, Cathy vi
Shafer, Heather Leah v, vi
shaman 19, 38, 63, 67, 163, 225
sheep-goat effect (SGE) 26–28, 44, 45, 54, 55, 76, 112, 235; *see also* psi hitting (ψH); psi missing (ψM); Schmeidler, Gertrude Raffel
Shermer, Michael 83, 130–31
shifting time 125, 126
Shishkin, I.F. 220, 229
shoes 176
Shushan, Gregory 162, 163
Sidgwick, Eleanor Mildred Balfour 22, 52, 108
Sidgwick, Henry 22, 40, 52, 106, 108
Simard, Suzanne 225–26

Sinclair, Upton 49
sitter 99, 101–5, 108–15, 120
skeptic 21, 22, 31, 51, 55, 64, 75, 76, 83, 86, 87, 97, 108, 109, 112, 114, 126, 136, 141, 145, 164, 170, 190, 191, 202, 210, 212, 225, 231, 233, 235; *see also* criticism
Soal, Samuel George 41, 56
Society for Psychical Research (SPR) 4, 18, 22–25, 35, 40, 71, 101, 103–6, 108, 109, 119
Socrates 143
somatosensory evoked potential (SSEP) 186, 189, 190
Soviet Union 47, 49, 66, 67; *see also* Russia
Spetzler, Robert F. 185–89, 190
Spiritualism 19, 21–23, 25, 34, 40, 63, 64, 96–98, 100, 101, 104, 105, 119, 137
spontaneous cases 18, 23, 43, 44, 55, 59, 63, 68, 70, 79, 82, 113, 142, 159, 160, 186, 189, 190, 209, 216; *see also* anecdotes; experiment
spontaneous ignition 63; *see also* pyrokinesis
Sri Lanka 85–88
standstill 185–86; *see also* hypothermic cardiac arrest
Stargate 29, 49, 225
statistical significance 29, 40, 41, 47, 52–54, 57, 74–75, 113, 171, 174, 192, 212
statistics 12, 18, 26, 40–43, 52, 54, 55, 56–59, 73, 74, 89, 126, 151, 166, 174, 192, 211, 223
Stevenson, Ian 78–90, 92
Stockholm 46, 48
string theory 220
suicide 88, 131, 145, 161
Sullivan, Al 179; *see also* flapping arms; Louis
super-psi 12, 91, 92
supervenience 215
survival 3, 10, 11, 12, 23, 30–32, 92, 101, 104, 107–9, 114, 140, 167, 179, 201, 236; *see also* afterlife
Swann, Ingo Douglas 49
Swedenborg, Emanuel 21, 46, 48, 49, 51

tachyon 220
Tafel, Rudolf Leonhard 48, 51
tailed test 57
Tao, Terence 223
Targ, Elisabeth 225
Targ, Russell 43, 47, 49, 76
target 18, 28, 29, 39, 43–46, 55, 57, 111, 112, 178, 191–99, 200–2, 211, 212
Tart, Charles T. 46, 47, 49, 57, 178, 200, 202, 220
telekinesis 63

246 Index

telepathy 4, 8, 9, 17, 19, 23, 24, 35, 38–41, 44, 46–48, 53, 57, 103–5, 108, 109, 111, 114, 174, 187, 192, 210–212, 216; *see also* ganzfeld
teleportation 65
television 27, 58, 115, 118–39, 144, 147, 190
theory 4, 11, 13, 14 20, 24, 32, 35, 42, 43, 51, 53, 54, 58, 66, 70, 80, 90, 92, 113, 126, 167, 171, 172, 187, 202, 207, 208, 212, 213, 215–230, 235, 238; *see also* philosophy
Theosophy 83, 84, 103
thermodynamics 216
Thomas, Drayton 108, 109, 111
thoughtography 63, 71–72
Thouless, Robert Henry 26, 41
Three Mile Island 175
Tibet 67, 80, 162–63, 165
time shifting 125, 126
time symmetry 216, 220, 224; *see also* delayed choice quantum eraser experiment; positron
Titanic 46, 51
transistors 224
Trickster 54, 225, 235
tunnel 18, 32, 161, 163, 168, 199
Turkey 48, 164
Tylor, Edward Burnett 80
Tyrrell, George Nugent Merle 24, 33, 42

Ullman, Montague 28, 43, 47, 57
ultraviolet caatastrophe 207
Utts, J. 58

Van Camp, Carol 10, 236, 238
van Lommel, Pim 159, 161, 191, 192, 198, 219, 222–223

Van Praagh, James 115, 118, 121–22, 125, 126, 128
Vasiliev, Leonid Leonidovich 47, 66, 68
Vasquez, Julio 68–69
veridical perception 12, 161, 166–68, 170, 174–79, 185, 186, 190–93, 195–202
Vienne, archbishop of 48
violence 88
Volk, Steve 223
von Huegel, Friedrich 157
von Neumann, John Louis 222
von Weizaecker, Carl Friedrich 4, 222, 235

Walker, Evan Harris 222
Walker, Kenneth 25, 32–33
warm reading 126, 130, 131
Washington, Wendy Donlin 10, 236, 237
Watt, Carolyn A. 5, 13, 14, 45, 46, 54, 58, 168, 226
wave equation 32, 221–24, 235; *see also* Schroedinger, Erwin
Wesley, John 51
white crow 102–103, 216
Wigner, Eugene 202, 217, 222, 225, 235
Williams, Montel 121, 125, 132
Williamson, W. Paul 150
witch 19, 334, 135–36
Woerlee, Gerald 186–91, 194, 200, 201
Woodruff, Joseph Leroy 56
world wars 3, 7, 8, 40, 53, 107, 178, 232; *see also* Dieppe raid
wormhole 220

Zener cards 26, 28, 41–43
Zhang, Baosheng 67–68

www.ingramcontent.com/pod-product-compliance
Lightning Source LLC
Chambersburg PA
CBHW032036300426
44117CB00009B/1086